Culture and International Economic Law

Globalization and international economic governance offer unprecedented opportunities for cultural exchange. Foreign direct investments can promote cultural diversity and provide the funds needed to locate, recover and preserve cultural heritage. Nonetheless, globalization and international economic governance can also jeopardize cultural diversity and determine the erosion of the cultural wealth of nations. Has an international economic culture emerged that emphasizes productivity and economic development at the expense of the common wealth?

This book explores the 'clash of cultures' between international law and international cultural law, and asks whether States can promote economic development without infringing their cultural wealth. The book contains original chapters by experts in the field. Key issues include how international courts and tribunals are adjudicating culture-related cases; the interplay between Indigenous peoples' rights and economic globalization; and the relationships between culture, human rights, and economic activities.

The book will be of great interest and use to researchers and students of international trade law, cultural heritage law, and public international law.

Valentina Vadi is a Reader (Associate Professor) in international economic law at Lancaster University, in the UK. She formerly was an Emile Noël Fellow at the Jean Monnet Centre for International and Regional Economic Law, New York University, and a Marie Curie Postdoctoral Fellow at Maastricht University.

Bruno de Witte is Professor of European Union law at Maastricht University, and part-time Professor at the Robert Schuman Centre of the European University Institute (EUI) in Florence.

Routledge Research in International Economic Law

Culture and International Economic Law

Edited by
Valentina Vadi and
Bruno de Witte

LONDON AND NEW YORK

First published 2015
by Routledge
2 Park Square, Milton Park, Abingdon, Oxon, OX14 4RN

and by Routledge
711 Third Avenue, New York, NY 10017

Routledge is an imprint of the Taylor & Francis Group, an informa business

British Library Cataloguing in Publication Data
A catalogue record for this book is available from the British Library

Library of Congress Cataloging-in-Publication Data
A catalog record for this book has been requested

ISBN: 978-0-415-72326-8 (hbk)
ISBN: 978-1-315-84973-7 (ebk)

Typeset in Garamond
by Florence Production Ltd, Stoodleigh, Devon, UK

Contents

Notes on contributors

Lucky Belder is Assistant Professor at the Centre of Intellectual Property Rights (CIER) of the Molengraaff Institute for Civil Law, University of Utrecht. She is a member of the working group on Culture, Communication and Information of the Dutch UNESCO Commission and advisor on intellectual property, cultural heritage, information policies and cultural diversity. In that capacity she was a member of the Dutch delegation to several Sessions of the Committee of the UNESCO Convention on the Protection and Promotion of the Diversity of Cultural Expressions and the Convention on the Safeguarding of Intangible Heritage. She is also member of the expert-group on Cultural Diversity, hosted by the Dutch UNESCO Commission, that is to initiate and evaluate present and future projects regarding the Convention on the Protection and Promotion of Cultural Expressions. She is secretary to the board of editors of the leading Dutch journal on Intellectual property law IER published by Kluwer. L. Belder is initiator, project coordinator and researcher in the three year HERA/ EU-FP7 funded Research project *Cultural Heritage Institutions, Copyright and Cultural Diversity*, which is part of the international and interdisciplinary CULTIVATE project (2010–2013).

Louise Buckingham is completing a PhD in the Faculty of Law, University of New South Wales (UNSW). Her project is concerned with legal protection for traditional knowledge and traditional cultural expressions, particularly as they relate to international intellectual property regimes. She was the recipient of an Australian Postgraduate Award. Louise was previously the Senior Lawyer at the Australian Copyright Council and a Senior Solicitor at the Arts Law Centre of Australia. She has also delivered seminars and training as a consultant for Copyright Agency/Viscopy and has worked for large law firms and the INGO sector in Australia and the UK.

Mira Burri is a Senior Research Fellow at the Swiss National Centre of Competence in Research (NCCR): Trade Regulation, and a lecturer in international media law at the University of Bern. At the NCCR, she leads the research cluster on new technologies and trade governance.

Mira's research focus has been on the interaction between digital technologies and the law, in particular, in shaping new media and cultural policies. She has published pieces in peer-reviewed journals, such as the *Journal of International Economic Law*, the *Journal of World Trade* and the *Common Market Law Review*. Mira is the author of *EC Electronic Communications and Competition Law* (Cameron May, 2007) and *Classification of Services in the Digital Economy* (Springer, 2012; together with Weber). She has co-edited the publications: *Free Trade versus Cultural Diversity* (Schulthess, 2004); *Digital Rights Management: The End of Collecting Societies?* (Staempfli et al., 2005); *Intellectual Property and Traditional Cultural Expressions in a Digital Environment* (Edward Elgar, 2008); *Governance of Digital Game Environments and Cultural Diversity* (Edward Elgar, 2010); and *Trade Governance in the Digital Age* (Cambridge University Press, 2012).

Mira is a member of the editorial board of the *International Journal of Communication Law and Policy* and of the *International Journal of Cultural Property*. She has acted as a consultant to the European Parliament on cultural diversity matters.

Rachael Craufurd Smith is a Senior Lecturer at the University of Edinburgh, specialising in media, the regulation of culture and European Union law. In 2003/4 she was a Jean Monnet Fellow at the European University Institute, Florence. She is a qualified solicitor and has worked both in the International and Policy and Planning Departments of the BBC, focussing on the impact of European Community Law on the public broadcasting sector. Rachael also worked as a trainee in the Internal Market DG of the European Commission and was a Fellow for a number of years at Trinity, Corpus Christi and St John's Colleges, and a University Lecturer at the University of Oxford.

She has written widely on media law and currently heads the University of Edinburgh team working on the EU funded Mediadem project, which seeks to promote free and independent media. Rachael was a co-founding editor of *The Journal of Media Law*, launched by Hart Publishing in 2009.

Antonietta Di Blase is Full Professor of International Law in the University of Rome 'Roma Tre' Law School. She is a Member of the editorial board of the *Rivista di Diritto Internazionale Privato e Processuale* and of the Board of teachers of the International Doctoral School 'Tullio Ascarelli' at the University of Roma Tre. She is also a member of the Scientific Committee of the International Centre of Studies on Alberico Gentili (S. Ginesio). Professor Di Blase holds an honours J.D. Degree from the University of Rome 'La Sapienza', Law School (Italy). Before joining the University of 'Roma Tre', Professor Di Blase held professorships of international law and/or international economic law at the University of Bologna Law School (1 November 2002–1 November 2006), the LUISS University-Guido Carli of Rome (1996–2001); and the University of Camerino (1994–2002). She also was former Director of the Department of Public Law of the University of Camerino (1995–1996), where she was also Dean of the Law School (1996–2001). She has published widely in the area of international law and international economic law.

Yvonne Donders is Professor of International Human Rights and Cultural Diversity and Executive Director of the Amsterdam Center for International Law (ACIL) at the Faculty of Law of the University of Amsterdam. She graduated from Utrecht University in international relations and completed her PhD at the Law Faculty of Maastricht University on cultural human rights and the right to cultural identity. Her research interests include public international law; international human rights law, in particular economic, social and cultural rights and human rights and cultural diversity. She teaches courses on international law and international human rights law and gives lectures on cultural rights and cultural diversity.

Yvonne Donders worked from March 2011 to October 2012 as project manager (one day per week detachment) at the National Human Rights Institute of the Netherlands (College voor de Rechten van de Mens), assisting the transformation from Equal Treatment Commission to NHRI. Previously Yvonne Donders worked as Programme Specialist on Economic, Social and Cultural Rights in the Division of Human Rights and Struggle against Discrimination of UNESCO's Secretariat in Paris. Yvonne Donders is a member of the European Expert Network on Culture (EENC), the National Commission for UNESCO and Chair of the Dutch United Nations Association (Nederlandse Vereniging voor de Verenigde Naties, NVVN).

Francesco Francioni holds the Chair of International Law at the European University Institute in Florence and the University of Siena, and is a Visiting Professor at the University of Texas Law School. He has been legal advisor of the Italian Ministry of Foreign Affairs in many international negotiations concerning the cultural heritage and the environment. He was president of the World Heritage Committee of the UNESCO in 1997 and 1998. He is a graduate in law from the University of Florence and from Harvard University.

Federico Lenzerini holds a Juris Doctor *magna cum laude* from the University of Siena (Italy) and a PhD in international law from the University of Bari (Italy), 2003. He is a Professor of Public International Law, Private International Law, European Union Law and the Law of Cultural Property at the University of Siena. Occasionally, he has worked as a consultant to the United Nations Educational, Scientific and Cultural Organization (UNESCO) and as Legal Advisor of the Italian Ministry of Foreign Affairs at international negotiations concerning the protection of cultural heritage. He is a member of the Committee on Biotechnology of the International Law Association (ILA), Rapporteur of the ILA Committee on the Rights of Indigenous Peoples, and member of the ILA Committee on Cultural

Heritage Law. In addition, he has been a Visiting Professor at the Tulane University of New Orleans and at the St. Thomas University Law School, Miami (FL), USA, in the context of the LLM Programme on Intercultural Human Rights, 2009–2012. He is a Professor at the 'European Master for the Conservation and Management of Cultural Property', organized by the Faculty of Literature of the University of Siena and a Professor at the Tulane-Siena Summer School on International Law and the Arts, 2009–2012; and was a Visiting Professor at the Academy of European Law, European University Institute, Session on Human Rights Law, June-July 2011. His main areas of research include the international protection of human rights; the rights of Indigenous peoples; the international protection of cultural heritage; the rights of refugees and the right of asylum; international environmental law and international trade law.

Lucas Lixinski is a Senior Lecturer at the University of New South Wales Faculty of Law (Sydney, Australia). He holds a PhD from the European University Institute (Florence, Italy), an LLM in International Human Rights Law from Central European University (Budapest, Hungary), and an LLB from the Federal University of Rio Grande do Sul (Porto Alegre, Brazil). He has recently published a monograph titled *Intangible Cultural Heritage in International Law* with Oxford University Press. In addition to intangible cultural heritage, his research focuses on a broader structural critique to orthodox international cultural heritage law, relying on insights from critical theory.

Evangelia Psychogiopoulou is a lawyer and research fellow at the Hellenic Foundation for European and Foreign Policy (ELIAMEP). A graduate from the Faculty of Law of the Kapodistrian University of Athens, she holds a DEA in European and Community Law from the University of Paris I, Panthéon-Sorbonne (2001), and a Master of Research in Law from the European University Institute (2003). In 2007, she successfully defended her PhD thesis on the accommodation of cultural diversity considerations in EU law and policies (Art. 167.4 TFEU) at the European University Institute. Her research interests lie in the fields of EU law, with emphasis on EU cultural and media policies, and human rights protection. She has held research and management positions at the Academy of European Law (Florence, Italy), the Directorate General Education and Culture of the European Commission and UNESCO. Her articles have appeared, among others, in *European Foreign Affairs Review*, *European Law Journal*, *European Law Review*, and *Legal Issues of Economic Integration*. Her recent publications include: *The Integration of Cultural Considerations in EU Law and Policies* (Martinus Nijhoff Publishers, 2008); *The European Court of Human Rights and the Rights of Marginalised Individuals and Minorities in National Context* (Martinus Nijhoff Publishers, 2010, ed.); and *Understanding Media Policies: A European Perspective* (Palgrave Macmillan, 2012, ed.).

Sarah Sargent is currently a Lecturer at the University of Buckingham, United Kingdom. She holds a Bachelor of Arts (*cum laude*) degree from Kansas State University, a Juris Doctor degree from the University of Denver, an LLM (with distinction) from the University of Leicester and a PhD from De Montfort University. She has previously practised law in the United States, and was involved with the issues on the rights of Indigenous children in state fostering and adoption. She is a co-founder and past president of the not-for-profit organisation of the Kansas Association of Counsel for Children, which is an affiliate of the National Association of Counsel for Children. Dr Sargent was also a member of an Advisory Committee of the Kansas Judicial Council that studied and proposed statutory changes for fostering and juvenile offender laws.

Her research interests are culture and cultural heritage with a focus on children's, Indigenous and human rights in public international law. She has published articles on children's rights and Indigenous rights, and is the editor of a forthcoming book on the impact of the United Nations Declaration on the Rights of Indigenous Peoples on Indigenous rights.

Valentina Vadi is a Reader (Associate Professor) in international economic law at Lancaster University, in the UK. She formerly was an Emile Noël Fellow at the Jean Monnet Centre for International and Regional Economic Law, New York University, and a Marie Curie Postdoctoral Fellow at Maastricht University. Dr Vadi has also lectured at Hasselt University (Belgium), the University of Rome III (Italy), the China EU School of Law (PR China) and Maastricht University (The Netherlands). Dr Vadi's main areas of research are in international economic law as well as international cultural law. She has published more than seventy articles in these areas in top journals, including the *Stanford Journal of International Law*, the *European Journal of International Law*, the *Columbia Human Rights Law Review* and others. She is the co-editor (with Hildegard Schneider) of *Art, Cultural Heritage and the Market: Legal and Ethical Issues* (Springer, 2014). Valentina Vadi is the author of *Cultural Heritage in International Investment Law and Arbitration* (Cambridge University Press, *forthcoming* 2014) and *Public Health in International Investment Law and Arbitration* (Routledge 2012).

Ana Filipa Vrdoljak is the author of *International Law, Museums and the Return of Cultural Objects* (Cambridge University Press, 2006) and numerous academic articles on international law, cultural heritage and human rights. She is currently completing a European Commission funded book project entitled 'Law and Cultural Heritage in Europe'. She has taught courses and been invited to present at international conferences on these issues in Asia Pacific, Europe and North America. Dr Vrdoljak is also a Visiting Professor, Legal Studies Department, Central European University, Budapest. She is a member of the Cultural Heritage Law Committee and Rights of Indigenous Peoples Committee, International Law Association, and Board Member of the International Cultural Property Society (US) and

Advisory Board, International Journal of Cultural Property (Cambridge University Press). She is co-General Editor of the Cultural Heritage Law and Theory: International and Comparative book series. She was a Marie Curie Fellow and Jean Monnet Fellow at the Law Department of the European University Institute, in Florence; and a visiting scholar at the Lauterpacht Centre for International Law, at the University of Cambridge; at the Global Law School, New York University, and the Faculty of Law of the University of New South Wales. She holds a Doctor of Philosophy (in Law) from the University of Sydney.

Bruno de Witte is Professor of European Union law at Maastricht University, and part-time professor at the Robert Schuman Centre of the European University Institute (EUI) in Florence. He is co-director of the Maastricht Centre for European Law. Previously, from 2000 to 2010, he was professor of EU law at the EUI, and co-director of the Academy of European Law there, and prior to that, he was professor at Maastricht University from 1989 to 2000. He studied law at the University of Leuven and the College of Europe and obtained a doctorate at the European University Institute in 1985, on 'The Protection of Linguistic Diversity through Fundamental Rights'.

Bruno De Witte's principal interest is the constitutional law of the European Union, with a particular focus on the relation between international, European and national law, the protection of fundamental rights, law-making and treaty revision procedures, and internal market law and non-market values. His second main field of interest is the law of cultural diversity, with a particular focus on language law, the protection of minorities and the relation between market integration and cultural diversity in European Union law.

Bruno is also a member of the Ius Commune Research School. He is a member of the editorial board of the European Law Journal, the European Human Rights Law Review, the Revista Española de Derecho Europeo, and the Revista de Llengua I Dret. He is a member of the advisory board of the *European Journal of International Law*, the *European Constitutional Law Review*, the *Maastricht Journal of European and Comparative Law*, the *European Journal of Law Reform*, and the *Zeitschrift für öffentliches Recht*, and correspondent of the Rivista Italiana di Diritto Pubblico Comunitario. He currently teaches the course of Advanced EU law in the Master programmes of Maastricht University. He has supervised some thirty-five doctoral dissertations, partly at the European University Institute and partly at Maastricht University.

Selected representative publications: Editor of the volume *Ten Reflections on the Constitutional Treaty for Europe* (2003) and co-editor of the volumes, *Social Rights in Europe* (2005), *Constitución Europea y Constituciones nacionales* (2005), *Genesis and Destiny of the European Constitution* (2007), *The Framework Convention for National Minorities – a Useful Pan-European Instrument?* (2008), and *EU Foreign Relations Law – Constitutional Fundamentals* (2008).

1 Introducing culture and international economic law

Valentina Vadi[1] and Bruno de Witte[2]

Introduction

Can states promote economic development without infringing their cultural wealth? Culture represents inherited values, ideas, beliefs, and traditions, which characterize social groups and their behaviour. Culture is not a static concept but rather a dynamic force, which evolves through time and shapes countries and civilizations. As such, culture has always benefitted from economic exchange. Nowadays globalization and international economic governance have spurred a more intense dialogue and interaction among nations: thus, they offer unprecedented opportunities for cultural exchange. In parallel, foreign direct investment and financial transactions can promote cultural diversity and provide the funds needed to locate, recover and preserve cultural heritage.

Nonetheless, globalization and international economic governance can also jeopardize cultural diversity and determine the erosion of cultural heritage. While trade in cultural products can lead to cultural homogenization and even to cultural hegemony, foreign direct investments have an unmatched penetrating force with the ultimate capacity to change landscapes and erase memory. At the same time, the increase in global trade and foreign direct investment (hereinafter FDI) has determined the creation of legally binding and highly effective regimes which demand that states promote and facilitate trade and FDI. Has an international economic culture emerged that emphasizes productivity and economic development at the expense of the common wealth?

Against this background, this book aims to explore the 'clash of cultures' between international (economic) law and international cultural law[3] exploring

1 Reader, Lancaster University. Valentina Vadi has received funding from the European Union Seventh Framework Programme (FP7/2007–2013) under grant agreement n. 273063 for conducting research in the area of cultural heritage and international and European law. The views expressed in this chapter are the author's only and do not necessarily reflect those of the European Union. The usual disclaimer applies.
2 Professor of EU Law, Maastricht University and European University Institute. Bruno De Witte authored section 1 (Structure of the book).
3 J.A.R. Nafziger 'Cultural Heritage Law: The International Regime' in J.A.R. Nafziger and T Scovazzi (eds) *Le Patrimoine Culturel de l'Humanité* (Leiden: Martinus Nijhoff 2008).

some key questions which remain unaddressed by the relevant literature thus far.[4] The clash of cultures between economics and culture has been scrutinized through a number of perspectives. While economists have used economics lenses to observe this interplay, international law scholars have focused on the well-known *trade v. culture* debate. However, several facets of the interplay remain underexplored. For instance, is economic globalization affecting the protection of cultural heritage? How are international (economic) courts and tribunals adjudicating culture–related cases? Has any grass root resistance developed to cope with the threats posed by economic globalization? Is there a global (economic) resistance to cultural governance, often perceived as anti-democratic and at times infringing individual (economic) freedom and/or the same cultural rights it would aim to reinforce? This book addresses these questions, bringing greater attention from a number of perspectives to an increasingly important and under explored topic within international law.

Structure of the book

The book is divided into four parts: the first part introduces the main themes and challenges to be addressed. Parts II, III and IV explore the interplay between culture and international economic law, international intellectual property law, and European law respectively.[5]

Part I addresses the interplay between culture and economic globalization in international law and human rights law. While the general linkage between economic globalization and human rights more generally is beyond the scope of the book, the book focuses on the interaction between culture and economic interests in human rights law to provide a powerful counter narrative to the analogous interplay between culture and economic interests in international economic law. In a sense, Part I is a sort of prologue, to understand how the linkage between culture and economic interests has been approached by human rights courts. This part allows fruitful comparisons between the adjudication of human rights courts and tribunals, on the one hand, and international economic *fora*, on the other, to verify whether there is convergence or divergence between these different streams of international law. Has there

---

4   The book stems from an academic conference organized in June 2013 at Maastricht University, the Netherlands, financed by the Faculty of Law and the European Commission.

5   The views in this edited volume are those of the individual authors and do not necessarily correspond to those of the editors. The editing was also relatively non-intrusive, in order to allow each author to maintain their own voice and perspective. The use of particular designations of countries or territories does not imply any judgment by the publisher or the editors as to the legal status of such countries or territories, of their authorities and institutions or of the delimitation of their boundaries. The mentioning of names of specific companies or products does not imply any intention to infringe proprietary rights, nor should it be construed as an endorsement or recommendation by the editors. The authors are responsible for having obtained the necessary permission to reproduce, translate or use material from sources already protected by copyright.

been judicial borrowing between courts belonging to different subsystems of international law, or is there a fragmentation? Answering this question contributes to the ongoing debate on the unity or fragmentation of international law while allowing the interpreter to verify whether there is coalescence of general principles of law demanding the protection of cultural heritage in times of peace. Part I contextualizes international economic law in the broader framework of international law because, in the editors' view, international economic law is not a self-contained regime, but is rather a part of international law. Therefore, it may be useful to ascertain whether and how international economic law is addressing the interplay between culture and economic activities contextualizing the analysis in the broader matrix of international law. This juxtaposition is significant because arbitral tribunals often refer to human rights cases in arbitral awards.

In Part I, Francioni focuses on the interplay between culture, human rights and economic globalization in international law, highlighting that on the one hand, 'economic globalization has spurred a movement towards the recognition of some "cultural human rights", such as the right to cultural identity, the right to access and participate in community culture, linguistic rights, rights related to the preservation of minorities, and more recently, Indigenous peoples' rights'.[6] On the other hand, Francioni also reflects that 'the protection of culture and cultural heritage is becoming a component of international economic law and an important consideration in the adjudication of international economic disputes'.[7]

Donders develops this thread further, focusing on the interplay between culture, human rights, and economic activities in international human rights jurisprudence. Donders argues that 'human rights should be taken into account in connecting cultural diversity and economy'.[8] Such a connection is also increasingly reflected in a number of international law instruments, including the UNESCO Convention on the Protection and Promotion of the Diversity of Cultural Expressions.[9] Donders explores the tripartite linkage between economic activities, culture and human rights, investigating the jurisprudence of international human rights courts concerning Indigenous peoples. States have often granted concessions for economic activities on lands inhabited by Indigenous tribes. This practice has raised a number of human rights concerns, and human rights courts have increasingly adjudicated on the legitimate boundaries between the human rights of Indigenous peoples, including their cultural rights, and the states' developmental needs.

---

6 See Francioni's chapter in this volume.
7 Ibid.
8 See Donders' chapter in this volume.
9 Convention on the Protection and Promotion of the Diversity of Cultural Expressions, Paris, 20 October 2005, in force 18 March 2007. 2440 UNTS 311.

Part II explores the interplay between culture and economic interests in international economic law, including international investment law, international trade law and international financial law. In this part, Vadi questions whether international economic law puts emphasis on economic development and favours macroeconomic notions of growth regardless of actual or potential infringement of cultural entitlements. To answer this question, she focuses on a cases study, analysing the specific interplay between Indigenous cultural heritage and economic interests in the jurisprudence of international economic courts and tribunals. In particular, she examines the *Seal Products* dispute,[10] and the *John Andre v. Canada* case,[11] both of which concern Indigenous heritage and economic activities.

Lenzerini examines the interplay between the protection of Indigenous heritage and foreign direct investments in international investment law and arbitration. He points out that land plays a crucial role in the preservation of the identity of Indigenous peoples. As Indigenous heritage is protected under international law, and the 2007 United Nations Declaration on the Rights of Indigenous Peoples[12] has gained momentum, Lenzerini argues that Indigenous heritage should be taken into account when states consider the feasibility of investment projects in Indigenous peoples' traditional lands. He also highlights that in some circumstances, investments risk jeopardizing 'the spiritual relationship of Indigenous peoples with their ancestral lands', thus leading to results that are incompatible with the protection of Indigenous heritage. To prevent such negative outcomes, Lenzerini calls for proper consultations between state representatives and communities of Indigenous peoples to obtain the free prior and informed consent of the latter. He also argues that whenever an investment project may seriously jeopardize the cultural integrity of the Indigenous communities concerned, the requirement of a prior informed consent should become compulsory.

Moving to international financial law, Sarah Sargent examines the policies of the International Finance Corporation (IFC), which is the arm of the World Bank which provides advice, loans, equity and technical assistance to stimulate private sector investment in developing countries, with regard to Indigenous cultural heritage. For projects that rely on international sources of financing, compliance with the IFC standards for cultural heritage protection are a condition of financing.[13] The IFC's performance standards include specific

---

10   *European Communities – Certain Measures Prohibiting the Importation and Marketing of Seal Products*, Panel report, 25 November 2013, WT/DS369/2. Online. Available http://wto.org/english/tratop_e/dispu_e/cases_e/ds400_e.htm (accessed 25 May 2014).

11   *John R. Andre v. Government of Canada*, Notice of Intent to Submit Claim to Arbitration Pursuant to Chapter Eleven of the North American Free Trade Agreement, 19 March 2010, para. 8. Online. Available http://international.gc.ca/trade-agreements-accords-commerciaux/assets/pdfs/JohnR_Andre_FiledNOI.pdf (accessed 25 May 2014).

12   United Nations Declaration on the Rights of Indigenous Peoples (UNDRIP), GA res. 61/295, 13 September 2007.

13   See A. Mason, 'International Project Financing and Cultural Heritage Protection' 19 *International Journal of Cultural Property* (2012) 556, 557.

standards on cultural heritage and Indigenous rights respectively. Sargent compares the interpretation of free prior and informed consent (FPIC) within the IFC Performance Standard and Guidance Notes on Indigenous Rights to the interpretation of the same right in the context of the United Nations Declaration on the Rights of Indigenous Peoples (UNDRIP).

Moving to international trade law, Mira Burri explores the *trade vs culture* debate, tracing its evolution from the *exception culturelle* battle, which Canada and a number of European countries fought during the Uruguay Round of trade negotiations which led to the establishment of the World Trade Organization (WTO)[14] to the victory (of cultural proponents) represented by the inception of the 2005 UNESCO Convention on Cultural Diversity. The chapter examines the different developmental stages of the debate, contextualizing it in the current discourse on global governance.

Vrdoljak concludes Part II by examining the international exchange and trade in cultural objects. In particular, she discusses the operation of the 1970 Convention on the Means of Prohibiting and Preventing the Illicit Import, Export, and Transfer of Ownership of Cultural Property,[15] the 1976 Recommendation concerning the International Exchange of Cultural Property,[16] and the debates relating to each of them which followed, especially concerning the transposition and operation of these instruments in domestic law. She then discusses the significance of international exchange in the legal protection of cultural heritage.

Part III focuses on the interplay between culture and economic interests in international intellectual property law. Since the inception of the Agreement on Trade Related Aspects of Intellectual Property Rights (TRIPS Agreement),[17] intellectual property has been governed under the aegis of the World Trade Organization, despite earlier criticisms as to the connection between international trade and intellectual property. Di Blase focuses on the issue of traditional knowledge (TK) and the challenges posed by its regulation. In fact, the TRIPS Agreement does not seem well equipped to govern traditional knowledge. The classic rules on copyright and patents adopt a proprietary approach in that they aim to provide inventors with an adequate economic

---

14 Marrakesh Agreement Establishing the World Trade Organization, 15 April 1994, 33 ILM 1144 (1994).

15 Convention on the Means of Prohibiting and Preventing the Illicit Import, Export and Transfer of Ownership of Cultural Property, Paris, 14 November 1970, in force 24 April 1972. 823 UNTS 231.

16 Recommendation Concerning the International Exchange of Cultural Property, 19th session of the General Conference of the United Nations Educational, Scientific and Cultural Organization, Nairobi, 26 October to 30 November 1976. Online. Available http://portal.unesco.org/en/ev.php-URL_ID=13132&URL_DO=DO_TOPIC&URL_SECTION=201.html (accessed 8 December 2013).

17 Agreement on Trade-Related Aspects of Intellectual Property Rights, 15 April 1994, Marrakesh Agreement Establishing the World Trade Organization, Annex 1C, 33 ILM 1197 (1994).

reward, in addition to providing effective legal remedies against the unfair use of the products of the innovation. Furthermore, TK has a cumulative nature, and it may be very difficult to single out the creator or inventor of a given product of ingenuity. Di Blase also points out that the current IP rules do not take into account the linkage between intangible and tangible TK (the latter entailing the appropriate use of land and natural resources). Both tangible and intangible elements – Di Blase argues – 'concur in the social and cultural identity of the local communities'.[18] In this respect, Di Blase compares the approach of the World Trade Organization with that of the World Intellectual Property Organization (WIPO).[19] Di Blase concludes with some reflections on what would be the best approach for the protection of TK, assessing whether some legal safeguards should be incorporated into the TRIPs Agreement, or whether establishing a *sui generis system*, whose principles would prevail over intellectual property rights, would constitute a preferable option.

Following this thread, Lucas Lixinski and Louise Buckingham investigate the promises and pitfalls of the supposedly complementary relationship between the intellectual property and heritage regimes in the field of culture, focusing on the interplay between intangible cultural heritage (ICH) and traditional cultural expressions (TCEs). Lixinski and Buckingham pinpoint that while both concepts refer to cultural expressions in the realm of what is popularly known as folklore, they have different focuses, approaches and connections to different institutional settings – UNESCO for ICH, and WIPO for TCEs. Lixinski and Buckingham argue that 'ICH and TCEs are, in some respects, fundamentally at odds with one another'.[20]

Belder explores the linkage between copyright and digitization – meaning the process of storing information in a digital format of cultural heritage – focusing on the online *Europeana* as a key study. *Europeana* is a website providing free access to digitized collections of books, paintings, films, museum objects and archival records throughout Europe. Endorsed by the European Commission, this European cultural heritage database aims to provide access to the cultural wealth of European heritage and possibly to foster education, research and tourism, facilitating research as well as access to the public. In particular, Belder focuses on the role that private actors may play in the context

---

18 See Di Blase's chapter in this volume.
19 The World Intellectual Property Organization (WIPO) is a specialized agency of the United Nations established in 1970, following the entry into force of the 1967 WIPO Convention. As stated in its website, 'It is dedicated to developing a balanced and accessible international intellectual property (IP) system, which rewards creativity, stimulates innovation and contributes to economic development while safeguarding the public interest.' The mission of WIPO is 'the promotion of innovation and creativity for the economic, social and cultural development of all countries through a balanced and effective international IP system'. See WIPO A User's Guide'. Online. Available http://wipo.int/freepublications/en/general/1040/wipo_pub_1040.html (accessed 8 December 2013).
20 See Lixinski and Buckingham's chapter in this volume.

of the digitization of cultural heritage, and explores the contribution of Public Private Partnership (PPP) in this sense. Belder clarifies the copyright aspects in PPP contracts also in the light of the current revision process of European Copyright law and the Digital Agenda.[21]

Part IV focuses on the interplay between economic interests, culture and European Law. Part IV examines European media policies, as media law can facilitate or hinder the distribution of cultural products and is an essential component of cultural governance – consider for example, the recent British musical invasion of the US; or the US audiovisual invasion of the EU. The EU is selected as a case study due to the fact that the EU has adopted a unique approach merging cultural and economic concerns rather than adopting exception clauses in its treaty making. The book questions whether or not this holistic approach works, and whether it is contributing to the development of international economic law.[22] The interaction between EU law and international economic law with regard to cultural matters is also proven by the number of culture related investment and trade disputes which have seen the EU or member states as respondent and/or actor. Finally, in a broad sense, some aspects of EU law are also components of international economic law, albeit European integration has now moved beyond pure economic integration.

De Witte explores the linkage between market integration and cultural diversity in EU law. His contribution provides a micro-analysis of the policies adopted by the Commission and the Court of Justice in particular fields, pinpointing the patchy record of the Court. In addition, he examines the legislative and regulatory measures adopted by the EU institutions for 'mainstreaming' the concern for cultural diversity. He concludes that while the protection of cultural diversity is acknowledged as a duty under the EU Treaties, it occurs only occasionally and half-heartedly in the EU's legislative practice. However, the EU institutions are more sanguine about the need to protect cultural diversity against market forces when it comes to formulating the EU's *external* trade policy in the context of the WTO or in bilateral negotiations.

Craufurd Smith scrutinizes the interplay between culture and economic interests charting 'the complex and contested development of EU media law'. She maps the 'calls for the EU to engage more directly in such issues as media pluralism and media ownership transparency' and examines the case for developing the human rights dimension in EU media law and policy, alongside

---

21 The *Digital Agenda for Europe* (DAE) aims 'to reboot Europe's economy and help Europe's citizens and businesses to get the most out of digital technologies'. See Digital Agenda for Europe. Online. Available http://ec.europa.eu/digital-agenda/node/1584 (accessed 8 December 2013).

22 For an analogous approach, see H. Schneider and P. Van Den Bossche (eds) *Protection of Cultural Diversity from a European and International Perspective* (Antwerpen/ Oxford: Intersentia 2008).

the implications for the relationship between the EU and Council of Europe in establishing guidelines and standards for the media in Europe in the future. Finally, the author addresses the key question of precisely which position the EU holds with regard to mass media issues: a cultural policy or just business as usual?

Psychogiopoulou concludes Part IV exploring the interplay between culture and economic interests in the EU's external economic relations. Since the inception of the *European Agenda for Culture in a Globalizing World* in 2007, enhancing the role of culture in the external relations of the European Union (EU) has represented one of the key objectives of the European Commission. Not only is the emphasis on cultural cooperation in conformity with EU law,[23] but it is also in line with the provisions of the UNESCO Convention on the Protection and Promotion of the Diversity of Cultural Expressions to which the EU is party. The chapter explores the ways in which culture has been integrated into the EU's external economic relations, and in particular into its common commercial policy. After scrutinizing a few early efforts by European institutions to accommodate cultural diversity concerns in the EU common commercial policy, the chapter analyses a number of *protocols on cultural cooperation* that accompany multilateral and bilateral trade agreements entered into by the EU. Designed to facilitate cultural exchanges, such protocols frame 'a strengthened policy dialogue on culture and cultural diversity'.[24] The chapter explores the main features and characteristics of these protocols and identifies and explains possible analogies and differences so as to verify whether culture and cultural diversity are incorporated in the EU's trade policy in a systematic and consistent manner.

Common threads

The book is timely given the pressing and urgent need for the protection of cultural heritage and the promotion of economic activities in international law, the recent flourishing of scholarly interest in the area of international cultural law and economic governance respectively, and the increase in cases related to aspects of cultural heritage. The recent boom in culture related cases has brought the interplay between economic globalization and cultural governance to the forefront of scholarly debate and public scrutiny because of the public policy implications of such cases. Research needs to be done in order to verify whether international adjudication pays due respect to cultural matters, and more generally, what impact cultural concerns have on the

---

23 See Article 167(3) of the Treaty on the Functioning of the European Union (TFEU), which mandates the EU and its member states 'to foster cooperation with third countries and the competent international organizations in the sphere of culture' and Article 167(4) TFEU, according to which 'the Union shall take cultural aspects into account in its action under other provisions of the Treaties'.
24 See Psychogiopoulou's chapter in this volume.

structure of international economic law. This section aims at highlighting some emerging features and common threads of the debate.

With regard to the plethora of disputes which have arisen in the relevant fields, several common threads can be discerned. First, the polyphonic nature of the debate on the interplay between culture and economic interests is pinpointed. Not only is the topic interdisciplinary (attracting the interest of multiple constituencies, including lawyers and economists to name but a few) and intra-disciplinary (involving different subsets of international law), it is also polyphonic because it is multilayered at national, regional and international levels, and involves both public and private actors. The emergence of claims involving cultural elements highlights the transformation of the notion of international law from the classical image of it being the law applicable among states to a new, more dynamic, understanding of international law as a discipline in which private actors also matter. Heritage protection and economic development have become a subject of transnational law. Private actors can play a dual role with regard to heritage protection. On the one hand they can threaten heritage protection with projects involving the exploitation of natural resources.[25] On the other, they can perform some positive roles, engaging in private-public partnerships, providing funds for the recovery and preservation of heritage,[26] developing eco-tourism projects[27] etc. Local communities also have an important role to play in the protection of cultural heritage.

The debate on culture and economic interests in international (economic) law can contribute to the *democratization* of international law, bringing claims from its former 'periphery' to the centre of the legal debate.[28] On the one hand, non-state entities, such as individuals and even entire groups of Indigenous peoples, used to be mere 'objects' of international law 'on the periphery of the international legal order' but are now increasingly playing an active role in international relations.[29] On the other hand, the claims concerning cultural elements reflect complex historical legacies.[30]

---

25 For a paradigmatic case, see *Glamis Gold Ldt v. United States of America*, Award, 8 June 2009, available at www.state.gov/s/l/c10986.htm (accessed 30 July 2014).

26 J.A.R. Nafziger, 'A Brief Sketch of the Relationship between Non-State Actors and the World Heritage Convention' 19 *International Journal of Cultural Property* (2012) 550–552.

27 N. Affolder, 'Company Reserves: Corporations, Natural Heritage, and Protected Areas of Law' 19 *International Journal of Cultural Property* (2012) 553–556.

28 A. Becker Lorca, 'Universal International Law: Nineteenth Century Histories of Imposition and Appropriation' 51(2) *Harvard International Law Journal* (2010) 475–552.

29 R. Higgins 'Conceptual Thinking about the Individual in International Law' in R. Falk, F. Kratochwil and S. Mendlovitz (eds) *International Law: A Contemporary Perspective* (Boulder CO: Westview Press 1985), pp. 476–494.

30 A. Anghie, 'Finding the Peripheries: Sovereignty and Colonialism in Nineteenth-century International Law' 40 *Harvard International Law Journal* (1999) 1–80; K. Miles, *The Origins of International Investment Law – Empire, Environment and the Safeguarding of Capital* (Cambridge: Cambridge University Press 2013).

Second, the debate on the interplay between culture and economic interests can contribute to the *humanization* of international (economic) law, making it more porous to other interests and needs which include the respect for human dignity and fundamental human rights. Cultural heritage is not just objects. It embodies different meanings to different audiences: adjudicators should capture these different values.

Third, this debate contributes to international cultural law, in that it counteracts *heritigization* processes which emphasize the protection of heritage because of its mere intrinsic features ('heritage is heritage').[31] The debate about culture and economic interests contextualizes heritage within a broader framework, that of international law. In other words, cultural objects are to be seen against the background of human history. Heritage is not an abstract value; rather it matters to a variety of actors who attach different narratives to the same objects. The debate on culture and economic interests ultimately highlights the human dimension of international cultural law.[32]

Fourth, the debate about the interplay between culture and economic interests contributes to the consolidation of cultural rights' place in the human rights pantheon. While cultural rights have been marginalized historically vis-à-vis civil and political rights, they have recently undergone a renaissance – as shown by the number of studies published in the past decade.[33] The debate on culture and economic interests reinforces, and is reinforced by, the discourse on cultural rights. Cultural rights are connected to other human rights, including self-determination, freedom of expression, religious freedoms and others. More generally, a human rights-based approach to cultural heritage centres on the human dimension of heritage discourse expressing the need to put people and human values at the centre of an enlarged concept of cultural heritage.

Finally, the debate on culture and economic interests allows for some reflection on the meaning of justice. Does the existing legal framework preclude access to justice and to effective remedies? The Vienna Convention on the Law of Treaties (VCLT)[34] requires adjudicators to settle disputes 'in conformity with the principles of justice and international law'.[35] This will have to be a case by case assessment.

---

31   C. De Cesari 'World Heritage and Mosaic Universalism' 10 *Journal of Social Anthropology* (2010) 299–324.

32   F. Francioni 'The Human Dimension of International Cultural heritage Law' 22 *European Journal of International Law* (2011) 9–16.

33   Y. Donders and V. Volodin (eds) *Human Rights in Education, Science and Culture: Legal Developments and Challenges* (Paris: UNESCO/Ashgate 2007); E. Stamatopoulou *Cultural Rights in International Law* (Leiden: Martinus Nijhoff 2007); F. Francioni and M. Scheinin (eds) *Cultural Human Rights* (Leiden/Boston, MA: Brill 2008).

34   Vienna Convention on the Law of Treaties (VCLT), in force 27 January 1980. 1155 UNTS 331, 8 ILM 679.

35   VCLT, preamble.

The book has an international law focus rather than a comparative one, mainly focusing on the case law of international and regional courts and tribunals. Therefore, it falls generally within the area of international law, and specifically within the areas of international economic law, international investment law, European law, intellectual property law and cultural heritage law. While national cases will be mentioned by way of reference, the book has an international focus, with cases involving North and Latin America, Australia, Asia and Africa. Its contributors come from North and South America, Oceania and Europe, thus reflecting a range of different perspectives and approaches and the polyphonic nature of international law.

While the book aims to be exhaustive, it also brings up questions, which in this context are simply identified, to promote further debate. For instance, the book identifies areas where different values conflict and proposes possible tools for improving the synergy between culture and economic globalization; however, it leaves institutional reforms to another day. Rather it focuses on legal tools that *de jure condito* can help interpreters and policy makers to bring coherence to the field. This book aims at contributing some reflection on a range of selected issues to the rich mosaic of the discussion concerning the interplay between culture and economic interests in international economic law. Further studies will be needed to map other emerging cases and the ongoing dialogues between adjudicators, policy makers and the public and private parties involved.

The place of the book in the literature

The book goes beyond the state of the art, contributing to the fields of international cultural law and international economic law by mapping their interaction in a systematic fashion. The interplay between the protection of cultural heritage and the pursuit of economic interests in international and European law has heretofore been approached in a fragmented and incomplete fashion adopting a variety of perspectives and methods. In particular, the available literature can be placed in five broad categories: 1) examination of the interplay between international trade and cultural policies;[36] 2) examination of the interplay between international investment law and cultural policies;[37]

---

36 See e.g. T. Voon *Cultural Products and the World Trade Organization* (New York: Cambridge University Press, 2007); P. Van den Bossche, *Free Trade and Culture* (Amsterdam: Boekmanstudies 2007).

37 See e.g. F. Lenzerini, 'Property Protection and Protection of Cultural Heritage' in S. Schill (ed.) *International Investment Law and Comparative Public Law* (Oxford: Oxford University Press 2010), chapter 17; V. Vadi, *Cultural Heritage in International Investment Law and Arbitration* (Cambridge: Cambridge University Press 2014).

3) international cultural law scholarship;[38] 4) cultural rights scholarship;[39] and 5) examination of the EU cultural policy.[40]

In recent years international economic law scholars have begun to explore the complex interplay between global economic governance and cultural policies.[41] Scholars have acknowledged that, while economic liberalization may have positive effects on public well-being, it may also negatively affect some fundamental interests and values such as cultural policies.[42] While some authors have already analysed the interaction between trade and culture,[43] and others have investigated the parallel linkage between foreign direct investment and culture,[44] most have approached the relevant cases from a mere international or European law standpoint, leaving cultural policy arguments aside.

In parallel, international cultural law scholars have neglected the emerging cases due to their focus on more traditional aspects of cultural governance.[45] For instance, while some scholars have pinpointed the emergence of international cultural law as a distinct field of law, others have addressed the interplay between given specimens of the cultural wealth of nations and economic interests, leaving the broader picture aside. On the other hand, in the human rights discourse, cultural rights have been neglected for a long time and have been less developed than civil, political, economic, and social rights.[46] Only in the past decade have cultural rights begun to receive increased

---

38 See e.g. J.A.R. Nafziger, R. Kirkwood Paterson and A. Dundes Renteln (eds) *Cultural Law – International Comparative and Indigenous* (Cambridge: Cambridge University Press 2010); C. Forrest *International Law and the Protection of Cultural Heritage* (Abingdon: Routledge 2010); B. Hoffmann (ed.) *Art and Cultural Heritage: Law, Policy and Practice* (Cambridge: Cambridge University Press 2006).

39 See, for instance, F. Francioni and M. Scheinin (eds) *Cultural Human Rights* (Leiden/Boston, MA: Martinu Nijhoff 2008); E. Stamatopoulou *Cultural Rights in International Law* (Leiden: Martinus Nijhoff 2007); S. Borelli and F. Lenzerini (eds) *Cultural Heritage, Cultural Rights, Cultural Diversity* (Leiden/Boston, MA: Martinus Nijhoff 2012).

40 See, for instance, M. Pantel 'Unity in Diversity: Cultural Policy and EU Legitimacy' in T.F. Banchoff and M.P. Smith (eds) *Legitimacy and the European Union: The Contested Polity* (London: Routledge 1999) 46–65.

41 See e.g. F. Macmillan, 'Development, Cultural Self-Determination, and the World Trade Organization', in A Perry-Kessaris (ed.) *Law in Pursuit of Development: Principles into Practice?* (London: Routledge 2009); R. Coombe, 'Legal Claims to Culture in and Against the Market: Neoliberalism and the Global Proliferation of Meaningful Difference' 1 *Law Culture and the Humanities* (2005) 35–52.

42 J. Stiglitz, *Globalization and Its Discontents* (New York: Norton & Co. 2002).

43 See note 34 above.

44 See note 35 above.

45 See, however, R.K. Paterson and A. Telesetsky 'Heritage Inc.: A Mini-Symposium on Heritage Protection and Private Actors' 19 *International Journal of Cultural Property* (2012) 549–571.

46 V. Vadi, 'The Cultural Wealth of Nations in International Law' 21 *Tulane Journal of International and Comparative Law* (2012) 87–133.

attention. However, human rights scholars have only partially touched upon the interplay between economic globalization and cultural rights. The book contributes greatly to the fields of international cultural law and international law mapping their interaction.

Conclusions

The emergence of a number of conflicts and disputes of international resonance has put the interplay between culture and economic interests at the forefront of legal debate. Recent developments in international law seem to indicate the emergence of a new sensitivity in regulating cultural heritage and addressing related disputes. Whether general principles of law or even customary law requiring the protection of cultural heritage in times of peace have emerged is open to debate.

This chapter has highlighted some emerging features of the debate; pinpointing the interdisciplinary, intra-disciplinary and polyphonic nature of the debate on the interplay between culture and economic interests in international law. Not only is the topic interdisciplinary – attracting the interest of multiple constituencies – but it is also intra-disciplinary – involving different subsets of international law – and polyphonic because it involves both public and private actors. The emergence of investment treaty arbitrations and forms of participation to the proceedings by NGOs and local communities highlights the transformation of the notion of international law from the classical view of it being merely the law among states to today's more dynamic understanding of international law as a discipline in which private actors also matter.

In turn, this leads to a humanization of international law, making it more permeable to other interests which go beyond the *raison d'état* and include the respect for human dignity and fundamental human rights. Cultural heritage has a dual dimension – cultural and economic at the same time – taking on different meanings for different audiences. Adjudicators should acknowledge these different values. In this sense, the debate on the interplay between culture and economic interests contributes to the humanization of international law by putting humanity first.

This debate is contributing to international cultural law in that it counteracts *heritigization* processes which emphasize the protection of heritage because of its mere intrinsic features. The debate about the interplay between culture and economic interests contextualizes heritage within a broader framework – that of the human history. Heritage is not an abstract value; rather it matters to a variety of actors who attach different narratives to the same goods. Finally, these disputes also allow for further reflection on the meaning of justice in international relations.

Bibliography

Affolder, N. 'Company Reserves: Corporations, Natural Heritage, and Protected Areas of Law' 19 *International Journal of Cultural Property* (2012) 553–556.

Anghie, A. 'Finding the Peripheries: Sovereignty and Colonialism in Nineteenth-century International Law' 40 *Harvard International Law Journal* (1999) 1–80.

Becker Lorca, A. 'Universal International Law: Nineteenth Century Histories of Imposition and Appropriation' 51(2) *Harvard International Law Journal* (2010) 475–552.

Borelli S. and F. Lenzerini (eds) *Cultural Heritage, Cultural Rights, Cultural Diversity* (Leiden/Boston, MA: Martinus Nijhoff 2012).

Coombe, R. 'Legal Claims to Culture in and Against the Market: Neoliberalism and the Global Proliferation of Meaningful Difference' 1 *Law Culture and the Humanities* (2005) 35–52.

De Cesari, C. 'World Heritage and Mosaic Universalism' 10 *Journal of Social Anthropology* (2010) 299–324.

Donders Y. and V. Volodin (eds) *Human Rights in Education, Science and Culture: Legal Developments and Challenges* (Paris: UNESCO/Ashgate 2007).

Forrest, C. *International Law and the Protection of Cultural Heritage* (Abingdon: Routledge 2010).

Francioni F. 'The Human Dimension of International Cultural Heritage Law' 22 *European Journal of International Law* (2011) 9–16.

Francioni F. and M. Scheinin (eds), *Cultural Human Rights* (Leiden/Boston, MA: Martinus Nijhoff 2008).

Higgins, R. 'Conceptual Thinking about the Individual in International Law' in R. Falk, F. Kratochwil and S. Mendlovitz (eds) *International Law: A Contemporary Perspective* (Boulder, CO: Westview Press 1985), pp. 476–494.

Hoffmann B. (ed.) *Art and Cultural Heritage: Law, Policy and Practice* (Cambridge: Cambridge University Press 2006).

Lenzerini, F. 'Property Protection and Protection of Cultural Heritage' in S. Schill (ed.) *International Investment Law and Comparative Public Law* (Oxford: Oxford University Press 2010), pp. 201–218.

Macmillan, F. 'Development, Cultural Self-Determination, and the World Trade Organization' in A. Perry-Kessaris (ed.) *Law in Pursuit of Development: Principles into Practice?* (London: Routledge 2009), pp. 68–96.

Mason, A. 'International Project Financing and Cultural Heritage Protection' 19 *International Journal of Cultural Property* (2012) 556–560.

Miles, K. *The Origins of International Investment Law – Empire, Environment and the Safeguarding of Capital* (Cambridge: Cambridge University Press 2013).

Nafziger, J.A.R. 'Cultural Heritage Law: The International Regime' in J.A.R. Nafziger and T. Scovazzi (eds) *Le Patrimoine Culturel de l'Humanité* (Leiden: Martinus Nijhoff 2008), p. 145.

Nafziger, J.A.R. 'A Brief Sketch of the Relationship between Non-State Actors and the World Heritage Convention' 19 *International Journal of Cultural Property* (2012) 550–552.

Nafziger, J.A.R., R. Kirkwood Paterson and A. Dundes Renteln (eds) *Cultural Law – International Comparative and Indigenous* (Cambridge: Cambridge University Press 2010).

Pantel, M. 'Unity in Diversity: Cultural Policy and EU Legitimacy' in T.F. Banchoff and M.P. Smith (eds) *Legitimacy and the European Union: The Contested Polity* (London: Routledge 1999), pp. 46–65.

Paterson R.K. and A. Telesetsky, 'Heritage Inc.: A Mini-Symposium on Heritage Protection and Private Actors' 19 *International Journal of Cultural Property* (2012) 549–571.

Schneider H. and P. Van Den Bossche (eds) *Protection of Cultural Diversity from a European and International Perspective* (Antwerpen/ Oxford: Intersentia 2008).

Stamatopoulou, E. *Cultural Rights in International Law* (Leiden: Martinus Nijhoff 2007).

Stiglitz, J. *Globalization and Its Discontents* (New York: Norton & Co. 2002).

Vadi, V. 'The Cultural Wealth of Nations in International Law' 21 *Tulane Journal of International and Comparative Law* (2012) 87–133.

Vadi, V. *Cultural Heritage in International Investment Law and Arbitration* (Cambridge: Cambridge University Press 2014).

Van den Bossche, P. *Free Trade and Culture* (Amsterdam: Boekmanstudies 2007).

Voon, T. *Cultural Products and the World Trade Organization* (New York: Cambridge University Press 2007).

WIPO A User's Guide'. Online. Available: www.wipo.int/freepublications/en/general/1040/wipo_pub_1040.html (accessed 8 December 2013).

International instruments

Agreement on Trade-Related Aspects of Intellectual Property Rights, 15 April 1994, Marrakesh Agreement Establishing the World Trade Organization, Annex 1C, 33 ILM 1197 (1994).

Convention on the Protection and Promotion of the Diversity of Cultural Expressions, Paris, 20 October 2005, in force 18 March 2007. 2440 UNTS 311.

UN Declaration on the Rights of Indigenous Peoples, GA res. 61/295, 13 September 2007.

Agreement Establishing the World Trade Organization, 15 April 1994, 33 ILM 1144 (1994).

Convention on the Means of Prohibiting and Preventing the Illicit Import, Export and Transfer of Ownership of Cultural Property, Paris, 14 November 1970, in force 24 April 1972. 823 UNTS 231.

Recommendation Concerning the International Exchange of Cultural Property, 19th session of the General Conference of the United Nations Educational, Scientific and Cultural Organization, Nairobi, 26 October to 30 November 1976. Online. Available: http://portal.unesco.org/en/ev.php-URL_ID=13132&URL_DO=DO_TOPIC&URL_SECTION=201.html (accessed 8 December 2013).

Treaty on the Functioning of the European Union (TFEU), OJC 115, 9/5/2008, p. 47.

Vienna Convention on the Law of Treaties (VCLT), in force 27 January 1980. 1155 UNTS 331, 8 ILM 679.

Cases

European Communities – Certain Measures Prohibiting the Importation and Marketing of Seal Products, Panel Report, 25 November 2013, WT/DS369/2. Online. Available: www.wto.org/english/tratop_e/dispu_e/cases_e/ds400_e.htm (accessed 25 May 2014).

Glamis Gold Ldt v. United States of America, Award, 8 June 2009. Available: www.state.gov/s/l/c10986.htm (accessed 30 July 2014).

John R. Andre v. Government of Canada, Notice of Intent to Submit Claim to Arbitration Pursuant to Chapter Eleven of the North American Free Trade Agreement, 19 March 2010. Online. Available: www.international.gc.ca/trade-agreements-accords-commerciaux/assets/pdfs/JohnR_Andre_FiledNOI.pdf (accessed 25 May 2014).

Part I

Culture and economic interests in international law

2 Culture, human rights and international law

Francesco Francioni

Introduction

The emergence of culture in the international law discourse is the tip of the iceberg of a slow but constant process which tends to deconstruct the very concept of the state as we have known it from the Greek *polis* to the modern nation, a model that has divided human beings between *rulers* and *subjects*, in a defined sovereign space, the national territory. The present discourse on culture and international law reflects the rupture of this model and the emergence of new claims of recognition for different cultural groups in increasingly pluralistic societies, and for the role of culture, rather than mere politics, in the organization of social bodies. Individuals and groups demand recognition of their right to the unimpeded enjoyment of their freedom to participate in the shaping and development of their societies as cultural communities. This claim is increasingly framed in terms of human rights.

However, the relationship between culture and human rights has not been an easy one in the more than fifty years of international standards setting and scholarship. In 1945, the Lemkin genocide convention project placed culture at the heart of the definition of genocide and recognized that the intentional destruction of a human group, as shown by the appalling experience of the Shoah, was inseparable from the attack on the collective entity of the group as such and of its specific culture.[1] But the 1948 Convention rejected the concept of cultural genocide and linked the *actus reus* of the crime to the

---

1 R. Lemkin, *Axis Rule in Occupied Europe: Laws of Occupation – Analysis of Government – Proposals for Redress*, 2nd edn (first published 1944), Clark, NJ: Lawbook Exchange, Ltd 2008; B. Whitaker, 'Revised and Updated Report on the Question of the Prevention and Punishment of the Crime of Genocide', 2 July 1985, UN Doc. E/CN.4/Sub.2/1985/6; D.D. Anayiotos, 'The Cultural Genocide Debate: Should the UN Genocide Convention include a Provision on Cultural Genocide, or Should the Phenomenon be Encompassed in a Separate International Treaty?', *New York International Law Review*, Vol. 22, No. 2, 2009, 99–129; W.A. Schabas, *Genocide in International Law: The Crime of Crimes*, 2nd edn, Cambridge: Cambridge University Press, 2009.

physical destruction of 'a national, ethnical, racial or religious group as such'.[2] Similarly, the 1948 Universal Declaration of Human Rights consciously avoided recognizing rights of culturally distinct groups and minorities as specific subjects of human rights, opting rather for an absolute, natural law conception of human rights that left little room for cultural relativism to play a role in the field. This approach was also reinforced by the fear that such recognition of specific cultural rights for groups would have destabilizing effects on the internal structure of the states, as seen in the experience of minorities' protection in the post-World War I period.

From a more general point of view, the difficult relationship between culture and human rights can be explained by the fact that, since 1948, the human rights movement has been informed by an idea of human rights as rights of the individual, whereas culture by definition is a societal phenomenon. This latter concept implies the recognition of the collective interest of a human group in the preservation of its way of life, including language, religious beliefs, artistic heritage and child education. This also explains the paucity of human rights provisions expressly devoted to the protection of culture in contemporary instruments on the protection of fundamental rights.[3]

In spite of this past resistance, today a different approach to culture is beginning to emerge in international law. The internationalization of the economy and the revolution in information and communication technology increase the opportunities for cultural interaction between nations and, at the same time, spur an intense interest in local culture and traditions as an antidote to the alienating effects of globalization. Preservation of the plurality and diversity of cultures is thus becoming a major concern for the international community, as is witnessed by the adoption of the 2005 UNESCO Convention on the Protection and Promotion of the Diversity of Cultural Expressions.[4] The universal support for the 1972 World Heritage Convention, which embodies the spirit of representativity of the outstanding examples of the cultures of the world,[5] is evidence of the international concern for the

---

2   Article II Convention on the Prevention and Punishment of the Crime of Genocide, adopted by the UN General Assembly on 9 December 1948, and entered into force on 12 January 1951, 78 UNTS 277. This Article also includes in the definition of genocide acts that do not involve the physical destruction of the individual members of the group: namely the forcible transfer of children of the group to another group. This is as far as the Convention goes in acknowledging that acts not involving physical destruction, but only socio-cultural dismemberment of the group, may amount to genocide.

3   See F. Francioni and M. Scheinin (eds), *Cultural Human Rights*, Leiden/Boston, MA: Martinus Nijhoff, 2008, pp. 2 ff.

4   UNESCO Convention on the Protection and Promotion of the Diversity of Cultural Expressions, adopted by the General Conference of UNESCO at its 33rd Session, Paris, 20 October 2005, reprinted in *Standard Setting in UNESCO*, vol. II, UNESCO, 2007, pp. 326 ff.

5   Convention concerning the Protection of the World Cultural and Natural Heritage, adopted by the General Conference of UNESCO at its 17th session, Paris, 16 November 1972. Ibid., supra note 4 p. 135. For a commentary, see F. Francioni (ed.), *The 1972 World Heritage Convention: a Commentary*, Oxford: Oxford University Press, 2008.

identification and preservation of the diversity of the tangible expressions of the cultures of the world. Other important indicators of the growing role that culture plays in the present evolution of international law are the intensification of interest in minority protection – also with regard to the new phenomenon of minorities formed by immigrant populations – and the powerful movement on the rights of Indigenous peoples. This movement has led to the adoption of the 2007 UN Declaration of the Rights of Indigenous Peoples, a declaration that is by and large inspired by the pre-eminent objective of safeguarding the specific way of life of Indigenous peoples as cultural communities.[6]

If we take into account these developments, several normative perspectives can be explored on the relationship between culture and international law as a prologue to this book on culture and international economic law. The first one concerns the way in which culture has contributed to the shaping of certain individual rights, such as the right to access and participate in a community's cultural life, the right to preserve one's cultural identity, as well as collective rights, in particular minorities' and Indigenous peoples' rights.

The second line of analysis relates to the human dimension of cultural heritage, a dimension that is the result of a dynamic evolution of the concept and scope of cultural heritage, from a material conception prevalent in the Western civilization to the living culture and the 'intangible' cultural heritage, which includes social practices and tradition that are an integral part of the social fabric of any nation or group.[7]

The third aspect to be analysed is linked to the above evolution and concerns the role of international human rights as a limit to the recognition and safeguarding of the culture and cultural heritage of a specific community.

The fourth aspect of the interaction between culture and human rights stems from the emerging consensus that grave offences against the culture and cultural heritage of other peoples, both in times of war and peace, must be criminalized and prosecuted under international law.

A fifth aspect of the relationship would concern the impact of culture on international trade and international investment law. But I will not cover this aspect in this chapter since it constitutes the object of the specific contributions elsewhere in this volume.

The influence of culture in the shaping of human rights

Several provisions can be identified among the post-World War II instruments on the protection of human rights in which culture is treated as a component

---

6 United Nations Declaration on the Rights of Indigenous Peoples, GA Resolution A/res/61/295, 13 September 2007.
7 UNESCO Convention on the Safeguarding of the Intangible Cultural Heritage, adopted by the General Conference of UNESCO at its 32nd session, Paris, 17 October 2003, reprinted in *Standard Setting in UNESCO*, op. cit. p 297 ff.

of specific categories of rights. Article 27 of the 1948 Universal Declaration proclaims 'the right freely to participate in the cultural life of the community'. This right is articulated in terms of an individual entitlement ('everyone has the rights') rather than of a communal right of a group to perform and transmit is own culture. The individual connotation of this right is reinforced by para. 2 of Article 27, which proclaims the right of everyone to the protection of the moral and material interest resulting from the literary, artistic and scientific production of which 'he is the author'. Indirect support for culture can also be found in Article 26 of the Universal Declaration, which proclaims the right to education, with the general aim to strengthen 'respect for human rights and fundamental freedoms' and to promote 'tolerance and friendship among all nations, racial and religious groups' as well as the right of parents 'to choose the kind of education that shall be given to their children'.

These provisions were the basis for the drafting of the more detailed provisions of Article 15 and Article 13 of the 1966 International Covenant on Economic, Social and Cultural Rights (ICESCR). The first article reiterates the right of everyone to take part in cultural life, to enjoy the benefits of scientific progress, and also the right of authors to benefit from the protection of the moral and material interests vesting in their artistic production. Article 13 of the ICESCR expands the concept and scope of the right to education by establishing an obligation of the state parties to ensure free and universal primary education[8] and give equal opportunity for all to access secondary and higher education.[9] Of particular importance for the present discussion is the recognition in para. 3 of Article 13 of the liberty of 'individuals and bodies' to organize and direct their own educational institutions, a provision that certainly takes into account the role of education in the maintenance and transmission of the cultural specificity of a group.

If we move from universal human rights to regional systems, apart from a generic reference to 'cultural development' in Article 22 of the African Charter,[10] no meaningful provision on culture can be found in either the 1950 European Convention or the 1969 American Convention. However, subsequent protocols have added a cultural dimension to the rights protected under these instruments. This is the case with the 1999 Protocol of San Salvador, an additional protocol of the American Convention, on economic, social and cultural rights,[11] whose Article 14 enunciates the right to take part in cultural life, and, with respect to the European Convention, Additional Protocol 1,

---

8   Article 13 para. 2(a) of the ICESCR.
9   Article 13 para. 2(b) and (c) of the ICESCR.
10 'All peoples shall have the right to their economic, social and cultural development '. Article 22 para. 1 of the African Charter of Human And Peoples' Rights (Banjul Charter), adopted by the Organisation of African Unity on 27 June 1981, entered into force, 21 October 1986. OAU Doc. CAB/LEG/67/3/Rev. 5.
11 Organization of American States, *Additional Protocol to the American Convention on Human Rights in the Area of Economic, Social and Cultural Rights* ('*Protocol of San Salvador*'), 16 November 1999, A-52, www.refworld.org/docid/3ae6b3b90.html (accessed 4 September 2013).

whose Article 2 establishes the right to education, including the right of parents to the respect of their religious and philosophical beliefs, which obviously includes the cultural traditions associated with such beliefs. This right could provide a strong guarantee against state interference with the practice by groups of their specific culture. However, this is not an absolute right. As the case law of the European Court demonstrates, it is to be construed within the context of the ample margin of appreciation that every state party enjoys in the implementation of Article 2 in harmony with the system of religious traditions and cultural values prevailing in the state.[12]

At the level of European Union law, consideration for culture can be found in the lapidary provision of Article 22 of the EU Charter of fundamental rights, which commits the Union to the respect of cultural, religious and linguistic diversities.[13] This finds its corresponding provision in Article 167 of the Lisbon Treaty which commits the Union to respecting and promoting the diversity of its cultures as a component of the policies that it pursues under other provisions of the Treaties.[14]

If we look beyond human rights treaties, many important UNESCO instruments are devoted to culture. Among them, we can recall the 1966 Declaration of the Principles of International Cultural Cooperation,[15] the 1976 Recommendation on Participation by the People at Large in Cultural Life and their Contribution to It,[16] the 2003 Recommendation on the Promotion of Multilingualism,[17] the 1989 Recommendation on the Safeguarding of Traditional Culture and Folklore,[18] and the 2001 Universal Declaration on Cultural Diversity.[19] All these instruments belong to the category of soft law, and, although they are not formally binding, they carry a considerable normative weight owing to the fact that they were adopted by a universal body such as the General Conference of UNESCO, with some of them carrying the more solemn title of 'Declaration'. In addition, some of these instruments were later developed into formally binding law. This is the case with the 2003

---

12 See *Lautsi and others v. Italy*, European Court of Human Rights, Application no. 30814/06, Judgment (Grand Chamber) of 18 March 2011.

13 EU Charter of Fundamental Rights, first adopted in Nice on 7 December 2000 and then proclaimed, with some modifications, in Strasbourg on 12 December 2007, Official Journal of the EU n. C 303, 14 December 2007.

14 Article 167, para. 4 of the Lisbon Treaty.

15 Declaration of the Principles of International Cultural Cooperation, adopted by the General Conference of UNESCO on 4 November 1966. Text reprinted in *Standard Setting in UNESCO*, op. cit., pp. 669 ff.

16 1976 Recommendation on Participation by the People at Large in cultural Life and their Contribution to It, text reprinted in *Standard Setting in UNESCO*, op. cit., p. 487 ff.

17 2003 Recommendation on the Promotion of Multilingualism, text reprinted in *Standard Setting in UNESCO*, op. cit., p. 660 ff.

18 1989 Recommendation on the Safeguarding of Traditional Culture and Folklore, text reprinted in *Standard Setting in UNESCO*, op. cit., p. 605 ff.

19 2001 Universal Declaration on Cultural Diversity, text reprinted in *Standard Setting in UNESCO*, op. cit., pp. 707 ff.

Convention on the Safeguarding of Intangible Cultural Heritage,[20] and the 2005 Convention on the Protection and Promotion of the Diversity of Cultural Expressions.[21]

Among the binding instruments, a special position is occupied by the 2005 Council of Europe's Faro Convention on the Value of Cultural Heritage for Society. This convention focuses on the role of citizens in managing their cultural environment and it is the first instrument to identify cultural heritage as a connecting factor in the building of European identity, and to connect cultural heritage to human rights. This approach has a strong potential for those countries where an imposed official state political culture in the recent past had suppressed genuine popular traditions and living culture. It is important also for the multicultural challenge posed by the settlement of migrant communities in Europe that wish to retain their linguistic, cultural and religious traditions.[22]

More recently, the link between international human rights and culture has found expression in the 2007 UN Declaration on the Rights of Indigenous Peoples.[23] Culture is the dominant theme of the Declaration, which is pervaded by the principle that '[i]ndigenous peoples have the right to practice and revitalize their cultural traditions and customs'.[24]

In spite of the absence of a specialized forum for the enforcement of cultural norms, judicial and arbitral practice is also contributing to the identification and consolidation of the linkage between culture and human rights. The International Court of Justice had the opportunity to highlight the importance of cultural heritage in the context of genocide in *Bosnia-Herzegovina v. Serbia*[25] and then to uphold, in *Navigational and Related Rights*, the cultural traditions of local communities as a component of their right to the preservation of forms of subsistence economy (fishing).[26] In the area of international economic law, which is most relevant to the theme of this book, arbitral practice in the field of investment protection shows a systematic opening of the adjudication process to considerations of culture and cultural heritage protection.[27]

---

20 2003 Convention on the Safeguarding of Intangible Cultural Heritage, text reprinted in *Standard Setting in UNESCO*, op. cit., pp. 297 ff.

21 2005 Convention on the Protection and Promotion of the Diversity of Cultural Expressions, text reprinted in *Standard Setting in UNESCO*, op. cit., pp. 326 ff.

22 See *Khurshid Mustafa and Tarzibachi v. Sweden*, ECtHR Application no. 238883/06, Judgment, 16 December 2008.

23 2007 UN Declaration on the Rights of Indigenous Peoples, adopted by the General Assembly, 13 September 2007, A/Res/61/295.

24 Article 11 of the UNDRIP. See also Articles 27, 31 and 34 of the UNDRIP.

25 *Genocide Case (Bosnia-Herzegovina v. Serbia)*, Judgment of 10 February 2007

26 *Navigational and Related Rights (Costa Rica v. Nicaragua)*, Judgment of 13 July 2009, paras 134–144.

27 See *SPP Ltd v. Egypt*, ARB/84/3, 20 May 1992; *Glamis Gold Ltd v. United States*, ICSID Award, 8 June 2009; *Parkering AS v. Lithuania*, ICSID case No. ARB/05/08, Award, 11 September

The human rights dimension of cultural heritage

This aspect of the relationship between culture and international law relates to the transformative process that has taken place with regard to the concept and scope of cultural heritage in international law and practice. The transformation consists in the dynamic evolution that the concept of 'cultural heritage' has undergone from the material connotation of 'cultural property' and 'cultural objects', understood as tangible goods of artistic, historical and archaeological value, to the 'immaterial' notion of heritage coinciding with living tradition and customs of a cultural community. The concept of 'cultural property' was inaugurated with the 1954 Hague Convention for the Protection of Cultural Property in the event of Armed Conflict[28] whose definition covered only monuments and material objects according to the prevailing Western tradition and understanding of art and culture. The scope of this notion was extended with the 1972 World Heritage Convention, which included natural heritage and a new notion of cultural heritage as a representation of the variety of the exceptionally important cultural traditions of the world. In this sense, the 1972 Convention is an antecedent of the 2005 Convention on the Protection and Promotion of the Diversity of Cultural Expressions. But the decisive step towards the international recognition of the human dimension of cultural heritage was the launching by UNESCO of the Living Human Treasures and the Masterpieces of Oral and Intangible Heritage programmes, which finally led to the adoption of the 2003 UNESCO Convention on the Safeguarding of Intangible Cultural Heritage.[29] The dematerialization of cultural heritage and the widening of the scope of international protection to cover living culture and 'intangible heritage' has a potential for enhancing cultural human rights, but may also pose the risk of hidden conflicts and discrepancies. For example, the safeguarding of intangible cultural heritage may run counter to the specific protection of intellectual property rights (IPRs), as recognized by Article 15(1) of the International Covenant on Economic, Social and Cultural Rights. This is acknowledged in the 2003 Convention, which contains a saving clause (Article 3 b) on IPRs. At the same time, intangible cultural heritage may entail the performance of racist practices, expressions of religious intolerance or forms of inhumane treatment of animals that run counter to the shared sense of human dignity or to basic considera-tion of humanity. These potential conflicts are foreseen by the 2003 Conven-tion, which requires, as a condition for consideration of heritage under the Convention, the compatibility of proposed intangible cultural heritage with 'existing international human rights instruments, as well as with requirements

2007. On these cases, see F. Francioni, 'Plurality and Interaction of Legal Orders in the Enforcement of Cultural Heritage Law', in F. Francioni and J. Gordley (eds), *Enforcing International Cultural Heritage Law*, Oxford: Oxford University Press, 2013, pp. 22 ff.

28 1954 Hague Convention for the Protection of Cultural Property in the event of Armed Conflict, reprinted in *Standard Setting in UNESCO*, op. cit. pp. 65 ff.

29 *Supra*, n. 7.

of mutual respect among communities, groups and individuals, and of sustainable development'.[30]

And this brings us to the negative role of human rights as limits to the recognition and protection of cultural expressions under international law.

Human rights as limits to the international protection of cultural expressions

This facet of the relationship between culture and international human rights presents two distinct types of conflicts. The first one a) is between the *collective right* of the group as a cultural community to maintain its distinct customs and the *individual right* of members of the group to enjoy personal freedom and self-determination in the pursuit of their project of good life. The second type of conflict b) arises when the cultural tradition of the community is in itself incompatible with international law standards.

a) The first conflict has arisen in a number of cases brought before international human rights courts and monitoring bodies. The classic case is *Lovelace v. Canada* which involved the claim of a Canadian woman who had left her native tribe to marry outside the Indigenous community. When she later divorced her non-native husband, she sought permission to return and buy a home in her native land but was refused access to programmes permitting the purchase of a house on the alleged ground that, under customary rules of the tribe, she had lost her Indian status after her marriage. Deference of Canadian law to the law of the Indigenous peoples foreclosed the possibility of enforcing the claimant's right to have access to a home in Canadian courts. The Human Rights Committee decided the case in favour of the personal right of the woman. But the decision was not made on the basis of an assumed prevalence of the individual right of the group's member over the collective right of the community to maintain its cultural traditions. Rather, the Committee found that Canada had failed to ensure the observance of the principle of non-discrimination on the basis of gender: the refusal of the right to return applied only to women who had left the tribe and not to male members. Another manifestation of this type of conflict concerns property rights and the community's interest in preserving certain forms of cultural heritage. A state may enact laws and regulations for the protection of a cultural landscape and then see such regulations challenged in court on the basis of the individual right to property and to the peaceful enjoyment of his/her possessions, as provided under Article 1, Protocol 1 to the European Convention on Human Rights. Emblematic of this situation is the case *Fondi Sud v. Italy*, in which Italy was found liable to pay a substantial reparation (49 million Euros) for the economic damage suffered by the applicants as a consequence of the confiscation of real estate development and demolition of buildings disfiguring the landscape and coastline in the southern region of Apulia. The

---

30   Article 2(1) of the UNESCO Convention on the Safeguarding of Intangible Cultural Heritage.

development and the construction of the building had been found in breach of national law on heritage and landscape and condemned in a series of national judgments. But since the development and building had been originally permitted by local authorities, the Strasbourg Court held that the confiscation and demolition amounted to an *ex post facto* application of criminal sanctions (Article 7) and to violation of property rights (Article 1, protocol 1).[31] Conversely, cultural human rights may be claimed by individuals to challenge public regulations on land management and landscape conservation. In *Chapman v. United Kingdom* the Roma applicants were claiming the right as a minority to live in a trailer in defiance of United Kingdom regulation on land use and landscape protection. Here the cultural claim failed because of the overriding importance of the public interest in land management in an environmentally sensitive area;[32] but also because of the absence of a specific cultural provision on minority rights in the European Convention system. The applicants had based their case on the alleged violation of Articles 8 (private and family life) and 14 (non-discrimination) of the Convention.[33]

b) The second type of conflict, concerning the incompatibility of the relevant cultural expression and internationally recognized human rights, may arise with regard to material expressions of art and heritage which symbolize ideas and beliefs which are offensive to human dignity. This is the case with monuments celebrating racism or memorializing slavery or periods of history marked by gross violations of human rights. This becomes a sensitive problem when such monuments are located in a public place or in a politically significant space such as a government building or an historical site. In this case the preservation of the cultural property may yield to the political-cultural aim of removing the memory of a discredited past.[34]

But the most frequent clash between culture and human rights is likely to occur in the area of intangible cultural rights, where cultural traditions may involve gender segregation and discrimination, as well as practices entailing the violation of physical integrity, self-mutilation, female genital cutting and other forms of physical violence. This potential clash is acknowledged in the text of the 2003 Convention on the Safeguarding of Intangible Cultural

---

31 *Fondi Sud v. Italy*, Judgment of 10 May 2012, Application no. 75909/01.

32 *Chapman v. United Kingdom*, Judgment of 18 January 2001, Application no. *27238/95*.

33 It is to be noted, however, that the Court recognized a possible future consensus among the member states of the Council of Europe regarding the special needs of minorities and an obligation to protect their security, identity and lifestyle. As a matter of fact a general consensus in this direction had been expressed within the Council of Europe at the time of the adoption of the Framework Convention for the Protection of National Minorities of 1 February 1995, which provides that states parties submit a report to the Council of Europe containing 'full information on the legislative and other measures taken to give effect to the principles set out in this framework Convention' (Article 25).

34 See the illuminating analysis of S. Levinson, *Written in Stone: Public Monuments in Changing Societies*, Durham, NC: Duke University Press, 1998, and, of the same author, 'Political Change and the Creative Destruction of Public Space', in F. Francioni and M. Scheinin (eds), *Cultural Human Rights*, Leiden/Boston, MA: Martinus Nijhoff, 2008, pp. 341 ff.

Heritage, whose Article 2 provides that:

> consideration shall be given solely to such intangible cultural heritage as is compatible with existing international human rights instruments, as well as with requirements of mutual respect among communities, groups and individuals.

Similar provisions can be found in the 2005 Convention on Cultural Diversity (Articles 2(1) and 5(1)), and in Article 46(2) of the 2007 UN Declaration on the Rights of Indigenous Peoples. However, these provisions provide only a partial solution to the problem. First, the exclusion of cultural practices that are incompatible with human rights only operates within the limited scope of the relevant convention and for the purpose of its operation. This means that with regard to the Convention on Intangible Heritage, the human rights test may only serve the purpose of barring the inscription of a particular cultural heritage in the Representative List of the Intangible Cultural Heritage of Humanity pursuant to Article 16. The 2005 Convention on Cultural Diversity does not contemplate a similar list, but provides for a Fund and a Committee which may evaluate the compatibility of a given cultural expression with human rights. Besides, the above treaty provisions only apply prospectively, once the treaties have entered into force, and in no way can they impact on problematic cultural practices that may have already received some form of international recognition.[35]

International criminalization of cultural offences

This aspect of the intersection between culture and human rights is a relative late comer in the development of international law. Regrettably, international law scholarship has long neglected the connection between the protection of cultural heritage and egregious violations of human rights. It took the descent into sheer barbarity of the Yugoslav war of the 1990s and the subsequent infamous destruction of the ancient art and heritage by the ruling Taliban in Afghanistan – later replicated in Mali and Syria – to direct scholars and public opinion to the link between attacks on culture and violations of human rights. It became evident, as a matter of fact, that much of the cultural destruction of monuments, religious buildings, libraries and historical sites in these wars was not the collateral effect of the conduct of hostilities but the result of deliberate targeting of cultural objects with the purpose of 'cleansing' the attacked territory, not only of the human presence, but also of the symbols and cultural traces of the enemy's life and presence in the territory. So, on 9 November 1993, Croatian artillery bombed and destroyed the ancient Mostar bridge, not for military necessity, but because the bridge symbolized

---

35   This is the case with items included in the UNESCO program of Masterpieces of Oral and Intangible Heritage, which was not subject to the human rights test.

the peaceful coexistence and the material and cultural connection of the Muslim and Christian communities on the two sides of the river. For the same reason Serbs destroyed mosques in Bosnia and Muslims destroyed Orthodox churches and monasteries in Kosovo. When, in March 2001, the Taliban finally carried out its threats to destroy the great Buddhas of Bamiyan, the world reacted with incredulity and indignation. Yet, the experience of the Yugoslav war had provided ample evidence that attacks on culture and cultural heritage had become a systematic method of conducting war by other 'means' and extending the brutality of ethnic cleansing to cultural persecution and cultural extinction.

Over the past two decades, the link between attacks on culture and grave violations of human rights has emerged at the level of international law and has taken precise legal connotations in the form of international crimes.[36] This is witnessed by the criminalization of offences against cultural heritage in the Statute of the International Criminal Tribunal of Former Yugoslavia (ICTY), Article 3(d), and in the Statute of the International Criminal Court, Article 8. The 1999 Second Protocol to the 1954 Hague Convention has introduced a detailed regime of individual criminal responsibility for attacks against cultural property in time of conflict, international and non-international (Articles 15–20), which goes beyond the general provisions of the 1954 Convention and the 1907 Hague Convention IV. In 2003 the UNESCO General Conference adopted by unanimous vote the Declaration Concerning the Intentional Destruction of Cultural Heritage, which restates the principle of state responsibility and individual criminal liability for deliberate acts of destruction of cultural heritage of great importance for humanity.[37] What is more important, a chain of case law has developed in the judicial practice of international criminal tribunals which has articulated and clarified the different aspects of the legal connection between wilful destruction of cultural heritage and breaches of human rights. First, this practice has clarified and expanded the concept and scope of cultural property relevant to the commission of a war crime.[38] Second, it has established that intentional destruction of cultural property is an independent count of criminal liability under the law of armed conflict, and that, when the destruction is carried out with a discriminatory intent, it amounts to a crime against humanity, i.e. the crime of persecution.[39] Third, in cases of attacks on cultural property recognized as being of exceptional

36 For a review of the role of courts in the development of this area of the law, see F. Lenzerini, 'The Role of International and Mixed Criminal Courts in the Enforcement of International Norms Concerning the Protection of Cultural Heritage', in F. Francioni and J. Gordley (eds), *Enforcing International Cultural Heritage Law*, Oxford: Oxford University Press, 2013, pp. 40 ff.

37 Articles VI and VII of the Declaration, adopted on 17 October 2003. Text in *Standard Setting in UNESCO*, op. cit. pp. 729 ff.

38 See *Prosecutor v. Blaskic*, Case IT-95–14-T, Trial Chamber, Judgment of 3 March 2000; *Kordic v. Cerkez*, Case IT-95-14/2 T, Trial Chamber, Judgment of 26 February 2001.

39 *Kordic-Cerkez*, op. cit.

importance and registered as such in the inventory of competent international organizations, the attacks involve the breach of an *erga omnes* obligation and entail an aggravated responsibility.[40] Finally, the ICTY has held that the deliberate and systematic destruction of cultural heritage of a particular ethnic group may constitute evidence of the 'specific intent' (*mens rea*) required for the commission of the crime of genocide.[41]

Conclusions

I started this chapter by referring to the early debates on the role of culture at the time of the drafting of the 1948 Genocide Convention with its failure to accept the notion that causing the cultural extinction of a group may amount to the crime of genocide. Sixty years later we have seen how cultural destruction, when combined with the physical elimination of a group, may become a psychological component of the crime of genocide. In this period, culture has played an increasingly important role in the progressive development of international law. It has contributed to the identification of a cultural dimension of internationally recognized human rights, as well as to the fashioning of a new category of collective cultural rights that belong to the collective body of the group, as in the case of Indigenous peoples. An important impact of culture on the contemporary development of international law is at the intersection between heritage law and international criminal law. The emergence of the category of international cultural crimes in the past twenty years is a reminder that culture can also have a destructive effect, when it becomes the source of intolerance and ill feelings towards 'others' and their different culture. Far from ceding to the temptation of offering a romantic vision of 'cultural traditions', capable of trumping other norms of international law, in this chapter I have tried to show how the recognition and protection of culture by international law remains contingent upon its compatibility with the universally accepted standards of human rights, human dignity and mutual respect among different cultural communities.

Bibliography

African Charter of Human and Peoples' Rights (Banjul Charter), adopted by the Organisation of African Unity on 27 June 1981, entered into force, 21 October 1986. OAU Doc. CAB/LEG/67/3/Rev. 5.

Anayiotos, D.D., 'The Cultural Genocide Debate: Should the UN Genocide Convention include a Provision on Cultural Genocide, or should the Phenomenon be Encompassed in a Separate International Treaty?', *New York International Law Review*, Vol. 22, No. 2, 2009, 99–129.

---

40 *Prosecutor v. Strugar*, Case IT-01.42-T, Trial Chamber II, Judgment of 31 January 2005.
41 *Prosecutor v. Krstic*, Case IT-98-33-T. Judgment of the Trial Chamber, 2 August 2001, affirmed by the Appellate Chamber 19 April 2004.

Convention concerning the Protection of the World Cultural and Natural Heritage, adopted by the General Conference of UNESCO at its 17th session, Paris, 16 November 1972.

Convention on the Prevention and Punishment of the Crime of Genocide, adopted by the UN General Assembly on 9 December 1948, and entered into force 12 January 1951, 78 UNTS 277.

Declaration of the Principles of International Cultural Cooperation, adopted by the General Conference of UNESCO on 4 November 1966, reprinted in Standard Setting in UNESCO.

EU Charter of Fundamental Rights, first adopted in Nice on 7 December 2000 and then proclaimed, with some modifications, in Strasbourg on 12 December 2007, Official Journal of the EU n. C 303, 14 December 2007.

Francioni, F. (ed), *The 1972 World Heritage Convention: a Commentary*, Oxford: Oxford University Press, 2008.

Francioni, F., 'Plurality and Interaction of Legal Orders in the Enforcement of Cultural Heritage Law', in F. Francioni and J. Gordley (eds) *Enforcing International Cultural Heritage Law*, Oxford: Oxford University Press, 2013, pp. 9–21.

Francioni, F. and Scheinin, M. (eds), *Cultural Human Rights*, Leiden/Boston, MA: Martinus Nijhoff, 2008.

Lemkin, R., *Axis Rule in Occupied Europe: Laws of Occupation – Analysis of Government – Proposals for Redress*, 2nd edn (first published 1944), Clark, NJ: Lawbook Exchange Ltd, 2008.

Lenzerini, F., 'The Role of International and Mixed Criminal Courts in the Enforcement of International Norms Concerning the Protection of Cultural Heritage', in F. Francioni and J. Gordley (eds), *Enforcing International Cultural Heritage Law*, Oxford: Oxford University Press, 2013, pp. 40 ff.

Levinson, S., *Written in Stone: Public Monuments in Changing Societies*, Durham, NC: Duke University Press, 1998.

Levinson S. 'Political Change and the Creative Destruction of Public Space', in F. Francioni and M. Scheinin (eds), *Cultural Human Rights*, Leiden/Boston, MA: Martinus Nijhoff Publishers, 2008, pp. 341 ff.

Organization of American States, *Additional Protocol to the American Convention on Human Rights in the Area of Economic, Social and Cultural Rights ('Protocol of San Salvador')*, 16 November 1999, A-52. Online. Available: http://refworld.org/docid/3ae6b3b90.html (accessed 4 September 2013).

Schabas, W.A., *Genocide in International Law: The Crime of Crimes*, 2nd edn, Cambridge: Cambridge University Press, 2009.

UNESCO Convention on the Safeguarding of the Intangible Cultural Heritage, adopted by the General Conference of UNESCO at its 32nd session, Paris, 17 October 2003, reprinted in Standard Setting in UNESCO.

UNESCO Convention on the Protection and Promotion of the Diversity of Cultural Expressions, adopted by the General Conference of UNESCO at its 33rd Session, Paris, 20 October 2005, reprinted in Standard Setting in UNESCO.

United Nations Declaration on the Rights of Indigenous Peoples, GA Resolution A/res/61/295, 13 September 2007.

Whitaker, B., 'Revised and Updated Report on the Question of the Prevention and Punishment of the Crime of Genocide', 2 July 1985, UN Doc. E/CN.4/Sub.2/1985/6.

Cases

Case *Bosnia-Herzegovina v. Serbia and Montenegro (Genocide Case)*, Judgment of 10 February 2007.

Case *Chapman v. United Kingdom*, Judgment of 18 January 2001, Application no. 27238/95.

Case *Fondi Sud v. Italy*, Judgment of 10 May 2012, Application no. 75909/01.

Case *Glamis Gold Ltd v. United States*, ICSID Award, 8 June 2009.

Case *Khurshid Mustafa and Tarzibachi v. Sweden*, ECtHR Application no. 238883/06, Judgment, 16 December 2008.

Case *Kordic v. Cerkez*, Case IT-95–14/2 T, Trial Chamber, Judgment of 26 February 2001.

Case *Lautsi and others v. Italy*, European Court of Human Rights, Application no. 30814/06, Judgment (Grand Chamber) of 18 March 2011.

Case *Navigational and Related Rights (Costa Rica v. Nicaragua)*, Judgment of 13 July 2009.

Case *Parkering AS v. Lithuania*, ICSID, Case No. ARB/05/08, Award, 11 September 2007.

Case *Prosecutor v. Blaskic*, Case No. IT-95–14-T, Trial Chamber, Judgment of 3 March 2000.

Case *Prosecutor v. Krstic*, Case No. IT-98–33-T, Judgment of the Trial Chamber, 2 August 2001, affirmed by the Appellate Chamber 19 April 2004.

Case Prosecutor v. Strugar, Case IT-01.42-T, Trial Chamber II, Judgment of 31 January 2005.

SPP Ltd v. Egypt, ARB/84/3, 20 May 1992.

3 The cultural dimension of economic activities in international human rights jurisprudence

Yvonne Donders[1]

Introduction

Cultural diversity and human rights are mutually linked: human rights protect and promote cultural diversity while cultural diversity also forms an important aspect of the enjoyment of human rights. Cultural diversity and the economy are also increasingly connected, for example through cultural industries, trade in cultural goods, but also the protection of cultural heritage. The relationship between the three – human rights, cultural diversity and the economy – is, however, not fully clear. For instance, while cultural expressions such as paintings, books and films, fall within the scope of the right to freedom of expression, the trade in these products is not necessarily part of this human right. While the right to access to cultural heritage is considered part of the right to take part in cultural life, the economic issues related to the management of cultural heritage are not necessarily part of the human rights dimension.

One of the areas in international human rights law where the link between human rights, culture and economy has been recognized and elaborated is the protection of rights of Indigenous peoples against state-authorized economic activities, such as mining and logging operations. Several states have authorized (semi-) private companies to carry out economic activities on land where Indigenous peoples live and where those peoples carry out *their own* economic activities. Precisely because these economic activities of Indigenous peoples have a strong cultural dimension, they may fall within the realm of the protection of international human rights law. The uses to which such land is put by Indigenous peoples, for example fishing, hunting or herding and breeding activities, have an economic dimension in that they provide labour, income and trade possibilities, but the way these economic activities are carried

1 Prof. Dr. Yvonne Donders is Professor of International Human Rights and Cultural Diversity and Executive Director of the Amsterdam Center for International Law at the Faculty of Law of the University of Amsterdam. She thanks Martin Reuling, Research Master student, for his valuable help in collecting jurisprudence.

out has a strong cultural dimension. The use of the land and the ways animals are kept, killed and used, are firmly connected to the cultural identity of the community concerned, which triggers human rights protection. These rights of Indigenous peoples have to be balanced against the interest of the state to promote economic development.

This chapter explores how international supervisory bodies have dealt with this balance and which criteria they have set down to assess the interference by states with the rights of Indigenous peoples to the protection of their economic activities. Section 1 examines the concept of economic activities with a cultural dimension. Section 2 scrutinizes the jurisprudence of the UN Human Rights Committee. Section 3 critically assesses the jurisprudence of the Inter-American Court of Human Rights and the African Commission on Human and Peoples' Rights. The conclusion summarizes the findings and sums up the various criteria.

Economic activities with a cultural dimension

Economic activities are not as such protected under international human rights law, but they can be protected under several human rights provisions if they have cultural value that links these activities to human dignity and thereby to human rights. The best example of such economic activities with cultural value are activities related to the use of land by Indigenous peoples, for instance for fishing, hunting or reindeer herding. As such, land rights are not included in general international human rights instruments. They are, however, recognized in international instruments on Indigenous peoples, for instance ILO Convention 169 on Indigenous and Tribal Peoples[2] and the UN Declaration on the Rights of Indigenous Peoples.[3] These have inspired international human rights monitoring bodies to read land rights into several human rights norms.

The state, as the main duty bearer of human rights implementation, can limit human rights, including land rights. One of the reasons to do so is economic development. The state may itself, or via contracts with private companies, wish to explore certain territories in order to economically develop a region. The general criteria for limiting human rights are that the measures should be provided by law, should have a legitimate aim and should be necessary and proportionate. There have been several cases before international human rights bodies brought by Indigenous communities against states concerning limitations of the use of land or expropriation, which were allegedly in violation of international human rights norms. In these cases, a balance was to be sought between the interest of the Indigenous people to have their economic activities with a cultural dimension respected and protected and the

---

2   ILO Convention 169 concerning Indigenous and Tribal Peoples in Independent Countries, adopted 27 June 1989, entered into force 5 September 1991.
3   UN Declaration on the Rights of Indigenous Peoples, GA Res. 61/295, 13 September 2007.

general interest of the state to promote economic development. Supervisory bodies have dealt with these cases under different human rights provisions, such as the right to (private) life, property, the right to health and the right to enjoy culture, when these economic activities impacted on the land and culture of the Indigenous peoples. The following sections explore the criteria used to assess the balance between economic development and the protection of cultural activities with an economic dimension.

UN level: Article 27 ICCPR and the Human Rights Committee

Article 27 ICCPR

The provision in international human rights law most often used to defend economic activities with a cultural dimension is Article 27 of the International Covenant on Civil and Political Rights (ICCPR),[4] which reads as follows:

> In those States in which ethnic, religious or linguistic minorities exist, persons belonging to such minorities shall not be denied the right, in community with the other members of their group, to enjoy their own culture, to profess and practise their own religion, or to use their own language.

The scope and normative content of this provision have been elaborated by the supervisory body of the ICCPR, the Human Rights Committee (HRC), in its Concluding Observations on state reports, its views on individual complaints and in its General Comment on Article 27.

The subjects of Article 27 are all persons belonging to an ethnic, religious or linguistic minority. The meaning of the term 'minority' remains disputed, and to date states have not agreed on a legal definition. The question revolves around whether *Indigenous peoples* could be considered minorities. During the drafting of Article 27, some states explicitly stated that they did *not* consider Indigenous peoples to be minorities.[5] However, from the practice of the HRC it becomes clear that Indigenous peoples fall within the scope of Article 27. The HRC declared cases of Indigenous peoples admissible under Article 27.[6] In dealing with state reports the HRC has encouraged states to take measures

---

4 International Covenant on Civil and Political Rights, adopted by General Assembly resolution 2200A (XXI) of 16 December 1966, entered into force 23 March 1976.
5 Among these states were, for example, Chile and Australia. See C. Tomuschat, 'Protection of Minorities under Article 27 of the International Covenant on Civil and Political Rights', in: *Völkerrecht als Rechtsordnung. Internationale Gerichtsbarkeit Menschenrechte: Festschrift für Hermann Mosler*, Berlin/Heidelberg/New York: Springer Verlag, 1983, p. 962.
6 Among others, *Kitok v. Sweden* Comm. No. 170/1984 and 197/1985; *Ominayak v. Canada*, Comm. No. 167/1984; *Lovelace v. Canada*, Comm. No. 24/1977; *Länsman v. Finland*, Comm. No. 671/1995. These cases are discussed in more detail below.

under Article 27 to protect the culture, language and religion of Indigenous peoples and this reference to Indigenous peoples is not disputed by states.[7] In addition, in its General Comment on Article 27, the HRC reaffirmed that members of Indigenous peoples can fall within the scope of Article 27.[8]

Economic activities may also benefit from the protection of Article 27 ICCPR if they fall within the scope of the term 'culture'. The HRC endorses a broad concept of culture, which includes, for example, 'a particular way of life associated with the use of land resources, especially in the case of Indigenous peoples'.[9] Traditional activities such as fishing or hunting are thus protected under Article 27.

As regards state obligations, Article 27 is formulated in negative terms, 'persons belonging to such minorities shall not be denied the right to . . . enjoy their own culture'. At the time, this was done to avoid the possible stimulation of minority consciousness.[10] Nowadays, the HRC maintains that states have both negative and positive obligations under this provision, including financial efforts, for example with regard to effective minority participation in decisions that affect them.[11] States have not principally objected to this approach.[12] Positive measures of protection are not only required against the acts of the state party itself, but may also be required against actions of third parties, which could be companies.[13]

Cases by the Human Rights Committee

The HRC has dealt with several cases under Article 27 ICCPR concerning the traditional use of land in relation to the enjoyment of culture. One of the first cases was that of the *Lubicon Lake Band v. Canada*.[14] The complaint concerned the fact that the government had allowed the expropriation of land for the benefit of private corporate interests including gas and oil exploration. The Band argued that such industrialization, by destroying its environmental

---

7   R. Cholewinski, 'State Duty towards Ethnic Minorities: Positive or Negative?', *Human Rights Quarterly*, 1988, Vol. 10, No. 3, 361–362; N.S. Rodley, 'Conceptual Problems in the Protection of Minorities: International Legal Developments', *Human Rights Quarterly*, 1995, Vol. 17, No. 1, 61–62; M. Nowak, *UN Covenant on Civil and Political Rights – CCPR Commentary*, Kehl-Strasbourg-Arlington: Engel, 2nd rev. edn, 2005, pp. 650–652.

8   Human Rights Committee, *General Comment 23 on Article 27*, fifteenth session, 1994, paras 5.1 and 7.

9   Ibid., para. 7.

10 M. Nowak, *UN Covenant on Civil and Political Rights – CCPR Commentary*, Kehl-Strasbourg-Arlington: Engel, 2nd rev. edn, 2005, pp. 638–642, 646–647.

11 Human Rights Committee, *General Comment 23 on Article 27*, paras 6.2, 6, 3 and 7.

12 R. Cholewinski, 'State Duty towards Ethnic Minorities: Positive or Negative?', *Human Rights Quarterly*, 1988, Vol. 10, No. 3, pp. 344, 346–359.

13 Human Rights Committee, *General Comment 23 on Article 27*, para. 6.1.

14 *Bernard Ominayak, Chief of the Lubicon Lake Band v. Canada*, Comm. No. 167/1984, 26 March 1990.

and economic base, constituted a violation of Article 1 ICCPR recognizing the right of peoples to self-determination.[15] The HRC determined that it could not deal with cases under Article 1, because it could only deal with alleged violations of individual rights.[16] It concluded, however, that many of the claims presented by the applicants raised issues under Article 27 and the enjoyment of culture. In a brief reasoning, it stated that historical inequities and the recent developments threatened the way of life and the culture of the Lubicon Lake Band, and therefore constituted a violation of Article 27.[17] Although land issues were cited in relation to Article 27, the HRC did not give an extensive legal reasoning for the applicability of Article 27, and no substantiation of its determination that Article 27 had been violated.

At that time, not all members of the HRC agreed to have land issues fall within the scope of enjoyment of culture in Article 27 and to let traditional activities of the Indigenous people prevail over economic development in this case. In an individual opinion, one of the Committee members doubted whether the expropriation of land for commercial interests constituted a violation of the Band members' right to enjoy their own culture. According to this member, the right to enjoy one's culture should not imply that the Band's traditional way of life should be preserved at all costs. Moreover, the refusal by a community to change its traditional way of life could hinder the economic development of the society as a whole.[18]

In various cases brought by individuals of the Sami people, the HRC confirmed that land issues and economic activities do fall under Article 27 where this land is important for the culture of a given community. These cases concerned the use of land by the Sami to breed and herd reindeer in the context where the government had granted permission for companies to use the land for logging, mining or forestry. In these cases, the HRC elaborated the criteria to be used to determine whether the limitation of Article 27 constituted a violation of that provision.

In the case of *Ivan Kitok v. Sweden*,[19] concerning a Swedish citizen of Sami ethnic origin who was denied membership of the Sami community because he had not been practising reindeer husbandry for a period of over three years, the HRC reaffirmed that the economic activity of reindeer husbandry is an essential component of the Sami culture and, as such, falls under Article 27. The HRC applied the criteria of reasonable and objective justification to assess

---

15 *Lubicon Lake Band v. Canada*, paras 29.1, 29.5 and 29.9.
16 The HRC decided that it could not deal with collective rights under Article 1, since the ICCPR's Optional Protocol (Article 1) stipulates that only individuals who are victims of violations of rights under the ICCPR can submit claims. The HRC argued that an individual could not be a victim of a collective right to self-determination. Since communities as such do not have *locus standi* before the HRC, all cases under Article 1 are inadmissible. *Lubicon Lake Band v. Canada*, paras 32.1 and 32.2.
17 *Lubicon Lake Band v. Canada*, § 32.2 and 33.
18 *Lubicon Lake Band v. Canada*, Appendix I.
19 *Ivan Kitok v. Sweden*, Comm. No. 197/1985, 27 July 1988.

the limitation of Article 27. The decisive factor, however, was the *impact* of the measures taken on the enjoyment of culture. In the *Kitok* case the HRC concluded that the impact of the measures on Kitok was limited, since he was allowed, although not as a right, to herd reindeer. It found the measures taken to have been objectively justified by the welfare of the minority as a whole and consequently concluded that no violation of Article 27 had occurred.[20]

Two other important Sami cases were the *Länsman* cases against Finland.[21] Both cases concerned reindeer breeders of Sami ethnic origin who claimed a violation of Article 27 because government authorities allowed stone quarrying and logging and road construction, respectively, on lands traditionally used for reindeer herding.[22] In both cases, the HRC argued that reindeer herding did not seem to be affected very much by the quarrying and logging activities. The HRC concluded that the impact of the measures taken by the authorities on the enjoyment of culture was limited to such an extent that it did not constitute a violation of Article 27 ICCPR.[23]

In these cases, the HRC did, however, express its concern about the permits issued by the authorities to private companies. In these and several other cases the HRC took interim measures to prevent irreparable harm to the environment, which the claimants argued was vital for their culture. This indicates that the HRC was initially concerned that the measures could constitute a violation of the ICCPR. The HRC also warned Finland that future activities might constitute a breach of Article 27 if they had a significant negative impact on reindeer breeding and the enjoyment of the Sami culture.[24]

The way the HRC used its impact criterion has been criticized, mainly because the HRC did a *quantitative* comparison between the area allocated to the disputed projects and the total area used by the Sami for reindeer herding, paying insufficient attention to the *qualitative* aspect, namely the specific importance of a certain area and its potential impact on the future livelihood of the community.[25]

In the case of *Anni Äärelä and Jouni Näkkäläjärvi v. Finland* more attention was paid to the quality of the land. In this case, the applicants argued that the land concerned was the best winter grazing available and consequently of strategic importance. The HRC argued that it did not have sufficient information from both parties in order to 'draw independent conclusions on

20 *Ivan Kitok v. Sweden*, paras 4.3, 9.2, 9.7, 9.8.
21 *Ilmari Länsman et al. v. Finland*, Comm. No. 511/1992, 26 October 1994 and *Jouni E. Länsman et al. v. Finland*, Comm. No. 671/1995, 30 October 1996.
22 *Ilmari Länsman et al. v. Finland*, para. 2.1, 2.3, 3.1; *Jouni E. Länsman et al. v. Finland*, paras 2.1–2.9.
23 *Ilmari Länsman et al. v. Finland*, para. 9.1–9.8; *Jouni E. Länsman et al. v. Finland*, paras 10.1–10.6.
24 *Jouni E. Länsman et al. v. Finland*, para. 10.7.
25 M. Scheinin, 'The Right to Enjoy a Distinct Culture: Indigenous and Competing Uses of Land' in: Th. S. Orlin, A. Rosas and M. Scheinin (eds), *The Jurisprudence of Human Rights Law: A Comparative Interpretive Approach*, Turku/Abo: Institute for Human Rights, 2000, pp. 170, 175, 212.

the factual importance of the area to husbandry and the long-term impacts on the sustainability of husbandry, and the consequences under Article 27'.[26] The HRC subsequently argued that it could not conclude that there was a violation of Article 27. This case illustrates the difficulty of determining the importance of a certain piece of land and consequently of the use of an impact assessment as a tool to assess whether a limitation is permissible or not.

In the case of *Poma Poma v. Peru*, the HRC concluded that the limitation of the applicants' rights did constitute a violation of Article 27. This case concerned an authorization given by the state to withdraw water from Indigenous land, thereby preventing the Indigenous people from raising llamas.[27] As regards the impact of the measures taken, the HRC specified that these must respect the principle of proportionality so as not to endanger the very survival of the community.[28] In this case, the HRC added the criterion that Indigenous participation in the decision-making process has to be effective 'which requires not mere consultation, but the free, prior and informed consent of the member of the community'.[29] The HRC found that the community was not sufficiently consulted, that no studies were undertaken to assess the impact of the measures and that these measures substantively compromised the way of life and culture of the claimant. Consequently, it concluded that there had been a violation of Article 27 ICCPR.

The impact of economic activity also played a decisive role in the case of *Apirana Mahuika et al. v. New Zealand*.[30] The petitioners were New Zealand Maoris claiming that their rights under Article 1 and Article 27 ICCPR had been violated by the New Zealand government in a dispute over fishing rights. The HRC repeated that it could not express its views on Article 1 on self-determination. However, it argued that 'the provisions of Article 1 may be relevant for the interpretation of other rights protected by the Covenant, in particular Article 27'.[31] The HRC confirmed that the use and control of fisheries constitutes part of the Maori culture. It based its final decision on an assessment of the impact on the traditional life forms of the community and on the question whether this community was given sufficient opportunity to participate in the decision-making process. The HRC concluded that New Zealand had engaged in a process of broad consultation with the Maori and had taken the necessary steps to ensure that the fisheries settlement was compatible with Article 27 ICCPR. Accordingly, no breach of Article 27 was found.[32]

---

26 *Anni Äärelä and Jouni Näkkäläjärvi v. Finland*, Comm. No. 779/1997, 24 October 2001, para. 7.6.
27 *Angela Poma Poma v. Peru*, Comm. No. 1457/2006, 24 April 2009.
28 Ibid., para. 7.6.
29 Ibid., para. 6,7
30 *Apirana Mahuika et al. v. New Zealand*, Comm. No. 547/1993, 27 October 2000.
31 Ibid., para. 9.2.
32 Ibid., paras 9.3–9.8, 10.

It is interesting to note that in the *Apirana Mahuika* case, the HRC confirmed its dynamic approach to the concept of culture as developed in the *Länsman* cases. In the *Länsman* cases, the HRC had argued that Article 27 not only protects the *traditional* economic activities of a community. The fact that, for example, technological innovations are used in these economic activities does not imply that Article 27 is no longer applicable. In *Apirana Mahuika* the HRC again asserted that Article 27 not only protects traditional means of livelihood, but also allows for adaptation of those means to the modern way of life and technology.[33]

In order for economic activities and land claims to fall within the enjoyment of culture, a close relationship between them must be demonstrated. In *J.G.A. Diergaardt (the late Captain of the Rehoboth Baster Community) et al. v. Namibia*,[34] this relationship was not sufficiently demonstrated. Diergaardt and others claimed that their rights under Article 27 had been violated by the Namibian government by the expropriation of land. Since the community consisted mainly of cattle raising farmers, the claimants argued that 'the confiscation of all property collectively owned by the community robbed the community of the basis of its economic livelihood, which in turn was the basis of its cultural, social and ethnic identity.'[35]

The HRC repeated that economic activities including the use of land may fall within the scope of Article 27 if there is a direct link with the culture of the community involved. In this case, however, the HRC was not convinced that such a direct link existed, because cattle grazing was no longer an exclusive activity of the community. It concluded that, 'although the link of the Rehoboth community to the lands in question dates back some 125 years, it is not the result of a relationship that would have given rise to a distinctive culture'. The HCR found no violation of Article 27 ICCPR.[36]

In the case of *Hopu and Bessert v. France*,[37] the HRC brought economic activities and land rights within the scope of Article 17 ICCPR on respect for private life and Article 23 on rights of the family.[38] The HRC had to disregard Article 27 ICCPR in this case, because France made a reservation on Article 27 ICCPR.[39] In the case of *Hopu and Bessert* several Indigenous Polynesians

33   Scheinin, 'The Right to Enjoy a Distinct Culture: Indigenous and Competing Uses of Land', 2000, p. 169.
34   *J.G.A. Diergaardt (the late Captain of the Rehoboth Baster Community) et al. v. Namibia*, Comm. No. 760/1997, UN Doc. CCPR/C/69/D/760/1997, 6 September 2000.
35   Ibid., para. 3.1.
36   Ibid., para. 10.6.
37   *Francis Hopu and Tepoaitu Bessert v. France*, Comm. No. 549/1993, 29 July 1997.
38   Ibid., paras 4.3 and 4.4.
39   France submitted a declaration that since the French Constitution prohibits all distinctions between citizens on grounds of origin, race or religion, no minorities exist in France. Consequently, Article 27 would not be applicable with regard to France. In 1989, the HRC concluded that this declaration should be considered a binding reservation in accordance with the Vienna Convention on the Law of Treaties (1969). See *T.K. v. France*, Comm. No. 220/1987, 8 November 1989, para. 8.6.

claimed ownership of a piece of land in Tahiti where the French-Polynesian authorities had started to build a hotel. The land contained a traditional Indigenous burial ground and a fishing lagoon.[40] According to the logic of the HRC's case law, this case would fall under Article 27, but because of the French reservation,[41] the HRC decided to deal with the case under rights to family life, arguing that the relationship of the claimants with their ancestors was an important element of their identity and played a defining role in their family life.[42] The HRC concluded that the construction of a hotel on the traditional burial grounds of the Polynesians constituted an interference with the right to privacy and family life, which was neither reasonable nor justified.[43]

In assessing whether the state has found a proper balance between the general interest of economic development and the interests of the Indigenous people related to their land and economic activities, the HRC has developed the following set of criteria. The state may limit the rights of the Indigenous peoples concerned if the measures are provided by law, if these measures have a reasonable and objective justification, if the measures do not have such an impact as to fully deny the rights of the community concerned and if the community was seriously involved in the decision-making process, including seeking their prior and informed consent.

Regional level: the Americas and Africa

The criteria developed by the HRC have been similarly used, and further elaborated upon, by regional supervisory bodies, notably within the Inter-American and the African human rights system.[44] Since the regional human rights treaties do not contain a provision similar to Article 27 ICCPR, the

---

40 *Hopu and Bessert v. France*, paras 1 and 2.
41 Five HRC members dissented and argued that the declaration was not of relevance to overseas territories under French sovereignty. Individual opinion by Committee members Elizabeth Evatt, Cecilia Medina Quiroga, Fausto Pocar, Martin Scheinin and Maxwell Yalden (partly dissenting).
42 Several HRC members dissented, arguing that the term 'family' does not include all members of one's ethnic community. Accordingly, in order to fall under Articles 17 and 23, the burial grounds should be connected to the direct family, which could not be established by the authors. They also argued that the HRC emphasized the history and culture of the claimants, which referred to cultural values – protected under Article 27 – and not to family rights or privacy. Individual opinion by Thomas Buergenthal, David Kretzmer, Nisuke Ando and Lord Colville (dissenting).
43 *Hopu and Bessert v. France*, para. 10.3.
44 Within the Council of Europe, there was only one case similar to those under Article 27 ICCPR before the European Commission of Human Rights: *G. and E. v. Norway* (Application Nos. 9278/81 and 9415/81, decision of 3 October 1983, Decisions and Reports, vol. 35 (1984), pp. 30–45). The case concerned a plan by the Norwegian authorities to build a water dam and a hydro-electric power station in a valley used by the Sami for reindeer herding, fishing and hunting. The Commission dealt with the case under Article 8 on respect for private life and home. It found that the impact on the private life and traditional activities of the Sami was limited and concluded that the interference was justified as it was in accordance with the law and necessary in a democratic society in the interest of the economic well-being

cases were dealt with under various other rights, including the right to life, the right to property, the right to health and the right to respect for private life.

Cases by the Inter-American Commission and Court on Human Rights

The Inter-American Commission and Inter-American Court on Human Rights have dealt with various cases concerning economic activities of Indigenous peoples and they have elaborated a comprehensive set of criteria to assess the interference by the state for reasons of economic development, often referring to the work of the HRC.

One of the earliest cases was that of *Yanomami v. Brazil*,[45] in which the complainants argued that the Brazilian government had failed to protect the Yanomami by permitting the construction of highways and mining activities on ancestral lands of the tribe. The Inter-American Commission concluded that Brazil had violated several rights in the American Declaration of Human Rights, such as the right to life, personal security, residence and health.[46] The Commission also invoked Article 27 ICCPR,[47] which is all the more interesting, since Brazil was not a party to the ICCPR at that time.[48]

In the famous case of *Awas Tingni v. Nicaragua*,[49] the Inter-American Court concluded that Nicaragua had violated the right to property (Article 21 of the Inter-American Convention on Human Rights) by not delimiting and demarcating the communal property of the Awas Tingni and by authorizing third parties to exploit this land and resources. The Court ordered Nicaragua to demarcate and recognize the Awas Tingni's ownership title over the land in accordance with the community's values and customs.[50] The Court explained the connection between land rights and the culture of an Indigenous community as follows:

> [T]he close relationship that the communities have with the land must be recognized and understood as a foundation for their cultures, spiritual life, cultural integrity and economic survival. For Indigenous communities,

---

of the country. The Commission did not pay much attention to the involvement of the community in the process.

45 OAS Doc. OEA/Ser.l/V/II.66, doc. 10, rev. 1, Case No. 7615 (Brazil), Inter-American Commission Res. No. 12/85, 5 March 1985, *Annual report of the Inter-American Commission on Human Rights*, 1984–1985, 1 October 1985.

46 Ibid., para. 1, p. 33.

47 Ibid., para. 7, p. 31.

48 Brazil ratified the International Covenant on Civil and Political Rights on 24 January 1992.

49 Inter-American Court of Human Rights, *Case of the Mayagna (Sumo) Indigenous Community of Awas Tingni versus the Republic of Nicaragua*, Judgment of 31 August 2001.

50 *Case of the Mayagna (Sumo) Indigenous Community of Awas Tingni versus the Republic of Nicaragua*, paras 151, 153, 155.

the relationship with the land is not merely one of possession and production, but also a material and spiritual element that they should fully enjoy, as well as a means through which to preserve their cultural heritage and pass it on to future generations.[51]

In the *Yakye Axa case* and the *Sawhoyamaxa case*,[52] the Inter-American Court found that Paraguay had violated the right to property as laid down in Article 21 of the Convention by failing to ensure the effective use and enjoyment of ancestral land by the respective Indigenous communities.[53] It ordered Paraguay to return the ancestral land or to provide an alternative piece of land and to pay monetary compensation, all in accordance with the cultural practices of the communities.[54] The Court reaffirmed the strong link between ancestral land and resources, which are not only means of subsistence, but parts of the community's cultural identity.[55]

The case of the *Sarayaku v. Ecuador* concerned the granting of a permit by the state to a private oil company to carry out oil exploration and exploitation activities in the ancestral territory of the Indigenous people of Sarayaku, without prior consultation with, or consent by, the community.[56] The Sarayaku claimed to be prevented from pursuing their traditional economic and cultural activities, such as farming, hunting, fishing and gathering, in violation of their rights to property (Article 21), to life and to a fair trial (Articles 4, 8 and 25), to freedom of movement (Article 22) and to humane treatment (Article 5). The Court reaffirmed that the Indigenous community has the right to be consulted, as well as the right to communal property. It held that limitations to these rights should be provided for by law, be necessary, proportional and aimed at achieving a legitimate objective in a democratic society without denying a people their livelihood.[57] It further repeated that the safeguards to be guaranteed by the state included an appropriate and participatory process guaranteeing the right to consultation, an environmental impact assessment, and, where applicable, the reasonable sharing of the benefits arising from the exploitation of natural resources with the community as a form of just compensation.[58] The Court extensively prescribed how the consultation should

---

51 Ibid., para. 149.
52 Inter-American Court of Human Rights, *Case of Yakye Axa Indigenous Community v. Paraguay*, Judgment of 17 June 2005; Inter-American Court of Human Rights, *Case of the Sawhoyamaxa Indigenous Community v. Paraguay*, Judgment of 29 March 2006.
53 *Yakye Axa Indigenous Community v. Paraguay*, para. 242–1; *Sawhoyamaxa Indigenous Community v. Paraguay*, para. 248–2.
54 *Yakye Axa Indigenous Community v. Paraguay*, para. 242–6 and 242–13; *Sawhoyamaxa Indigenous Community v. Paraguay*, paras 226 and 248–6.
55 *Yakye Axa Indigenous Community v. Paraguay*, para. 135; *Sawhoyamaxa Indigenous Community v. Paraguay*, para. 118.
56 Inter-American Court of Human Rights, *Case of the Kichwa Indigenous People of Sarayaku v. Ecuador*, Judgement of 27 June 2012. Series C, No. 245.
57 *Kichwa Indigenous People of Sarayaku v. Ecuador*, para. 156.
58 *Kichwa Indigenous People of Sarayaku v. Ecuador*, para. 157.

take place. It should be adequate and accessible with sufficient and reliable information being provided, and it should be done in advance, in good faith and in an attempt to reach an agreement.[59] As regards the environmental impact assessment, the Court noted that, in this case, it was carried out by a private company subcontracted by the oil company, without being monitored by the state and without the participation of the Sarayaku people. The study did not take into account the social, spiritual and cultural impact that these development activities might have on them.[60] The Court found that Ecuador had violated the right to communal property of the Sarayaku people in relation to their right to cultural identity.

These cases show that the Inter-American Commission and Court have followed the criteria developed by the HRC – such as participation, consultation and impact assessment – and further elaborated upon them.

Cases by the African Commission on Human and Peoples' Rights

The African Commission on Human and Peoples' Rights has dealt with several cases concerning Indigenous peoples and their lands that have concerned economic activities and culture.[61]

The case of the *Ogoni v. Nigeria* concerned the involvement of the state in human rights violations directly and indirectly related to the activities of oil company Shell, with which the Nigerian National Petroleum company had a joint venture.[62] The issues included the contamination of environment, destruction of homes, burning of crops, and the killing of animals – all of which implied violations of the rights to health (Article 16), property (Article 14) and family rights (Article 18). Nigeria was accused of condoning the situation, by providing security forces to the companies and by not investigating the alleged violations or providing information to the Ogoni.

---

59 *Kichwa Indigenous People of Sarayaku v. Ecuador*, paras 184–209.
60 *Kichwa Indigenous People of Sarayaku v. Ecuador*, para. 207.
61 The African Commission has for some time been hesitant to use the term 'Indigenous peoples'. It found this term not to be applicable to the African context, because it considered all Africans to be Indigenous to Africa, being pre-colonial and original to the continent. See Kaeleboga N. Bojosi and George Mukundi Wachira, 'Protecting Indigenous Peoples in Africa: An Analysis of the Approach of the African Commission on Human and Peoples' Rights', *African Human Rights Law Journal*, 2006, Vol. 6, 382–406; Jeremie Gilbert, '"Indigenous Peoples" Human Rights in Africa: The Pragmatic Revolution of the African Commission on Human and Peoples' Rights', *International Comparative Law Quarterly*, 2011, Vol. 60, 245–270.
62 African Commission on Human and Peoples' Rights, *The Social and Economic Rights Action Center and the Center for Economic and Social Rights v. Nigeria*, Comm. No. 155/96 (2001).

The *Ogoni* case is interesting, because it explicitly referred to the indirect horizontal effect of human rights treaties. States are not only responsible for preventing and solving violations of state actors, but they also have the responsibility to protect individuals from violations by private parties, including companies.[63] In the *Ogoni* case, the African Commission reaffirmed that a state also violates human rights when it allows private persons, including companies, to act freely and with impunity to the detriment of human rights. The responsibility is not triggered by the act itself, but by a lack of due diligence to prevent the violation or to respond properly. In this case it found that Nigeria had not exercised due diligence towards the acts of oil companies and had violated various provisions of the African Charter. It recommended Nigeria, *inter alia*, to conduct an investigation into the human rights violations and prosecute persons involved in them; to ensure adequate compensation to victims and undertake a comprehensive clean-up of lands and rivers damaged by oil operations; and to ensure that appropriate environmental and social impact assessments be prepared for any future oil development.[64]

In the case of the *Endorois v. Kenya* land rights were more directly invoked.[65] The case of the Endorois concerned their forceful removal from their ancestral lands in the Lake Bogoria area. The economic reason for their removal was that the government wanted to turn the land into a game reserve. The Endorois community argued that the fertile land was used for raising their cattle, as well as for cultural and religious ceremonies. The Kenyan government had promised to compensate the families, providing them with other pieces of fertile land, as well as a 25 per cent share in the benefits of tourism and 85 per cent of the employment of the region. Apart from the fact that the Endorois complained that this compensation was not carried out, they also claimed that such compensation could not replace their cultural link to the land. The Endorois also complained about mining concessions that were granted by the Kenyan authorities to private companies, which risked pollution of the water they used for themselves as well as their livestock.[66] The Endorois reclaimed their land and asked for compensation, maintaining that Kenya had violated

63 *The Social and Economic Rights Action Center and the Center for Economic and Social Rights v. Nigeria*, para. 57.
64 *The Social and Economic Rights Action Center and the Center for Economic and Social Rights v. Nigeria*, para. 69.
65 *Centre for Minority Rights Development (Kenya) and Minority Rights Group International on Behalf of Endorois Welfare Council v. Kenya*, Communication 276/2003, decision adopted by the African Commission on Human and Peoples' Rights in May 2009 and endorsed by the African Union in January 2010. See, also, Jeremie Gilbert, '"Indigenous Peoples" Human Rights in Africa: The Pragmatic Revolution of the African Commission on Human and Peoples' Rights', International Comparative Law Quarterly, Vol. 60, 2011, 245–270.
66 *Centre for Minority Rights Development (Kenya) and Minority Rights Group International on Behalf of Endorois Welfare Council v. Kenya*, paras 2, 3, 6, 7, 12, 14.

the rights to religion (Article 8), property (Article 14), culture (Article 17), natural resources (Article 21) and development (Article 22) of the African Charter on Human and Peoples' Rights.

The African Commission argued that limitations of the rights of the Endorois were to be established by law and not to be applied in a way that would completely vitiate their rights.[67] It argued that it was not convinced that the restrictions on the rights of the Endorois were justified, since there was no significant public interest or other justification, including economic development. The African Commission was of the view that allowing the Endorois to use the land would not detract from the goal of developing the area for economic reasons.[68] In relation to the right to property, the Commission also concluded that the general interest was not a sufficiently legitimate aim to remove the people from their land. It noted that '[t]he "public interest" test is met with a much higher threshold in the case of encroachment of Indigenous land rather than individual private property'.[69] The Commission applied two requirements for measures to be legitimate: consultation, including consent, and compensation.[70] It found that the Endorois were not sufficiently consulted and did not effectively participate in the process. Moreover, the state had not conducted a prior environment and social impact assessment. Neither was prompt and full compensation paid.[71] As regards the right to culture, the Commission referred to the work of the HRC on Article 27 ICCPR reaffirming that economic activities could fall within the concept of culture.[72] The Commission stated that 'any development or investment projects that would have a major impact within the Endorois territory, the State has a duty not only to consult with the community, but also to obtain their free, prior, and informed consent, according to their customs and traditions'.[73]

The Commission concluded that the rights to freedom of religion, property, culture and development were violated. It recommended the state to recognize ownership rights of the Endorois, return their ancestral lands to the Endorois, guarantee the Endorois community unrestricted access to Lake Bogoria and surrounding sites for religious and cultural rites and for grazing their cattle; to pay adequate compensation to the community for all the loss suffered, and to pay royalties to the Endorois from existing economic activities and ensure that they benefit from employment possibilities within the Reserve. All these measures were to be taken in close consultation with the Endorois community.[74]

67   Ibid., para. 172.
68   Ibid., para. 173.
69   Ibid., para. 212.
70   Ibid., paras 225–226.
71   Ibid., para. 228, 231.
72   Ibid., para. 243.
73   Ibid., para. 291.
74   Ibid., recommendations, p. 80.

Conclusions: criteria for the protection of the cultural dimension of economic activities

This chapter shows that economic activities of Indigenous peoples and minorities can be protected by international human rights law as long as they have an established link with the culture of the community involved. The most prominent examples of such activities relate to Indigenous peoples and the use of their land. Indigenous peoples use their land for subsistence and economic activities and benefits, but these activities also form part of their cultural and spiritual identity and link with the land. On the other hand, this must be balanced with states that want to use the land, including for economic purposes, either themselves or via permits given to private companies to use the land.

In assessing whether an interference by the state with the rights of the community amounts to a violation of these rights, it appears that a common approach is emerging among international and regional monitoring bodies. The regional bodies, notably the African Commission and the Inter-American Commission and Court, extensively cited the work of the HRC while the African Commission also referred to cases by the Inter-American Court and the European Court of Human Rights, showing a dialogue between the different international supervisory bodies on these issues.

The first criterion is that, in order for the economic activities of the community to be protected under human rights, the link between these activities and the culture of the community must be established. It is the link with culture that makes these activities eligible for human rights protection. Such protection may fall under the right to enjoy culture, or under other human rights, such as the right to property or respect for private life and family. The state has positive obligations with regard to these rights, not only to prevent violations by its own actions, but also to protect against (potential) violations by third parties, including companies.

This does not mean that all state measures concerning land of Indigenous peoples are automatically violations of their rights. Human rights are seldom absolute and limitations are possible, as long as these limitations fulfil certain general criteria. They need to be provided by law, have a legitimate aim and be necessary and proportionate. Most state measures are indeed provided by law and the promotion of the general welfare or of economic development are generally considered to be legitimate aims that a government may pursue. The assessment therefore focuses on the necessity and the proportionality of the measures concerned.

The criteria for necessity and proportionality have been elaborated by the various monitoring bodies, notably the Inter-American Court of Human Rights. First, the community must be seriously involved in the process leading to the adoption of the measures that concern them. This does not merely mean participation or consultation, but their free, prior and informed consent needs to be sought. Second, the state is obliged to carry out an objective assessment of the impact of the measures on the economic, social and cultural situation of the community concerned. The state should avoid that the measures have such an impact as to in fact annul the rights. Third, if certain measures are taken on the land of Indigenous peoples, the state should ensure that the community shares in the economic benefits that result from the exploitation of the land. Finally, if land has to be confiscated and the community indeed has to move, proper means of compensation need to be provided, which should be determined and carried out in full respect of the culture and customs of the community concerned. The problem remains, however, that precisely this cultural aspect of land is often hard to compensate.

This set of criteria should give states' executives and legislators sufficient guidance if they wish to interfere with the land rights of Indigenous peoples for reasons of economic development, as well serving the national judiciary in its role of monitoring this process. The practical application is, however, sometimes more complicated, especially where states fail to respect these criteria or ignore recommendations by the international monitoring bodies. Communities thereby continue to face the risk that their economic and cultural activities on their land may have to give way to state promoted economic development.

Bibliography

Bojosi, K.N. and Mukundi Wachira, G., 'Protecting Indigenous Peoples in Africa: An Analysis of the Approach of the African Commission on Human and Peoples' Rights', *African Human Rights Law Journal*, 2006, Vol. 6, 382–406.

Cholewinski, R., 'State Duty towards Ethnic Minorities: Positive or Negative?', *Human Rights Quarterly*, 1988, Vol. 10, No. 3, 344–371.

Donders, Y.M., *Towards a Right to Cultural Identity?*, Antwerp: Intersentia, 2002.

Francioni, F. and Scheinin, M. (eds), *Cultural Human Rights*, Leiden: Martinus Nijhoff Publishers, 2008.

Gilbert, J., '"Indigenous Peoples" Human Rights in Africa: The Pragmatic Revolution of the African Commission on Human and Peoples' Rights', *International and Comparative Law Quarterly*, 2011, Vol. 60, 245–270.

Nowak, M., *UN Covenant on Civil and Political Rights – CCPR Commentary*, Kehl-Strasbourg-Arlington: Engel, 2nd rev. edn, 2005.

Rodley, N.S., 'Conceptual Problems in the Protection of Minorities: International Legal Developments', *Human Rights Quarterly*, 1995, Vol. 17, No. 1, 48–71.

Scheinin, M., 'The Right to Enjoy a Distinct Culture: Indigenous and Competing Uses of Land' in: Th.S. Orlin, A. Rosas and M. Scheinin (eds), *The Jurisprudence of Human Rights Law: A Comparative Interpretive Approach*, Turku/Abo:Institute for Human Rights, 2000, pp. 159–222.

Tomuschat, C., 'Protection of Minorities under Article 27 of the International Covenant on Civil and Political Rights', in: *Völkerrecht als Rechtsordnung.Internationale Gerichtsbarkeit Menschenrechte: Festschrift für Hermann Mosler*, Berlin/Heidelberg/New York: Springer Verlag, 1983, p. 962.

Cases – Human Rights Committee

Lovelace v. Canada, Comm. No. 24/1977, 30 July 1981.

Kitok v. Sweden, Comm. No. 170/1984 and 197/1985, 27 July 1988.

T.K. v. France, Comm. No. 220/1987, 8 November 1989.

Bernard Ominayak, Chief of the Lubicon Lake Band v. Canada, Comm. No. 167/1984, 26 March 1990.

Ilmari Länsman et al. v. Finland, Comm. No. 511/1992, 26 October 1994.

Jouni E. Länsman et al. v. Finland, Comm. No. 671/1995, 30 October 1996.

Francis Hopu and Tepoaitu Bessert v. France, Comm. No. 549/1993, 29 July 1997.

J.G.A. Diergaardt (the late Captain of the Rehoboth Baster Community) *et al. v. Namibia*, Comm. No. 760/1997, 6 September 2000.

Apirana Mahuika et al. v. New Zealand, Comm. No. 547/1993, 27 October 2000.

Anni Äärelä and Jouni Näkkäläjärvi v. Finland, Comm. No. 779/1997, 24 October 2001.

Angela Poma Poma v. Peru, Comm. No. 1457/2006, 24 April 2009.

Cases – Inter-American Commission and Court on Human Rights

IACommHR, Case No. 7615 (Brazil), Inter-American Commission Res. No. 12/85, 5 March 1985, *Annual report of the Inter-American Commission on Human Rights*, 1984–1985, 1 October 1985, OAS Doc. OEA/Ser.l/V/II.66, doc. 10, rev. 1.

IACtHR, *Case of Velasquez Rodriquez v. Honduras*, Judgment of 29 July 1988, Series C, No. 4.

IACommHR, *Case of Maya Indigenous Communities and their Members v. Belize*, 5 October 2000, IACHR Report No. 78/00, Case No. 12.053.

IACommHR, *The Human Rights Situation of the Indigenous People in the Americas*, OEA/Ser.L/V/II.108 doc. 62, 20 October 2000.

IACtHR, *Case of Mayagna (Sumo) Indigenous Community of Awas Tingni v. The Republic of Nicaragua*, Judgment of 31 August 2001

IACtHR, *Case of Maya Indigenous Communities of the Toledo District Belize*, 12 October 2004, IACHR Report No. 40–04, Case No. 12.053.

IACtHR, *Case of Yakye Axa Indigenous Community v. Paraguay*, Judgment of 17 June 2005.

IACtHR, *Case of the Sawhoyamaxa Indigenous Community v. Paraguay*, Judgment of 29 March 2006.

IACtHR, *Case of the Kichwa Indigenous People of Sarayaku v. Ecuador*, Judgment of 27 June 2012. Series C, No. 245.

Cases – African Commission on Human and Peoples' Rights

African Commission on Human and Peoples' Rights, *The Social and Economic Rights Action Center and the Center for Economic and Social Rights v. Nigeria*, African Commission on Human and Peoples' Rights, Comm. No. 155/96 (2001).

African Commission on Human and Peoples' Rights, *Centre for Minority Rights Development (Kenya) and Minority Rights Group International on Behalf of Endorois Welfare Council v. Kenya*, Communication 276/2003, decision adopted by the African Commission on Human and Peoples' Rights in May 2009 and endorsed by the African Union in January 2010.

Part II

Culture and economic interests in international economic law

4 Cultural heritage in international economic law

Valentina Vadi

Introduction

Can the protection of cultural heritage and the promotion of economic development be reconciled in international and European law? The protection of cultural heritage is a fundamental public interest that is closely connected to fundamental human rights and is deemed to be among the best guarantees of international peace and security. There is no single definition of cultural heritage. While culture represents inherited values, ideas, and traditions, which characterize social groups and their behaviour, heritage indicates something to be cherished and handed down from one generation to another. Cultural heritage is a multifaceted concept which includes both tangible (i.e. monuments, sites, cultural landscapes etc.) and intangible cultural resources (i.e. food, music, cultural practices etc.). On the one hand, the protection and the sustainable use of cultural heritage may foster economic development, enabling communities and individuals to respond to major economic and social changes.[1] On the other hand, development may be conceived as a process for expanding cultural freedom.[2] As a result, there can be positive synergies between the promotion of trade and foreign direct investment on the one hand and the protection of cultural heritage on the other.

However, this is not always the case. Although economic globalization and international economic governance have spurred a more intense dialogue and interaction among nations – potentially promoting cultural diversity and providing the funds to recover and preserve cultural heritage – these phenomena can also jeopardize cultural heritage. Asymmetry in flows and exchanges of cultural goods can lead to cultural homogenization. In parallel, foreign direct investments in the extractive industries have the ultimate capacity of changing cultural landscapes. At the same time, the increase in global trade, economic integration and foreign direct investment has determined the creation of legally

---

1 A. Sen, 'How Does Culture Matter?', in V. Rao and M. Walton (eds), *Culture and Public Action* (Stanford University Press 2004) 37–58.
2 A. Sen, *Development as Freedom* (Oxford: Oxford University Press 1999).

binding and highly effective regimes which demand that states promote and facilitate trade and foreign direct investment.

This study aims to investigate whether and how international law and European Union (EU) law govern cultural phenomena and respond to the challenges posed by economic globalization. Despite decades of protection of cultural heritage in many states, widespread non-compliance with norms protecting cultural heritage by individuals and corporations and lack of enforcement by states has been the norm rather than the exception. The protection of cultural heritage under international law has emerged after WWII through a series of international conventions and the formation of customs,[3] and appears both vertically and horizontally fragmented.[4] The vertical fragmentation is reflected in the coexistence of different layers of heritage protection, at the national, regional and international levels.[5] Meanwhile, horizontal fragmentation is evident in the varied sources of cultural heritage law. The incremental and *ad hoc* adoption of conventions and soft law instruments by the United Nations Educational, Scientific and Cultural Organization (UNESCO)[6] has not led to a homogenous and well-coordinated system: 'instead more regimes are being established, depending on the kind of properties and on the public interest at stake'.[7]

More importantly, while international economic law presents sophisticated and highly effective dispute settlement mechanisms which have produced a growing body of jurisprudence, about fifty per cent of UNESCO treaty law lacks a dispute settlement provision *tout court*.[8] Given the increasing relevance of international law governing cultural heritage, the rise of cultural heritage related disputes, and the lack of dedicated courts or tribunals, international economic *fora*, such as the World Trade Organization (WTO)[9] panels and Appellate Body (AB) on the one hand and investment treaty arbitral tribunals on the other have adjudicated a number of cases that feature cultural elements. Given the fact that international economic *fora* present a distinct culture,[10] it is important to scrutinize this emerging jurisprudence through a cultural lens,

3 See J. Nafziger, 'The Development of International Cultural Law', *American Society of International Law. Proceedings of the Annual Meeting* (2006).
4 L. Casini, '*Italian Hours*: The Globalization of Cultural Property Law', 9 *International Journal of Constitutional Law* (2011) 373.
5 Ibid. 387.
6 UNESCO Constitution, preamble. Constitution of the United Nations Educational, Scientific, and Cultural Organization, Paris, 16 November 1945, in force 4 November 1946, 52 UNTS 1947, 276.
7 Casini, '*Italian Hours*', 373.
8 S. Von Schorlemer, 'UNESCO Dispute Settlement', in A.A. Yusuf (ed.), *Standard-Setting in UNESCO – Normative Action in Education, Science and Culture Essays in Commemoration of the Sixtieth Anniversary of UNESCO* (Leiden/Boston, MA: Martinus Nijhoff 2007 78.
9 Agreement Establishing the World Trade Organization, 15 April 1994, 33 ILM (1994).
10 See D. Steger, 'The Culture of the WTO: Why It Needs to Change', 10 *Journal of International Economic Law* (2007) 483–495 and A. Bjorklund, 'The Emerging Civilization of Investment Arbitration', 113 *Penn State Law Review* (2009) 1269.

just as such cases are examined by international courts and tribunals from an international economic law perspective and without a specific mandate (and expertise) to ascertain the adequate protection of cultural heritage.

In contrast to general international law, culture lies at the heart of the European Union project. Not only is culture one of the pillars on which the European Union is founded, but it also constitutes a vital element in the European Union's international relations. At the normative level, the EU has been enabled to take action in the field of culture since the inception of the Maastricht Treaty.[11] Cultural elements such as cultural and linguistic diversity are expressly listed among the objectives of the EU[12] and are included in a series of specific provisions.[13] The strategic importance of culture is manifold. Cultural exchanges help in preventing conflicts, foster economic development and promote human rights and fundamental freedoms.[14] Since the adoption of the 2007 European Agenda for Culture in a Globalising World,[15] culture has increasingly been perceived as a strategic factor of political, social and economic development. Culture plays a fundamental role in the knowledge-based economy, and its economic potential is particularly evident with respect to cultural and creative industries and sustainable cultural tourism.[16]

Against this background, the objectives of the EU in the field have been two-fold. *First*, the EU has aimed to promote an understanding of European cultures throughout the world and to protect European cultural heritage, thus contributing to the vitality of the European economy of culture.[17] *Second*, it has aimed to promote external cultural policies that encourage dynamism and balance in the exchange of cultural goods and services with third countries in order to preserve and promote cultural diversity.[18] As Party to the UNESCO Convention on the Protection and the Promotion of the Diversity of Cultural Expressions,[19] the European Commission has adopted a rather proactive stance

11 Article 151 TEU. The Treaty on European Union (TEU) was signed on 7 February 1992 and entered into force on 1 November 1993. Article 151 TEU now corresponds to Article 167 TFEU. Treaty on the Functioning of the European Union, Consolidated version, 53 OJEU 30 March 2010, 2010 C83/01.
12 Article 2 of the TFEU expressly states that the EU shall respect its rich cultural and linguistic diversity, and shall ensure that Europe's cultural heritage is safeguarded and enhanced.
13 See e.g. Article 165 of the TFEU on education.
14 Council of the European Union, Council Conclusions on the Promotion of Cultural Diversity and Intercultural Dialogue in the External Relations of the Union and its Member States, Brussels, 20 November 2008 at 2.
15 The European Agenda for Culture in a globalising world was proposed by the European Commission in May 2007 and endorsed by the Council of the European Union and by the European Council in November and December 2007 respectively.
16 Council of the European Union, Council Conclusions on the Promotion of Cultural Diversity and Intercultural Dialogue in the External Relations of the Union and its Member States, Brussels, 20 November 2008 at 2.
17 Ibid. at 4.
18 Ibid.
19 Convention on the Protection and Promotion of the Diversity of Cultural Expressions, adopted 20 October 2005, in force 18 March 2007.

to ensure that the promotion of cultural diversity is given due consideration when free trade agreements are made.[20] It remains to be seen whether and how the mainstreaming of culture in the European legal framework has reverberated on the jurisprudence of the Court of Justice of the European Union (CJEU), and whether it may constitute a model of successful integration between the protection of cultural heritage and economic development and/or whether it may contribute to the development of general principles of law requiring the protection of cultural heritage in times of peace. While some research has been done with regard to the existence of such principle in wartime,[21] the parallel question as to whether such principle exists in times of peace has not received scholarly attention. Finding out whether such a principle also exists in peacetime would be significant because general principles and customary international law are binding on states irrespective of their adhesion to specific treaties.

For instance, as Europeans perceive the hunting of seals to be morally objectionable, the European Union has banned the trade in seal products except those derived from hunts traditionally conducted by the Inuit and other Indigenous communities for cultural and subsistence reasons. However, the Inuit contested the regulation and alleged that the derogation in their favour was merely an empty gesture, as it would not prevent the market for seal products from collapsing. After the Court of Justice of the European Union (CJEU) declined jurisdiction on jurisdictional grounds, the Canadian and Norwegian governments brought the seal ban before the WTO, contending that the ban violated relevant trade obligations. Several questions arise in this context: is the Indigenous exemption in conformity with relevant international economic law obligations? Is it adequate to ensure the conservation of Indigenous hunting practices, constituting a form of intangible cultural heritage?

The survey of this and similar disputes shows that international economic law has developed limited institutional machinery – such as limited exceptions – for the protection of cultural heritage through dispute settlement. Given the significant and consistently increasing number of international disputes in which cultural elements are an issue, the interaction between international cultural law and economic globalization deserves further scrutiny.

The aims of the chapter are to address the question as to whether the existing legal framework adequately protects cultural heritage vis-à-vis economic globalization and to offer concrete ways to reconcile economic development with cultural concerns. The protection of cultural heritage is not an end in itself, but is closely related to human rights, human dignity and economic

---

20 Article 167(4) TFEU *inter alia* requires the Union to take culture into account in all its actions under other provisions of the Treaties so as to respect and to promote the diversity of its cultures ('mainstreaming').

21 R. O'Keefe, *The Protection of Cultural Property in Armed Conflict* (Cambridge: Cambridge University Press 2001).

development. The underlying hypothesis of this chapter is that development should be conceived as a broad concept, inclusive not only of mere economic growth, but also of human flourishing and well-being, to which cultural elements are crucial.

The chapter proceeds as follows. After analysing and critically assessing three case studies from the jurisprudence of different international and regional economic *fora* dealing with the interplay between economic activities and Indigenous cultural heritage, it examines some tools for reconciling the opposing interests. Finally some conclusions are drawn.

Indigenous heritage v. economic interests in international economic law

Indigenous cultural heritage is a special type of heritage which reflects the inner beliefs and cultural practices of Indigenous peoples, and it is of fundamental importance to mankind as a whole for its uniqueness and for its contribution to cultural diversity. According to General Comment 23:

> [C]ulture manifests itself in many forms, including a particular way of life associated with the use of land resources, especially in the case of Indigenous peoples. [Cultural rights] may include such traditional activities as fishing or hunting. . . . The enjoyment of those rights may require positive legal measures of protection and measures to ensure the effective participation of members of minority communities in decisions that affect them. . . . The protection of these rights is directed to ensure the survival and continued development of the cultural, religious and social identity of the minorities concerned, thus enriching the fabric of society as a whole.[22]

Arbitral tribunals and the WTO dispute settlement mechanism have increasingly dealt with elements of Indigenous cultural heritage. The protection of Indigenous heritage has intersected with international trade law in determining clashes between Indigenous culture, free trade and animal protection. In parallel, a potential tension exists when a state adopts cultural policies interfering with foreign investments as these may be deemed to amount to indirect expropriation or a violation of other investment treaty provisions.

The question arises of whether international economic law is open to encapsulating cultural concerns in its *modus operandi*. Given the impact that arbitral awards and reports can have on Indigenous peoples' lives and culture, some scrutiny and critical assessment of this jurisprudence is of the utmost relevance. In general terms, investment disputes with Indigenous cultural

---

22 UN Human Rights Comm., *General Comment No. 23: The Rights of Minorities* (Art. 27), paras 7, 9, UN Doc. CCPR/C/21/Rev.1/Add.5, 8 April 1994.

elements are characterized by the need to balance the protection of Indigenous cultural heritage by the host state and the economic entitlements of foreign investors. Trade disputes with Indigenous cultural elements can relate to the legitimacy of positive measures adapted by the WTO member states to foster Indigenous subsistence and cultural practices. Such measures can be perceived to be in violation of the Most Favoured Nation (MFN) and National Treatment (NT) provisions. While the collision between culture and economic globalization has many facets, this chapter will focus on a specific type of controversy which has recently come to the fore: the clash between economic globalization and cultural practices relating to subsistence harvest.

Reindeer herding, Indigenous cultural heritage and the promotion of foreign investments

In *John Andre v. Canada*, a US-based businessman lodged a Notice of Intent to arbitrate, alleging losses arising from legislative measures affecting his caribou-hunting outfitter in Northern Canada.[23] The claimant had 360 caribou hunting licences (called Caribou Quota Tags), and organized hunting camps for tourists and hunters who would travel from locations outside Canada to the aboriginal land in Canada's North West Territories (NWT).[24] In 2007, the government of the NWT decided to grant only seventy-five Caribou Quota Tags per outfitter.[25] Outfitters with prior commitments to clients would therefore be required to buy Caribou Quota Tags from their competitors.[26] The claimant complained that the relevant authorities cut the number of hunting licences in a discriminatory manner.[27] As many of the local outfitters only used seventy-five to one hundred Caribou Quota Tags or less per year, the claimant alleged that the government developed a strategy to minimize the negative effect on local outfitters and maximize the negative effects on the outside investors.[28] The investor thus claimed to have been targeted as a non-resident of Canada and to have been discriminated against on the basis of his US nationality.[29]

The press subsequently reported that, while the ban initially also included the aboriginal caribou hunt, the NWT government and the Tlicho aboriginal government jointly agreed to impose a total hunting ban only on non-

23 *John R. Andre v. Government of Canada*, Notice of Intent to Submit Claim to Arbitration Pursuant to Chapter Eleven of the North American Free Trade Agreement, 19 March 2010, para. 8.
24 Ibid., para. 12.
25 Idid., para. 51.
26 Ibid.
27 Ibid., para. 35.
28 Ibid., para. 51.
29 Ibid., para. 35.

aboriginal hunters and commercial hunting outfitters.[30] In other words, while the sport hunting of caribou was to be outlawed,[31] the aboriginal subsistence hunting would be permitted.

This differential treatment may be justified under human rights law. The annual Fall hunt allows the Indigenous tribes to preserve their traditional culture and to rely on caribou meat in the winter. A number of cases at the international, regional, and national levels provide evidence of the recognition of Indigenous peoples' cultural rights in this sense. In the *Kitok* case, the Human Rights Committee stated that reindeer husbandry, as a traditional livelihood of the Indigenous Saami people, is an activity protected under Article 27 ICCPR.[32] In *Jouni Lansman v. Finland*, the Committee found that reindeer herding fits into the definition of cultural activities.[33] In reaching this conclusion, the Committee recognized that the subsistence activities of Indigenous peoples are an integral part of their culture.[34]

An 'Aboriginal exemption' is a common feature of natural resource conservation legislation. A number of international environmental treaties which protect certain species include derogations to their main principles to 'accommodate the needs of traditional subsistence users of such species',[35] thus protecting traditional hunting practices linked to the cultural heritage of the communities concerned.[36] It remains to be seen whether the case will move forward and, if so, how the arbitral tribunal will adjudicate on this matter.

Indigenous culture and the protection of free trade before the Court of Justice of the European Union: the EU seals disputes

Since European consumers perceive seal hunting as cruel and inhuman, largely because of the means through which the seals are hunted, the European Union (EU) has adopted a comprehensive regime governing seal products.[37]

---

30 'New Plan for Canadian Bathurst Caribou Herd Management', *Eye on the Arctic*, 2 June 2010. Online. Available: http://eyeonthearctic.rcinet.ca/en/news/canada/35-geopolitics/232-new-plan-for-canadian-bathurst-caribou-herd-management (accessed 25 May 2014).

31 'Debate over N.W.T. Caribou Hunting Goes Public', *CBC News*, 9 February 2010. Online. Available: www.cbc.ca/canada/north/story/2010/02/09/nwt-caribou-debate.html. (accessed 25 May 2014).

32 *See Ivan Kitok v. Sweden* (Communication No. 197/1985), UN Human Rights Comm., para. 4.2, UN Doc. CCPR/C/33/D/197/1985, 27 July 1988.

33 *Jouni Lansman v. Finland* (Communication No. 671/1995), UN Human Rights Comm., para. 10.2, UN Doc. CCPR/C/58/D/671/1995, 22 November 1996.

34 UN Human Rights Comm., *General Comment No. 23: the Rights of Minorities* (Art. 27), paras 7, 9, UN Doc. CCPR/C/21/Rev.1/Add.5, 8 April 1994.

35 Convention on Conservation of Migratory Species Article 3(5), 23 June 1979, 19 ILM 11.

36 For instance, the 1946 International Convention for the Regulation of Whaling retains aboriginal rights to subsistence whaling. International Convention for the Regulation of Whaling Article III(13)(b), 2 December 1946, 161 UNTS 72.

37 Regulation (EC) 1007/2009 of the European Parliament and of the Council of 16 September 2009 on Trade in Seal Products, 2009 OJ (L. 286) 36.

The EU seal regime prohibits the importation and sale in the EU of any seal product except:

(a) those derived from hunting conducted in a traditional fashion by Inuit and other Indigenous communities and which contribute to their subsistence;[38] and

(b) those that are by-products of a hunt regulated by national law and with the sole purpose of sustainable management of marine resources.[39]

In addition, seal products for personal use may be imported but may not be placed on the market.[40] The EU allowed the exception for Indigenous hunts because of the international law commitments of its member states and of the Declaration on the Rights of Indigenous Peoples.[41]

Recently, however, the Canadian Inuit filed a lawsuit before the Court of Justice of the European Union (CJEU) for the annulment of the EU regulation.[42] As mentioned, the regulation expressly recognizes hunting as an integral part of the Inuit culture and exempts the Inuit people from the ban. However, since the Inuit people do not export seal products themselves, but export them via non-Indigenous exporters, they alleged that the derogation in their favour would be merely an 'empty box'[43] as it would not prevent the market for seal products from collapsing.

The General Court, however, declared the action for annulment to be inadmissible.[44] The General Court found that Regulation 1007/2009 was a legislative act and that under Article 263(4) of the Treaty on the Functioning of the European Union (TFEU)[45] the applicant should be *directly* and *individually* concerned in order to bring their action before the Court. Yet, the Court held that the applicants were concerned by the regulation 'like any other trader who places seal products on the market'.[46] Therefore, they did not satisfy the conditions of admissibility for the purposes of Article 263(4) TFEU. The applicants appealed against this Order, alleging that the Court erred in law, and that, more generally, Article 263(4) TFEU was in breach of the Charter of Fundamental Rights of the European Union[47] and Articles 6 and 13 of the

---

38 Ibid., Article. 3(1).
39 Ibid., Article 3(2)(b).
40 Ibid., Article 3(2)(a).
41 Ibid., point 14.
42 *See Inuit Tapiriit Kanatami and Others v. Parliament and Council*, Case T 18/10 R, Online. Available: http://curia.europa.eu/jcms/jcms/j_6/ (accessed 5 June 2014).
43 Ibid., para. 103.
44 General Court, *Inuit Tapiriit Kanatami and Others v. Commission*, Case T-18/10 Order of 6 September 2011.
45 Treaty on the Functioning of the European Union, Consolidated version, 53 OJEU 30 March 2010, 2010 C83/01.
46 CJEU, General Court, *Inuit Tapiriit Kanatami and Others v. Commission*, Case T-18/10 Order of 6 September 2011, para. 90.
47 Charter of Fundamental Rights of the European Union, OJC 364/1 (2000).

European Convention for the Protection of Human Rights and Fundamental Freedoms.[48] The Grand Chamber dismissed the appeal upholding the analysis of the General Court. According to the Grand Chamber,

> the conditions of admissibility laid down in the fourth paragraph of Article 263 TFEU must be interpreted in the light of the fundamental right to effective judicial protection, but such an interpretation cannot have the effect of setting aside the conditions expressly laid down in that Treaty.[49]

As the case was dismissed on jurisdictional grounds, it is of limited relevance with regard to the substantive interaction between cultural heritage and trade. Nevertheless, it remains significant because it shows the difficulties that individual actors face when they are affected by international norms governing international trade. From its inception, the CJEU has taken a rather restrictive approach on the *locus standi* of natural and legal persons – that is, the question as to whether the applicant is entitled to have the Court decide the merits of a particular dispute. The Court's interpretation of the criteria requiring direct and individual concern – the so-called *Plaumann* test[50] – is very restrictive and EU law scholars have called for a rethinking of such a stance in order to facilitate access to the Court.[51] The Lisbon Treaty[52] has modified the conditions of *locus standi*, and the wording of Article 263 TFEU no longer requires individual concern when natural or legal persons challenge 'regulatory acts' which do not require 'implementing measures'. However, a restrictive interpretation of 'regulatory acts' as excluding 'legislative acts' did still lead the Court to dismiss the action of the Inuit.

Indigenous culture and the protection of free trade before the WTO dispute settlement mechanism

Parallel to the litigation before the ECJ, Canada and Norway brought claims against the European Union (European Communities or EC in the WTO jargon) before the WTO Dispute Settlement Body for partially overlapping and partially diverging reasons. The Panel reports were circulated on 25 November 2013.[53] The Appellate Body Reports were circulated on 22 May

---

48 Convention for the Protection of Human Rights and Fundamental Freedoms, 213 UNTS 222.

49 CJEU, Grand Chamber, Judgment of the Court, 3 October 2013, para. 98.

50 *Plaumann & Co v. Commission*, Case 25/62, 15 July 1963.

51 For commentary, see e.g. M. Wathelet and J. Wildemeersch, 'Recours en annulation: Une première interprétation restrictive du droit d'action élargu des particuliers?', *Journal des Tribunaux – Droit Européen* (2012) 77–78.

52 Treaty of Lisbon Amending the Treaty on European Union and the Treaty Establishing the European Community, 13 December 2007, 2007 OJ (C306) 1.

53 *European Communities – Measures Prohibiting the Importation and Marketing of Seal Products*, WT/DS400/R and WT/DS401/R, 25 November 2013, Reports of the Panel.

2014.[54] After a brief scrutiny of the arguments of the claimants, the reports of the Panel and the Appellate Body (AB) will be examined.

Canada and Norway argued that the Indigenous communities condition (IC condition) and the marine resource management condition (MRM condition) violated the non-discrimination obligation under Article I:1 and III:4 of the GATT 1994[55] as such conditions accord seal products from Canada and Norway treatment less favourable than that accorded to like seal products of domestic origin, mainly from Sweden and Finland as well as those of other foreign origin, in particular from Greenland.[56] In fact, the majority of seals hunted in Canada and Norway would not qualify under the exceptions, 'while most if not all of Greenlandic seal products are expected to conform to the requirements under the IC exception'.[57] Therefore, according to the complainants, the EU Seal Regime would *de facto* discriminate against Canadian and Norwegian imports of seal products.[58] In fact, the EU Seal Regime would restrict virtually all trade in seal products from Canada and Norway within the European Union.[59]

Moreover, the complainants argued that while the EU measures did not prevent seal products derived from seals killed inhumanely from being sold on the EU market,[60] they could prevent seal products derived from seals killed humanely such as those killed in their commercial hunts from being placed on the market.[61] According to the complainants 'seal welfare concerns exist equally in all seal hunts, irrespective of the type of hunt. Furthermore . . . all seal hunts [including IC hunts] have commercial dimensions',[62] and contribute to the subsistence of coastal communities.[63] They maintained that the EU's exemption for trade in traditional Inuit seal products would prove to be ineffective, particularly in the face of the collapse of the larger market.[64]

The claimants also contended that the EU Seal Regime constituted a quantitative restriction on trade which was inconsistent with Article XI of the GATT 1994 and that it created an unnecessary obstacle to trade that was inconsistent with Article 2.2 of the Agreement on Technical Barriers to Trade (TBT Agreement)[65] because it was more restrictive of trade than was necessary

54   *European Communities – Measures Prohibiting the Importation and Marketing of Seal Products*, WT/DS400/AB/R and WT/DS401/AB/R, 22 May 2014, Reports of the Appellate Body.
55   General Agreement on Tariffs and Trade 1994, 15 April 1994, Marrakesh Agreement Establishing the World Trade Organization, Annex 1A, 1867 UNTS 187.
56   Reports of the Panel, para. 7.2.
57   Ibid., paras 7.161 and 7.164.
58   Ibid., para. 7.141.
59   Ibid., para. 7.46.
60   Ibid., para. 7.4.
61   Ibid., para. 7.226.
62   Ibid., para. 7.178.
63   Ibid., para. 7.228.
64   Ibid., para. 7.162.
65   Agreement on Technical Barriers to Trade (TBT Agreement) 33 ILM 1125 (1994).

to achieve a legitimate objective.[66] In addition, Norway contended that the EU Seal Regime violated relevant provisions of the Agreement on Agriculture.[67] Finally, the complainants submitted that the EU Seal Regime nullified or impaired benefits set down by Article XXIII:1(b) of the GATT 1994.[68]

The Panel found that the seal products produced by Indigenous peoples and those not hunted by Indigenous peoples were like products.[69] The Panel acknowledged the existence of a number of international law instruments, including the United Nations Declaration on the Rights of Indigenous Peoples focusing on the preservation of cultural heritage and control over resources.[70] The Panel also referred to a number of WTO countries adopting analogous Inuit exceptions.[71] These sources were taken into account as 'factual evidence'.[72]

Despite the reference to these instruments, however, the Panel concluded that the design and application of the IC measure was not even-handed because the IC exception was available *de facto* to Greenland.[73] Therefore, the Panel report held, *inter alia*, that the exception provided for Indigenous communities under the EU Seal Regime violated Article 2.1 of the TBT Agreement because it accorded more favourable treatment to seal products produced by Indigenous communities than that accorded to like domestic and foreign products.[74] The Panel concluded that the same exception also violated Articles I:1 and III:4 of the GATT 1994 because an advantage granted by the EU to seal products derived from hunts traditionally conducted by the Inuit was not accorded immediately and unconditionally to like products originating in Canada.[75]

Finally, the Panel examined the question as to whether the seal products regulation is justified under any of the exceptions under Article XX of the GATT 1994, and in particular under Article XX(a) on public morals. The Panel observed that ethical considerations did play a role in the public debate which preceded the adoption of the EU Seal Regime,[76] and found that 'the legislative history of the measure suggests a link between the public concerns on seal welfare and an ethical or moral consideration'.[77] The Panel concluded

---

66 Reports of the Panel, para. 7.2.
67 Agreement on Agriculture, 15 April 1994, Marrakesh Agreement Establishing the World Trade Organization, Annex 1A, 1867 UNTS 410.
68 Reports of the Panel, para. 7.2.
69 As usual, the Panel assessed the likeness of products on criteria such as: (a) the properties of the product; (2) the end-uses of the products; (3) consumers' tastes and habits; and (d) the tariff classification of goods. Ibid., para. 7.136.
70 Ibid., para. 7.292.
71 Ibid., para. 7.294.
72 Ibid., footnote 475.
73 Ibid., para. 7.317.
74 Ibid., para. 8(2).
75 Ibid., para. 8(3)(a).
76 Ibid., para. 7.395.
77 Ibid., para. 7.405.

that 'animal welfare is an issue of ethical or moral nature in the European Union'.[78] Therefore the Panel found that the EU Seal Regime was necessary to protect public morals. Yet, it determined that the regime had a discriminatory impact that could not be justified under the *chapeau* of Article Article XX(a) of the GATT 1994.[79]

Immediately after the release of the reports, Canada, Norway and the European Union each appealed certain issues of law and legal interpretations developed in the Panel reports.[80] While the Appellate Body confirmed that the EU Seal Regime *de facto* discriminated like products under Articles I:1 (Most Favoured Nation) and III:4 (National Treatment) of the GATT 1994, it reversed the Panel's finding that by laying down product characteristics the EU Seal regime constitutes a technical regulation governed by the TBT Agreement.[81] The AB held that the EU Seal Regime does not prescribe any characteristics on the seal products; rather, it regulates the placing on the EU market of these products.[82]

The AB also confirmed that the ban on seal products can be justified on moral grounds under Article XX(a) the GATT. However, it held the regime did not meet the requirements of the *chapeau* of Article XX of the GATT 1994, criticizing the way the exception for Inuit hunts has been designed and implemented.[83] *Inter alia*, the AB emphasized that 'the lack of a precise definition of the subsistence criterion introduces a degree of ambiguity into the requirements for the IC exception under the EU Seal regime'.[84] It noted that the IC exception contained no anti-circumvention clause,[85] and pinpointed that 'seal products derived from . . . commercial hunts could potentially enter the EU market under the IC exception'.[86] The AB concluded that 'the European Union has not justified the EU Seal Regime under Article XX(a) of the GATT 1994'.[87]

---

78   Ibid., para. 7.409.

79   Ibid., para. 7.651.

80   *European Communities – Measures Prohibiting the Importation and Marketing of Seal Products*, Notification of an Appeal by Canada, WT/DS400/8, 24 January 2014; European Communities – Measures Prohibiting the Importation and Marketing of Seal Products, Notification of an Appeal by Norway, 29 January 2014, WT/DS401/9.

81   Ibid., para. 5.59.

82   *European Communities – Measures Prohibiting the Importation and Marketing of Seal Products*, Reports of the Appellate Body, para. 5.58. Eminent scholars had suggested this line of interpretation. See e.g. R. Howse and J. Langille, 'Permitting Pluralism: The *Seal Products* Dispute and Why the WTO Should Accept Trade Restrictions Justified by Noninstrumental Moral Values', 37 *Yale Journal of International Law* (2012), 367–432.

83   *European Communities – Measures Prohibiting the Importation and Marketing of Seal Products*, Reports of the Appellate Body, para. 5.339.

84   Ibid., para. 5.324.

85   Ibid., para. 5.327.

86   Ibid., para. 5.328.

87   Ibid., para. 6.1(d)(iii).

Therefore, the European Union will have to refine the Seal Regime to demonstrate good faith, insert anti-circumvention rules and thus comply with the *chapeau* requirements. In this regard, Howse suggested that 'the European authorities appoint a special commission, comprised of veterinary experts, animal ethicists, member state animal welfare authorities, animal rights activists and Indigenous communities representatives, which would recommend steps that can be taken. . . . to improve seal welfare in Indigenous hunts'.[88] However, as noted by some commentators, 'these concerns should be relatively easy for the EU to address'.[89] Ultimately, the flaws found by the Panel and the AB were not with the ban itself, but with the specific implementation of the ban's exception for Indigenous peoples.

Critical assessment: a clash of cultures?

The case studies analysed here highlight several different clashes: the clash between international economic law and domestic regulatory autonomy; the clash between an international economic culture and a local Indigenous culture; and the clash between animal welfare and traditional cultural practices. These cases also show that there may be both synergy and collision between economic interests and the protection of (Indigenous) cultural heritage. On the one hand, the seal products dispute shows that free trade can enhance Indigenous peoples' cultural practices, and that trade can be a mechanism of economic subsistence and cultural empowerment. Yet, there is a friction between the non–discrimination principle, as applied in international trade law, and positive measures, i.e. those exceptions or measures adopted by states to protect specific sectors of society. On the other hand, the interplay between international investment law and Indigenous entitlements can jeopardize the latter, if it is not monitored.

At a procedural level, international and regional economic *fora* constitute an uneven playing field: often the affected communities do not have direct access to these *fora* – as is the case for investment tribunals (unless the Indigenous peoples qualify as investors) and WTO panels and the Appellate Body. Before such tribunals, the arguments of local communities, including Indigenous peoples, need to be espoused by their home government. While local communities can (and have) present(ed) *amicus curiae* briefs reflecting their specific interests, the investment tribunals and the WTO panels and Appellate Body are not legally obliged to consider such briefs – rather they have the capacity to do so should they deem it appropriate. Even when direct access is theoretically admissible, as a matter of fact, it may be overly difficult to gain

---

88 See R. Howse, 'WTO Seals: the Gestures of Good Faith the AB is demanding of the EU in return for Public Morals Justification', International Economic Law and Policy Blog, 25 May 2014.

89 R. Howse, J. Langille and K. Sykes, 'Sealing the Deal: The WTO's Appellate Body Report in EC-Seal Products', 18(12) *ASIL Insights* (2014).

access to the relevant economic forum – the dispute brought by the Inuit before the CJEU constituting a paradigmatic example in this regard.

More substantively, international economic *fora* are tribunals of limited jurisdiction and cannot adjudicate on eventual infringements of Indigenous peoples' rights – except for the CJEU. In a number of disputes brought before the WTO and arbitral tribunals, the arguments in support of free trade and foreign direct investment are intertwined with Indigenous claims. In the *Andre v. Canada* case, it is uncertain whether the arbitral tribunal will consider the Indigenous exception as a legal *acquis* under human rights law. With regard to the seal products dispute, while the cultural entitlements of Indigenous peoples are referred to by the defendant,[90] the panel found that the commercial aspect of IC hunts to be related more to the 'need [of Inuit communities] to adjust to modern society rather than to continuing their cultural heritage of bartering'.[91] In general terms, the Panel and the AB's reports considered the arguments of the claimant and defendant carefully – as it is customary.[92] Yet, the rehearsal of these arguments does not necessarily mean that the Panel and the AB endorse them.

International economic *fora* have become a key pillar of global governance attracting a number of 'culture and trade' and 'culture and investment' related disputes. Are the WTO adjudicative bodies and investment treaty tribunals operating as open, rather than self-contained, regimes under public international law? Some scholars and practitioners have pinpointed that 'trade and other societal values incorporated in the WTO framework ought to be recognized as equals; a liberal trade bias to interpret each and every rule in the WTO package is to be excluded'.[93] Similar arguments have been made in the context of investment treaty arbitration, highlighting that 'excessive compartmentalisation impedes coherence; it emphasises the particular over the universal; it may defeat important policy objectives of the international community by leading to competition and clashes between regimes'.[94] Neither the WTO nor international investment governance are 'mono-cultures';[95] rather they deal with a variety of issues and sectors, ranging from agriculture to intellectual property to telecommunications. Furthermore, international

---

90   See e.g. *EC –Seal products*, AB Reports, para. 5.143 (stating that 'With regard to the IC exception, the European Union states that EU legislators considered that the subsistence of Inuit and other Indigenous communities and the preservation of their cultural identity "provide benefits to humans which, from a moral point of view, outweigh the risk of suffering inflicted upon seals as a result of the hunts conducted by those communities.")

91   *EC – Seal Products*, Panel Report, para. 7.287.

92   *EC–Seal Products*, Panel Reports, para. 7.294 and AB Reports, footnote 1559 (both quoting the arguments of the parties).

93   M.C.E.J. Bronckers, 'More Power to the WTO?', 4 *Journal of International Economic Law* (2001) 41–65, 41.

94   M. Waibel, 'International Investment Law and Treaty Interpretation', in R. Hoffmann and C. Tams (eds), *International Investment Law and General International Law* (Baden-Baden: Nomos 2011) pp. 29–52, 30.

95   Bronckers, 'More Power to the WTO?', 45.

economic *fora* have a proven track record of effective dispute settlement. Customary canons of treaty interpretation also require systematic interpretation.[96]

Yet, the existence of highly sophisticated dispute settlement mechanisms in international economic law risk eclipsing the values of other regimes, such as international cultural law, which lack a comparable mechanism. These cases show that economic globalization can affect non-economic matters, and that international economic *fora* may not be the most appropriate *fora* for disputes presenting cultural issues. At the institutional level, there seems to be 'a strict separation of powers between the competent international organizations'.[97] The Panel and the Appellate Body reports confirm previous jurisprudence on the interpretation of the agreements covered by the WTO and do not represent a significant departure from the WTO *acquis*. Very rarely have exceptions been successfully invoked by defendants in the adjudication of international trade disputes.[98]

The Seal Products dispute is likely to become a landmark case in the WTO jurisprudence, paving the way for other 'culture and trade' related disputes. For instance, the production of *foie gras* – that is the liver of a duck or a goose specially fattened – is banned in most EU member states because of animal concerns. However, not only do a few EU member states, such as France, produce this product, but they also consider it as a 'part of the[ir] protected cultural and gastronomic heritage'.[99] When California banned the production and consumption of *foie gras*, the relevant French authorities pledged to contest the Californian ban.[100] In addition, the importance of this case may well go beyond the limited boundaries of the WTO, as GATT XX-like exceptions have been inserted in a few investment treaties.[101]

The relationship between international economic law and other branches of international law, including international cultural law, should be addressed in terms of coordination between interrelated systems of public international law norms. Both WTO law and international investment law are public international law sub-systems, endowed with relative autonomy, but still open to the influence of international law, including international cultural law.

---

96 Vienna Convention on the Law of Treaties (VCLT), Vienna, 22 May 1969, entered into force on 27 January 1980, 1155 UNTS 331, Article 31(3)(c).

97 R. Neuwirth, 'The Future of the "Culture and Trade Debate": a Legal Outlook', 47(2) *Journal of World Trade* (2013) 391–420, 407.

98 J.F. Colares, 'A Theory of WTO Adjudication: From Empirical Analysis to Biased Rule Development', 42 *Vanderbilt Journal of Transnational Law* (2009) 383.

99 Article L654 of France Rural Code.

100 K. Willsher, 'Foie Gras: French Farmers Defend 'Tradition' after Ban in California', *The Observer*, 5 August 2012.

101 See e.g. Australia – Korea Free Trade Agreement, signed 8 April 2014. Online. Available: www.dfat.gov.au/fta/kafta/ (accessed 5 June 2014) and China – ASEAN Investment Agreement, signed on 15 August 2009 Online. Available: www.dti.gov.ph/dti/index.php?p=688 (accessed 5 June 2014).

It is not a question of direct application of international cultural law;[102] rather international economic law *fora* are called to incidentally evaluate the regulatory measures adopted by states to determine whether such measures can be justified even if *prima facie* they appear to be inconsistent with provisions of international economic law.

Conclusions

The analysed case studies illustrate a recently emerged facet of the complex interplay between culture and international economic law, highlighting a fundamental clash between local and global dimensions of regulation. Indigenous heritage is local, it belongs to specific places; economic governance has an international character. At the same time, Indigenous heritage also belongs to the international discourse; as a number of international law instruments protect Indigenous peoples' rights.

While the linkage between economic development and cultural concerns may lead to specific positive synergies, in certain circumstances economic activities may jeopardize cultural heritage. Exploring the reported disputes related to culture also tests the linkage between international economic law and general international law. Is international economic law a self-contained regime or is it an integral and responsive branch of international law? On the one hand, culture related cases before international economic *fora* show the (lack of) effectiveness of international cultural law when it comes to address emerging issues in relation to economic globalization. On the other, the power of attraction exercised by international economic *fora* towards culture related disputes risks over-emphasizing economic values vis-à-vis cultural values. International economic *fora* may not be the most suitable *fora* for settling this kind of dispute, as they may face difficulties in finding an appropriate balance between the different interests concerned. They are courts of limited jurisdiction, and cannot adjudicate on state violations of Indigenous peoples' entitlements.

A series of problematic cases involving elements of cultural heritage have shown the increasing interrelatedness of foreign investment and trade, on the one hand, and cultural heritage on the other. The survey of these cases shows that international law has only developed very limited institutional machinery – such as *amicus curiae* briefs, limited exceptions etc. – for the protection of cultural heritage through international economic law adjudication. It remains to be seen whether this developing jurisprudence can eventually lead to the

---

102 See P. Picone and A. Ligustro, *Diritto dell'Organizzazione Mondiale del Commercio* (Padova: CEDAM 2002) 633. In investment disputes, however, if the applicable law is the law of the host state and the host state is a party to a multilateral cultural treaty, then international cultural law would become relevant as part of the applicable law. For in depth analysis, see V. Vadi, *Cultural Heritage in International Investment Law and Arbitration* (Cambridge: Cambridge University Press 2014) 252.

emergence of general principles of international law requiring the protection of cultural heritage and the balance between private and public interests.

In conclusion, this chapter does not exclude the possibility that FDI and free trade can represent a potentially positive force for development. That said, when drafting and enforcing policies and practices concerning economic activities, states must be mindful of the implications for the culture of Indigenous peoples, as an excessive emphasis on economic development may endanger the protection of fundamental values. At the same time, international economic *fora* should adopt a holistic approach in interpreting and applying the relevant international economic agreements.

Bibliography

Bjorklund, A., 'The Emerging Civilization of Investment Arbitration', 113 *Penn State Law Review* (2009) 1269.

Bronckers, M.C.E.J., 'More Power to the WTO?', 4 *Journal of International Economic Law* (2001) 41–65.

Casini, L., '*Italian Hours*: The Globalization of Cultural Property Law', 9 *International Journal of Constitutional Law* (2011) 373.

Colares, J.F., 'A Theory of WTO Adjudication: From Empirical Analysis to Biased Rule Development', 42 *Vanderbilt Journal of Transnational Law* (2009) 383.

Howse, R., 'WTO Seals: The Gestures of Good Faith the AB is demanding of the EU in return for Public Morals Justification', International Economic Law and Policy Blog, 25 May 2014.

Howse, R. and J. Langille, 'Permitting Pluralism: The *Seal Products* Dispute and Why the WTO Should Accept Trade Restrictions Justified by Noninstrumental Moral Values', 37 *Yale Journal of International Law* (2012) 367–432.

Howse, R., J. Langille and K. Sykes, 'Sealing the Deal: The WTO's Appellate Body Report in EC-Seal Products', 18(12) *ASIL Insights* (2014).

Nafziger, J., 'The Development of International Cultural Law', *American Society of International Law. Proceedings of the Annual Meeting* (2006).

Neuwirth, R., 'The Future of the "Culture and Trade Debate": A Legal Outlook', 47(2) *Journal of World Trade* (2013) 391–420.

O'Keefe, R., *The Protection of Cultural Property in Armed Conflict* (Cambridge: Cambridge University Press 2001).

Picone P. and A. Ligustro, *Diritto dell'Organizzazione Mondiale del Commercio* (Padova: CEDAM 2002).

Sen, A., *Development as Freedom* (Oxford: Oxford University Press 1999).

Sen, A., 'How Does Culture Matter?', in V. Rao and M. Walton (eds), *Culture and Public Action* (Stanford University Press 2004) 37–58.

Steger, D., 'The Culture of the WTO: Why it Needs to Change', 10 *Journal of International Economic Law* (2007) 483–495.

Vadi, V. *Cultural Heritage in International Investment Law and Arbitration* (Cambridge: Cambridge University Press, 2014).

Von Schorlemer, S., 'UNESCO Dispute Settlement', in A.A. Yusuf (ed.), *Standard-Setting in UNESCO – Normative Action in Education, Science and Culture Essays in Commemoration of the Sixtieth Anniversary of UNESCO* (Leiden/Boston, MA: Martinus Nijhoff 2007) 78.

Waibel, M., 'International Investment Law and Treaty Interpretation', in R. Hoffmann and C. Tams (eds), *International Investment Law and General International Law* (Baden-Baden: Nomos 2011) 29–52.

Wathelet, M. and J. Wildemeersch, 'Recours en annulation: Une première interprétation restrictive du droit d'action élargu des particuliers?', *Journal des Tribunaux – Droit Européen* (2012) 77–78.

Willsher, K., 'Foie Gras: French Farmers Defend 'Tradition' After Ban in California', *The Observer*, 5 August 2012.

Legal instruments

Agreement Establishing the World Trade Organization, 15 April 1994, 33 ILM (1994).

Agreement on Agriculture, 15 April 1994, Marrakesh Agreement Establishing the World Trade Organization, Annex 1A, 1867 UNTS 410.

Agreement on Technical Barriers to Trade (TBT Agreement) 33 ILM 1125 (1994).

Australia – Korea Free Trade Agreement, signed 8 April 2014. Online. Available: www.dfat.gov.au/fta/kafta/ (accessed 5 June 2014).

Charter of Fundamental Rights of the European Union, OJC 364/1 (2000).

China – ASEAN Investment Agreement, signed on 15 August 2009 Online. Available: www.dti.gov.ph/dti/index.php?p=688 (accessed 5 June 2014).

Constitution of the United Nations Educational, Scientific, and Cultural Organization, Paris, 16 November 1945, in force 4 November 1946, 52 UNTS 1947, 276.

Convention for the Protection of Human Rights and Fundamental Freedoms, 213 UNTS 222, 4 November 1950.

Convention on Conservation of Migratory Species, 23 June 1979, 19 ILM 11.

Convention on the Protection and Promotion of the Diversity of Cultural Expressions, adopted 20 October 2005, in force 18 March 2007.

Council of the European Union, Council Conclusions on the Promotion of Cultural Diversity and Intercultural Dialogue in the External Relations of the Union and its Member States, Brussels, 20 November 2008.

General Agreement on Tariffs and Trade 1994, 15 April 1994, Marrakesh Agreement Establishing the World Trade Organization, Annex 1A, 1867 UNTS 187.

International Convention for the Regulation of Whaling Article III(13)(b), 2 December 1946, 161 UNTS 72.

Regulation (EC) 1007/2009 of the European Parliament and of the Council of 16 September 2009 on Trade in Seal Products, 2009 OJ (L. 286) 36.

Treaty of Lisbon Amending the Treaty on European Union and the Treaty Establishing the European Community, 13 December 2007, 2007 OJ (C306) 1.

Treaty on European Union, signed on 7 February 1992 and entered into force on 1 November 1993.

Treaty on the Functioning of the European Union, Consolidated version, 53 OJEU 30 March 2010, 2010 C83/01.

Vienna Convention on the Law of Treaties, Vienna, 22 May 1969, entered into force on 27 January 1980, 1155 UNTS 331.

Cases

Andre John R. v. Government of Canada, Notice of Intent to Submit Claim to Arbitration Pursuant to Chapter Eleven of the North American Free Trade Agreement, 19 March 2010.

European Communities – Measures Prohibiting the Importation and Marketing of Seal Products, WT/DS400/R and WT/DS401/R, 25 November 2013, Reports of the Panel.

European Communities – Measures Prohibiting the Importation and Marketing of Seal Products, WT/DS400/AB/R and WT/DS401/AB/R, 22 May 2014, Reports of the Appellate Body.

European Communities – Measures Prohibiting the Importation and Marketing of Seal Products, Notification of an Appeal by Canada, WT/DS400/8, 24 January 2014.

European Communities – Measures Prohibiting the Importation and Marketing of Seal Products, Notification of an Appeal by Norway, WT/DS401/9, 29 January 2014.

Inuit Tapiriit Kanatami and Others v. Commission, Case T-18/10, Order of 6 September 2011.

Inuit Tapiriit Kanatami and Others v. Commission, CJEU, Grand Chamber, Judgment of the Court, 3 October 2013.

Kitok Ivan v. Sweden (Communication No. 197/1985), UN Human Rights Comm., UN Doc. CCPR/C/33/D/197/1985, 27 July 1988.

Lansman Jouni v. Finland (Communication No. 671/1995), UN Human Rights Comm., UN Doc. CCPR/C/58/D/671/1995, 22 November 1996.

Plaumann & Co v. Commission, Case 25/62, 15 July 1963.

5 Investment projects affecting Indigenous heritage

Federico Lenzerini

Investment projects affecting Indigenous heritage: desecrating Indigenous peoples' ancestral land

> Our people have been the 'caretakers' of the land since time immemorial. Historically, our resources have always sustained us and been critical to our survival. We used our resources for food, bartering and trading for survival. Also, the lands and resources have always taken care of our social well-being as a people. Our lands are used for food, trading, hunting and plants for traditional medicines and teas. The water is used for spiritual baths, fishing for food, social and ceremonial purposes. We also sell fish to enhance our economic sustainability. As a People, we respect the land and resources by giving back, keeping it clean and looking after our homes. We conserve our resources by not taking more than what we need. We must not be greedy. The vision is to still have our resources for our grandchildren for many generations.[1]

The concept of Indigenous peoples' heritage is grounded on a complex idea based on their holistic vision of life, which is centred on their own view of the 'Cosmology' of the world. Indigenous heritage, therefore, includes all elements of tangible and – especially – intangible character which are essential for the relevant communities to exist as 'different' human groups as well as for transmitting their distinctive cultural identity to future generations. All elements of Indigenous heritage are inextricably linked to each other and include both material and spiritual features, where the line of separation between them is inescapably indefinite. In this context, ancestral lands – usually considered as the 'Mother Earth' to which the community belongs – play a central role in the preservation of the identity of Indigenous peoples. Also the concept of 'land' is, for Indigenous peoples, a complex one, which includes not only the land as such, but also natural resources – including both biological and mineral resources – as well as the invisible and spiritual elements that are perceived by the communities concerned as essential to ensure

---

1 See 'Cheam First Nation', June-August 2013. Online. Available: http://cheam.ca/Search?Search=nation (accessed 27 September 2013).

the necessary harmony in the world. The heritage of Indigenous peoples is today safeguarded by international law in the field, the development of which has ultimately resulted in the approval of the 2007 United Nations Declaration on the Rights of Indigenous Peoples.[2] This Declaration has achieved virtually universal support within the international community and, in some parts, is declaratory of customary international law.[3]

Against this background, this chapter proceeds as follows. The next section illustrates that investment projects can affect Indigenous heritage and therefore focuses on the obligation to consult Indigenous peoples before initiating investment projects in their ancestral lands. The third section examines the international practice in order to ascertain whether the requirement to obtain free, prior and informed consent has reached the status of an obligation under customary international law and to evaluate whether that requirement has merely 'procedural' connotations or whether, at least in some cases, it rather implies the existence of a real *veto power* in favour of Indigenous communities, allowing them to prevent the investment project from being carried out. In particular, reference will be made to the jurisprudence of investment tribunals, international human rights monitoring bodies – including the UN Committee on the Elimination of all Forms of Racial Discrimination, the Human Rights Committee, and the Committee on Economic, Social and Cultural Rights – and other competent institutions. The conclusions will then wrap up the gist of the argument.

The obligation to consult Indigenous peoples before initiating investment projects in their ancestral lands

In evaluating the feasibility of investment projects in Indigenous peoples' traditional lands, one necessarily needs to take into account the complexity of their vision of life – and, *a fortiori*, of their cultural heritage. This need produces special implications that sometimes result in the investment being absolutely incompatible with the necessity of properly safeguarding Indigenous peoples' rights. This happens, in particular, when an investment threatens to disrupt the essential elements of the spiritual relationship of Indigenous peoples with their ancestral lands. In light of this, it is essential that, before initiating any project of exploitation in Indigenous lands, the communities concerned are properly consulted with the purpose of obtaining their free, prior and informed consent.

This requirement is expressed in the form of an obligation by Article 15 para. 2 of the 1989 ILO Convention No. 169 concerning Indigenous and Tribal Peoples in Independent Countries,[4] according to which,

---

2 United Nations Declaration on the Rights of Indigenous Peoples (UNDRIP), GA Res. 61/295, UN Doc A/RES/61/295, 13 September 2007, 46 ILM 1013 (2007).
3 See, in this respect, note 6 below.
4 International Labour Organization Convention 169 Concerning Indigenous and Tribal Peoples in Independent Countries, 27 June 1989, 1650 UNTS 384.

[i]n cases in which the State retains the ownership of mineral or sub-surface resources or rights to other resources pertaining to lands, governments shall establish or maintain procedures through which they shall consult these peoples, with a view to ascertaining whether and to what degree their interests would be prejudiced, before undertaking or permitting any programmes for the exploration or exploitation of such resources pertaining to their lands. The peoples concerned shall wherever possible participate in the benefits of such activities, and shall receive fair compensation for any damages which they may sustain as a result of such activities.

This obligation, in reality, is quite soft – especially if one considers that it includes no reference to the requirement to seek the free, prior and informed consent of the communities concerned. Rather, the state is only under an obligation to ascertain whether and to what degree the interests of those communities would be prejudiced by programmes of exploration or exploitation of resources located in Indigenous lands, with no further requirement in terms of preventing or limiting such prejudices in the event that they are actually likely to be produced. On the other hand, it may well be asserted that an implicit requirement exists to 'design appropriate mitigation measures' in order to alleviate such prejudices.[5] In addition, the peoples concerned are entitled to participate in the benefits arising from the said programmes only *wherever possible*, the state being the actor with the competence to determine whether and to what extent such participation is *possible*. Last but not least, although according to the formulation of the provision in question it appears that the right of the Indigenous peoples concerned to receive fair compensation for any damages which they may sustain as a result of the programmes in point is not subject to the condition of compensation being *possible*, the problem exists of interpreting the meaning of the word 'damages'. The correct interpretation would appear to be one according to which the existence and gravity of the damage caused is to be evaluated from the perspective of the Indigenous communities concerned – therefore including the psychological pain endured as a consequence of the violence suffered by the land in light of its spiritual significance to the said communities. However, the very general wording used by Article 15 para. 2 in referring to 'damages' certainly paves the way for states to interpret such a concept according to their own views and needs. Moreover, the impact of Article 15 para. 2 of ILO Convention No. 169 is further reduced by the fact that the Convention has so far been characterized by a very low rate of ratification, with only 22 states being parties to it at the time of writing.[6]

5   See International Finance Corporation (IFC), 'ILO Convention 169 and the Private Sector. Questions and Answers for IFC Clients', March 2007. Online. Available: www.ifc.org/wps/wcm/connect/cba33980488556edbafcfa6a6515bb18/ILO_169.pdf?MOD=AJPERES (accessed 15 June 2013), p. 4.

6   See Ratification of C169 – Indigenous and Tribal Peoples Convention, 1989 (No. 169). Online. Available: www.ilo.org/dyn/normlex/en/f?p=1000:11300:0::NO:11300:P11300_INSTRUMENT_ID:312314 (accessed 27 September 2013).

Different considerations should be developed with respect to the UNDRIP. As noted by International Law Association's (ILA) Resolution No. 5/2012, adopted in Sofia in August 2012 with a overwhelming majority and no opposition, the UNDRIP, although technically a non-binding instrument, 'includes several key provisions which correspond to existing State obligations under customary international law';[7] in addition:

> [t]he provisions included in UNDRIP which do not yet correspond to customary international law nevertheless express the aspirations of the world's Indigenous peoples, as well as of States, in their move to improve existing standards for the safeguarding of Indigenous peoples' human rights. States recognised them in a 'declaration' subsumed 'within the framework of the *obligations* established by the Charter of the United Nations to promote and protect human rights on a non-discriminatory basis' and passed with overwhelming support by the United Nations General Assembly. This genesis leads to an expectation of maximum compliance by States and the other relevant actors. The provisions included in UNDRIP represent the parameters of reference for States to define the scope and content of their existing obligations – pursuant to customary and conventional international law – towards Indigenous peoples.[8]

The most relevant provisions with respect to the subject-matter of this contribution are Articles 19 and 32 of the UNDRIP. According to the former:

> States shall consult and cooperate in good faith with the Indigenous peoples concerned through their own representative institutions in order to obtain their free, prior and informed consent before adopting and implementing legislative or administrative measures that may affect them.

As for Article 32 of the UNDRIP, it establishes at para. 2 that:

> States shall consult and cooperate in good faith with the Indigenous peoples concerned through their own representative institutions in order to obtain their free and informed consent prior to the approval of any project affecting their lands or territories and other resources, particularly in connection with the development, utilization or exploitation of mineral, water or other resources.

The following paragraph adds that 'States shall provide effective mechanisms for just and fair redress for any such activities, and appropriate measures shall

---

7   Resolution 5/2012, 'Rights of Indigenous Peoples'. Online. Available: www.ila-hq.org/en/committees/index.cfm/cid/1024 (accessed 30 September 2013), para. 2.
8   Ibid., para. 3 (emphasis added).

be taken to mitigate adverse environmental, economic, social, cultural or spiritual impact.' Throughout the whole text of the UNDRIP the cultural rationale of the right in question emerges very clearly. For example, according to Article 12 of the UNDRIP, Indigenous peoples have 'the right to manifest, practise, develop and teach their spiritual and religious traditions, customs and ceremonies; the right to maintain, protect, and have access in privacy to their religious and cultural sites . . .'. Investment projects carried out in Indigenous lands can jeopardize such a right, when and to the extent that such projects may prevent the peoples concerned from performing their spiritual and religious traditions as well as to maintain, protect or have private access to their religious and cultural sites. Similar considerations may be developed, *mutatis mutandis*, with respect to Article 24 para. 1 of the UNDRIP – proclaiming the right of Indigenous peoples 'to their traditional medicines and to maintain their health practices, including the conservation of their vital medicinal plants, animals and minerals' – and to Article 26 para. 2 of the same declaration, according to which the said peoples 'have the right to own, use, develop and control the lands, territories and resources that they possess by reason of traditional ownership or other traditional occupation or use, as well as those which they have otherwise acquired'.

Provided that, according to contemporary international law, Indigenous peoples actually have a right to be properly consulted with the purpose of obtaining their free, prior and informed consent before any investment project is initiated on their traditional lands, the problem now consists of ascertaining the status of such a right, in particular from two different perspectives. First, it is necessary to determine whether such a right can be considered as having reached the status of an obligation under customary international law. Second, it is worthwhile to evaluate whether the right in question has a purely 'procedural' connotation – in the sense that states have only a duty to consult Indigenous peoples in good faith in view of obtaining their consent but, in the event that it is impossible to obtain it, they are entitled to carry out an investment project in Indigenous lands even in the absence of such a consent – or whether, at least in some cases, it actually implies the existence of a real *right to veto* in favour of Indigenous communities, allowing them to prevent the investment project from being performed. Both issues can be properly evaluated through examining the relevant international practice. Therefore, there is no need to assess them separately, at least at this stage of the present investigation.

The international practice

This section examines the relevant international practice in order to determine whether the right to free, prior and informed consent can be considered as having reached the status of an obligation under customary international law as well as evaluate whether the right in point has a simple 'procedural' connotation or whether, at least in some cases, it implies the existence of a real *veto power* in favour of Indigenous communities, allowing them to prevent the investment project from being performed. In particular, reference will be made to the jurisprudence of investment tribunals, international human rights monitoring bodies – including the UN Committee on the Elimination of all Forms of Racial Discrimination, the Human Rights Committee, and the Committee on Economic, Social and Cultural Rights – and other competent institutions.

First, a few recent investment arbitrations contribute to the emergence of international practice. Among them, the well-known *Glamis Gold* case is notable. In its award, the Arbitral Tribunal considered that certain measures taken by the government of the United States and the State of California, resulting in a restraint placed upon the open-pit mining operations of a Canadian mining corporation in the California Desert Conservation Area, were justified by the need to prevent 'a significant, unavoidable adverse impact to cultural resources and Native American sacred sites'.[9] The Tribunal agreed with the US government that investors' rights must be balanced with 'the harms caused to Native American sacred sites by open-pit mining',[10] and recognized that the measures affecting the investment were justified by the fact that the project 'presented a potential danger to Native American sacred sites'.[11]

Even more significant is the *Grand River* award. The controversy was triggered by a claim by a Canadian company, controlled by Aboriginal people, which exported tobacco to the United States. The claimants argued that the US *Master Settlement Agreement* (MSA) – compelling tobacco producers to contribute to funds necessary to compensate people affected by tobacco-related illnesses[12] – resulted in an indirect expropriation of its investment as well as in a violation of standards of fair and equitable treatment. Specifically referring to the right of Indigenous peoples to be consulted before implementing governmental policies or action significantly affecting them, the Tribunal asserted that:

> [i]t may well be, as the Claimants urged, that there does exist a principle of customary international law requiring governmental authorities to consult Indigenous peoples on governmental policies or actions significantly affecting them. One member of the Tribunal has written that there is such a customary rule. Moreover, a recent study by a committee of several international law experts assembled under the auspices of the International Law Association, after an exhaustive survey of relevant state

---

9 See *Glamis Gold, Ltd v. United States of America*, Arbitration under UNCITRAL Arbitration Rules, Award, 8 June 2009. Online. Available: www.state.gov/documents/organization/125798.pdf (accessed 15 June 2013), para. 760 f.
10 Ibid., para. 804.
11 Ibid., para. 814.
12 Master Settlement Agreement (MSA). Online. Available: http://ag.ca.gov/tobacco/pdf/1msa.pdf (accessed 15 June 2013).

and international practice, found a wide range of customary international law norms concerning Indigenous peoples, including 'the right to be consulted with respect to any project that may affect them.' As pointed out by the Claimants, the duty of states to consult with Indigenous peoples is featured in the UN Declaration of the Rights of Indigenous Peoples, particularly in its Article 19 as well as in several other articles. In its Counter-Memorial the Respondent maintained in sweeping terms that the Declaration does not represent customary international law, as did Canada in its non-disputing party submission. However, when questioned by the Tribunal on this point at the hearing, the Respondents' counsel stated that some parts of the Declaration could reflect fundamental human rights principles and emerging customary law.[13]

Although 'the possible existence of a customary rule calling for expanded consultation between governments and Indigenous peoples does not assist . . . an individual investor',[14] the Tribunal noted that:

> a good case could be made that consultations should have occurred with governments of the Indian tribes or nations in the United States whose members and sovereign interests could, and apparently are, being affected by the MSA and related measures to regulate commerce in tobacco. Retail tobacco businesses are in many Indian reservations across the country, constituting important sources of income and catalyzing other economic activity among Indigenous communities. The evidence before the Tribunal has shown many of the actual or potential effects of the MSA and related measures on reservation tobacco sales and distribution to reservations retailers. The United States federal government admits to the need for consultations with Indigenous communities on legislative and administrative measures affecting them, as a matter of federal policy if not as a matter of international law.[15]

The issue under discussion has also been extensively addressed by international human rights monitoring bodies and other competent institutions. For example, the UN Committee on the Elimination of all Forms of Racial Discrimination (CERD) in some cases has held the position according to which,

---

13 See *Grand River Enterprises Six Nations, Ltd et al. v. United States of America*, Arbitration under UNCITRAL Arbitration Rules, Award, 12 January 2011. Online. Available: www.state.gov/documents/organization/156820.pdf (accessed 15 June 2013), para. 210 (footnotes omitted). In quoting 'a committee of several international law experts assembled under the auspices of the International Law Association', the Tribunal refers to the Committee on the Rights of Indigenous Peoples, and particularly to its 'Hague Conference (2010) Report'. Online. Available: www.ila-hq.org/en/committees/index.cfm/cid/1024 (accessed 30 September 2013), Chapter 12 (pp. 44–52), written by the present author.

14 Ibid., para. 213.

15 Ibid., para. 212 (footnotes omitted); see also para. 185.

when it comes to 'exploitation of the subsoil resources of the traditional lands of Indigenous communities . . . merely consulting these communities prior to exploiting the resources' is not in line with the requirements of the 1965 International Convention on the Elimination of All Forms of Racial Discrimination,[16] therefore recommending that 'the prior informed consent of these communities be sought'.[17] This is consistent with the CERD's General Recommendation 23 of 1997, according to which states parties to the Convention are called to ensure that 'no decisions directly relating to [the] rights and interests [of Indigenous peoples] *are taken without their informed consent*'.[18] The CERD has reiterated this position on several occasions, albeit using quite inconsistent language. For instance, on some of these occasions the Committee has simply pointed out that states must 'seek the free informed consent of Indigenous communities' or that they must 'consult' with them, without specifying that such a consent is to be obtained as a precondition for carrying out exploitation projects on their traditional lands. Such inconsistency in the language used by the Committee makes it difficult to establish whether or not, and in which cases, the CERD considers the requirement of obtaining the consent of the Indigenous communities concerned as mandatory.[19]

The existence of a duty by states to '[c]onduct consultations with Indigenous peoples before granting licences for the economic exploitation of the lands where they live, and ensure that such exploitation in no circumstances infringes the rights acknowledged in the [International] Covenant [of Civil and Political Rights]' has also been emphasized by the Human Rights Committee in a number of cases.[20] Using a stronger language, the Committee on Economic, Social and Cultural Rights has stressed that states parties to the 1966 International Covenant on Economic, Social and Cultural Rights[21] 'should respect the principle of free, prior and informed consent of Indigenous peoples in all matters covered by their specific rights';[22] more specifically, states

16 Convention on the Elimination of All Forms of Racial Discrimination, in force 4 January 1969, 660 UNTS 195.
17 See 'Consideration of Reports submitted by States Parties under Article 9 of the Convention, Concluding Observations on Ecuador (Sixty second session, 2003)', UN Doc. CERD/C/62/CO/2 of 2 June 2003, para. 16.
18 See United Nations Commission on the Elimination of Racial Discrimination (CERD), General Recommendation No. 23: Indigenous Peoples, UN Doc. A/52/18, Annex V, 18 August 1997, para. 4(d) (emphasis added). Online. Available: www.unhchr.ch/tbs/doc.nsf/0/73984290d fea022b802565160056fe1c (accessed 16 June 2013).
19 For a more comprehensive assessment of the relevant practice of the CERD see ILA Committee on the Rights of Indigenous Peoples, 'Sofia Conference Report (2012)'. Online. Available: www.ila-hq.org/en/committees/index.cfm/cid/1024 (accessed 30 September 2013), pp. 4–6.
20 See, e.g., 'Concluding observations of the Human Rights Committee – Nicaragua', UN Doc. CCPR/C/NIC/CO/3 of 12 December 2008, para. 21(c).
21 International Covenant on Economic, Social and Cultural Rights (ICESCR) UNGA resolution 2200 (XXI) 16 December 1966, in force 3 January 1976, 993 UNTS 3.
22 See General Comment No. 21, 'Right of everyone to take part in cultural life (Art. 15, para. 1 (a), of the International Covenant on Economic, Social and Cultural Rights)', UN Doc. E/C.12/GC/21 of 21 December 2009, para. 37.

'should *obtain* [the] free and informed prior consent [of Indigenous peoples] when the preservation of their cultural resources, especially those associated with their way of life and cultural expression, are at risk'.[23]

With respect to the practice of regional human rights monitoring bodies, the jurisprudence of the Inter-American Court of Human Rights (IACHR) is noteworthy. First of all, in a judgment released in 2007, the Court affirmed that, 'regarding large-scale development or investment projects that would have a major impact within [an Indigenous or tribal people's] territory, the State has a duty, not only to consult with the [community concerned], *but also to obtain their free, prior, and informed consent, according to their customs and traditions*'.[24] Therefore, according to the IACHR, 'when dealing with major development or investment plans that may have a profound impact on the property rights of the members of the [people concerned] to a large part of their territory', 'in addition to the consultation that is always required when planning development or investment projects' there is the additional requirement of obtaining 'the free, prior, and informed consent of the [said people], in accordance with their traditions and customs'.[25]

This position has been reiterated by the Court in a later judgment, related to a claim brought in front of the IACHR by some Indigenous people with respect to the possible execution of a hydrocarbon concession in the Ecuadorian Amazon rainforest by a US oil and gas company.[26] In this case the Court found that Ecuador breached, *inter alia*, the right of the Sarayaku Indigenous community to be consulted before carrying out exploitation projects in their traditional lands, their land rights as well as their right to cultural identity, implicitly proclaimed by Article 21 of the 1969 American Convention of Human Rights (ACHR).[27] The judges stressed that:

> the failure to consult the Sarayaku People affected their cultural identity, since there is no doubt that the intervention in and destruction of their cultural heritage entailed a significant lack of respect for their social and cultural identity, their customs, traditions, worldview and way of life, which naturally caused great concern, sadness and suffering among them.[28]

23 Ibid., para. 55(e) (emphasis added).
24 See *Case of the Saramaka People v. Suriname*, Series C No. 172, Judgment of 28 November 2007, para. 134 (emphasis added).
25 Ibid., para. 137.
26 See *Case of the Kichwa Indigenous People of Sarayaku v. Ecuador*, Series C No. 245, Judgment of 27 June 2012.
27 American Convention of Human Rights (ACHR), OAS Treaty Series No. 36, 1144 UNTS 123. Article 21, para. 1 of the ACHR states that '[e]veryone has the right to the use and enjoyment of his property. The law may subordinate such use and enjoyment to the interest of society'.
28 See *Case of the Kichwa Indigenous People of Sarayaku v. Ecuador*, op. cit., para. 220.

The Court also emphasized that the state has a number of specific obligations which must be respected in order to guarantee the effective participation of Indigenous peoples in projects of exploitation to be carried out in their traditional territories; these obligations are:

> the obligation to consult the [. . .] community [concerned] in an active and informed manner, in accordance with its customs and traditions, within the framework of continuing communication between the parties. Furthermore, the consultations must be undertaken in good faith, using culturally-appropriate procedures and must be aimed at reaching an agreement. In addition, the people or community must be consulted in accordance with their own traditions, during the early stages of the development or investment plan, and not only when it is necessary to obtain the community's approval, if appropriate. The State must also ensure that the members of the people or the community are aware of the potential benefits and risks so they can decide whether to accept the proposed development or investment plan. Finally, the consultation must take into account the traditional decision-making practices of the people or community. Failure to comply with this obligation, or engaging in consultations without observing their essential characteristics, entails the State's international responsibility.[29]

The position held by the IACHR is echoed by the African Commission on Human and Peoples' Rights. In particular, in a case concerning oil production in the land of the Ogoni people, in Nigeria, carried out with the active involvement of the national government,[30] the Commission found that the environmental degradation and health problems suffered by the members of the Ogoni community had violated a number of provisions of the African Charter on Human and Peoples Rights (ACHPR).[31] The Commission also implicitly backed the argument of the claimants that the conduct of Nigeria was inconsistent with the ACHPR due to the fact that it did 'not involve the Ogoni Communities in the decisions that affected the development of Ogoniland'.[32] The Commission stressed that '[t]he intervention of multinational corporations may be a potentially positive force for development', but it is necessary that 'the State and the people concerned are ever mindful of the common good and the sacred rights of individuals and communities'.[33]

---

29 Ibid., para. 177 (footnotes omitted).
30 See *The Social and Economic Rights Action Center and the Center for Economic and Social Rights v. Nigeria*, Communication No. 155/96 (2001). Online. Available: www1.umn.edu/humanrts/africa/comcases/155-96.html (accessed 17 June 2012).
31 African [Banjul] Charter on Human and Peoples' Rights, 1981, 21 ILM 58, 1982.
32 See *The Social and Economic Rights Action Center and the Center for Economic and Social Rights v. Nigeria*, op. cit., para. 55.
33 Ibid., para. 69.

The examples analysed here[34] show that there is enough practice and evidence of *opinio juris* to assert that the right of Indigenous peoples to be consulted before investment projects are executed in their traditional lands now forms part of customary international law. However, if the said assumption is quite plain, it is more difficult to define the exact content of the right. As stressed in 2009 by the UN Special Rapporteur on the situation of human rights and fundamental freedoms of Indigenous people, James Anaya, 'the strength or importance of the objective of achieving consent varies according to the circumstances and the Indigenous interests involved'.[35] As a consequence, a 'significant, direct impact on Indigenous peoples' lives or territories establishes a strong presumption that the proposed measure should not go forward without Indigenous peoples' consent'.[36] In any event, the relevant practice assessed here shows that human rights monitoring bodies have not adopted a unanimous view, ranging from cases in which they recognize a 'simple' right in favour of Indigenous peoples to be consulted to instances where states are considered to be bound to obtain the consent of the communities concerned before initiating any project of exploitation of their traditional lands. Therefore, in trying to establish the content of the right in point one may start out from the assumption that, *as a minimum*, it takes the form of a *procedural* obligation imposed on states to properly consult Indigenous peoples. This seems to be confirmed by the formulation of Article 19 of the UNDRIP, which contemplates a duty of states to *consult* and cooperate in good faith with Indigenous peoples *in order to obtain* 'their free, prior and informed consent before adopting and implementing legislative or administrative measures that may affect them'. An identical formulation is used by Article 32 para. 2 of the UNDRIP with specific respect to projects affecting Indigenous peoples' lands or territories and other resources, 'particularly in connection with the development, utilization or exploitation of mineral, water or other resources'. In both provisions, the expression 'in order to obtain' seems to show that it is not mandatory to obtain such consent, but only to consult and cooperate in good faith with the purpose of obtaining it. The correctness of this interpretation is confirmed by a comparison of Articles 19 and 32 para. 2 of the UNDRIP with other provisions of the same instruments, showing that the Declaration uses a different wording to establish stricter obligations. For example, Article 28 para. 1 of the UNDRIP affirms that Indigenous peoples *have the right* to redress 'for the lands, territories and resources which they have traditionally owned or otherwise occupied or used, and which have been confiscated, taken, occupied, used or damaged *without their free, prior and informed consent*'.[37] Similarly, according to Article 29 para.

---

34 For a more comprehensive assessment of the relevant practice see ILA Committee on the Rights of Indigenous Peoples, 'Sofia Conference Report (2012)', op. cit., pp. 3–7.

35 See 'Report of the Special Rapporteur on the situation of human rights and fundamental freedoms of Indigenous people, James Anaya' (UN Special Rapporteur Report on consultation), UN Doc. A/HRC/12/34 of 15 July 2009, para. 47.

36 Ibid.

37 Emphasis added.

2 of the UNDRIP, 'States *shall take effective measures to ensure* that no storage or disposal of hazardous materials *shall take place* in the lands or territories of Indigenous peoples *without their free, prior and informed consent*.'[38] It follows that it is not possible to assert that Indigenous peoples have a full *right to veto* in all cases of investments or other projects of exploitation of their own traditional lands, although consultations with them must be carried out by the state in good faith, providing them with all necessary information in order to be able to properly understand all the implications which would arise from the execution of the project concerned,[39] making all possible efforts to actually obtain their consent, as well as through taking into proper account the specific needs of the community specifically involved in the concrete case.

This conclusion, however, may need to be reconsidered with regard to particular cases, especially those in the context of which a project of exploitation of Indigenous lands threatens to produce a significant violation of the fundamental rights of Indigenous peoples. This happens, for example, when the project in question would lead to the relocation of the communities concerned from their traditional territories[40] or would result in the taking of Indigenous peoples' cultural, intellectual, religious and spiritual property[41] as well as of their lands, territories and resources.[42] Consistently, ILA Resolution No. 5/2012 affirms that:

> States must . . . comply – according to customary and applicable conventional international law – with the obligation to recognise and promote the right of Indigenous peoples to autonomy or self-government, which translates into a number of prerogatives necessary in order to secure the preservation and transmission to future generations of their cultural identity and distinctiveness. These prerogatives include, inter alia, the right to participate in national decision-making with respect to decisions that may affect them, the right to be consulted with respect to any project that may affect them and *the related right that projects significantly impacting their rights and ways of life are not carried out without their prior, free and informed consent*.[43]

---

38 Emphasis added.
39 See, more comprehensively on this point, ILA Committee on the Rights of Indigenous Peoples, 'Sofia Conference Report (2012)', op. cit., p. 7.
40 See Article 10 UNDRIP, according to which 'Indigenous peoples shall not be forcibly removed from their lands or territories. No relocation *shall take place without the free, prior and informed consent* of the Indigenous peoples concerned and after agreement on just and fair compensation and, where possible, with the option of return' (emphasis added).
41 See Article 11(2) UNDRIP, affirming that 'States shall provide redress through effective mechanisms, which may include restitution, developed in conjunction with Indigenous peoples, with respect to their cultural, intellectual, religious and spiritual property taken without their free, prior and informed consent or in violation of their laws, traditions and customs.'
42 See supra text corresponding to n. 356.
43 See Resolution 5/2012, 'Rights of Indigenous Peoples', op. cit., para. 5 (emphasis added).

As emerges from the statement reproduced above, the discriminating factor allowing for a distinction to be made between the cases in which consultation is sufficient from those when it is essential to actually obtain the consent of the peoples concerned is represented by the *cultural impact* potentially caused by the investment or other measure of exploitation envisaged for Indigenous traditional lands. In fact, there is little doubt that, in the event that the absence of consent of the Indigenous community concerned would translate into a breach of one of the rights of Indigenous peoples that states are bound to guarantee and respect, obtaining such a consent becomes mandatory. As emphasized by the Human Rights Committee, 'before granting licences for the economic exploitation of the lands where they live', states have not only a duty to carry out consultations with the Indigenous communities concerned, but also to 'ensure that such exploitation in no circumstances infringes the rights' recognized to Indigenous peoples.[44] This said, if one considers that, as stressed by the Committee on Economic, Social and Cultural Rights,[45] the paramount purpose of safeguarding Indigenous peoples' rights is to preserve their autonomy and cultural integrity, guided by the overarching goal of preserving their cultural identity and, generally, cultural diversity,[46] then obtaining the free, prior and informed consent of the Indigenous peoples concerned should be mandatory when the planned project of exploitation threatens the essence of their cultural integrity. In other words, when an investment project may seriously prejudice the very cultural identity and integrity of the Indigenous communities concerned, these communities hold a *right to veto* with respect to the execution of such a project, as shown by relevant international practice.

Conclusions

When, in 1866, the United States' chief negotiator Ezra Booth Taylor approached the renowned Oglala Lakota Chief Red Cloud to convince him to cede part of the tribe's land to the government (so as to make a road and build a few forts for the seasonal requirements of the army), he promised that the 'Great Father' (the US President) would send presents. After listening to those words, Red Cloud replied: 'While this soldier goes to steal our land before the Indians say yes or no. The earth is my mother. For what presents should I sell my mother?'[47]

---

44 See 'Concluding observations of the Human Rights Committee – Nicaragua', op. cit., para. 21(c).
45 See General Comment No. 21, 'Right of everyone to take part in cultural life (Art. 15, para. 1 (a), of the International Covenant on Economic, Social and Cultural Rights)', op. cit., para. 55(e).
46 S. Wiessner, 'The Cultural Rights of Indigenous Peoples: Achievements and Continuing Challenges', *European Journal of International Law* 22, 2011, 121–140, pp. 138 f.
47 See J.G. Neihardt, *Black Elk Speaks*, Woodstock: Dramatic, 1996, p. 69.

The people of the West tend to have an attitude whereby they measure everything according to economic parameters. For several decades, modern international law has been shaped almost exclusively according to the view of life prevailing within the cultural model dominant in the modern world, therefore structuring its patterns and rules on the basis of an approach in the context of which the human being is suspended between economic interests and an atomistic conception of social and cultural relations. Only in recent times has a very positive evolution occurred, whereby the value of an alternative view of life based on a holistic approach has been acknowledged, and which has eventually obtained legal recognition especially in the human rights field, through a process characterized by an acceptance that the adjudication and enforcement of human rights may be influenced and conditioned by the cultural specificities of the human groups concerned.[48] Cultural identity has therefore become an essential value safeguarded by international law, to the point of representing a limit hindering certain activities threatening its integrity. As seen in the previous section, this undoubtedly applies to investments intended to be carried out in Indigenous peoples' ancestral lands, in light of the decisive role played by those lands in ensuring preservation of the cultural identity of the said peoples.

Certainly, much could be done to enhance the level of safeguarding of Indigenous peoples' heritage against the threats determined by investment projects. For example, rather than looking for sometimes complicated assessments of the impact that a specific investment project may have on Indigenous lands – in order to establish whether consultation is sufficient or it is necessary to obtain consent – the obligation of safeguarding Indigenous peoples' rights against the detrimental effects of investments could be included *ex ante* in investment agreements.[49] This would undoubtedly make everything easier, although the absence of such a clause in investment agreements does not change the substance, i.e. that the identity and rights of Indigenous peoples are in any event to be appropriately safeguarded against the harmful effects of investments.

Another important point to be noted is that the reflections developed with respect to Indigenous peoples may apply, in principle and *mutatis mutandis*, to other cultural groups. Although at present, and pursuant to the terms ascertained in the previous section, *positive* international law only recognizes the special rights of Indigenous peoples in particular, one may reasonably assert that the relevant rules might be applied by analogy to other human communities which possess their own traditional territories and/or heritage with a cultural connection equivalent to that which characterizes Indigenous peoples.

---

48 See generally, F. Lenzerini, *The Culturalization of Human Rights Law*, Oxford: Oxford University Press, 2014.

49 This point was highlighted by Professor Francesco Francioni at the Conference in Maastricht on 20 June 2013.

Bibliography

Foster, G.K., 'Foreign Investment and Indigenous Peoples: Options for Promoting Equilibrium Between Economic Development and Indigenous Rights', *Michigan Journal of International Law* 33, 2012, 627–691.

Lenzerini, F., *The Culturalization of Human Rights Law*, Oxford: Oxford University Press, 2014.

Neihardt, J.G., *Black Elk Speaks*, Woodstock: Dramatic, 1996.

Vadi, V., 'When Cultures Collide: Foreign Direct Investment, Natural Resources, and Indigenous Heritage in International Investment Law', *Columbia Human Rights Law Review* 42, 2011, 797–889.

Wiessner, S., 'The Cultural Rights of Indigenous Peoples: Achievements and Continuing Challenges', *European Journal of International Law* 22, 2011, 121–140.

Legal instruments

African [Banjul] Charter on Human and Peoples' Rights, 1981, 21 ILM 58, 1982.

ILO Convention No. 169 concerning Indigenous and Tribal Peoples in Independent Countries, 27 June 1989, 1650 UNTS 384.

Master Settlement Agreement (MSA). Online. Available: http://ag.ca.gov/tobacco/pdf/1msa.pdf (accessed 15 June 2013).

United Nations Declaration on the Right of Indigenous Peoples, 2007, GA Res 61/295, UN Doc. A/RES/61/295, 13 September 2007, 46 ILM 1013.

Cases

Case of the Kichwa Indigenous People of Sarayaku v. Ecuador, Series C No. 245, Judgment of 27 June 2012.

Case of the Saramaka People v. Suriname, Series C No. 172, Judgment of 28 November 2007.

Glamis Gold, Ltd v. United States of America, Arbitration under UNCITRAL Arbitration Rules, Award, 8 June 2009. Online. Available: www.state.gov/documents/organization/125798.pdf (accessed 15 June 2013).

Grand River Enterprises Six Nations, Ltd et al. v. United States of America, Arbitration under UNCITRAL Arbitration Rules, Award, 12 January 2011. Online. Available: www.state.gov/documents/organization/156820.pdf (accessed 15 June 2013).

The Social and Economic Rights Action Center and the Center for Economic and Social Rights v. Nigeria, Communication No. 155/96 (2001). Online. Available: www1.umn.edu/humanrts/africa/comcases/155–96.html (accessed 17 June 2012).

Other instruments

Report of the Special Rapporteur on the situation of human rights and fundamental freedoms of Indigenous people, James Anaya' (UN Special Rapporteur Report on consultation), UN Doc. A/HRC/12/34 of 15 July 2009.

Resolution 5/2012, 'Rights of Indigenous Peoples'. Online. Available: www.ila-hq.org/en/committees/index.cfm/cid/1024 (accessed 30 September 2013).

Sofia Conference Report (2012). Online. Available: www.ila-hq.org/en/committees/index.cfm/cid/1024 (accessed 30 September 2013).

United Nations Commission on the Elimination of Racial Discrimination (CERD), General Recommendation No. 23: Indigenous Peoples, UN Doc. A/52/18, Annex V, 18 August 1997.

6 What's in a name?

The contested meaning of free, prior and informed consent in international financial law and Indigenous rights

Sarah Sargent

Introduction

There has been an increasing focus on the way in which corporate activity related to economic development projects affects human rights. Traditionally human rights have been seen as the provenance of states. There is however a growing trend of seeing business enterprises and international financial institutions as having human rights obligations in their own right, separate and apart from state obligations. These human rights obligations arise and are expressed through several different means, including internal policies and procedures of international financial institutions (IFI) and through the framework of 'Protect, Respect and Remedy'[1] that is now embedded in the United Nations Guiding Principles on Business and Human Rights.[2] There is also a great deal of interest in pursuing development projects on lands where Indigenous peoples live. These bring together the potentially clashing interests of economic development financed through international financial institutions and the preservation and safeguarding of Indigenous culture.

It would be easy to begin a discussion by presuming these interests are necessarily in conflict with each other. Yet, the accuracy of this should be questioned. Indigenous communities may have an interest in development projects on their lands and be in favour of these going forward. This point is stressed by former United Nations Special Rapporteur on Indigenous Rights (UNSR) Professor James Anaya, in his July 2013 submission to the United Nations Human Rights Council.

> [I]t must not be assumed that the interests of extractive industries and Indigenous peoples are entirely or always at odds with each other . . .

---

1 J. Ruggie, *Just Business: Multinational Corporations and Human Rights*, New York: W.W. Norton and Company, 2013, 81–127.

2 *Guiding Principles on Business and Human Rights: Implementing the United Nations 'Protect, Respect and Remedy' Framework*, United Nations, 2011. Online. Available: www.ohchr.org/Documents/Publications/GuidingPrinciplesBusinessHR_EN.pdf (accessed 29 September 2013).

A number of situations have been brought to the attention of the Special Rapporteur in which Indigenous peoples have agreed to industrial-scale resource extraction within their territories or have even themselves taken initiatives for mining or development of oil and gas.[3]

An Indigenous interest in development, however, does not resolve any potentially clashing aims between economic development and the safeguarding of Indigenous cultural rights. Even an Indigenous interest in project development has the potential to result in conflicting goals, due to the sensitive and contentious issue of ownership and control over surface and subsurface natural resources. Whether it is the state that maintains ultimate control[4] or whether there is an overriding Indigenous claim is a dispute that is at the heart of debates over the meaning and usage of the principle of free, prior and informed consent (FPIC).

FPIC has been used by both international financial institutions and Indigenous rights advocates to safeguard Indigenous culture and cultural rights in the face of potential development. Is this common invocation of FPIC a means of bridging and balancing these interests?

This chapter explores this possibility. Exploring the meaning of FPIC is in itself a potentially large task, given the lack of agreement on what it means. It is both a principle of international law and a procedure embedded in the policies of international financial institutions (IFI) such as the International Finance Corporation (IFC). The discussion in this chapter focuses on the use of FPIC in IFC Performance Standards on Indigenous peoples[5] and in the United Nations Declaration on the Rights of Indigenous Peoples (UNDRIP).[6] There are three key issues to consider in addressing whether FPIC can be used to balance interests of economic development and Indigenous rights: 1) in what situations FPIC is to be used; 2) the meaning to be given to FPIC; and 3) underlying assumptions made about the ownership and control over the resources in question.

---

3 S.J. Anaya, 'Extractive Industries and Indigenous Peoples', 1 July 2013, A/HRC/24/41, para. 2.

4 For a discussion on issues of ownership and control over resources on Indigenous lands, see e.g. L. Aponte Miranda, 'Uploading the Local: Assessing the Contemporary Relationship Between Indigenous Peoples' Land Tenure Systems and International Human Rights Law Regarding the Allocation of Traditional Lands and Resources in Latin America', 10 *Oregon Review of International Law* 419, 2008.

5 The IFC is seen as being very influential in its use of FPIC, leading to other groups adopting FPIC as part of their operational standards. See E. Greenspan, 'ICCM Commits to Free Prior and Informed Consent Standard', 24 May 2013. Online. Available: politicsofpoverty.oxfam america.org/2013/05/24/icmm-commits-to-free-prior-informed-consent-standard/ (accessed 25 November 2013) (commenting that 'FPIC reflects a gradually turning tide which began to pick up momentum in 2011, when the World Bank's International Finance Corporation (IFC) announced a similar FPIC requirement').

6 United Nations Declaration on the Rights of Indigenous Peoples (UNDRIP), GA Res 61/295, UN Doc A/RES/61/295, 13 September 2007, 46 ILM 1013 (2007).

Differing views on when it is necessary to use FPIC are complicated by the lack of agreement on what FPIC is or means. This creates a great deal of uncertainty about what is necessary to comply with FPIC requirements. Much of the debate on the meaning of FPIC is centred on whether it is a consultation *process* with Indigenous groups, or a substantive *right* of Indigenous groups to veto proposed projects. Yet another view links FPIC to essential Indigenous rights, insisting that it cannot be understood as a stand-alone right in isolation from these.

Questions of ownership and control over natural resources on Indigenous lands underlie much of the debate on the meaning and use of FPIC.[7] This in turn raises issues of the relationship between the state, business enterprises and Indigenous groups. Whether they are seen as operating in partnership and on an equal footing, or if Indigenous interests are seen as subordinated to either those of the state or business interests has much to do with whether and how FPIC is employed. Also at issue is the role to be played by Indigenous groups. Are they to be seen as passive participants, only engaged in the consultation process? Or are they seen as active participants, who have their own interests in land and resource ownership and control, who themselves may wish to become engaged in the development projects?[8] Ultimately, this question of the framing of relationships is at the heart of Gordian knot debate over the meaning and usage of FPIC.

Ultimately this chapter concludes that the business model that has been proposed by former UNSR James Anaya for use by extractive industries in his 2013 report to the United Nations Human Rights Council can be used as a basis for any development on Indigenous land – and thus provide a stable basis for balancing interests and cutting through an otherwise intractable Gordian knot on the interests of international financial institutions in development and in the safeguarding of Indigenous rights. FPIC alone cannot balance these interests; rather, a balancing of interests must be found that looks beyond the principle of FPIC.

This chapter proceeds as follows. It first examines the development of the IFC Performance Standards on Indigenous Peoples (PS) in the larger context of the human rights obligations of business enterprises separate from those of states. In the second section it compares and contrasts the meaning given to FPIC by the IFC with that of two differing interpretations of FPIC provisions in the United Nations Declaration on the Rights of Indigenous Peoples

---

7 See generally S.J. Anaya, 'Indigenous Peoples' Participatory Rights in Relation to Decisions About Natural Resource Extraction: The More Fundamental Issues of What Rights Indigenous Peoples Have in Land and Resources', 22(1) *Arizona Journal of International and Comparative Law* 7, 2005.

8 Space does not permit a full scale discussion on the development of international legal personality of Indigenous peoples, largely seen as recognized through the approval of the UNDRIP. For further discussion on Indigenous legal personality, see R.L. Barsh, 'Indigenous Peoples in the 1990s: From Object to Subject of International Law?', 7 *Harvard Human Rights Journal* 33, 1994, 33.

(UNDRIP). The third section argues for the need to examine the relationship between states, Indigenous peoples and business enterprises in the context of proposed projects and suggests that a balancing of economic development and safeguarding of Indigenous cultural rights will not be found through the use of FPIC only; but rather in the principles set out in the business model proposed by UNSR Anaya. It argues that balancing of interests can be achieved through this model which provides for Indigenous groups as active participants in development. This may require a reformation of the conceptual view of Indigenous peoples within the IFC, and more broadly within international financial institutions.

Business and human rights

The current focus on the human rights obligations of businesses in international law cannot be overlooked as an important factor in striking a balance between economic development and the safeguarding of Indigenous culture. Businesses first began to explore their obligation to observe human rights in the development of corporate social responsibility policies. Some scholars argue that far from resulting from altruistic motives, corporate social responsibility policies were a direct response to poor images that resulted from highly publicized human rights abuses by large companies.[9] In this view, corporate social responsibility policies were developed to counteract the reputational damage done by such reports, and adopted as part of a risk-management strategy.[10]

The 2011 UN Guiding Principles on Business and Human Rights[11] and the recently created United Nations Working Group on the Issues of Human Rights and Transnational Corporations and the Forum on Business and Human Rights[12] are all recent indications of the growth in attention to the human rights obligations of businesses and corporate enterprises.

---

9   N. Deitelhoff and K. Dieter Wolf, 'Business and Human Rights: How Corporate Norm Violaters Become Norm Entrepreneurs', in T. Risse, S. Ropp and K. Sikkink, *The Persistent Power of Human Rights: From Commitment to Compliance*, Cambridge: Cambridge University Press, 2013, p. 223.

10 G. Sarfaty, 'Why Culture Matters in International Institutions: The Marginality of Human Rights at the World Bank', 103 *American Journal of International Law* 647, 2009, 648–649. See also M. Genasci and S. Pray, 'Extracting Accountability: The Implications of the Resource Curse for CSR Theory and Practice', 11 *Yale Human Rights and Development Law Journal* 37, 2008, 38–42.

11 Human Rights Council Resolution, A/HRC/Res 17/4, 16 June 2011. The text of the UN Guiding Principles. Online. Available: www.ohchr.org/Documents/Publications/Guiding PrinciplesBusinessHR_EN.pdf (accessed 25 November 2013).

12 See the Human Rights Council Resolution forming the new Working Group and Forum, 6 July 2011 A/HRC/Res/174. Online. Available: www.business-humanrights.org/media/ documents/un-human-rights-council-resolution-re-human-rights-transnational-corps-eng-6-jul-2011.pdf (accessed 15 June 2013).

The World Bank first issued policies on Indigenous peoples in 1982.[13] Despite this, it was reluctant to include FPIC in these policies.[14] In 2004, MacKay noted that the World Bank Group (WBG) had failed to include FPIC in its 'policy and practice'[15] despite the recommendations of two WBG commissioned reviews and calls of Indigenous groups that it do so.[16] This was representative of resistance to the inclusion of FPIC in its internal operations policies. MacKay comments that '[t]he WBG has . . . stated its opposition to FPIC on a number [of] occasions in the past eight years in response to Indigenous peoples long-standing demands that FPIC must be a fundamental component of WBG safeguard policies'.[17]

The inclusion of FPIC and the definition that it is given in internal international finance corporation policies can have significant influence on shaping views on the meaning of Indigenous rights. The importance of this should not be overlooked in an arena where there is no agreed upon meaning of FPIC, and the interpretations that are given to various facets of Indigenous rights can have immediate and sometimes detrimental consequences for the daily lives of Indigenous communities. The influence that such definitions have on the meaning of Indigenous rights, including that of FPIC, is not necessarily advantageous to Indigenous rights. Sawyer and Gomez comment upon the importance of understanding the:

> critical role that states and multinational corporations play in circum-
> scribing and containing what is understood as Indigenous rights. Indeed,
> case after case in this study demonstrates how a state-corporative alliance
> establishes a playing-field – even while advocating for Indigenous rights
> – that invariably furthers the interests of the extractive industries.[18]

There are also concerns on the move by international financial institutions to incorporate human rights standards into their operational policies. Anghie notes that this move is not motivated by a respect for human rights; rather it seems to co-opt the language of human rights to meet corporate aims:

> the principal danger is that important economic actors who are primarily
> concerned with profit and promotion of a problematic form of economic

---

13 F. MacKay, 'Indigenous Peoples and International Financial Institutions', in D. Bradlow and
    D. Hunter (eds), *International Financial Institutions and International Law*, The Netherlands:
    Kluwer Law International, 2010, p. 288.
14 F. MacKay, 'Indigenous Peoples' Right to Free, Prior and Informed Consent and the World
    Bank's Extractive Industries Review', 4(2) *Sustainable Development Law and Policy* 43, 2004,
    43.
15 Ibid., 43.
16 Ibid., 43.
17 Ibid., 43.
18 S. Sawyer and E.T. Gomez, 'Transnational Governmentality in the Context of Resource
    Extraction', in S. Sawyer and E.T. Gomez (eds) *The Politics of Resource Extraction: Indigenous
    Peoples, Multinational Corporations and the State*, Basingstoke: Palgrave Macmillan, 2012, p. 4.

development are increasingly appropriating and distorting the language of rights to justify and legitimize their own actions.[19]

A note of caution should be sounded then, when examining international financial institution definitions for FPIC. The meaning given may operate in such a way as to ultimately be beneficial to IFI interests, and yet at the same time, provide an *'illusion of inclusion'*[20] that operates to the detriment of Indigenous groups. As well, the meaning that is created influences daily activity and life of Indigenous peoples – making this a combination with the potential to have a devastating impact to the detriment of Indigenous culture rather than achieving a balancing of interests. This raises the question of whether policies such as the IFC's environmental and social sustainability performance standards can operate to balance economic interests and Indigenous cultural rights.

FPIC: consult, consent or more?

This section compares and contrasts the meaning and usage of FPIC in the IFC Performance Standards and in interpretations of FPIC provisions in the UNDRIP. Discussions on what meaning should be given to FPIC abound and there is no agreement or consensus on what the meaning of FPIC should be. The situations in which the IFC Performance Standards and the UNDRIP call for the use of FPIC vary widely. One of the fundamental arguments about FPIC is about what each of its component parts means.[21] Debate has centred on the meaning of 'consent' within the FPIC principle, as to whether it confers a right of Indigenous groups to veto projects, or whether it simply describes a method of consultation with Indigenous groups. Yet other views reject this dichotomy of either consultation or consent, and argue that FPIC in an Indigenous rights context takes on a very different meaning than cannot be captured in the debate over 'consent or consultation'.

FPIC in the performance standards of the International Finance Corporation

In 2012, the International Finance Corporation (IFC) issued revised Performance Standards (PS) for social and environmental sustainability which

19 A. Anghie, 'Time Present and Time Past: Globalization, International Financial Institutions, and the Third World', 32 *New York University Journal of International Law and Policy* 243, 2000, 254.
20 J. Corntassel, 'Toward Sustainable Self-determination: Rethinking the Contemporary Indigenous Rights Discourse', 33 *Alternatives* 105, 2008, 111. Emphasis in the original.
21 See for instance S. Baker, 'Why the IFC's Free, Prior and Informed Consent Policy Doesn't Matter (Yet) to Indigenous Communities Affected by Development Projects', University of San Francisco Law Research Paper No 2012–16. Online. Available: http://ssrn.com/abstract =2132887 (accessed 29 September 2013).

are meant to create a social[22] as well as legal licence[23] for engaging in project development. The IFC is the private-sector arm of the World Bank Group.[24] It is the 'largest global development institution focused exclusively on the private sector in developing countries'.[25] The IFC focuses on providing financial resources and assistance to developing states.[26] Its Performance Standard on Indigenous peoples is part of a package of eight environmental and social sustainability policies meant to promote ways of developing projects that are mindful of and ameliorate social and environmental harms that pursuing the project might entail.[27] Each Performance Standard is accompanied by Guidance Notes (GN) which provide further detailed information on the implementation of the standard. The IFC Performance Standards envision their content being carried out as a corporate responsibility of IFC clients, rather than the IFC itself.[28] A recent review on World Bank Group policies explains that 'The Performance Standards paradigm is based on an expectation that the clients, who are private business entities, will voluntarily adhere to Performance Standard requirements, with loan covenants that provide remedies if they do not.'[29]

While in an earlier 2006 standard, the IFC very clearly adopted a normative meaning for FPIC that was meant as a consultative process,[30] one of the most notable changes in the revised PS 7, dated 1 January 2012, is the reference to free, prior and informed *consent*, rather than free, prior and informed *consultation*. Yet, commentary in the Guidance Notes dispels any doubt that the new language embodies anything other than a consultation process. The GN state that FPIC does not 'confer [] any veto rights to individuals or sub-groups'[31]

---

22 Ruggie, op. cit, 10–11. See also MacKay, op. cit., 'Indigenous Peoples' Right to Free, Prior and Informed Consent', 45.

23 Ruggie, op. cit., 10–11.

24 About IFC. Online. Available: www.ifc.org/wps/wcm/connect/corp_ext_content/ifc_external_ corporate_site/about+ifc (accessed 30 September 2013).

25 Ibid.

26 Ibid.

27 IFC, Performance Standards on Environmental and Social Sustainability, 1 January 2012, para. 1. Online. Available: www.ifc.org/wps/wcm/connect/115482804a0255db96fbffd1a5d13d27/ PS_English_2012_Full-Document.pdf?MOD=AJPERES (accessed 30 September 2013).

28 The Independent Evaluation Group, 'Safeguards and Sustainability Policies in a Changing World: An Independent Evaluation of the World Bank Group Experience', 2010, 96. Online. Available: http://siteresources.worldbank.org/EXTSAFANDSUS/Resources/Safeguards_eval. pdf (accessed 29 September 2013).

29 Ibid., 96.

30 All of the 2006 IFC Performance Standards were revised after a review was completed on their efficacy in 2009. IFC's Policy and Performance Standards on Social and Environmental Sustainability and Policy on Discourse of Information: Report on the First Three Years of Application, International Finance Corporation, 29 July 2009. For commentary see R. Wasserstrom, *et al.*, op. cit, 2.

31 International Finance Corporation, Guidance Note 7, Indigenous Peoples, 1 January 2012, GN 22. Online. Available: www.ifc.org/wps/wcm/connect/e280ef804a0256609709ffd1a 5d13d27/GN_English_2012_Full-Document.pdf?MOD=AJPERES (accessed 29 September 2013).

nor does it 'contradict the state's right to develop its resources'.[32] The details of the consultation process to be pursued are set out in PS 7. First, it requires identifying any Indigenous groups who may be adversely affected by the planned project. The specific type of harm that might occur is to be identified, including any threats to 'culture' and 'cultural heritage'.[33] Harm is evaluated to see if it might result in adverse impacts. The PS indicates that 'adverse impacts may include impacts from loss of access to assets or resources or restrictions on land use resulting from project activities'.[34] The Guidance Notes elaborate on this, listing specific situations where FPIC is to be used, because of 'potentially adverse impacts':

– Impacts on lands and natural resources subject to traditional ownership or customary use;
– Relocation of Indigenous Peoples from lands and natural resources subject to traditional land or under customary use;
– Significant impacts on critical cultural heritage that is essential to the identity and/or cultural, ceremonial, or spiritual aspects of Indigenous Peoples lives, including natural areas with cultural and/or spiritual value such as sacred groves, sacred bodies of water and waterways, sacred trees and sacred rocks; or
– Use of cultural heritage, including knowledge, innovations, or practices of Indigenous Peoples for commercial purposes.[35]

In other words, the need to engage in FPIC is not triggered by *any* impact to the Indigenous community, but only those judged to be adverse, and then only in conjunction with the specific situations listed in the Performance Standards and Guidance Notes. When FPIC is triggered, the consultation process with the Indigenous community ensues. PS 7 recognizes the importance of engaging with Indigenous groups in terms and in a process that are appropriate for that group. The consultation is to be conducted in a manner allowing 'sufficient time for Indigenous Peoples' decision-making process'[36] and requires that the proposed project be discussed 'in a culturally appropriate manner'.[37]

At first reading, the contents of IFC Performance Standard 7 appear to be both sympathetic to the risks posed to Indigenous communities from development, but also focused on preventing unnecessary harm to Indigenous culture. The detailed process that is given for engaging Indigenous

32 Ibid., GN 26.
33 International Finance Corporation, Performance Standard, Indigenous Peoples, 1 January 2012, para. 8. Online. Available: www.ifc.org/wps/wcm/connect/1ee7038049a79139b845faa8c6a8312a/PS7_English_2012.pdf?MOD=AJPERES (accessed 29 September 2013).
34 PS 7,4, footnote 8.
35 Guidance Note 7, GN 27. Emphasis added.
36 PS 7, para. 10.
37 Ibid.

communities also appears to focus on safeguarding Indigenous culture even while finding ways for development to go forward. In particular, the opening paragraph for PS 7 appears to be overtly sensitive to the plight of Indigenous groups and the risk that they face as a result of development, including the risk that such projects might pose to Indigenous culture:

> Indigenous Peoples are particularly vulnerable if their lands and resources are transformed, encroached upon, or significantly degraded. Their language, cultures, religions, spiritual beliefs, and institutions may also come under threat. As a consequence, Indigenous Peoples may be more vulnerable to the adverse impacts associated with project development than non-Indigenous communities. This vulnerability may include loss of identity, culture, and natural resource-based livelihoods, as well as exposure to impoverishment and disease.[38]

FPIC is clearly meant to operate as a process that safeguards Indigenous culture threatened by proposed development.

Yet, is this an accurate assessment of the Performance Standard? Does such Performance Standard provide an adequate safeguard to Indigenous culture? Other interpretations of FPIC have been put forward by the International Law Association and the UNSR which differ so greatly from that of the IFC as to appear irreconcilable.

FPIC in the ILO Convention No 169

The origins of FPIC are sometimes raised as providing interpretive authority in the current disagreement over its meaning. With claims made that FPIC originated as a principle within the context of international Indigenous rights,[39] it might be thought that its first use would be one that is helpful to support the UNDRIP meaning. In fact, this is not the case. While FPIC as an international norm may have originated in the ILO Convention No 169,[40] that instrument and usage does not provide an authoritative interpretation and application of the principle. While this chapter has focused on the content of UNDRIP, it is worth noting that in addition to ILO Convention 169 and UNDRIP, FPIC is seen to be implicitly located within other international human rights instruments, and is strongly associated with a right to self-determination.[41]

---

38 Ibid., para. 1.
39 Wasserstrom *et al.*, op. cit., 5.
40 International Labour Organization Convention 169 Concerning Indigenous and Tribal Peoples in Independent Countries, 27 June 1989, 1650 UNTS 384 (hereinafter ILO Convention 169).
41 See e.g. MacKay, 'Indigenous Peoples' Right to Free, Prior and Informed Consent', op. cit., 50–51, commenting that '[a]lthough not spelled out, FPIC is certainly required pursuant to the right of self-determination as set forth in Common Article 1 of the International Covenants on Human Rights as part of Indigenous peoples' rights to freely determine their political

The ILO Convention No 169 has not escaped the current international debate on the meaning of free, prior and informed consent. The meaning of the ILO Convention requirements for consultation with Indigenous peoples was the subject of commentary in the 2011 Report of the ILO Committee of Experts.[42] The Committee of Experts commentary draws a distinction between provisions of the Convention which refer to *consultation*, and provisions which refer to free and informed *consent*.[43] It notes that 'free and informed *consent* is required where relocation of these peoples from lands which they occupy is considered necessary as an exceptional measure'.[44] The comments make clear that where consultation is required, such consultation is not to be considered as providing Indigenous groups the right or power to veto.[45] But the commentary from the Committee of Experts, having distinguished the provisions of the Convention that require consultation from those which requires free and informed consent, and providing some explanation on what consultation does and does not entail, is simply silent on whether consent provides Indigenous groups with a power to veto a planned relocation – the only situation in which the Convention calls for free and informed consent. It leaves unclear whether there is a real difference between *consent* and *consultation*.

FPIC in the United Nations Declaration on the Rights of Indigenous Peoples

The principle of free, prior and informed consent is contained in many articles throughout the UNDRIP. Arguably, within all of these articles is an overriding aim of protection of Indigenous culture and cultural rights.[46] It is required in Article 10, in relation to the relocation of Indigenous peoples from their lands.[47] Article 11 provides protections with respect to Indigenous 'cultural, intellectual, religious and spiritual property'.[48] Article 28 requires redress for lands taken without free, prior and informed Indigenous consent.[49] Article 29 requires this for the storage or disposal of hazardous materials on Indigenous lands.[50] Additionally there are two other articles that refer to FPIC that are of particular importance in considering their relation to economic development interests: Article 19 and Article 32(2). Article 19 provides that 'States shall

status, freely pursue the economic social and cultural development and freely dispose of their natural wealth and resources'.
42 Report of the Committee of Experts and the Application of Conventions and Recommendations, International Labour Conference, 100th Session, 2011.
43 Ibid., pp. 787–788.
44 Ibid., p. 787. Emphasis added.
45 Ibid., pp. 787–788.
46 See also Lenzerini's chapter in this volume.
47 UNDRIP Article 10.
48 UNDRIP Article 11.
49 UNDRIP Article 28.
50 UNDRIP Article 29.

consult and cooperate in good faith with the Indigenous peoples concerned through their own representative institutions in order to obtain their free, prior and informed *consent* before adopting and implementing legislative or administrative measures that may affect them.'[51] Article 32(2) states that:

> States shall *consult* and cooperate in good faith with the Indigenous peoples concerned through their own representative institutions in order to obtain their free and informed *consent* prior to the *approval* of any project affecting their lands or territories and other resources, particularly in connection with the development, utilization or exploitation of mineral, water or other resources.[52]

Read together, the plain language of these articles seems to suggest that FPIC is a substantive right to veto or approve – and not simply a process of consultation – in respect of projects that would take place on Indigenous lands. Article 19 juxtaposes the words of consult and consent, as does Article 32(2) which additionally refers to 'approval'. An interpretation that invokes the doctrine of state permanent sovereignty over natural resources would indicate that state approval is needed. This would be an interpretation consistent with the IFC FPIC provisions. Even so, this provision could be read that no state approval can be given unless Indigenous groups have specifically acquiesced by giving permission for the project to proceed. This recognizes both Indigenous and state interests in projects on Indigenous lands. This interpretation creates the right of an Indigenous veto. The UNDRIP itself provides no further explanation on this content, nor does it offer any definition for FPIC. The interpretation conundrum has been the subject of study by the International Law Association Committee on Indigenous Rights. Its Final Report comments there is no right of veto conferred by UNDRIP Articles 19 and 32(2) in the instances of development on land.[53] The Final Report does argue that the UNDRIP confers a right of veto via FPIC in some limited situations:

> however, such a right [to veto] seems to exist with respect to measures of relocation of Indigenous peoples from their lands or territories, measures resulting in the taking of Indigenous peoples' cultural, intellectual, religious and spiritual property or lands, territories and resources, as well as measures of storage or disposal of hazardous materials in the lands or territories of Indigenous peoples.[54]

---

51 UNDRIP Article 19. Emphasis added.
52 UNDRIP Article 32(2). Emphasis added.
53 International Law Association, Rights of Indigenous Peoples, Sofia Conference 2012, Final Report, 6–7.
54 Ibid., 7.

This commentary indicates the complexity and lack of agreement on the situational definitions that have been given to FPIC. The interpretation given in the Final Report suggests that FPIC will have different meanings within the same instrument, and the meaning that it is given is dependent upon the situation in which it is being used. This is potentially confusing, in that there is no variation of language within the respective UNDRIP provisions that would indicate when FPIC is a consultative process and when it is a substantive right of veto.

The Final Report commentary – however detailed – is far from settling the matter on the meaning of FPIC. In some instances, its positions may appear to be compatible with that of the IFC, in those situations where both agree that FPIC consists of a consultation process. The UNDRIP, however, does not contain the detail of FPIC consultative requirements that the IFC PS does. This leaves open the question of what is required of a consultative process under the UNDRIP. As well, UNDRIP Article 32(2) calls for a much broader application of FPIC than does PS 7 notably not limited to impacts that are deemed to be *adverse.*

The endorsement of the Final Report by the UNSR might be seen as putting to rest any differences that the UNSR and the ILA have over the normative interpretations of FPIC within the UNDRIP.[55] But this is not the case. Other statements made by the UNSR suggest that there are perhaps situations within the ambit of Article 32(2) that do confer an Indigenous right of veto – in far more situations than are suggested by the Final Report commentary. UNSR Anaya explains that:

> The primary substantive rights of Indigenous peoples that may be implicated in natural resources development and extraction . . . include, in particular, rights to property, culture, religion and non-discrimination in relation to lands, territories, and natural resources . . . rights to health and physical well-being in relation to a clean and healthy environment; *and rights to set and pursue their own priorities for development, including development of natural resources, as part of their fundamental right to self-determination.*[56]

These are inclusive of at least some of the circumstances in which the Final Report indicates that FPIC entails a right to veto. The Final Report and the UNSR position do not provide detailed clarity on when FPIC is required to be used, or what it means – consult, consent, or more – in any given situation. The comments do not resolve the disagreement or contradictions in the position on FPIC.

55 Ibid., 31–32.
56 S.J. Anaya, Report of the Special Rapporteur on the Rights of Indigenous Peoples, A/HRC/21/47, 12 July 2012, para. 50 (emphasis added). Online. Available: http://unsr. jamesanaya.org/docs/annual/2012_hrc_annual_report_en.pdf (accessed 29 September 2013).

The role of Indigenous peoples in economic development

For a very long span of time in international law, Indigenous groups were seen as lacking legal personality.[57] A view of Indigenous groups as mostly passive recipients – objects rather than subjects of international law – seems inherent in the IFC depiction of FPIC. Yet with the 2007 approval of the UNDRIP, Indigenous groups are now recognized as 'peoples'[58] and thus perceived as active participants in international law. That Indigenous groups have the capacity for legal personality and active engagement – or, at the very minimum, are important non-state actors – is implicit in a view that there is, at least in some circumstances, an Indigenous right to a veto. FPIC then, can be seen as an expression of assumptions about the role of Indigenous peoples, and their relationships to the state and to business enterprises.

In his submission to the Human Rights Council in July 2013, the UNSR called for the use of a new business model to be used by extractive industries for projects on Indigenous lands. This model requires the recognition of an Indigenous right to development of their own resources, even if states are seen as having ownership and control of the resources in question. The UNSR comments that:

> even when the State claims ownership of subsurface or other resources under domestic law, Indigenous peoples have the right to pursue their own initiatives for extraction and development of natural resources within their territories, at least under the terms generally permitted by the State for others.[59]

This calls for a much broader recognition of an Indigenous stake in development than is provided by the IFC. The IFC PS 7 does recognize that Indigenous groups may have some interest or should be accorded some benefit from projects on their land – but again in limited circumstances. PS 7 calls for benefit sharing when the project will use 'natural resources that are central to the identity and livelihood of the Affected Communities of Indigenous Peoples and their usage thereof exacerbate livelihood risk'.[60] Any further Indigenous interests in resources benefits from projects on their land are not recognized by PS 7. It does not contemplate Indigenous groups themselves playing a role in development of natural resources. The business model acknowledges, but does not answer, the question of Indigenous ownership of natural resources in preference to any state claims. That this issue has been

57 See Barsh, op. cit.
58 UNDRIP Article 3.
59 S.J. Anaya, Report of the Special Rapporteur on the Rights of Indigenous Peoples, 'Extractive Industries and Indigenous Peoples', A/HRC/24/41 2013, para. 9, 5. Online. Available: http://unsr.jamesanaya.org/study/extractive-industries-and-Indigenous-peoples-report-of-the-special-rapporteur-on-the-rights-of-Indigenous-peoples (accessed 29 September 2013).
60 PS 7, para. 7. See also Final Report, 6.

avoided in FPIC debates is not surprising if one takes on board the view of MacKay that 'FPIC is viewed by some as a mechanism to avoid much more sensitive and politically charged discussions about Indigenous ownership of the subsoil.'[61] According to MacKay, Indigenous rights to subsurface resources mean that 'Indigenous peoples, should they so choose, would be free to consent to arrangements with third parties, including the state, for exploitation of *their* resources through mutually acceptable agreements'.[62]

This argument seems to have come of age with the 2013 UNSR submission to the UN Human Rights Council. The model does not go so far as to provide a definitive statement of Indigenous penultimate ownership and control over development or resource extraction. It does stress, however, the priority and preference to be accorded Indigenous initiatives to develop projects on their own land, and further, contemplates the possibility of active Indigenous engagement in projects: 'When Indigenous peoples choose to pursue their own initiatives for natural resources extractions within their own territories, States and the international community should assist them to build the capacity to do so, and States should privilege Indigenous peoples' initiatives over non-Indigenous initiatives.'[63]

As well, the UNSR model calls for a very broad application of FPIC. It distinguishes between consultation and consent, and is very clear that the two concepts cannot be conflated in the way that they are in PS 7. The demands of the business model are that '[i]n all instances of proposed extractive projects that might affect Indigenous peoples, *consultations* with them should take place and *consent* should at least be sought, even if consent is not strictly required'.[64]

The UNSR report leaves no doubt that consent entails an ability to veto a proposed project.[65] It clarifies that FPIC is much more than a right to approve or reject projects, pointing out the human rights nature of consent within FPIC and what is needed for it to safeguard Indigenous culture. According to the UNSR:

> [the FPIC] is not a free-standing devise of legitimation. The principle does not contemplate consent as simply a yes to a predetermined decision, or as a means to validate a deal that disadvantages affected Indigenous peoples. When consent is given, not just freely and on an informed basis, but also on just terms that are protective of Indigenous peoples rights, it will fulfil its human rights safeguard role.[66]

This provides a way in which FPIC is able to be used as a principle that both balances interests and provides a safeguard for Indigenous culture. This is done

---

61   MacKay, 'Indigenous Peoples' Right to Free, Prior and Informed Consent', op. cit., 54.
62   Ibid.
63   UNSR 2013, op. cit., para. 81.
64   Ibid., para. 27. Emphasis added.
65   Ibid., para. 30.
66   Ibid.

in a framework that contemplates the option for Indigenous groups to be active participants in development, and further points out the responsibility of states and the international community to assist with these endeavours. The IFC, as part of that international community, then, has a role to play supporting development by Indigenous groups.

Conclusions

The FPIC Performance Standard 7 specifically addresses the need to safeguard Indigenous culture, and recognizes the particular risks that Indigenous communities face from development projects. This is in itself a noteworthy achievement. The Performance Standard and Guidance Notes also provide guidelines for engaging with Indigenous communities and the importance of recognizing and following Indigenous community customary practice as part of the negotiation and consultation that make up the FPIC process. Whatever other criticisms might be levelled at PS 7 and its Guidance Notes, it should be acknowledged as an advancement from earlier positions which did not address FPIC in safeguard policies and procedures.

Moreover, while the PS are also criticized as creating too much uncertainty and placing too large a burden of risk on private companies,[67] they do make an effort to provide detailed guidance on what businesses need to do to adhere to human rights responsibilities. This is important in an international atmosphere that is increasingly focused on the human rights obligations of businesses, independent from the human rights obligations of states.

Yet, whether IFC will respond to the UNSR Human Rights Council call for a new business model remains to be seen. From a human rights perspective, it will be important for the IFC to present itself as compatible with prevailing human rights norms. From a business perspective, this is also true, as shown by the discussion in this chapter on the motivations businesses have to observe and voluntary take on human rights obligations.

Resolution and a way to balance rights and interests is dependent upon two things – the business model and role of and for Indigenous groups that perhaps ultimately is seen as the most legitimate across the international community, including states, international financial institutions, business enterprises and Indigenous communities. Otherwise, the IFC and the UNDRIP will continue on distinctly different tracks. Resolution might be found as well through an agreement to incorporate into PS 7 the business model suggestions of the UNSR, in particular these important elements: 'mitigation of power imbalances; information gathering and sharing; provision for adequate timing of consultations, in an environment free of pressure, and assurance of Indigenous peoples' participation through their own representative institutions'.[68]

---

67 Wasserstrom *et al.*, op. cit., 8.
68 UNSR, July 2013, para. 91.

Seen from this view, the UNSR business model and the IFC PS are not so very far apart. Many of those elements are already in place in PS 7. A change of view of Indigenous groups to that of active participants and potential clients of the IFC, or working in concert with businesses to develop projects would also contribute towards the achievement of the goals called for by the UNSR. It would also require viewing FPIC as related to the realization of other Indigenous rights that could, in some situations, result in an Indigenous right to a veto. Since the IFC relies upon its corporate clients to carry out the requirements of its Performance Standards, there exists a real opportunity for implementation of the UNSR's business model. The IFC business clients would be responsible for conducting their work in accordance with those principles. PS 7 could be adjusted to be inclusive of the UNSR business model, and adherence to this made part of the Performance Standard requirements. Definitional divides on FPIC would of necessity be resolved through amending the Performance Standards to be inclusive of the UNSR business model principles. This then has the potential to create a 'framework of genuine partnership'[69] and is one in which an appropriate and effective balance can be struck. Short of that, it is unlikely there will be a balancing of the competing interests of economic development and Indigenous rights to culture.

Bibliography

'About IFC', Online. Available: www.ifc.org/wps/wcm/connect/corp_ext_content/ifc_external_corporate_site/about+ifc (accessed 30 September 2013).

Anaya, S.J., 'Indigenous Peoples' Participatory Rights in Relation to Decisions About Natural Resource Extraction: The More Fundamental Issues of What Rights Indigenous Peoples Have in Land and Resources', 22(1) *Arizona Journal of International and Comparative Law* 7, 2005.

Anaya, S.J., 'Report of the Special Rapporteur on the Rights of Indigenous Peoples', A/HRC/21/47, 12 July 2012.

Anaya, S.J., 'Report of the Special Rapporteur on the Rights of Indigenous Peoples, 'Extractive Industries and Indigenous Peoples', A/HRC/24/41 2013.

Anghie, A., 'Time Present and Time Past: Globalization, International Financial Institutions, and the Third World', 32 *New York University Journal of International Law and Policy* 243, 2000.

Aponte Miranda, L., 'Uploading the Local: Assessing the Contemporary Relationship Between Indigenous Peoples' Land Tenure Systems and International Human Rights Law Regarding the Allocation of Traditional Lands and Resources in Latin America', 10 *Oregon Review of International Law* 419, 2008.

Baker, S., 'Why the IFC's Free, Prior and Informed Consent Policy Doesn't Matter (Yet) to Indigenous Communities Affected by Development Projects', University of San Francisco Law Research Paper No 2012–16.

Barsh, R.L., 'Indigenous Peoples in the 1990s: From Object to Subject of International Law?', 7 *Harvard Human Rights Journal* 33, 1994.

---

69 Ibid., para. 92.

Corntassel, J., 'Toward Sustainable Self-determination: Rethinking the Contemporary Indigenous Rights Discourse', 33 *Alternatives* 105, 2008.

Deitelhoff, N. and Dieter Wolf, K., 'Business and Human Rights: How Corporate Norm Violaters Become Norm Entrepreneurs', in T. Risse, S. Ropp and K. Sikkink, *The Persistent Power of Human Rights: From Commitment to Compliance*, Cambridge: Cambridge University Press, 2013, pp. 222–258.

Doyle, C. and Carino, J., 'Making Free Prior and Informed Consent a Reality: Indigenous Peoples and the Extractive Sector', 2013. Online. Available: wwwpiplinks.org/making fpicareality (accessed 30 September 2013).

Genasci, M. and Pray, S., 'Extracting Accountability: The Implications of the Resource Curse for CSR Theory and Practice', 11 *Yale Human Rights and Development Law Journal* 37, 2008.

Greenspan, E., 'ICCM Commits to Free Prior and Informed Consent Standard', 24 May 2013. Online. Available: http://politicsofpoverty.oxfamamerica.org/2013/05/24/icmm-commits-to-free-prior-informed-consent-standard/ (accessed 30 September 2013).

Guiding Principles on Business and Human Rights: Implementing the United Nations 'Protect, Respect and Remedy' Framework, United Nations, 2011.

Human Rights Council Resolution, A/HRC/Res 17/4, 16 June 2011.

IFC's Policy and Performance Standards on Social and Environmental Sustainability and Policy on Discourse of Information: Report on the First Three Years of Application, International Finance Corporation, 29 July 2009.

The Independent Evaluation Group, *Safeguards and Sustainability Policies in a Changing World: An Independent Evaluation of the World Bank Group Experience*, 2010.

International Finance Corporation, Guidance Note 7, Indigenous Peoples, 1 January 2012.

International Finance Corporation, Performance Standards on Environmental and Social Sustainability, 1 January 2012.

International Finance Corporation, Performance Standard 7, Indigenous Peoples, 1 January 2012.

International Law Association, Rights of Indigenous Peoples, Sofia Conference 2012, Final Report.

MacKay, F., 'Indigenous Peoples' Right to Free, Prior and Informed Consent and the World Bank's Extractive Industries Review', 4(2) *Sustainable Development Law and Policy* 43, 2004.

MacKay, F., 'Indigenous Peoples and International Financial Institutions', in D. Bradlow, and D. Hunter, (eds), *International Financial Institutions and International Law*, The Netherlands: Kluwer Law International, 2010, pp. 287–320.

Report of the Committee of Experts and the Application of Conventions and Recommendations, International Labour Conference, 100th Session, 2011.

Ruggie, J., *Just Business: Multinational Corporations and Human Rights*, New York: W.W. Norton & Company, 2013.

Sarfaty, G., 'Why Culture Matters in International Institutions: The Marginality of Human Rights at the World Bank', 103 *American Journal of International Law* 647, 2009.

Sawyer, S. and Gomez, E.T., 'Transnational Governmentality in the Context of Resource Extraction', in S. Sawyer, and E.T. Gomez, (eds), *The Politics of Resource Extraction: Indigenous Peoples, Multinational Corporations and the State*, Basingstoke: Palgrave Macmillan, 2012, pp. 1–8.

United Nations Declaration on the Rights of Indigenous Peoples, GA Res 61/295, UN Doc A/RES/61/295, 13 September 2007, 46 ILM 1013 (2007).

7 The trade versus culture discourse

Tracing its evolution in global law

Mira Burri

Introduction

The intensified flows of goods, services, peoples and ideas across borders intrinsic to globalization have had numerous and multi-faceted effects. Those affecting culture have been perhaps the most controversial, as it is difficult to identify the spill-overs across economic and non-economic areas and across borders, just as it is equally hard to qualify the effects of these spill-overs as positive or negative. The debate also tends to be politically and even emotionally charged, which has so far not proven advantageous to establishing a genuine dialogue, nor to finding solutions. This contention and the divergent interests of major players in the international community have been reflected in the institutions and rules of global law. It is the objective of this chapter to explore this institutional architecture, in particular its main (and opposing) constituent *fora* of the World Trade Organization (WTO) and the United Nations Educational Social and Cultural Organization (UNESCO). The chapter traces the evolution of these institutions and their interaction over time, as well as the underlying objectives, demands and strategies of the key proponents in the trade versus culture discourse, which ultimately shaped the existent law and policy. The chapter concludes with an appraisal of the present state of affairs and by situating the discussion in the contemporary global governance landscape.

The origins of the trade versus culture discourse

The early years of the discourse on trade and culture evolved under the dictum of cultural exceptionalism, and were marked by attempts to carve out cultural from other – mostly economic – policies, in particular on the international scene. Although the idea of state protection of cultural identity has existed for many years, possibly going as far back as the origins of sovereignty,[1] the

---

1 D.S. Petito, 'Sovereignty and Globalization: Fallacies, Truth, and Perception', *New York Law School Journal of Human Rights* 17, 2001, 1139–1172.

real policy debates on the relationship between trade and culture began only after World War I. The reason was two-pronged and had to do with the changing nature of the medium, on the one hand, and the particularities of that historical period, on the other. In the former sense, although printed media, such as books, newspapers and magazines, were the first manifestation of industrialized cultural production, they had relatively low tradability, due to their cultural specificity and the use of local language.[2] Audiovisual media, especially film, in contrast, proved more suitable for engaging and appealing to a broader, also foreign, audience.

Timing also mattered. After World War I, the European cinema industry was suffering and clearly losing the battle against Hollywood, which had emerged as the new centre of global visual entertainment.[3] As a reaction to this shift of power and fearing both the economic and cultural impact of Hollywood, many European governments introduced measures to protect their domestic film industries, mostly in the form of import and screen quotas. These measures were reflected in the General Agreement on Tariffs and Trade (GATT) 1947. Article IV thereof permitted quotas for 'the exhibition of cinematograph films of national origin during a specified minimum proportion of the total screen time', while preserving GATT's general ban on quantitative restrictions on imports (Article XI). The screen quotas are proof of the sought-after (and accepted by the GATT Members) cultural exception, as well as of its narrow focus on audiovisual media.

The idea that some measures protecting national cultural industries may be justified was also taken up in bilateral and regional *fora*. In 1988, the Canadian negotiators celebrated a major victory, as they succeeded in introducing a 'cultural exclusion' clause in the Canada–US Free Trade Agreement (CUSFTA).[4] Five years later, this exclusion became part of the North American Free Trade Agreement (NAFTA) too.[5] It should be noted, however, that this cultural clause was coupled with a retaliation provision that significantly limited by design its practical use.

To be sure, the stakes were much higher in the multilateral context, and the trade versus culture battle truly escalated during the Uruguay Round of trade negotiations (1986–1994). The reasons for this heightened tension are various but certainly the most important has to do with the round's special mandate. One should be reminded that the Uruguay Round was not only aimed at dismantling tariff barriers, as had been the convention with other

2 M.E. Footer and C.B. Graber, 'Trade Liberalisation and Cultural Policy', *Journal of International Economic Law* 3, 2000, 115–144, pp. 116–117.
3 J. Trumpbour, *Selling Hollywood to the World: US and European Struggles for Mastery of the Global Film Industry, 1920–1950*, Cambridge: Cambridge University Press, 2007; C.M. Bruner, 'Culture, Sovereignty, and Hollywood: UNESCO and the Future of Trade in Cultural Products', *International Law and Politics* 40, 2008, 351–436; J.P. Singh, *Negotiation and the Global Information Economy*, Cambridge: Cambridge University Press, 2008.
4 Canada – US Free Trade Agreement, 22 December 1987–2 January 1988, 27 ILM 281 (1988).
5 North American Free Trade Agreement, 17 December 1992, 32 ILM 289 (1993).

GATT talks, but was a much further reaching undertaking that ultimately led to the establishment of the WTO with a new structure and an unprecedentedly effective dispute settlement mechanism.[6] The WTO, which became operational on 1 January 1995, included certain domains that had previously been unaffected by international trade regulation – most notably, intellectual property (by means of the Agreement on Trade-related Aspects of Intellectual Property Rights, TRIPS)[7] and services (by means of the General Agreement on Trade in Services, GATS).[8]

The slogan of the time was 'exception culturelle' and its supporters strived to exempt any product or service that is culture-related from the rules of the negotiated WTO Agreements. Still, and this should be kept in mind, the main focus of the efforts was on the exclusion of audiovisual services.[9] Reflecting this, during the Uruguay trade talks, a Working Group on Audiovisual Services was established with the task of considering whether the special cultural considerations related to the audiovisual sector demanded its total exclusion from the scope of the services agreement, or whether a dedicated annex to the Agreement could provide a solution.[10] The opinions differed profoundly, and even the diplomatic vernacular of trade representatives could not conceal the chasm between those in favour of free trade and those in favour of shielding (national) culture. While Canada and audiovisual media exporters, such as India, Brazil and Hong Kong were important actors,[11] it is noteworthy that the greatest clash on media matters was between the then European Community (EC) and the United States.[12] The conflict shaped, and continues to define, the discourse on trade and culture that maps onto key architectural choices in global law.

6 J.H. Jackson, *The World Trading System: Law and Policy of the International Economic Relations*, Cambridge, MA: MIT Press, 1997.
7 Agreement on Trade Related Aspects of Intellectual Property Rights (TRIPS Agreement), 15 April 1994, Marrakesh Agreement establishing the World Trade Organization, Annex 1C, 33 ILM 1997 (1994).
8 General Agreement on Trade in Services (GATS), 15 April 1994, Marrakesh Agreement Establishing the World Trade Organization, Annex 1B, 33 ILM 1167 (1994).
9 Pursuant to the technical classification scheme, which WTO Members applied during the negotiations, these included: motion picture and video tape production and distribution services; motion picture projection services; radio and television services; radio and television transmission services; sound recording and others. WTO, Services Sectoral Classification List Doc.MTN.GNS/W/120, 1991.
10 WTO, Working Group on Audiovisual Services, Communication from the European Communities, Draft Sectoral Annex on Audiovisual Services, MTN.GNS/AUD/W/2, 1990.
11 WTO, Working Group on Audiovisual Services, ibid.
12 Singh, op. cit., pp. 122–23 and *passim*. It is fair to say that the EC was not united in this approach and there were various opinions within the Community – with France being very pro-active and Germany and Britain somewhat reluctant. The Commission, headed at the time by Jacques Delors, acted as a strong policy entrepreneur in shaping the views of the Member States. See G. Ross, *Jacques Delor and European Integration*, Oxford: Polity, 1995, p. 115; D.A. Levy, *Europe's Digital Revolution: Broadcasting Regulation, the EU and the Nation State*, London: Routledge, 1999; Singh, op. cit., p. 127.

While generally the EC sought to secure sufficient wiggle room for cultural policy measures, at that point of time, it was also particularly keen to preserve the quotas recently introduced through the Television without Frontiers Directive (TVWF),[13] and to make them permissible at the international level.[14] Rhetorically, the Community pursued its goals by relying on a set of arguments relating to the specific qualities of cultural goods and services. The EC argued that because of these specific qualities specific policies were needed, which can correct the market failures in the relevant markets and ensure welfare.[15] The cultural identity line of defence has also been prominent in the EU tactics – on the one hand, by emphasizing the importance of the audiovisual industry to European identity and unity, and by highlighting the harmful effects of the American entertainment industry, on the other.[16] Overall, this strategy has been politically strengthened by the enduring negative attitude towards globalization and its effects upon culture shared by key domestic constituencies.[17]

The US, having been successfully lobbied by the entertainment industry,[18] countered the European offensive. The US was opposed to any cultural exception, regardless of its form. Its strongest argument was that it amounted to disguised protectionism, especially considering the intrinsic difficulty of defining 'national' and 'culture'. It also stressed consumers' freedom of choice, as well as other positive effects of free trade in cultural products.[19] Being

---

13 The TVWF contained two provisions specifically targeting culture. Article 4 TVWF calls upon Member States to ensure that broadcasters allocate a majority of time on TV channels, to Europe-made programmes (the so-called 'European works'). Article 5 TVWF is intended to secure that a minimum proportion of viewing time (10 per cent) is reserved to European works created by independent producers, or alternatively that a minimum programme budget is allocated to independent productions.

14 M. Burri, 'Trade *versus* Culture in the Digital Environment: An Old Conflict in Need of a New Definition', *Journal of International Economic Law* 12, 2009, 17–62.

15 Failures typical of markets for cultural goods and services are: (i) failures due to economies of scale in production and distribution; (ii) failures due to the nature of competition in products with public goods aspects; (iii) failures due to the impact of externalities on the pricing of cultural products; and (iv) failures due to collective action problems. See P. Sauvé and K. Steinfatt, 'Towards Multilateral Rules on Trade and Culture: Protective Regulation or Efficient Protection?', in Productivity Commission & Australian National University (eds), *Achieving Better Regulation of Services*, Canberra, AU: AusInfo, 2000, pp. 323–346.

16 Singh, op. cit., pp. 132–133.

17 D. Held, A. McGrew, D. Goldblatt and J. Perraton, *Global Transformations: Politics, Economics and Culture*, Stanford, CA: Stanford University Press, 1999; T. Cowen, *Creative Destruction: How Globalization Is Changing the World's Cultures*, Princeton, NJ: Princeton University Press, 2002; A. Giddens, *Runaway World: How Globalisation is Reshaping Our Lives*, London: Routledge, 2002.

18 P.S. Grant and C. Wood, *Blockbusters and Trade Wars: Popular Culture in a Globalized World*, Vancouver, CA: Douglas and McIntyre, 2004, pp. 352–376; Singh, op. cit., pp. 134–138.

19 WTO, Working Group on Audiovisual Services, Note on the Meeting of 5 and 18 October 1990 (MTN.GNS/AUD/2).

cautious about pushing too far on the cultural identity issue, the US consistently framed the whole debate as one on trade *not* culture.[20]

The law of the WTO and the agreement to disagree

The cultural exception agenda only partially attained its goals. On the eve of the Marrakesh talks, without striking any concrete deal, the EU and the US basically agreed to disagree on addressing cultural matters,[21] and this is reflected in the design and substance of WTO law, in particular in the rules on trade in services.

While no services sector is excluded from the scope of the GATS,[22] there are a number of inbuilt flexibilities, which allow for limitations to be placed on the opening up of certain sectors that are sensitive to domestic constituencies.[23] While under the GATT, which regulates trade in goods, obligations regarding national treatment and quantitative restrictions apply across the board, the GATS framework adopted a 'positive list' approach. Thereby, WTO Members can choose the services sectors and sub-sectors in which they are willing to make market access (Article XVI GATS) and/or national treatment (Article XVII GATS) commitments, and can define their modalities. Even the MFN obligation – that is, the duty to treat equally all like foreign services and services suppliers, which is fundamental to the entire trade system, can be subject to limitation under the GATS (Article II:2).

As a result of this malleability in design, almost all Members, with the exception of the US, Japan and New Zealand, have been reluctant to commit and have listed significant MFN exemptions.[24] Indeed, audiovisual media is the least liberalized services sector.[25] What is interesting when looking at

20 Singh, op. cit., pp. 134–135.
21 As legend would have it, early in the morning of 14 December 1994, just before the US President's Fast Track Authority was to expire, Leon Brittan, as EU representative, offered the US Trade Representative (USTR) Mickey Kantor a deal to bind the television quota at 49 per cent as part of an audiovisual services agreement and to continue negotiations on box office receipt taxes in France, as well as on blank video and audio tapes taxes. After discussions with President Clinton and Hollywood representatives, the US turned the deal down instead of signing something to which the lobbies at home would have opposed. See, E.H. Preeg, *Traders in a Brave New World: The Uruguay Round and the Future of the International System*, Chicago, IL: University of Chicago Press, 1995, p. 172; Singh, op. cit., pp. 135–136.
22 Except for services supplied in the exercise of governmental authority, Article I:3(b) GATS.
23 F.S. Galt, 'The Life, Death, and Rebirth of the "Cultural Exception" in the Multilateral Trading System: An Evolutionary Analysis of Cultural Protection and Intervention in the Face of American Pop Culture's Hegemony', *Washington University Global Studies Law Review* 3, 2004, 909–935.
24 M. Roy, 'Audiovisual Services in the Doha Round: Dialogue de Sourds, the Sequel?', *Journal of World Investment and Trade* 6, 2005, 923–952.
25 WTO, European Communities and their Member States, Final List of Article II (MFN) Exemptions, GATS/EL/31, 1994; WTO, European Communities and their Member States, Schedule of Specific Commitments, Trade in Services, Supplement 3, GATS/SC/31/Suppl. 3, 1997.

the Members' commitments for audiovisual services – and most illustratively those of the EU – is that they reflect a resolute 'all-or-nothing' approach. The scheduling flexibility permitting a wide variety of commitments ranging between full liberalization and absolute non-commitment is not utilized. This is odd because, at least for some sub-sectors, government regulation and trade restrictions are not common (*e.g.* for sound recording). In a more systemic sense, this compromises one of the core purposes of an international trade agreement, i.e. to provide predictability and stability.[26]

Despite this state of affairs, which permits almost unlimited possibilities for measures protecting domestic cultural industries and/or discriminating against foreign products and services, the Uruguay Round's 'Agreement to Disagree' was not a real solution for cultural proponents. As the trade *forum* could not provide an adequate design for safeguarding cultural concerns, a change of venue seemed to many appropriate. It was at that time that the concept of 'cultural diversity' was introduced into the trade and culture discourse and embraced by the former cultural exception advocates.[27] This re-conceptualization seemed to cast aside some of 'the negativism and the latent "anti-Americanism" of the "cultural exception" rhetoric'.[28] Cultural diversity had a positive but also a more proactive connotation, which was symptomatic of the more intensified developments in the following decade.

UNESCO and the search for a new institutional home

UNESCO is the special organization of the United Nations for cultural matters, among others. Yet, it was only in the 1990s that it took a concrete interest in protecting cultural diversity from the (alleged) negative effects of economic globalization. The repositioning began with the *World Decade for Cultural Development* (1988–1997) and UNESCO's role substantially expanded thereafter with the objectives of acknowledging the cultural dimension of development, affirming and enriching cultural identities, broadening participation in culture and promoting international cultural co-operation.[29] The idea of a legally binding instrument on cultural diversity came about as an afterthought in UNESCO. The process originally started under two *fora* unrelated

---

26 Roy, op. cit., pp. 940–941.
27 European Commission, The EU Approach to the WTO Millennium Round, COM(1999), 331 final, 8 July 1999.
28 C.B. Graber, 'The New UNESCO Convention on Cultural Diversity: A Counterbalance to the WTO', *Journal of International Economic Law* 9, 2006, 553–574, p. 555.
29 UNESCO, *UNESCO and the Issue of Cultural Diversity: Review and Strategy, 1946–2004*, Paris: UNESCO, revised version, 2004, p. 16. See also Resolution adopted by the General Assembly of the United Nations, World Commission on Culture and Development, A/Res./46/158, 19 December 1991; UNESCO, World Commission on Culture and Development, *Our Creative Diversity*, 2nd ed., Paris: UNESCO, 1996; UNESCO, *World Culture Report 1998: Culture, Creativity and Markets*, Paris: UNESCO, 1998; UNESCO, *World Culture Report 2000: Cultural Diversity, Conflict and Pluralism*, Paris: UNESCO, 2000.

to the UN agency – the International Network of Cultural Policy (INCP) and the International Network for Cultural Diversity (INCD).[30] It was only in 2003 that these efforts on international instrument on cultural diversity moved to UNESCO.[31] Relatively swiftly thereafter, the Convention on the Protection and Promotion of the Diversity of Cultural Expressions was adopted by the 33rd UNESCO General Conference. The US was also active in this process but, as one would have expected, it acted as a fervent adversary. It is indeed often argued that the US rejoined UNESCO in 2003 specifically because of the distressing prospect of a legally binding instrument on cultural diversity 'to be negotiated in a forum in which the United States had no formal input'.[32]

An appraisal of the UNESCO Convention on Cultural Diversity

The UNESCO Convention has been celebrated as an exceptional success in international treaty-making – as it was the first legally binding instrument on trade-related cultural matters, with a record of incredibly wide support and swift ratification. In the trade versus culture discourse, the Convention was intended to take up a critical role and counterbalance the highly institutionalized economic rules of the WTO[33] and ensure the attainment of cultural objectives at the global level. It is however questionable whether the UNESCO Convention provides a sufficient toolkit to achieve any of these goals.

The criticisms of the Convention are well documented[34] and its drawbacks can be grouped into three categories, relating to (i) the lack of binding obligations; (ii) its substantive incompleteness; and (iii) its ambiguous relation towards other international instruments. We discuss them briefly before considering the Convention's practical impact.

30 The INCP was a forum of cultural ministers, driven by a small group of countries, comprising Canada, Croatia, France, Greece, Mexico, Senegal, South Africa, Sweden and Switzerland. The INCD was a non-governmental organization (NGO), set up at the initiative of the Canadian Heritage in 1998 and intended to complement the efforts of the INCP by bringing together national cultural NGOs, artists and other activists. K. Acheson and C. Maule, 'Convention on Cultural Diversity', *Journal of Cultural Economics* 28, 2004, 243–256, p. 246.

31 UNESCO 32 C/Resolution 34, Desirability of Drawing up an International Standard-Setting Instrument on Cultural Diversity, 17 October 2003.

32 Bruner, op. cit., p. 383. While the US had been one of the parties involved in UNESCO's founding in 1945, in 1984 it left due to the starkly diverging views of the US and of developing countries and as a reaction to the 1980 MacBride report, which was viewed by the US as an assault on principles of free speech.

33 Graber, op. cit.

34 See M. Hahn, '"A Clash of Cultures?" The UNESCO Diversity Convention and International Trade Law', *Journal of International Economic Law* 9, 2006, 515–552; Graber, op. cit.; R. Craufurd Smith, 'The UNESCO Convention on the Protection and Promotion of Cultural Expressions: Building a New World Information and Communication Order?', *International Journal of Communication* 1, 2007, 24–55; Burri, 'Trade *versus* Culture in the Digital Environment: An Old Conflict in Need of a New Definition', op. cit.

(i) Although the UNESCO Convention is meant to be a binding instrument, in fact it has precious few obligations, and these are formulated as best effort duties for the Parties. There are only two provisions that can be said to be of a binding nature. The first resembles the WTO's enabling clause[35] and relates to the preferential treatment that developed countries must grant to cultural workers and cultural goods of developing countries.[36] The second, formulated in Article 17, creates an obligation for international co-operation in situations of serious threat to cultural expressions, construed in particular as assistance from developed to developing countries. Even this pair of obligations is vague and unlikely to bring about radical change. The duties are also somewhat marginal to the proclaimed goal of cultural diversity.

Despite the limited obligations on the Parties to take action to protect and promote cultural diversity, the Convention formulates an extensive block of rights to that end. Article 6(2) provides a non-exhaustive list of measures that the Parties may adopt. The list is virtually all encompassing.[37] This approach, adding up to the Convention's broad and fuzzy definition of 'cultural diversity,'[38] and the lack of proportionality or necessity tests, opens the door to state activism in a wide range of economic sectors that affect culture in one way or another. The value added by the Convention's Operational Guidelines in assisting efforts to concretize targeted action and ensure balanced choices can be deemed minimal so far.[39]

(ii) Despite its seemingly broad scope, the UNESCO Convention is in fact not comprehensive enough to secure the protection and promotion of cultural diversity. Some of the missing critical pieces are related to the centrality of state sovereignty, which is intrinsic to the UNESCO Convention as all rights and obligations stemming from the Convention are attributed to states.[40] This may be understandable for an intergovernmental treaty but cultural rights do not correspond to national boundaries.[41] The fact that the UNESCO Convention subscribes to respecting and safeguarding human rights[42] may partly remedy this situation but it is still disappointing that specific cultural

---

35 GATT, Decision of 28 November 1979 (L/4903), Differential and More Favourable Treatment, Reciprocity and Fuller Participation of Developing Countries ('Enabling Clause').

36 Article 16 UNESCO Convention.

37 See Article 6(2)(a)–(h) UNESCO Convention. For a taxonomy of cultural policy measures, see Footer and Graber, op. cit., pp. 122–126.

38 Article 4(1) UNESCO Convention defines 'cultural diversity' as referring 'to the manifold ways in which the cultures of groups and societies find expression. These expressions are passed on within and among groups and societies.'

39 All guidelines are available at www.unesco.org/new/en/culture/themes/cultural-diversity/diversity-of-cultural-expressions/the-convention/operational-guidelines/ (accessed 24 January 2013).

40 Article 2(2) UNESCO Convention.

41 A. Eide, 'Cultural Rights as Individual Human Rights', in A. Eide, C. Krause and A. Rosas (eds), *Economic, Social and Cultural Rights*, The Hague: Kluwer Law International, 2001, 2nd edn, pp. 289–301; E. Stamatopoulou, *Cultural Rights in International Law*, Leiden: Brill, 2007.

42 Articles 2(1), 2(3) and 7 UNESCO Convention.

rights – such as access to education or use of language of choice – did not make it into the text.[43] Nor are the specific rights of Indigenous peoples[44] or media organizations, journalists or individuals appropriately safeguarded.

Moreover, a vital element omitted from the regulatory domain of the UNESCO Convention, except for the brief remark in the preamble,[45] is intellectual property. This omission is odd, since intellectual property rights (IPRs) have as their core objective the protection and promotion of creativity and innovation, and are thus an indispensable element of all processes related to the creation, distribution of and access to cultural content.[46]

(iii) A significant drawback of the Convention in terms of the critical role it was supposed to play as a counter-force to economic globalization (as epitomized by the WTO) is its 'conflict of laws' provision. This crucial norm fails to ensure any meaningful interface with the rules of the WTO (or any of the other existing international agreements) in case of a conflict between them.[47] Article 20 of the Convention provides simultaneously that, '[n]othing in this Convention shall be interpreted as modifying rights and obligations of the Parties under any other treaties to which they are parties,'[48] and that, 'without subordinating this Convention to any other treaty,' Parties shall foster mutual supportiveness between the Convention and the other treaties to which they are parties.[49] Evidently, this rather paradoxical formulation excludes the modification of rights and obligations of the Parties under other existing treaties.[50]

To sum up the critique of the UNESCO Convention's text, one can maintain that it is an instrument of soft rather than hard law,[51] which largely

43 Craufurd Smith, op. cit., pp. 28, 37.
44 Despite few mentions: Recitals 8, 13 and 15 of the preamble, Articles 2(3) and 7(1)(a) UNESCO Convention.
45 Recital 17 of the UNESCO Convention's preamble.
46 See e.g. J.E. Cohen, 'Creativity and Culture in Copyright Theory', *UC Davis Law Review* 40, 2005, 1151–1205; M. Burri, 'Cultural Protectionism 2.0: Updating Cultural Policy Tools for the Digital Age', in S. Pager and A. Candeub (eds), *Transnational Culture in the Internet Age*, Cheltenham, UK: Edward Elgar, 2012, pp. 182–202.
47 For all possible causes of conflict, see A. Dahrendorf, 'Free Trade Meets Cultural Diversity: The Legal Relationship between WTO Rules and the UNESCO Convention on the Protection of the Diversity of Cultural Expressions', in H. Schneider and P. van den Bossche (eds), *Protection of Cultural Diversity from an International and European Perspective*, Antwerp: Intersentia, 2008, pp. 31–84.
48 Article 20(2) UNESCO Convention.
49 Ibid.
50 Graber, op. cit., pp. 565–568; Hahn, op. cit., pp. 540–546; P.T. Stoll, 'Article 20. Relationship to Other Treaties: Mutual Supportiveness, Complementarity and Non-subordination', in S. von Schorlemer and P.T. Stoll (eds), *The UNESCO Convention on the Protection and Promotion of the Diversity of Cultural Expressions: Explanatory Notes*, Heidelberg: Springer, 2012, pp. 519–543; G.C. Shaffer and M.A. Pollack, 'Hard vs. Soft Law: Alternatives, Complements, and Antagonists in International Governance', *Minnesota Law Review* 94, 2010, 706–799, p. 772.
51 Shaffer and Pollack, op. cit., p. 771.

avoids controversies and, while affirming state sovereignty in cultural policy matters, fails to provide adequate guidance on how to design appropriate, future-oriented instruments capable of protecting and promoting cultural diversity in a world of profound rule fragmentation and complexity and of rapid technological change.[52]

The impact of the UNESCO Convention

Yet, the impact of the Convention needs to be explored beyond its textual basis,[53] both with regard to the WTO – as the defined 'adversary' and natural institutional counterpart in the trade versus culture context – and outside the forum of the WTO in the broader and multi-level landscape of governance.

The Convention's impact vis-à-vis the WTO

Despite the great number of states that have ratified the UNESCO Convention, its impact on the WTO regime is likely to be minimal. This is due to the weakness of the Convention but also due to the closed and less responsive system of the WTO. The impressive track-record of the UNESCO Convention cannot mask the much more complicated political economy behind it, as different states have ratified it for very different reasons.[54] Although the Canadian and French delegations,[55] assisted by a number of NGOs, were fairly efficient during the Convention's negotiation,[56] this mobilization is not strong enough to go beyond the weak regulatory charge of the Convention and matter when 'real' trade interests are at stake. At present, it is unlikely that a negotiating bloc will form within the WTO to push for more culture-oriented solutions – such as including some sort of 'cultural exception,'[57] an express clause for culture in the general exception provisions of the GATT (Article

---

52 Craufurd Smith, 'The UNESCO Convention', pp. 53–54; M. Burri, 'Trade and Culture in International Law: Paths to (Re)conciliation', *Journal of World Trade* 44, 2010, 49–80; Burri, 'Cultural Protectionism 2.0: Updating Cultural Policy Tools for the Digital Age', op. cit.

53 K.J. Alter and S. Meunier, 'The Politics of International Regime Complexity', *Perspectives on Politics* 7, 2009, 13–24, p. 16.

54 For instance, Brazil, Japan and India have all ratified the Convention but remain equally willing to engage in further liberalization of the audiovisual sector. See Pauwels, C., J. Loisen and K. Donders, 'Culture Incorporated; or Trade Revisited? How the Position of Different Countries Affects the Outcome of the Debate on Cultural Trade and Diversity', in N. Obuljen and J. Smiers (eds), UNESCO's Convention on the Protection and Promotion of the Diversity of Cultural Expressions: Making It Work, Zagreb, edited by Nina Obuljen and Joost Smiers: Institute for International Relations, 2006, pp. 125–158.

55 Supported by Germany, Greece, Mexico, Monaco, Morocco and Senegal, and a number of Francophone UNESCO Member States.

56 Acheson and Maule, op. cit.

57 Burri, 'Trade *versus* Culture in the Digital Environment: An Old Conflict in Need of a New Definition', op. cit.

XX) and the GATS (Article XIV), or listing cultural diversity as one of the objectives of the WTO in the Preamble of the WTO Agreement.[58]

Although Doha is not stalling because of the trade versus culture debate, the requests and offers tabled so far reveal precious few new commitments and no future-oriented rule-design that could address cultural matters at their intersection with economic interests. The legacy line of separation between the EU and the US with their respective pro-culture and pro-trade positions – if we are to describe them in a typified manner[59] – clearly persists. This is particularly palpable in the audiovisual services sector, which has been the most contentious in this clash.[60] Despite the widely shared recognition by key WTO Members that the audiovisual sector has changed dramatically,[61] in particular due to the sweeping transformations caused by the Internet, there is little sign of an agreement emerging.

One could argue that the trade versus culture status quo has indeed been perpetuated through the UNESCO Convention. This has had multiple effects for the WTO outside the narrow domain of audiovisual services. The spill-over effects are felt in the discussions on advancing liberalization and coherent multilateral regulation in the 'neighbouring' areas of telecommunications and electronic commerce.[62] Overall, the WTO is, in many senses, rendered incapable of appropriately addressing trade in the Internet age,[63] despite the organization's inherent flexibility and potential to adapt.[64] This may be deemed a negative rather than a positive development.[65]

Against the backdrop of this political deadlock, many observers have hoped that when a new 'trade versus culture' case emerges, the WTO adjudication – as a uniquely powerful mechanism of dispute resolution at the international

---

58 There are plenty of proposals that fall into this category. For an overview as well as references to the authors, see Burri, 'Trade *versus* Culture in the Digital Environment: An Old Conflict in Need of a New Definition', op. cit., 46–53.

59 See e.g. Bruner, op. cit.

60 See WTO, Communication from the European Communities and its Member States, Conditional Revised Offer, TN/S/O/EEC/Rev.1, 2005; WTO Council for Trade in Services, Audiovisual Services, Background Note by the Secretariat, S/C/W/310, 2010.

61 C.B. Graber, 'Audio-visual Policy: The Stumbling Block of Trade Liberalisation', in D. Geradin and D. Luff (eds), *The WTO and Global Convergence in Telecommunications and Audiovisual Services*, Cambridge: Cambridge University Press, 2004, 165–214, pp. 166–170; Roy, op. cit., pp. 931–936.

62 S. Wunsch-Vincent, 'Trade Rules for the Digital Age', in M. Panizzon, N. Pohl and P. Sauvé (eds), *GATS and the Regulation of International Trade in Services*, Cambridge: Cambridge University Press, 2008, 497–529, pp. 501–505; R.H. Weber and M. Burri, *Classification of Services in the Digital Economy*, Zurich: Staempfli & Berlin: Springer, 2012.

63 M. Burri and T. Cottier (eds), *Trade Governance in the Digital Age*, Cambridge: Cambridge University Press, 2012.

64 See e.g. R. Cooney and A. Lang, 'Taking Uncertainty Seriously: Adaptive Governance and International Trade', *European Journal of International Law* 18, 2007, 523–551.

65 Burri, 'Trade *versus* Culture in the Digital Environment: An Old Conflict in Need of a New Definition', op. cit.

level – would provide a final resolution to the conflict, possibly also clarifying the status of the UNESCO Convention and its relationship with the WTO rules.[66] The *China – Publications and Audiovisual Products* case,[67] decided in favour of the United States in 2009, proved the contrary. China's attempt to apply the UNESCO Convention as a shield for some measures in the media domain remained futile and the Convention's impact on the WTO rules was dismissed.[68]

Interestingly, the Panel did leave a door open for further consideration of cultural concerns, as it interpreted broadly the public morals exception under Article XX(a) GATT.[69] It acknowledged China's claim that 'reading materials and finished audiovisual products are so-called "cultural goods"' and these are 'of a unique kind with a potentially serious negative impact on public morals'.[70] Despite the fact that the Panel found that the measures at issue were not 'necessary within the meaning of Article XX(a),'[71] this may be interpreted as newly enhanced flexibility of the WTO rules with regard to culture, which can be used in the future (albeit the *chapeau* test of Articles XX GATT and XIV GATS still remains hard to pass).

The Convention's impact outside the WTO

As noted earlier, the standstill in the WTO in trade and culture matters, which has only been confirmed by the UNESCO Convention, has had repercussions outside the WTO. The situation with digital trade and the inability of the WTO to tackle the relevant questions because of the issue-overlaps with culture is illuminating. It is symptomatic of the overall intensified power-plays, which lead to increased fragmentation of both negotiation themes and negotiation *fora*. The lack of solutions within the WTO context has driven, and will continue to drive, Members to pursue bilateral or regional paths to advance their policy priorities. The United States, in particular, has made

---

66 Graber, op. cit., pp. 567, 571; Voon, T., 'UNESCO and the WTO: A Clash of Cultures?', International and Comparative Law Quarterly 55:3, 2006, 635–652.

67 WTO Appellate Body Report, *China – Measures Affecting Trading Rights and Distribution Services for Certain Publications and Audiovisual Entertainment Products (China – Publications and Audiovisual Products)*, WT/DS363/AB/R, adopted 21 December 2009, confirming in most essential points WTO Panel Report, *China – Measures Affecting Trading Rights and Distribution Services for Certain Publications and Audiovisual Entertainment Products (China – Publications and Audiovisual Products)*, WT/DS363/R, adopted 12 August 2009.

68 WTO Appellate Body Report, *China – Publications and Audiovisual Products*, para. 4.207, referring to Article 20 UNESCO Convention.

69 Following the meaning of the term in Article XIV(a) GATS as broadly interpreted in *US – Gambling*. See WTO Panel Report, *United States – Measures Affecting the Cross-Border Supply of Gambling and Betting Services (US – Gambling)*, WT/S285/R, adopted 10 November 2004, paras 6.461 and 6.465.

70 WTO Panel Report, *China – Publications and Audiovisual Products*, para. 7.751.

71 Ibid. para. 7.913.

substantial efforts to ensure implementation of its Digital Agenda[72] through a number of preferential trade agreements (PTAs). The agreements reached since 2002 with Australia, Bahrain, Chile, Morocco, Oman, Peru, Singapore, the Central American countries,[73] and most recently with Panama, Colombia and South Korea, contain only minimal restrictions on digital products, applying a negative scheduling approach (in contrast to the standard GATS positive pick-and-choose mode) and also tackle some 'deep' e-commerce regulatory issues.[74] The Trans-Pacific Partnership (TPP) Agreement may be going even further.

It should be noted that the United States has shown some deference to the culturally inspired measures of its PTA partners in the field of audiovisual services. It permitted some policy space for those measures, as long as they are 'frozen' at their present level,[75] and often to the exclusion of newer digital media. It is also noteworthy that the leeway given to the US partners with respect to trade in cultural products tends to reflect the negotiating capacity of the states involved – the smaller the country, the more concessions it makes.[76] Policy room thus may often be substantially reduced and countries (especially the poorer ones) may not be able to appropriately address diverse public interests in the field of media – particularly digital media. In effect, this constrains the possibilities for implementing the UNESCO Convention in the said domains and distorts any present or future trade/culture balance.

The impact of the Convention on its own parent organization, UNESCO, and its authority can be deemed sizeable, as it has subsequently become a hub of new activities. The UNESCO Convention has also effectively contributed to promoting the notion of cultural diversity and establishing it as a global public good, as a distinct regulatory objective worth pursuing in a wide range of activities and venues, both domestically and internationally. This mobilization should not be underestimated and may have multiple spill-over effects. The first test of these effects has been the reporting exercise that some of the Convention's ratifying Parties underwent in 2012 – four years after the UNESCO Convention's entry into force.

The evidence provided in the countries' reports can be analysed with mixed conclusions. The overall impact of the activities so far seems somewhat small in practical terms, especially when domestic implementation is concerned. It

---

72 See S. Wunsch-Vincent, 'The Digital Trade Agenda of the US: Parallel Tracks of Bilateral, Regional and Multilateral Liberalization', *Aussenwirtschaft* 1, 2003, 7–46.

73 The DR-CAFTA includes Costa Rica, El Salvador, Guatemala, Honduras, Nicaragua and the Dominican Republic.

74 See Wunsch-Vincent, 'The Digital Trade Agenda of the US', op. cit., pp. 28–35; Wunsch-Vincent 'Trade Rules for the Digital Age', op. cit., pp. 516–523.

75 T. Voon, 'A New Approach to Audiovisual Products in the WTO: Rebalancing GATT and GATS', *UCLA Entertainment Law Review* 14, 2007, 1–32, pp. 25–26.

76 I. Bernier, 'The Recent Free Trade Agreements of the United States as Illustration of Their New Strategy regarding the Audiovisual Sector', April 2004. Online. Available: www.coalition suisse.ch/doss_sc/unesco_ccd/bernier_us_ftas_and_av_sector1.pdf (accessed 22 January 2013), p. 15.

is sometimes hard to differentiate between instruments and interventions which were specifically designed to address the UNESCO Convention's objectives and others that were simply adopted as part of the 'business as usual' of national cultural policies. As positive achievements one could list the development of best practices, the building of statistical resources and the impact assessments of the tools applied, which may in the longer run improve the efficiency of the measures and dispel some of the protectionist fears the UNESCO Convention has instilled.[77] In international affairs, the EU Protocols on Cultural Cooperation are an innovative tool,[78] the application and further development of which should be closely followed. Generally speaking, it may take time before some of the longer-term effects of the Convention, as alluded earlier, are felt, as institution building is often involved and patterns and practices need to settle.

More broadly, one should assess the Convention's impact against the backdrop of the contemporary global governance,[79] to which the UNESCO Convention was a reaction and in which it is now embedded. Trade and culture are, in many senses, a prime example of fragmented global governance with many, parallel and partially overlapping international regimes that are not hierarchically ordered. The inherent complexity of the system and its various multi-directional and multi-effect interactions caused a reduction in the clarity of the Convention's legal obligations as well as the introduction of overlapping sets of rules to address, among others, issues of trade, culture, intellectual property, development and human rights.

We find the theoretical framework of international regime complexity, which examines these existing multiple, overlapping and non-hierarchical regimes and their interaction,[80] particularly fitting to capture the many facets of the UNESCO Convention's effects and the evolution of the trade versus culture discourse. This framework would suggest that fragmentation is an

---

77 M. Burri, 'The UNESCO Convention on Cultural Diversity: An Appraisal Five Years after its Entry into Force', *International Journal of Cultural Property* 20, 2014, 357–380.

78 See the chapter by Psychogiopoulou in this volume.

79 See e.g. M. Kahler and D.A. Lake (eds), *Governance in a Global Economy: Political Authority in Transition*, Princeton: Princeton University Press, 2003; J.L. Dunoff and J.P. Trachman (eds), *Ruling the World?: Constitutionalism, International Law, and Global Governance*, Cambridge: Cambridge University Press, 2009; T. Cottier and P. Delimatsis, *The Prospects of International Trade Regulation: From Fragmentation to Coherence*, Cambridge: Cambridge University Press, 2011.

80 Alter and Meunier talk of 'international regime complexity' to signify the presence of nested, partially overlapping, and parallel international regimes that are not hierarchically ordered and stress that the lack of hierarchy is particularly typical of the international level. See Alter and Meunier, op. cit., p. 13. This follows up on important work on the notion of 'regime complex'. See K. Raustiala and D.G. Victor, 'The Regime Complex for Plant Genetic Resources', *International Organization* 58, 2004, 277–309; L.R. Helfer, 'Regime Shifting in the Intellectual Property System', *Perspective on Politics* 7, 2009, 39–44; and L.R. Helfer, 'Regime Shifting: The TRIPs Agreement and New Dynamics of International Intellectual Property Lawmaking', *The Yale Journal of International Law* 29, 2004, 1–83.

evolving quality of regimes, contingent on actors' preferences and bargains. So, it observes that 'where state preferences are similar, lawyers overcome fragmentation by crafting agreements that resolve conflicts across regimes, and thus legal ambiguity is transitory. Where preferences diverge, states block attempts to clarify the rules and thus ambiguity persists, allowing countries to select their preferred rule or interpretation.'[81]

As discussed above, and perhaps to the detriment of the system, the EU and the US have starkly diverging positions on the matters of trade and culture. The EU–US distributive conflict is also highly likely to continue, so that the UNESCO and the WTO regimes are exceedingly unlikely to 'converge into a new synthesis, but rather will remain in conflict for a prolonged period'.[82] The deadlock in the WTO realm with regard to cultural products and services may have led to overall greater levels of uncertainty and unpredictability regarding the WTO trade liberalization commitments and the ways forward, both in terms of future commitments and rule design. The UNESCO and related *fora* focusing on cultural policies will remain soft in character and impact, largely contributing to further fragmentation in institutional and rule architecture.

Conclusions: on the present and future of the trade versus culture discourse

The chapter mapped the evolution of the trade versus culture discourse in particular by looking at the international institutions embodying both sides of the conflict – the WTO and UNESCO and their interaction. The chapter highlighted the path dependence in the positions of the major stakeholders, the EU and the US, and how this mattered in shaping institutional choices. In many senses very little has changed since the conclusion of the Uruguay talks in 1994, when the cultural exception battle reached its peak. Although the UNESCO Convention on Cultural Diversity may be (and has been) interpreted – especially right after its adoption – as a breakthrough and a solid attempt to counterbalance trade and culture, economic and non-economic interests, we showed that both its text and actual impact disappoint in important aspects. As it appears that within the closed venues of UNESCO and the WTO no radical, if any, change can be expected, it is interesting to trace the effects of this deadlock on other venues, as actors seek to accommodate their interests and preferences elsewhere. At the regional level, especially as PTAs increase in number and depth of regulatory convergence,[83] they are also taking on many of the issues left unresolved as trade and culture clash, such as in the field of digital trade. There is still, however, no future-oriented

---

81 Alter and Meunier, op. cit., p. 16.
82 Shaffer and Pollack, op. cit., p. 773.
83 WTO, *The WTO and Preferential Trade Agreements: From Co-existence to Coherence*, Geneva: WTO, 2011.

solution offered for the actual reconciliation of trade and cultural concerns. And there may never be as the theoretical conjectures of international regime complexity suggest and as a concrete recent reminder of this path-dependent discourse reveals. The latter concerns a decision of the EU Parliament on the occasion of the negotiation of the Transatlantic Trade and Investment Partnership (TTIP) Agreement between the EU and the US. While the European Parliament did give a green light to the TTIP, it expressly asked, under the substantial influence of France, that cultural and audiovisual services, including online services, are excluded from the negotiating mandate in order to safeguard the 'cultural exception' and protect the cultural and linguistic diversity of the EU countries.[84] So, it seems that we are pretty much back to square one, at least in terms of the political debate.

The perpetuation of the trade versus culture quandary may be unfortunate. On the one hand, it does not reflect the reality that culture and trade are 'inextricably related'.[85] On the other hand, we argued that it triggers, or at least does not obstruct, the proliferation of fragmented institutions and rules – thereby increasing overall complexity and rendering the governance of key global public goods more difficult.[86] As a factor that exacerbates this state, one could add rapid technological development, in particular in the field of digital media. We have argued elsewhere[87] that this may have led, among other things, to an acute mismatch between the 'old' cultural exception policies and the practical reality of contemporary cultural creation, distribution and consumption.[88] Persistent path dependence in both trade and cultural law and policies has hindered innovative solutions so far.

Bibliography

Acheson, K. and C. Maule, 'Convention on Cultural Diversity', *Journal of Cultural Economics* 28, 2004, 243–256.

Alter, K.J. and S. Meunier, 'The Politics of International Regime Complexity', *Perspectives on Politics* 7, 2009, 13–24.

Benkler, Y., *The Wealth of Networks: How Social Production Transforms Markets and Freedom*, New Haven, CT: Yale University Press, 2006.

Bernier, I., 'The Recent Free Trade Agreements of the United States as Illustration of their New Strategy Regarding the Audiovisual Sector', April 2004. Online. Available: www.coalitionsuisse.ch/doss_sc/unesco_ccd/bernier_us_ftas_and_av_sector1.pdf (accessed 20 October 2014).

---

84 European Parliament, Resolution on EU Trade and Investment Negotiations with the United States of America (2013/2558(RSP)), paras 11–12.

85 R.J. Neuwirth, 'The Future of the "Culture and Trade Debate": A Legal Outlook', *Journal of World Trade* 47, 2013, 391–420, p. 395.

86 E. Brousseau, T. Dedeurwaerdere and B. Siebenhüner (eds), *Reflexive Governance for Global Public Goods*, Cambridge, MA: MIT Press, 2012.

87 Burri (2012), op. cit.

88 Y. Benkler, *The Wealth of Networks: How Social Production Transforms Markets and Freedom*, New Haven, CT: Yale University Press, 2006.

Braithwaite, J. and P. Drahos, *Global Business Regulation*, Cambridge: Cambridge University Press, 2000.

Brousseau, E., T. Dedeurwaerdere and B. Siebenhüner (eds), *Reflexive Governance for Global Public Goods*, Cambridge, MA: MIT Press, 2012.

Bruner, C. M., 'Culture, Sovereignty, and Hollywood: UNESCO and the Future of Trade in Cultural Products', *International Law and Politics* 40, 2008, 351–436.

Burri, M., 'The New Audiovisual Media Services Directive: Television without Frontiers, Television without Cultural Diversity', *Common Market Law Review* 44, 2007, 1689–1725.

Burri, M., 'Trade *versus* Culture in the Digital Environment: An old Conflict in Need of a New Definition', *Journal of International Economic Law* 12, 2009, 17–62.

Burri M., 'Trade and Culture in International law: Paths to (re)conciliation', *Journal of World Trade* 44, 2010, 49–80.

Burri, M., 'Cultural Protectionism 2.0: Updating Cultural Policy Tools for the Digital Age', in S. Pager and A. Candeub (eds), *Transnational Culture in the Internet Age*, Cheltenham, UK: Edward Elgar, 2012, pp. 182–212.

Burri, M., 'The UNESCO Convention on Cultural Diversity: An Appraisal Five Years After its Entry into Force', *International Journal of Cultural Property* 20, 2013, 357–380.

Burri, M. and T. Cottier (eds), *Trade Governance in the Digital Age*, Cambridge: Cambridge University Press, 2012.

Cohen, J.E., 'Creativity and Culture in Copyright Theory', *UC Davis Law Review* 40, 2005, 1151–1205.

Cooney, R. and A. Lang, 'Taking Uncertainty Seriously: Adaptive Governance and International Trade', *European Journal of International Law* 18, 2007, 523–551.

Cottier, T. and P. Delimatsis, *The Prospects of International Trade Regulation: From Fragmentation to Coherence*, Cambridge: Cambridge University Press, 2011.

Cowen, T., *Creative Destruction: How Globalization Is Changing the World's Cultures*, Princeton, NJ: Princeton University Press, 2002.

Craufurd Smith, R. (ed.), *Culture and European Union Law*, Oxford: Oxford University Press, 2004.

Craufurd Smith, R., 'The UNESCO Convention on the Protection and Promotion of Cultural Expressions: Building a New World Information and Communication Order?', *International Journal of Communication* 1, 2007, 24–55.

Craufurd Smith, R., 'The Evolution of Cultural Policy in the EU', in P. Craig and G. De Búrca (eds), *The Evolution of EU Law*, Oxford: Oxford University Press, 2011, pp. 872–895.

Dahrendorf, A., 'Free Trade Meets Cultural Diversity: The Legal Relationship Between WTO Rules and the UNESCO Convention on the Protection of the Diversity of Cultural Expressions', in H. Schneider and P. van den Bossche (eds), *Protection of Cultural Diversity from an International and European Perspective*, Antwerp: Intersentia, 2008, pp. 31–84.

Dunoff, J.L. and J.P. Trachman (eds), *Ruling the World?: Constitutionalism, International Law, and Global Governance*, Cambridge: Cambridge University Press, 2009

Eide, A. 'Cultural Rights as Individual Human Rights', in A. Eide, C. Krause and A. Rosas (eds), *Economic, Social and Cultural Rights*, The Hague: Kluwer Law International, 2001, 2nd edn, pp. 289–310.

European Commission, The EU Approach to the WTO Millennium Round, COM(1999), 331 final, 8 July 1999.

Footer, M.E. and C.B. Graber, 'Trade Liberalisation and Cultural Policy', *Journal of International Economic Law* 3, 2000, 115–144.

Galt, F.S., 'The Life, Death, and Rebirth of the "Cultural Exception" in the Multilateral Trading System: an Evolutionary Analysis of Cultural Protection and Intervention in the Face of American Pop Culture's Hegemony', *Washington University Global Studies Law Review* 3, 2004, 909–935.

Giddens, A., *Runaway World: How Globalisation is Reshaping Our Lives*, London: Routledge, 2002.

Graber, C.B., 'Audio-visual Policy: The Stumbling Block of Trade Liberalisation', in D. Geradin and D. Luff (eds), *The WTO and Global Convergence in Telecommunications and Audiovisual Services*, Cambridge: Cambridge University Press, 2004, pp. 165–214.

Graber, C.B., 'The New UNESCO Convention on Cultural Diversity: A Counterbalance to the WTO', *Journal of International Economic Law* 9, 2006, 553–574.

Grant, P.S. and C. Woods, *Blockbusters and Trade Wars: Popular Culture in a Globalized World*, Vancouver, CA: Douglas & McIntyre, 2004.

Hahn, M., '"A Clash of Cultures?" The UNESCO Diversity Convention and International Trade Law', *Journal of International Economic Law* 9, 2006, 515–552.

Held, D., A. McGrew, D. Goldblatt and J. Perraton, *Global Transformations: Politics, Economics and Culture*, Stanford, CA: Stanford University Press, 1999.

Helfer, L.R., 'Regime Shifting: The TRIPs Agreement and New Dynamics of International Intellectual Property Lawmaking', *The Yale Journal of International Law* 29, 2004, 1–83.

Helfer, L.R., 'Regime Shifting in the International Intellectual Property System', *Perspective on Politics* 7, 2009, 39–44.

Jackson, J.H., *The World Trading System: Law and Policy of the International Economic Relations*, Cambridge, MA: MIT Press, 1997.

Kahler, M. and D.A. Lake (eds), *Governance in a Global Economy: Political Authority in Transition*, Princeton, NJ: Princeton University Press, 2003

Levy, D.A., *Europe's Digital Revolution: Broadcasting Regulation, the EU and the Nation State*, London: Routledge, 1999.

Neuwirth, R.J., 'The Future of the "Culture and Trade Debate": A Legal Outlook', *Journal of World Trade* 47, 2013, 391–420.

Pauwels, C., J. Loisen and K. Donders, 'Culture Incorporated; or Trade Revisited? How the Position of Different Countries Affects the Outcome of the Debate on Cultural Trade and Diversity', in N. Obuljen and J. Smiers (eds), *UNESCO's Convention on the Protection and Promotion of the Diversity of Cultural Expressions: Making It Work*, Zagreb: Institute for International Relations, 2006, pp. 125–158.

Petito, D.S., 'Sovereignty and Globalization: Fallacies, Truth, and Perception', *New York Law School Journal of Human Rights* 17, 2001, 1139–1172.

Preeg, E.H., *Traders in a Brave New World: The Uruguay Round and the Future of the International System*, Chicago, IL: University of Chicago Press, 1995.

Raustiala, K. and D.G. Victor, 'The Regime Complex for Plant Genetic Resources', *International Organization* 58, 2004, 277–309.

Ross, G., *Jacques Delor and European Integration*, Oxford: Polity, 1995.

Roy, M., 'Audiovisual Services in the Doha Round: Dialogue de Sourds, the Sequel?', *Journal of World Investment and Trade* 6, 2005, 923–952.

Sauvé, P. and K. Steinfatt, 'Towards Multilateral Rules on Trade and Culture: Protective Regulation or Efficient Protection?', in Productivity Commission & Australian National University (eds), *Achieving Better Regulation of Services*, Canberra, AU: AusInfo, 2000, pp. 323–346.

Shaffer, G.C. and M.A. Pollack, 'Hard vs. Soft Law: Alternatives, Complements, and Antagonists in International Governance', *Minnesota Law Review* 94, 2010, 706–799.

Singh, J.P., 'Culture or Commerce? A Comparative Assessment of International Interactions and Developing Countries at UNESCO, WTO, and Beyond', *International Studies Perspectives* 8, 2007, 36–53.

Singh, J.P., *Negotiation and the Global Information Economy*, Cambridge: Cambridge University Press, 2008.

Stamatopoulou, E., *Cultural Rights in International Law*, Leiden: Brill, 2007.

Stoll, P.T., 'Article 20. Relationship to Other Treaties: Mutual Supportiveness, Complementarity and Non-subordination', in S. von Schorlemer and P.T. Stoll (eds), *The UNESCO Convention on the Protection and Promotion of the Diversity of Cultural Expressions: Explanatory Notes*, Heidelberg: Springer, 2012, pp. 519–543.

Trumpbour, J., *Selling Hollywood to the World: US and European Struggles for Mastery of the Global Film Industry, 1920–1950*, Cambridge: Cambridge University Press, 2007.

Tuthill, L. and M. Roy, 'GATS Classification Issues for Information and Communication Technology Services', in M. Burri and T. Cottier (eds), *Trade Governance in the Digital Age*, Cambridge: Cambridge University Press, 2012, pp. 157–178.

UNESCO, *Our Creative Diversity*, 2nd edn, Paris: UNESCO, 1996.

UNESCO, *World Culture Report 1998: Culture, Creativity and Markets*, Paris: UNESCO, 1998.

UNESCO, *World Culture Report 2000: Cultural Diversity, Conflict and Pluralism*, Paris: UNESCO, 2000.

UNESCO, *UNESCO and the Issue of Cultural Diversity: Review and Strategy, 1946–2004*, Paris: UNESCO, 2004.

Weber, R.H. and M. Burri, *Classification of Services in the Digital Economy*, Zurich: Staempfli and Berlin: Springer, 2012.

WTO, *The WTO and Preferential Trade Agreements: From Co-existence to Coherence*. Geneva: WTO, 2011.

Wunsch-Vincent, S., 'The Digital Trade Agenda of the US: Parallel Tracks of Bilateral, Regional and Multilateral Liberalization', *Aussenwirtschaft* 1, 2003, 7–46.

Wunsch-Vincent, S., 'Trade Rules for the Digital Age', in M. Panizzon, N. Pohl and P. Sauvé (eds), *GATS and the Regulation of International Trade in Services*, Cambridge: Cambridge University Press, 2008, pp. 497–529.

Voon, T., 'UNESCO and the WTO: A Clash of Cultures?', *International and Comparative Law Quarterly* 55:3, 2006, 635–652.

Voon, T., 'A New Approach to Audiovisual Products in the WTO: Rebalancing GATT and GATS', *UCLA Entertainment Law Review* 14, 2007, 1–32.

Legal instruments

Agreement on Trade Related Aspects of Intellectual Property Rights (TRIPS Agreement), 15 April 1994, Marrakesh Agreement establishing the World Trade Organization, Annex 1C, 33 ILM 1997 (1994).

Canada–US Free Trade Agreement, 22 December 1987–2 January 1988, 27 ILM 281 (1988).

Convention on the Protection and Promotion of the Diversity of Cultural Expressions (CCD), Paris, 20 October 2005, in force 18 March 2007, 2440 UNTS 311.

General Agreement on Trade in Services (GATS), 15 April 1994, Marrakesh Agreement Establishing the World Trade Organization, Annex 1B, 33 ILM 1167 (1994).

North American Free Trade Agreement, 17 December 1992, 32 ILM 289 (1993).

Cases

WTO Appellate Body Report, *China – Measures Affecting Trading Rights and Distribution Services for Certain Publications and Audiovisual Entertainment Products (China – Publications and Audiovisual Products)*, WT/DS363/AB/R, adopted 21 December 2009.

WTO Panel Report, *China – Measures Affecting Trading Rights and Distribution Services for Certain Publications and Audiovisual Entertainment Products (China – Publications and Audiovisual Products)*, WT/DS363/R, adopted 12 August 2009.

WTO Panel Report, *United States – Measures Affecting the Cross-Border Supply of Gambling and Betting Services (US – Gambling)*, WT/S285/R, adopted 10 November 2004.

8 International exchange and trade in cultural objects

Ana Filipa Vrdoljak[1]

Introduction

The legal protection of movable cultural heritage at the international level has been defined by a perennial tug-of-war between forces promoting international exchange and those seeking regulation of the transfer of the cultural objects. Shifts over the last century in how the balance between these twin aims is achieved reflect changes in the composition of Member States of intergovernmental organizations and their corresponding changing priorities. In the early twentieth century, the balance fostered under the League of Nations favoured a cosmopolitan view promoting the circulation and interchange of cultural material to further knowledge and mutual understanding between peoples. The balance sought in the late twentieth century emphasized the importance of states being able to host representative national collections on their own territory. More recently, this position appears to be tempered by moves to make cultural objects exhibited in international exhibitions immune from seizure or suit while on temporary loan. These moves are justified on the grounds reminiscent of those articulated a hundred years before.

The evolving recalibration of these dual priorities is the central focus of this chapter. First, I consider the antecedent efforts of the United Nations Educational, Scientific and Cultural Organization (UNESCO)'s predecessor the International Committee for Intellectual Cooperation and International Museum Office's early initiative to draft a multilateral agreement for the protection and return of cultural objects. Next, I reassess the operation of UNESCO's mandate with specific reference to the negotiations for the 1970 Convention on the Means of Prohibiting and Preventing the Illicit Import, Export, and Transfer of Ownership of Cultural Property and 1976 Recommendation concerning the International Exchange of Cultural Property. Finally, there is a brief examination of regional and domestic instruments regulating the trade in cultural objects and promoting temporary loans abroad. This focus serves as an entry point for a broader discussion of the significance of international exchange in the legal protection of cultural heritage.

---

1 Professor and Associate Dean (Research), Faculty of Law, The University of Technology Sydney.

Early initiatives and the International Committee of International Cooperation

The earliest multilateral efforts to regulate the international trade in cultural objects were instigated under the auspices of the League of Nations' International Committee for Intellectual Cooperation (ICIC). These initiatives can only be understood within the context of the ICIC's ethos: the promotion of peace among nations through the pursuit of intellectual cooperation across borders.[2] It was in this milieu that the ICIC's executive arm in Paris, the International Institute of Intellectual Cooperation, organized a number of international conferences in the 1930s through its International Museum Office (*Office international des musées* (OIM)).[3] When summarizing the findings of the 1931 Athens Conference, Jules Destrée noted that there was general agreement that the preservation and protection of masterpieces which 'represent[ed] civilisation's highest power of self-expression' was the concern of the entire international community and should be manifested in the 'idea of international solidarity' and mutual assistance.[4] He argued that there was a need for the public to appreciate its own cultural heritage but also to be inculcated with the 'spirit of international solidarity' which was best achieved through the international movement for exchange and cooperation between museums and other collecting institutions. He suggested that by necessity this restricted 'the right of national ownership' insofar as it is 'a selfish character'. Accordingly, it was necessary for countries to modify their laws to facilitate these endeavours.[5] This sentiment was reiterated in the Resolution concerning the Protection of Historical Monuments and Works of Art adopted in 1932 (1932 Resolution) by the League of Nations.[6] It guided the organization's initiatives in the field of movable heritage until its demise in 1945. The Resolution requested that Member States enact domestic laws permitting the transfer of cultural objects 'of no interest' to their national museums and limiting the scheduling of cultural objects 'to those of the special interest to the artistic or archaeological heritage of the country'.[7]

While the OIM conferences were organized to foster technical preservation and protection of movable and immovable heritage, it became clear that there

2 F.S. Northedge, *International Intellectual Co-operation with the League of Nations: Its Conceptual Basis and Lessons for the Present*, PhD Thesis, University of London, 1953, p. 28.
3 Including the Rome Conference of 1930 covering the preservation of paintings and sculptures and the Athens Conference of 1931 covering restoration and preservation of architectural monuments.
4 Anon., 'League of Nations' Intellectual Co-operation Organisation', *Information Bulletin*, Oct–Nov 1932, 165–166.
5 Ibid.
6 Adopted by the ICIC on 23 July 1932, and approved by the Assembly of the League of Nations on 10 October 1932.
7 J. Destrée, Annual Report of the President of the Directors' Committee of the International Museums Office, Note by the Secretary, of the Intellectual Co-operation Organisation, 1 July 1932, ICIC/273, 7; and Recommendation 4, 1932 Resolution.

was also a 'legal' aspect, 'in the form of international agreements'.[8] The 1932 Resolution called on states to assist each other in recovering scheduled objects which had been stolen or illicitly exported.[9] At the behest of the Italian Committee on Intellectual Co-operation, a convention guaranteeing the integrity of national collections was a central recommendation of the Resolution.[10] The draft International Convention on the Repatriation of Objects of Artistic, Historical or Scientific Interest which have been Lost, or Stolen or Unlawfully Alienated or Exported (1933 OIM draft) clearly reflected the motivation of states, like Italy, that had passed stringent export control laws, designed to 'make surreptitious traffic in works of art more difficult'.[11] Solidarity and mutual aid in the context of this draft was pursued to make such laws more effective.[12] The only trigger for the proposed Convention's operation was the alienation or export of the object contrary to national legislation.[13]

The 1933 OIM draft applied to 'movable or immovable objects of an artistic, historical or scientific character'.[14] However, it did not distinguish between cultural objects contained in museum collections and those from archaeological excavations, as was illustrated by a controversy regarding stelae illicitly exported from Egypt and offered for sale on the European market.[15] The OIM confirmed that the definition of objects covered by the proposed convention included *'fragments de monuments'*.[16] Nevertheless, subsequent drafts of the convention did not cover objects from archaeological excavations.

In response to concerns raised by states to the 1933 draft, the subsequent iteration was 'drastically' altered.[17] The draft International Convention for the Protection of National Historic or Artistic Treasures (1936 OIM draft) tightened its operation and no longer provided unfettered aid to national laws.[18] Drawing inspiration from the Pan-American Union's treaty covering movable heritage adopted during the same period,[19] the definition of cultural objects covered by the 1936 OIM draft was broadened to include 'objects of remarkable palæontological, archæological, historic or artistic

---

8 Anon. 'International Cooperation in the Sphere of Art', *League of Nations Official Journal*, vol. 13, 1932, 1776–1777.

9 Anon., op. cit., 1776.

10 C. de Visscher, 'International Protection of Works of Art and Historic Monuments', *Documents and State Papers*, 1949, 857.

11 Destrée, op. cit. 7. See De Visscher, op. cit., Appendix B, 865–866.

12 De Visscher, op. cit., 821.

13 1933 OIM Draft, Art. 1.

14 1933 OIM Draft, Art. 1.

15 J. Capart to S.S. Pacha, Egyptian ambassador to Washington, 10 April 1933, OIM.IV.27.I, pp. 172–173.

16 Foundoukidis to Destrée, n.d.: OIM.IV.27.I, p. 168, Records of the Office international des musées, UNESCO Archives, Paris.

17 Visscher, op. cit., 859.

18 Visscher, op. cit., Appendix B, 866–868.

19 Pan American Union (PAU) Treaty on the Protection of Movable Property of Historic Value, 15 April 1935, in force 17 July 1936, OASTS No. 28.

interest'.[20] With the inclusion of two words: 'national' and 'treasures', in the title and preamble of this draft, there is a subtle, but significant, recalibration of the balance between national and cosmopolitan objectives towards the views championed by the ICIC.[21] It redefined its purpose as the protection of cultural objects considered by the future State Parties to be of national importance, with the claimant state as the 'sole judge of the nature and value of such objects'.[22] Also, it provided that the proposed convention's operation could be extended to objects in private collections, provided they were scheduled as being 'of national concern' and subject to export control.[23] These amendments were retained and extended in the 1939 redraft.

During the inter-war period, the promotion of free trade and equal access to cultural resources was most pronounced in the international regulation of archaeological sites, which reinforced the principles set down by the mandate system.[24] The tension created between the solidarity for domestic laws for the protection of national cultural heritage and the promotion of international exchange (and by extension the international art trade) was encapsulated in the complete overhaul of Article 1 in the final OIM draft in 1939. It quarantined its application to scheduled objects only. Iraq had unsuccessfully requested a return to the original wording where the convention's operation was triggered by the lack of export authorization.[25] It observed that: '[W]here illegal and secret excavations . . . [are] extremely difficult to control. . . . It follows that stolen objects cannot be always known and therefore not registered by the authority concerned.'[26] In response, it was argued that the inclusion of objects removed from clandestine excavations would 'compromise' the proposed convention because such objects, by their nature, could not satisfy the requirement of 'prior possession . . . the indispensable condition of the [restitution] claim'.[27]

The recommendations contained in the Charter adopted at the International Conference on Excavations (1937 Cairo Charter),[28] complemented the obligations of the 1936 OIM draft by emphasizing accessibility to the cultural 'resources' from archaeological sites. The primary recommendation required museums to 'satisfy themselves that nothing in its intrinsic character or the circumstances in which it is offered . . . warrants the belief that the object is

20 1936 OIM Draft Art. 1(1).
21 Second preambular recital and Art.1(1), 1936 OIM draft.
22 1936 OIM Draft Art. 1(2).
23 1936 OIM Draft Art. 17.
24 See A.F. Vrdoljak, *International Law, Museums and the Return of Cultural Objects*, Cambridge: Cambridge University Press, 2006, pp. 85–87.
25 Iraqi delegation to Secretary General, League of Nations, 21 May 1936, OIM.IV.27.II, pp. 162–163.
26 Ibid.
27 ICIC, Report of the Committee on the Work of its Nineteenth Plenary Session, 9 August 1937, C.327.M.220.1937.XII, p. 69.
28 See E. Foundoukidis and OIM, *Final Act of the International Conference on Excavations*, Paris: OIM, 1937; and *Mouseïon*, 1937, vol. 39–40, pp. 251–255.

the result of clandestine excavation or any other illicit operation'.[29] If suspicion was aroused, they were to notify the relevant authorities. The government and museum should then assist with the repatriation of the object to its country of origin.[30] However, to curb illicit trade and enable museums to fulfil their 'scientific and education mission', states were encouraged to provide legal means of acquiring archaeological materials, with the OIM to facilitate the resolution of any dispute between the country of origin and a collecting institution.[31] Euripide Foundoukidis, head of the OIM, noted that these recommendations were significant because 'they complete[d] legal clauses that figure[d] in the [1936 OIM draft]'.[32] The commentary on the Cairo Charter made it clear that the OIM draft which required cooperation for the return of scheduled cultural objects could not be readily extended to archaeological material.[33] Instead, a 'moral agreement among museums' was the preferred route because 'these institutions display an ever more enlightened spirit of international solidarity and understanding'.[34]

During the same period, the OIM was also working on international initiatives that augmented the international exchange of cultural objects through international exhibitions and the circulation of casts. The League of Nations adopted the Recommendation regarding International Art Exhibitions which made the OIM the central repository of information concerning all international exhibitions.[35] The aim was overtly educative as reflected in its opening words: '[I]international art exhibitions are calculated to promote intellectual *rapprochement*, the education of public taste, and the progress of historical and artistic research.'[36] While almost exclusively concerned with logistical aspects, it did request that governments take all steps necessary to facilitate the importation and return of loaned objects.[37] Also, to better encourage the release on loan, collecting institutions approached to loan objects for an international exhibition could request the loan of 'an equivalent work of art' during the period of the exhibition or another form of compensation.[38]

The draft International Convention for the Protection of National Collections of Art and History (1939 OIM draft) prepared in the aftermath

---

29   Recommendation 15, Section III, Cairo Charter.
30   Recommendations 16 and 17, Section III, Cairo Charter.
31   Section II, Recommendation 13(b) and (c); and Section III, Recommendations 18, 21 and 22, Cairo Charter. It also recommends the conclusion of bilateral agreements under the auspices of the OIM: Recommendation 27.
32   The Cairo Charter in Section II covering the system of excavation and international collaboration recalled the 1932 Resolution.
33   Foundoukidis and OIM, op. cit., p. 5.
34   Foundoukidis and OIM, op. cit., p. 3; and Preamble, Section III, Cairo Charter.
35   Recommendation regarding International Art Exhibitions, adopted at the seventeenth session of the Assembly of the League of Nations, 23 November 1936, CL.207, 1936, XII.
36   Ibid.
37   Para. 14, 1936 Recommendation.
38   Para. 7, 1936 Recommendation.

of the Cairo Conference and on eve of the Second World War, saw a further tightening of its application.[39] The expansive operation of earlier drafts was wound back because of the lack of uniformity in national legislative schemes or agreement on the notion of public ownership, and a desire not to impede unduly the international art trade.[40] Charles de Visscher explained that 'restitution form[ed] the essential and also the most solid basis of the proposed convention'.[41] The types of objects covered by the convention had not been altered from the 1936 draft. Yet, how they attracted its operation was severely circumscribed. Objects in public (and private) collections had to be scheduled by State Parties prior to their illicit removal.[42] Therefore, the key to restitution was that the claimed object was 'known to that administration and inventorie[d] by' the claimant states.[43] Also, the drafting committee accepted that inalienability was not recognized by all states and the convention as drafted would severely undermine the international art trade.[44] Consequently, the draft required that the act triggering its operation be contrary to property rights 'under the criminal law of the claimant State'.[45]

The 1939 OIM draft also bolstered the OIM initiative to promote the universal appreciation of all cultures through the regulation of export for exhibition, loan, study or conservation.[46] The provision gave a 'legitimate owner' whose objects were abroad for an exhibition or repair, the same rights he or she would have in their own state.[47] This was augmented by the 1939 OIM draft explicitly providing that it would not apply retroactively.[48] Finally, it reaffirmed the precedence of 'diplomatic channels' as the first avenue for resolving disputes under the instrument.[49] This position departed from the judicial avenues incorporated in the 1933 OIM draft but accorded with the spirit of the 1937 Cairo Charter.[50]

The OIM draft was never adopted by the League of Nations. De Visscher when reflecting on these inter-war efforts observed that they endeavoured to

---

39 De Visscher, op. cit., pp. 869–871; and C. de Visscher, 'Le projet définitif établi en 1939 en vue de la conférence diplomatique', *Art et archeologie: recueil de législation comparée et de droit international*, 1939, vol. 1 78–79.
40 Visscher, 'Le projet définitif établi en 1939 en vue de la conférence diplomatique', op. cit., 89, 91.
41 C.327.M.220.1937.XII, 69.
42 1939 OIM Draft, Art. 1(3).
43 Ibid.
44 See De Visscher, op. cit., 'Le projet définitif établi en 1939 en vue de la conférence diplomatique', 89.
45 1939 OIM Draft Art. 2(1).
46 1939 OIM Draft Art. 2(2).
47 Ibid.
48 E. Foundoukidis to U. Aloisi, 15 March 1935, OIM.IV.27.II, pp. 104–105 referring to Art. 2(3) of the 1939 OIM Draft.
49 1939 OIM Draft Art. 4(1).
50 De Visscher, op. cit., 'Le projet définitif établi en 1939 en vue de la conférence diplomatique', 99.

marry two 'worthy' interests: the drive of a country to preserve cultural objects which represent its national heritage which may result in a 'chauvinistic idea' of export prohibitions which impeded the 'more lofty point of view' of the 'eminently universal educational role of the work of art throughout the world'.[51] It would take more than three decades for a multilateral agreement on the regulation of the trade in cultural objects to be realized in the post-war period – and the balancing it achieves was appreciably different from that of these inter-war OIM initiatives.

Current instruments and UNESCO

The United Nations Educational, Scientific and Cultural Organization (UNESCO) is the specialist United Nations' agency in the field of culture and succeeded the functions of the League of Nations' ICIC. It has a decidedly more global membership than its predecessor.[52] UNESCO's Constitution provides that it recommend the adoption of international agreements to 'promote the free flow of ideas by word and image' and 'maintain, increase and diffuse knowledge' including by facilitating the conservation and protection of the 'world's inheritance of books, works of art and monuments of history and science' and 'the exchange of publications, objects of artistic and scientific interests and other materials of information'.[53] By 1976, Deputy Assistant Director-General, Gérard Bolla noted that UNESCO had already adopted three conventions and six recommendations on culture which had the dual aims of 'identifying, protecting and presenting cultural property of Member States and, at the same time, of facilitating the development of cultural exchange, including the exchange of cultural objects'.[54] However, a clear distinction can be discerned between how the balance between these aims was achieved prior to the Second World War and following the war. The influx of new Member States into UNESCO and other intergovernmental organizations made a significant impact on propelling this shift.

The shift is encapsulated by the fact that one of UNESCO's first instruments covered the regulation of archaeological sites and objects. The UNESCO General Conference adopted the Recommendation on International Principles applicable to Archaeological Excavations in 1956 (1956 Recommendation).[55]

---

51 De Visscher, op. cit., 'International Protection of Works of Art and Historic Monuments' 859.

52 Agreement between UNESCO and the International Institute of Intellectual Co-operation dated 19 December 1946.

53 Arts 1 and 2, Constitution of UNESCO, 16 November 1945, in force 4 November 1946, 4 UNTS 275.

54 Draft Recommendation on the International Exchange of Cultural Property, 6 August 1976, 19C/25, Annex II, Report of the Special Committee of Governmental Experts, 2.

55 Resolution 4.32(c), of the ninth session of the General Conference of UNESCO, 5 December 1956.

The Recommendation clearly borrowed heavily from the Cairo Charter but its points of difference marked the changes which would permeate subsequent post-war initiatives in this field. It reaffirms that museums should ensure that archaeological objects which they may acquire are not the result of any unauthorized excavations, theft or otherwise illicitly removed from the country of origin. Further, if they are suspicious that the relevant authorities be notified and details of acquisitions be published.[56] It replicates the obligation to facilitate any requests for assistance in respect of restitution of objects clandestinely excavated, stolen or exported illicitly.[57] However, like the Cairo Charter, the Recommendation also urges '[e]ach Member State [to] consider ceding to, exchanging with, or depositing in foreign museums objects which are not required in the[ir] national museums'.[58] Furthermore, the fostering of bilateral agreements among Member States now extends to all aspects of the instrument.

These obligations are reiterated in the Recommendation on the Means of Prohibiting and Preventing the Illicit Export, Import, and Transfer of Ownership of Cultural Property adopted in 1964.[59] This Recommendation also urged the adoption of a multilateral instrument to curb the illicit trade in cultural objects but noted the obstacles to its realization, thereby counselling that bilateral and regional multilateral agreements be adopted in the interim.[60] Indeed, the United States in its reply to the draft Recommendation reaffirmed its continued objection to a multilateral agreement and annexed the views of the Association of Art Museum Directors (AAMD) of the United States and Canada in support.[61] The AAMD noted that North American and European museums had, with the 'aid of knowledgeable and enterprising dealers', displayed works which represented the 'cultural heritage of mankind'. It stated that while its members 'rigorously avoided the purchase of publicized stolen art objects' it was rare that the 'precise provenance of origin of an item' was known. It concluded that museums 'deserved encouragement . . . and not the threat of being impeded in this dedicated purpose'.[62] By contrast, in a 1962 Study, the International Council of Museums (ICOM) suggested that there was 'no contradiction' between the 'legitimate desire of States to preserve their national cultural heritage in their own territory' and the 'idea of a universal cultural heritage or a steady increase in international exchange in the cultural

---

56 Para. 30, 1956 Recommendation.
57 Para. 31, 1956 Recommendation.
58 Para. 23(e), 1956 Recommendation.
59 Paras 13 and 16, Recommendation on the Means of Prohibiting and Preventing the Illicit Export, Import and Transfer of Ownership of Cultural Property, adopted by the General Conference of UNESCO on 19 November 1964.
60 Means of Prohibiting the Illicit Export, Import and Sale of Cultural Property, Preliminary Report, 15 July 1963, UNESCO/CUA/123, 10.
61 Ibid.
62 Ibid.

field'.[63] However, it was not optimistic that a dedicated convention would be realized in the light of the failure of the OIM drafts, the poor take-up of the 1935 PAU treaty,[64] and the 1954 Hague Protocol,[65] and the diversity of national legal schemes covering movable heritage.[66]

Nonetheless, the momentum was for a multilateral agreement.[67] The campaign for an international instrument enabling the restitution of cultural objects to their country of origin, suspended because of the war, was put back on the international agenda by Mexico and Peru in 1960. This was the same year that the Declaration on the Granting of Independence to Colonial Countries and Peoples was adopted by the UN General Assembly, which in coming decades would significantly change the constituency of UNESCO and other intergovernmental organizations.[68] Many of these newly independent states were establishing a national collection and becoming acutely aware of cultural objects removed during colonization and the losses that continued following independence. The adoption of multilateral agreements for the regulation of the international trade in cultural materials and international exchange became integral to redressing this phenomenon. The 1964 Recommendation, the Convention on the Means of Prohibiting and Preventing the Illicit Import, Export and Transfer of Ownership of Cultural Property (1970 UNESCO Convention),[69] and UNIDROIT Convention on Stolen or Illegally Exported Cultural Objects (1995 UNIDROIT Convention),[70] reiterate several concerns that had coloured the inter-war OIM drafts. However, how they are articulated is decidedly different from their predecessors.

As the title of the 1970 Convention suggests, it is designed to facilitate the effectiveness of domestic laws concerning the transfer of cultural objects including export controls. It recognizes the 'indefeasible' right of each State Party to nominate certain cultural property as 'inalienable', and to legislate to prohibit exportation.[71] It also incorporates Iraq's 1936 proposal that cultural objects removed without an export certificate be defined as illicit.[72] Nonetheless, its transposition into the domestic law of States Parties, particularly

63   Technical and Legal Aspects of the Preparation of International Regulations to Prevent the Illicit Export, Import and Sale of Cultural Property, R. Brichet and ICOM, 14 April 1962, UNESCO/CUA/115.
64   Pan American Union (PAU) Treaty on the Protection of Movable Property of Historic Value, 15 April 1935, in force 17 July 1936, OASTS No. 28.
65   Protocol for the Protection of Cultural Property in the Event of Armed Conflict, 14 May 1954, in force 7 August 1956, 249 UNTS 358.
66   CUA/115, 10–11.
67   See UNESCO, Report on the Possibility of Drafting a Convention concerning the Illicit Export, Import and Transfer of Ownership of Cultural Property, 22 April 1968, 78EX/9, p. 3.
68   GA Res.1514(XV), 14 December 1960.
69   14 November 1970, in force 24 April 1972, 823 UNTS 231.
70   24 June 1995, in force 1 July 1998, (1995) 34 ILM 1322.
71   1970 Convention, Art. 13(d).
72   1970 Convention, Arts 3 and 6(b).

the emphasis on bilateral agreements by countries like the United States and Switzerland, has meant that it is far from the multilateral agreement that had been envisioned by its proponents.[73] The recognition of the export control laws of States Parties is even more circumscribed by the 1995 UNIDROIT Convention which articulates the applicable private international rules. The 1995 Convention contains a clear distinction between the legal framework governing the 'restitution' of cultural objects described as 'stolen' (Ch. II) and the 'return' of cultural material which had been 'illicitly exported' (Ch. III). Like the OIM drafts before it, the 1995 Convention requires a State Party to show that an illicitly exported object is of 'significant cultural importance' to it.[74]

An aspect of the Cairo Charter which was incorporated into the 1970 UNESCO Convention is the regulation of the conduct of individuals and organizations involved in the trade in cultural objects. The Convention calls on States Parties to establish 'rules in conformity with the ethical principles set forth in this Convention' for curators, collectors, art and antiquities dealers and to ensure that they adhere to them.[75] This has been augmented by the ICOM Code of Ethics of Acquisition which was originally adopted by its General Assembly in the same year as the UNESCO Convention.[76] Also, UNESCO finalized an International Code of Ethics for Dealers in Cultural Property in 1999 which recognizes the role 'the trade has traditionally played in the dissemination of culture' to museums and private collectors and the need to eliminate activities from the profession which foster traffic of 'stolen, illegally alienated, clandestinely excavated and illegally exported' objects.[77] Dealers who have 'reasonable cause' to believe that an object is illicitly removed or exported should not exhibit, appraise or retain it and must facilitate its return.[78] These provisions complement the 1995 UNIDROIT Convention. Like the OIM drafts and 1970 Convention before it (Art. 7 (b)(ii)), the 1970 Convention provides that the bona fide purchaser be compensated when a stolen item is returned.[79] However, this is subject to the possessor having acted with due diligence in the circumstances.[80]

---

73 See Swiss Federal Act on the International Transfer of Cultural Property of 20 June 2003; and US Convention on Cultural Property Implementation Act, 19 USC 2601.

74 1995 UNIDROIT Convention Art. 5(3).

75 1970 UNESCO Convention, Arts 5(f), 7(a) and 10. See also para. 8, 1964 Recommendation. While some States Parties has enacted laws regulating the activities of museum officials and dealers (e.g. France's Code of Ethics of Auction Houses of 2012) most have a voluntary professional code (e.g. Egypt's Antiquities Protection Law (No. 117 of 1983, amended 2010).

76 ICOM Code of Ethics of Acquisition adopted by the General Assembly in 1970, Code of Professional Ethics for Museums adopted 1984 and revised in 2006.

77 International Code of Ethics for Dealers in Cultural Property, adopted by the 30th session of the General Conference of UNESCO, November 1999.

78 Ibid. Arts 3, 4 and 5.

79 1995 Convention, Art. 4(1).

80 1995 UNIDROIT Convention, Art. 4(4) lists the following circumstances including 'the character of the parties, the price paid, whether the possessor consulted any reasonably

Countries that host large art markets continued to push for a distinction to be made between cultural objects located in museums and those removed from archaeological sites.[81] However, while these items are treated differently by the 1970 UNESCO Convention,[82] the treaty explicitly covers archaeological material.[83] This is in stark contrast to the inter-war OIM drafts. This fundamental shift is explained by changing circumstances in the intervening period including: the proliferation of newly independent states which irreversibly altered the dynamics within intergovernmental organizations like UNESCO, the growing public recognition in countries like the United States of the impact of illicit antiquities trade on the movable heritage of neighbouring countries, and the finalization of regional multilateral agreements covering archaeological excavations.[84] Likewise, the 1995 UNIDROIT Convention encompasses items removed from unlawful excavations within provisions covering stolen cultural objects. However, the time limit for claims is different from claims for objects from identified monuments, archaeological sites or public collections.[85]

These developments exemplify the recalibration, since the Second World War, of the balance between the aims of facilitating national laws concerning movable heritage, including export controls, and the promotion of the international exchange of cultural objects to foster appreciation of other cultures. International cooperation is defined by efforts to ensure that national laws regulating the transfer and export of cultural objects on a state's territory are rendered more effective.[86] The 1964 Recommendation calls on Members States, museums and all relevant institutions to collaborate to facilitate the return of cultural objects which have been illicitly exported.[87] These sentiments are replicated by the 1970 UNESCO Convention whose explicit purpose acknowledges that illicit transfer, export and import of cultural objects is 'one of the main causes of the impoverishment of the cultural heritage of countries of origin' and 'international cooperation constitutes one of the most efficient means of protecting each country's cultural property against [such] dangers'.[88] Likewise, the 1995 UNIDROIT Convention which is designed to facilitate the restitution of stolen or return of illicitly export objects to their countries of origin, in its preamble registers that States Parties are 'deeply concerned

---

accessible register of stolen cultural objects, and any other relevant information and documentation which it could reasonably have obtained, and whether the possessor consulted accessible agencies or took any other step that a reasonable person would have taken in the circumstances'.

81   16C/17, Annex II, para. 19.
82   1970 UNESCO Convention, Arts 7(b) and 9.
83   1970 UNESCO Convention, Art. 1(c).
84   See 1956 Recommendation.
85   UNIDROIT Convention, Art. 3.
86   Third and fourth preambular recitals, 1964 Recommendation.
87   Para. 16, 1964 Recommendation.
88   1970 UNESCO Convention, Art. 2.

by the illicit trade in cultural objects and the irreparable damage frequently caused by it'.[89]

However, UNESCO Member States had also adopted the Declaration of the Principles of International Cultural Cooperation in 1966 (1966 Declaration) which provides a cosmopolitan outlook in this field, reminiscent of the sentiments expressed in the inter-war period.[90] It recognizes that 'each culture has a dignity and value which must be respected and preserved' and that 'in the reciprocal influences they exert on one another, all cultures form part of the common heritage belonging to all mankind'.[91] Its preamble notes that 'the wide diffusion of culture . . . constitute[s] a sacred duty which all nations must fulfil in a spirit of mutual assistance and concern'. The 1970 UNESCO Convention in its opening preambular recitals references this Declaration and reaffirms that the 'interchange of cultural property among nations . . . enriches the cultural life of all peoples and inspires mutual respect and appreciation among nations'.[92]

While the *travaux* of the 1970 Convention suggested guarantees for the return of cultural property that had been loaned be included in the treaty, in order to facilitate international exchanges, no such provision appears in the final text.[93] By contrast, other contemporaneous multilateral initiatives do promote international exchange of cultural objects. The 1964 Recommendation provides that, to encourage 'legitimate exchange of cultural property', Member States should make items available for sale or exchange of the same type which have been prohibited from transfer or export.[94] The 1995 UNIDROIT Convention includes a provision which encourages the loan (and return) of cultural objects for international exhibitions.[95] The issue is treated at length in the Recommendation on the International Exchange of Cultural Property adopted in 1976,[96] which had its genesis in the aftermath of the 1970 UNESCO Convention. This synergy is captured in its preamble which observes that: '[T]he circulation of cultural property, when regulated by legal, scientific and technical conditions calculated to prevent illicit trading in and damage to such property, is a powerful means of promoting mutual understanding and appreciation among nations.'[97] And like the 1970 UNESCO Convention, it too opens with words which reflect the ethos of the 1966 Declaration on International Cultural Cooperation. The 1976 Recommendation signals that the 'systematic policy of exchanges among cultural institutions, by which each

---

89 Second preambular recital, 1995 UNIDROIT Convention.
90 Adopted by the General Conference of UNESCO on 4 November 1966.
91 1966 Declaration, Art. 2.
92 First and second preambular recitals, 1970 UNESCO Convention.
93 78EX/9 Annex, 11.
94 Para. 9, 1964 Recommendation.
95 1995 UNIDROIT Convention, Art. 5(2).
96 Recommendation concerning the International Exchange of Cultural Property adopted by the General Conference of UNESCO on 26 November 1976.
97 Third preambular recital, 1976 Recommendation.

would part with its surplus items in return for objects that it lacked . . . would also lead to a better use of the international community's cultural heritage which is the sum of all the national heritages'.[98]

Yet, like the 1970 UNESCO Convention and 1956 Recommendation, the 1976 Recommendation is distinguishable from its inter-war counterpart, the 1936 Recommendation regarding International Art Exhibitions. Whereas the latter was complemented by the promotion of the circulation of casts and reproductions to facilitate the acquisition of the knowledge and appreciation of other cultures, the late twentieth century instruments are driven by an objective closely aligned with the push to curb the illicit trade in cultural objects, namely, restitution. The *travaux* of the 1970 Convention noted that while the lawful transfer and exchange of cultural objects would not be forbidden, it did recognize the need to control its export and sale 'in the interests of the great cause of international understanding do not lead to the disappearance of the cultural heritage of certain States'.[99] Indeed, in the post-1945 period, international exchange has been advocated by the same states that championed a multilateral agreement on illicit export, import and transfer of cultural objects.[100] As the 1976 Recommendation notes the circulation of cultural property is 'still largely dependent on the activities of self-seeking parties', which leads to 'speculation which causes the price of such property to rise, making it inaccessible to poorer countries and institutions while at the same time encouraging the spread of illicit trading'.[101] Accordingly, there was a need to foster a licit trade in cultural material to counterbalance the illicit trade.[102] While this necessarily entailed advocacy for the relaxation of domestic laws, the UNESCO Secretariat rejected calls by some Member States to remove a reaffirmation of obligations curbing illicit traffic.[103] This reaffirmation is contained in the final text of the Recommendation (para. 15) and reiterated by the Universal Declaration on Cultural Diversity adopted by UNESCO in 2001.[104]

The international exchange of original objects between museums and the reconstitution of dismembered cultural objects was viewed as vital to the efforts of newly independent states to build up their own museum collections.[105] In the late twentieth century, international exchange did not mean

98   Eighth preambular recital, 1976 Recommendation.
99   Preliminary Report, 8 August 1969, SHC/MD/3, 3.
100 Expert Meeting on the Exchange between Museums of Original Objects, Measures to Facilitate International Exchange of Cultural Property, ICOM, 31 March 1966, UNESCO/IEMO/3, 1, 2 and 7.
101 Third preambular recital, 1976 Recommendation.
102 Ibid.
103 SHC/MD/32, 23. See Japan (para. 172) and Singapore (para. 172).
104 Universal Declaration on Cultural Diversity, Main Lines of an Action Plan for the Implementation, para. 13, adopted by the General Conference of UNESCO on 2 November 2001.
105 Expert Meeting on the Exchange of Original Objects between Museums and the Reconstitution of Dismembered Works of Art, Final Report, 26 August 1966, UNESCO/SHC/1.

short-term loans for the purpose of an international exhibition. Instead, the 1976 Recommendation defines it as 'any transfer of ownership, use or custody of cultural property between States or cultural institutions in different countries, whether in the form of a loan, deposit, sale or donation of such property'.[106] The *travaux* of the 1976 Recommendation makes plain that such international exchanges are rare and little heralded. Indeed, the Recommendation calls on Member States and their institutions to publicly circulate information about successful international exchanges to encourage future agreements.[107] Why this resistance and near silence? Countries calling for international exchanges as long-term loans or reconstitution of cultural objects are often motivated by the same objectives which drive restitution claims. Holding states and institutions resist such requests for similar reasons. Indeed, long-term loans are often the result of restitution claims. This is reflected in the mandate of the UNESCO Intergovernmental Committee for Promoting Return or Restitution which encourages international exchanges based on the 1976 Recommendation.[108]

Regional and national responses

Regulation of the transfer, export and import of cultural objects through mutual assistance between states has been addressed by almost every region. The relative strength of these initiatives is mirrored by the existence of intergovernmental organizations and the uptake of international agreements like the 1970 UNESCO and 1995 UNIDROIT Conventions by states within the region. Also, where a regional organization has adopted a specialist instrument in the field, Member States' domestic laws are more likely to be harmonized with it, rather than those at the international level.

The Organization of American States' Convention on the Protection of the Archaeological, Historical and Artistic Heritage of the American Nations[109] defines its dual purpose as the prevention of illicit export and import of cultural property and 'to promote cooperation among American states for mutual awareness and appreciation of their cultural property'.[110] Further, it also provides that objects on loan 'to museums, exhibitions, or scientific institutions that are outside the state to whose cultural heritage they belong shall not be subject to seizure as a result of public or private lawsuits'.[111]

---

106 Para. 1, 1976 Recommendation.

107 Parts II and III, 1976 Recommendation.

108 See Art. 4(7), Statute of the Intergovernmental Committee for Promoting the Return of Cultural Property to its Countries of Origin or its Restitution in case of Illicit Appropriation, adopted by the General Conference of UNESCO on 28 November 1978.

109 Resolution AG/Res.210(VI-O/76), OASTS No. 47.

110 Organization of American States' Convention on the Protection of the Archaeological, Historical and Artistic Heritage of the American Nations, Art. 1.

111 Ibid. Art. 16.

The Council of Europe and European Union have adopted their own specialist instruments for the protection and return of movable cultural heritage.[112] Following a review of its current legislative scheme covering mutual assistance in respect of export controls and restitution, the European Union established a panel of experts to prepare a toolkit covering good practice guidelines and codes of ethics on due diligence to tackle illicit trafficking in cultural objects, another group to consider means of simplifying the loan of artworks within Europe, and a study on the system of insuring, indemnifying and sharing liability for artworks.[113] Various reports have made recommendations concerning measures covering immunity from seizure or suit.[114]

The African Union's Charter for African Cultural Renaissance of 2006 makes explicit reference to the 1970 (and 1954 Hague) Convention in its preamble.[115] The Charter calls on African states to 'take steps to put an end to the pillage and illicit traffic of African cultural property to ensure that such cultural property is returned to the countries of origin'.[116] While the Charter does reference mutual cooperation between African states in the cultural field and the 1966 UNESCO Declaration, it does not list protection and return of cultural objects in the enumerated list. Further, it requires States Parties to organize art exhibitions and establish cultural exchange programmes, but makes no mention of immunity from seizure or suit.[117]

There is no intergovernmental organization which covers Asia as a whole and this explains the lack of related action in this field. However, under the

112 See Council of Europe: Convention on Offences relating to Cultural Property, ETS No. 119 adopted in 23 June 1985, not entered into force; and European Convention on the Protection of the Archaeological Heritage (revised) ETS No. 121, adopted 16 January 1992, entered into force 25 May 1995. For the European Union: Reg. no. 3911/92 of 9 December 1992 on the export of cultural goods, OJ L 395, 31.12.1992, p. 1; Reg. no. 116/2009 of 18 December 2008 on the export of cultural goods (codified version), OJ L 39, 10.2.2009, p. 1; and Directive 93/7/EEC of 15 March 1993 on the return of cultural objects unlawfully removed from the territory of a Member State, OJ L 74, 27.3.1993, p. 74 (as amended).

113 See CECOJI-CNRS-UMR 6224, Study on Preventing and Fighting Illicit Trafficking in Cultural Goods in the European Union, Final Report October 2011; Conclusions of the Council of European Union on preventing and combating crime against cultural goods, 13 and 14 December 2011; Conclusions of the Council and of the Representatives of the Governments of the Member States meeting within the Council, on the Work Plan for Culture 2011–2014 OJ C 325, 2.12.2010, p. 1. See Council Resolution of 24 November 2003, on cooperation between cultural institutions in the field of museums, OJ C 295, 5.12.2003, p. 1.

114 See EU, OMC Expert Working Group on the Mobility of Collections, Final Report and Recommendations to the Cultural Affairs Committee on Improving the means of increasing the Mobility of Collections, June 2010, pp. 11 and 21; Action Plan for the EU Promotion of Museum Collections' Mobility and Loan Standards, Helsinki: Finnish Ministry of Education, 2006, p. 12; Lending to Europe: Recommendations on Collection Mobility for European Museums, Rotterdam: Netherlands Ministry of Education, Culture and Science, 2005, para. 3.3.

115 Adopted by the Heads of State and Government of the African Union on 24 January 2006.

116 Charter for African Cultural Renaissance, Arts 26 and 27.

117 Ibid., Art. 31.

Declaration on Cultural Heritage of 2000,[118] the Association of South East Asian Nations (ASEAN) Member States agreed to facilitate regional and national efforts for the protection and restitution of movable heritage (paras 2 and 10) and 'mutual understanding of the cultures and values systems among the peoples of ASEAN' (Preamble). It too does not explicitly reference international exchange or granting immunity to facilitate temporary loans for exhibitions or study.

In every region, domestic legal regimes for the export of cultural objects provide for export authorization for the purposes of temporary loans for exhibitions, study or restoration.[119] Indeed, the relevant provision in the 1995 UNIDROIT Convention reinforces these efforts. Article 5(2) provides that an object temporarily exported for such purposes pursuant to domestic legislation and not returned according to the terms of the permit shall be deemed to be illegally exported.

However, states often do not have import control regimes and if they do they rarely cover objects temporarily imported for the purposes of an exhibition.[120] Australia had raised the failure of the draft 1976 Recommendation to properly address the issue of cultural objects acquired in the past but which could not be returned to the country of origin 'for loan, restoration, study of authentication etc., without risk of being seized because subsequent laws restrict the movement of that class of objects'.[121] It should be noted that some domestic laws do provide for the temporary import of such objects to encourage exhibitions of cultural materials which may not otherwise be accessible to their people.[122]

The spectre of possible restitution claims for cultural objects temporarily exported for an exhibition, study or restoration stymieing international exchange has led to demands from some lending states for stronger domestic

---

118 Adopted by the Foreign Ministers of the ASEAN Member Countries on 25 July 2000.
119 See for example France: Art. L111–7, National Heritage Code (Ordinance No. 2004–178); Switzerland: Art. 5(2), Federal Act on the International Transfer of Cultural Property (2003); Russian Federation: Art. 9, Law No. 4804–1 of 1993 on Export and Import of Objects of Cultural Value; Peru: Arts 36–39, Law No. 28296 of 2004 General Law of the Cultural Heritage of the Nation; Ecuador: Art. 40, Law on Cultural Patrimony No. 3501 of 1979 (as amended); Cambodia: Art. 57, Law on the Protection of Cultural Heritage of 1996 (in force 2006) NS/RKM/0196/26; China: Art. 60, Law of the People's Republic of China on Protection of Cultural Relics (Order No. 76 of 2002 and revised 2007); Mali: Art. 18, Decree No. 299 of 1986 regulating the Prospecting, Marketing and Export of Cultural Property; Egypt: Art. 10, Antiquities Protection Law (No. 117 of 1983, as amended); and Australia: s.10A, Protection of Movable Cultural Heritage Act 1986 (as amended).
120 See for example Russian Federation: Art. 9, Law No. 4804–1 of 1993.
121 International Instrument on the Exchange of Original Objects and Specimens among Institutions of Different Countries, 5 March 1976, Doc.SHC/MD/32, 4.
122 See for example, Australia: s. 12, Protection of Movable Cultural Heritage Act 1986 (Cth); Ecuador: Art. 57, General Regulation to the Law on Cultural Patrimony Decree No. 2733 of 1984, Art. 57; and South Africa: Art. 32(32), National Heritage Resources Act (No. 25 of 1999).

immunity from seizure and suit protections to be enacted by a borrowing state. Several countries have recently passed laws to make immune objects which are temporarily imported for an exhibition.[123] The potential for these laws to circumvent existing international obligations including those related to curbing the illicit trade in cultural objects is acknowledged.[124] Accordingly, guarantees of immunity under domestic law are often only provided after due diligence concerning title is demonstrated.[125] Restitution claims for objects on temporary loan have raised public awareness of contestations over title, provenance, and the broader historical and socio-economic context concerning the transfer and exchange of cultural materials, which should not be silenced.

Conclusion

The importance of the international exchange of cultural objects for fostering mutual understanding among people has been recognized since the earliest initiatives for the protection of movable heritage at the international level nearly a century ago. It remains a priority for the international community to this day. However, how it relates to efforts to regulate the transfer and restitution of cultural property has changed over time. As the 1966 Declaration makes clear, the diffusion of culture and its appreciation by other peoples can only occur with an acceptance that each culture forms part of the common heritage of all humanity and must be respected and preserved. For this reason, there has been an increasing acceptance of the importance of mutual assistance among states (and non-state actors) in curbing the illicit trade in cultural objects and stemming the losses it entails. The pursuit of this objective has not dampened with current efforts at the domestic and regional levels to facilitate international exhibitions. Indeed, it is telling that laws for immunity from seizure or suit for objects on temporary loan often require that due diligence has been undertaken in respect of title prior to the provision of such guarantees, in recognition of existing international rights and obligations concerning cultural heritage and human rights law. This present-day balance between encouraging international exchange and ensuring effective controls on the trade in cultural objects reflects an acceptance that these twin aims are not mutually exclusively – but can and must be mutually reinforcing.

123 See for example, Australia: Protection of Objects on Loan Act 2013 (Cth); UK: s.134, Tribunals, Courts, and Enforcement Act 2007 (UK) and Protection of Cultural Objects on Loan (Publication and Provision of Information Regulations; and US: Exemption from Judicial Seizure of Cultural Objects imported for Temporary Exhibition and Display, Pub. L. No. 89–259 (S.2273) 79 Stat.985 (1965), 22 USC 2459.

124 See Australian Government, Immunity from Seizure for Cultural Objects on Loan, Discussion Paper, Canberra: AGPO, 2011, p. 6; and OMC Expert Working Group, op. cit., p. 21.

125 Ibid. See for example, Swiss Federal Act on the International Transfer of Cultural Property of 2003, Arts 11 and 12; UK Protection of Cultural Objects on Loan (Publication and Provision of Information) Regulations 2008.

Bibliography

Anon. 'International Cooperation in the Sphere of Art', *League of Nations Official Journal*, vol. 13, 1932, 1776.

Anon. 'League of Nations' Intellectual Co-operation Organisation', *Information Bulletin*, Oct–Nov 1932, 165.

Australian Government, Immunity from Seizure for Cultural Objects on Loan, Discussion Paper, Canberra: AGPO, 2011.

Brichet, R. and ICOM, Technical and Legal Aspects of the Preparation of International Regulations to Prevent the Illicit Export, Import and Sale of Cultural Property, 14 April 1962, UNESCO/CUA/115.

CECOJI-CNRS-UMR 6224, Study on Preventing and Fighting Illicit Trafficking in Cultural Goods in the European Union, Final Report, October 2011.

Destrée, J., League of Nations, Intellectual Co-operation Organisation, International Museums Office, Annual Report of the President of the Directors' Committee of the International Museums Office, Note by the Secretary, of the Intellectual Co-operation Organisation, 1 July 1932, ICIC/273, 7.

De Visscher, C., 'Le projet définitif établi en 1939 en vue de la conférence diplomatique', *Art et archeologie: recueil de législation comparée et de droit international*, vol. 1, 1939, 78.

De Visscher, C., 'International Protection of Works of Art and Historic Monuments', *Documents and State Papers*, 1949, 857.

European Union, OMC Expert Working Group on the Mobility of Collections, Final Report and Recommendations to the Cultural Affairs Committee on Improving the means of increasing the Mobility of Collections, June 2010.

Finnish Ministry of Education, Action Plan for the EU Promotion of Museum Collections' Mobility and Loan Standards, Helsinki: Finnish Ministry of Education, 2006.

Foundoukidis, E. and OIM, Final Act of the International Conference on Excavations, Paris: OIM, 1937.

ICOM, Expert Meeting on the Exchange between Museums of Original Objects, Measures to Facilitate International Exchange of Cultural Property, prepared by ICOM, 31 March 1966, UNESCO/IEMO/3.

Netherlands Ministry of Education, Culture and Science, Lending to Europe: Recommendations on Collection Mobility for European Museums, Rotterdam: Netherlands Ministry of Education, Culture and Science, 2005.

Northedge, F.S., *International Intellectual Co-operation with the League of Nations: Its Conceptual Basis and Lessons for the Present*, PhD Thesis, University of London, 1953.

UNESCO, Means of Prohibiting the Illicit Export, Import and Sale of Cultural Property, Preliminary Report, 15 July 1963, UNESCO/CUA/123.

UNESCO, Expert Meeting on the Exchange of Original Objects between Museums and theReconstitution of Dismembered Works of Art, Final Report, 26 August 1966, UNESCO/SHC/1.

UNESCO, Report on the Possibility of Drafting a Convention concerning the Illicit Export, Import and Transfer of Ownership of Cultural Property, 22 April 1968, 78EX/9.

UNESCO, International Instrument on the Exchange of Original Objects and Specimens among Institutions of Different Countries, 5 March 1976, Doc.SHC/MD/32.

Vrdoljak, A.F., *International Law, Museums and the Return of Cultural Objects*, Cambridge: Cambridge University Press, 2006.

Part III

Culture and economic interests in international intellectual property law

9 Traditional knowledge

Cultural heritage or intellectual property right?

Antonietta Di Blase

Introduction

The first official international recognition of traditional knowledge (TK) as the intangible aspect inherent in genetic resources (GRs)[1] dates back to the 1992 Convention on Biological Diversity (CBD),[2] which makes it mandatory for states to ensure access to GRs and the transfer of relevant technologies in order to use biological resources in a sustainable manner for the benefit of present and future generations. In this framework, the CBD establishes the duty for each state:

> as far as possible and as appropriate . . . subject to its national legislation, [to] respect, preserve and maintain knowledge, innovations and practices of Indigenous and local communities embodying traditional lifestyles relevant for the conservation and sustainable use of biological diversity and promote their wider application with the approval and involvement of the holders of such knowledge, innovations and practices and encourage the equitable sharing of the benefits arising from the utilization of such knowledge, innovations and practices.[3]

TK is the result of the self-management in governing resources embedded in the social and cultural local practices of Indigenous and local communities, who have been working to make GRs compatible with the environment; it has the potential to indicate the ways and means for a sound use of resources, and therefore must be preserved and transmitted to future generations.[4]

---

1 In the official documents GRs are defined as 'material of plant or animal origin containing functional units of heredity' (i.e. capable of transmitting life).
2 Convention on Biological Diversity (CBD) signed on 5 June 1992, in force since 29 December 1993, 1760 UNTS 79, 31 ILM 818 (1992).
3 CBD, Art. 8 j.
4 In this paper TK is considered as distinct from culture and expressions of folklore which have been addressed separately – though in a complementary way – by the WIPO Intergovernmental Committee on IP, GRs, TK and Folklore (GRTKF Committee).

Within the CBD, the focus is on the need to encourage a sound use of GRs and, at the same time, safeguard the sovereign rights of GR-rich countries which host local and Indigenous communities. The latter are not recognized as right-holders, since their protection depends on the choice of the national government.

The multi-faceted aspects of TK have been addressed by a number of multilateral conventions including those protecting cultural rights and cultural heritage as having an intangible value for the whole of mankind.[5] The need to preserve TK was explicitly referred to in the UNESCO Convention for the Safeguarding of the Intangible Cultural Heritage (CSICH):[6] here, TK 'knowledge and practices concerning nature and universe' as well as 'traditional craftsmanship'[7] are listed among the expressions of cultural heritage, while TK as an instrument to preserve the identity of the local and Indigenous communities[8] is emphasized.[9]

This latter aspect found solemn support in the United Nations Declaration on the Rights of Indigenous Peoples,[10] where TK is referred to as a right vesting specifically in such peoples,[11] thus giving TK the features of a human right of a collective kind.[12] That perspective is not fully acknowledged in the Nagoya Protocol of 29 October 2010 (in force since 12 October 2014), which can be considered as the follow-up to the CBD. In the Protocol, it is left to the national government to find the ways and means of granting respect for

5 See V. Vadi, 'The Cultural Wealth of Nations in International Law', *Tulane J.I.L.* 21, 2012, 87 ff.

6 Convention for Safeguarding of the Intangible Cultural Heritage, 17 October 2003, in force 20 April 2006, 2368 UNTS 1.

7 CSICH, Art. 2.2.

8 CSICH, Art. 2.1.

9 The 2003 UNESCO Convention was adopted in the wake of a number of recommendations on cultural diversity, including the 1989 Recommendation on the Safeguarding of Traditional Culture and Folklore, the 2001 Universal Declaration on Cultural Diversity, and the 2002 Istanbul Declaration on Intangible Cultural Heritage. The FAO Treaty of 2001 on Plant Genetic Resources for Food and Agriculture considers TK in connection with food security.

10 United Nations Declaration on the Rights of Indigenous Peoples, 13 September 2007, 46 ILM 1013 (2007).

11 UNDRIP, Art. 31 (stating that '1. Indigenous peoples have the right to maintain, control, protect and develop their cultural heritage, traditional knowledge and traditional cultural expressions, as well as the manifestations of their sciences, technologies and cultures, including human and GRs, seeds, medicines, knowledge of the properties of fauna and flora, oral traditions, literatures, designs, sports and traditional games and visual and performing arts. They also have the right to maintain, control, protect and develop their intellectual property over such cultural heritage, traditional knowledge, and traditional cultural expressions').

12 See F. Francioni, 'Cultural Heritage and Human Rights: An Introduction', in F. Francioni and M. Scheinin (eds), *Cultural Human Rights*, Leiden/Boston, MA: Martinus Nijhoff Publishers, 2008, pp. 1–15; F. Macmillan, 'The Protection of Cultural Heritage: Common Heritage of Humankind, National Cultural "Patrimony" or Private Property?', *Northern Ireland L.Q.*, (forthcoming 2013); V. Vadi, 'When Cultures Collide: Foreign Direct Investment, Natural Resources, and Indigenous Heritage in International Investment Law', *Columbia Human Rights L.R.*, 42, 2011, 817 ff.

TK, to ensure that TK is accessed in conformity with the principles of prior and informed consent and involvement, and according to mutually agreed terms.[13] However, some progress has been made with respect to the CBD, since the Protocol requires 'user' countries to guarantee that access to TK is made in conformity with the CBD principles.

We shall not go into a detailed analysis of the instruments provided by the Nagoya Protocol for the settlement of inter-state disputes. We rather focus on the problem connected to the interplay between TK and IP entitlements. This aspect is relevant as TK is at the core of the struggle against bio-piracy, the latter being defined as a profit-oriented strategy consisting of an unwanted transfer of traditional practices and uses to the public domain or to persons external to the community, for commercial purposes, through the award of an IPR (especially patents or trade-marks). Given the transnational impact of trade and production connected with TK, its protection cannot be solely entrusted to the national government since the whole international community is involved in the protection of biodiversity and in the potential advantages of bio-industry. From this point of view, it is evident that limits to the registration and validity of TK-related IPRs should be widely recognized. This problem is not adequately addressed in the above-mentioned CBD[14] which confirms the terms and conditions of the international rules on IPRs and underlines the commitment of the Contracting Parties to cooperating in this regard, subject to national legislation and international law, in order to ensure that IPRs 'are supportive of and do not run counter to its objectives'.[15] An exception is present in Article 22.1 CBD ('Relationship with other conventions'), in cases where the exercise of IPRs would cause 'serious damage or threat to biological diversity'. Also the Nagoya Protocol expressly excludes the intention to derogate to other international instruments, except when the exercise of rights and obligations would cause serious damage or threat to biological diversity.[16] Of course, the exception extends to TK, given the close relationship between TK and biodiversity. Thus, in a dispute between two states concerning a serious infringement of TK, the CBD principles might be invoked as a limit to the commitments deriving from the Trade Related Aspects of Intellectual Property Rights (TRIPs Agreement).[17] However, no indications are given about the interpretation of the term 'serious'. Therefore, there is the risk that a IPRs-oriented approach might prevail in a case before the WTO bodies for TRIPs infringement.

There is much uncertainty as to how to make the protection of TK effective. In this chapter we shall try to ascertain whether a common trend towards

13 Nagoya Protocol, Art. 7. Online. Available: www.cbd.int/abs/text/default.shtml (accessed 10 October 2014).
14 CBD, Art. 16.2.
15 CBD, Art. 16.5.
16 Nagoya Protocol, Art. 4.1.
17 Agreement on Trade-Related Aspects of Intellectual Property Rights, 15 April 1994, Marrakesh Agreement Establishing the World Trade Organization, Annex 1C, 1869 UNTS 299, 33 ILM 1197 (1994).

building a new international TK title is emerging from national and international practice. Special reference will be made to the debates within the WIPO concerning the uniform model to be adopted by Members for the protection of TK, and to some relevant developments concerning the legislation of a number of GR-provider countries.

The main barriers to the adoption of common standards for the protection of TK

The majority of states seem to be conscious of the importance of TK as being strictly related to the general interests of cultural diversity and sustainable development. However, for the adoption of a common standard in compliance with the CBD principles it is necessary to remove any remaining ambiguities. The reasons for the different attitudes held by states are not only economic: heterogeneity is inherent in TK, being embedded in the local culture of communities. Devising uniform guidelines and rules means running the risk of collapsing the intrinsic richness of diversity into a single model.[18]

One of the most debatable points relates to the extent and limits of rights in TK. The majority of states have accepted the definition of TK 'associated' with GRs, along with the idea that the specific properties of GRs have been obtained over generations of experience and practices in the face of the challenges of the natural environment. However, the problem of determining the real extent of TK arises whenever a subject external to the community applies to obtain an IP title relating to a different use of the same resource (for instance the use of a plant as a food instead of a medication), or relating to derived products, having an indirect connection with the use previously practised by the local peoples. In favour of an extended notion of TK, it is possible to argue that the local and Indigenous communities must be accorded the merit of having contributed to the improvement and survival of a natural species, particularly in unfavourable environmental conditions. Such a definition of TK is expressly recognized by some Latin American countries, following the 1996 Decision 391 of the Andean Community on a Common Regime on Access to GRs:[19] it refers to TK as 'all know-how, innovation or individual or collective practice, with a real or *potential value*, that is associated

18 G. Dutfield, *Intellectual Property, Biogenetic Resources and Traditional Knowledge*, London: Sterling, 2004, p. 124. On the 'paradox' of devising a uniform title for systems intrinsically local see A. Taubman, 'Saving the Village: Conserving Jurisprudential Diversity in the International Protection of Traditional Knowledge', in K. E. Maskus and J. H. Reichman (eds), *International Public Goods and Transfer of Technology under a Globalized Intellectual Property Regime*, Cambridge: Cambridge University Press, 2005, p. 525.

19 Bolivia, Colombia, Ecuador, Peru and Venezuela are Members of the Andean Community. Res. 391 makes it mandatory for Members to 'recognise and value the rights and the authority of Indigenous, African-American and local communities to decide about their knowledge, innovations and traditional practices associated to GRs and their derived products' (Art. 7).

with the genetic resource, its by-products or the biological resource that contains them, whether or not protected by intellectual property regimes'. Otherwise, the Brazilian Provisional Measure No. 2.186–16 of 23 August 2001 *Genetic Heritage and Traditional Knowledge* also gives a comprehensive definition of TK as any 'information or individual or collective practices of an Indigenous or local community having real or potential value and associated with the genetic heritage'.[20] Such a broad definition is generally not accepted by the group of industrialized states.[21]

Another controversial point, having to do with the limits of TK, is the meaning of 'public domain'. It is a generally accepted principle, also seen under the TRIPs Agreement, that a product or a process which is in the public domain cannot be patented, and therefore can be used to patent a product or process deriving from that knowledge having the character of novelty. Nowadays, particular attention is given to the public domain in circumstances where IPRs are negatively evaluated from an ethical point of view because they constrain private subjects to buy the products of inventiveness. As regards TK, an argument goes that a certain level of public availability should be granted to all human beings because of its importance for food and health security and because of the intrinsic value of TK as a right of the Indigenous and local peoples, since it is an element of their identity.[22] For this reason, it should in principle be accessible for all and ineligible for exclusive private ownership.

Given the economic value assigned to TK and the need to draw the line between what can be the object of licit appropriation and what should be excluded from patentability, the public domain is a relevant parameter provided it is evaluated by taking into account the fact that TK holders are often not interested in establishing personal exclusive rights on GRs, but rather prefer to share them with members of other neighbouring groups. However it would be unjust to consider such a practice as allowing an unlimited use and appropriation also in consideration of the confidential or sacred elements which may be included in TK: the main element to consider is whether the

20 www.wipo.int/wipolex/en/details.jsp?id=5897. In favour of this interpretation see the decision by the Brazilian Federal Court of Acre, 22 May 2013, on the case *Ministério Público Federal v. Fábio F. Dias-ME et al.* (*murmuru case*). Online. Available: http://portal.trf1.jus.br/sjac/comunicacao-social/imprensa/noticias/justica-federal-profere-sentenca-no-caso-murmuru.htm (accessed 5 December 2013), para. 13.
21 See 'Joint Recommendation on Genetic Resources and Associated Traditional Knowledge' by the Delegations of Canada, Japan, Norway, Republic of Korea and the United States (doc. WIPO/GRTKF/IC/24/5, 26 March 2013), *Annex*, para. 1: 'Traditional knowledge associated with genetic resources' means *substantive* knowledge of the properties and uses of genetic resources held by Indigenous peoples or local communities and which directly leads to a claimed invention.'
22 See doc. WIPO/GRTKF/IC/17/INF/8, 24 November 2010, para. 5: 'Putting TK and Traditional cultural expressions into the public domain would violate the confidential character of many intangible, sacred and secret elements which belong to the living heritage and would accentuate the deterioration and illicit appropriation of cultural values.'

use and practice have been spread all over the country, even among peoples completely external to a regular intercourse between local communities, so as to make them easily accessible to the public from sources other than the original holder. In the latter case, TK can no longer be considered as the exclusive product of the peoples' skills and an element of the identity of the community. It would, therefore, be unreasonable to limit access.[23]

Moving on to the impact on TK protection of non-compliance with the rules and procedures, a distinction must be made between legislative systems where sanctions are provided, and other systems where non-compliance results in the invalidity of the titles obtained without due authorization. Following the Andean Community Decision 486 of 14 September 2000, relating to the Common Intellectual Property Regime,[24] Peru adopted Law No. 27811 on the Protection of Traditional Knowledge of Indigenous Peoples that provided for the refusal or invalidation of a licence as a sanction for misappropriation.[25] A ban on activities or contracts, the suspensions of registrations, licences or authorizations are also provided for under Art. 30 of the Brazilian Provisional Measure quoted above.

Other states, predominantly belonging to the group of industrialized countries, have not followed the same pattern. However, the Regulation of the European Parliament and of the Council of 16 April 2014 on 'Access to Genetic Resources and the Fair and Equitable Sharing of Benefits Arising from their Utilization in the Union'[26] makes it obligatory for individual or legal entities to ascertain that access to GRs occurred in the context of benefit-sharing and subject to mutually agreed terms; it envisages a certificate of compliance (*i.e.* an access permit or its equivalent) issued by a competent national authority, that is made available to the Access-and-Benefit Clearing House (*i.e.* a global information-sharing portal established under the Nagoya Protocol). The permit can be discontinued if it appears that access was not in keeping with those requirements. This Regulation is capable of impacting on the procedures for the award of patents by the European Patent Office (EPO),

---

23 G. Dutfield, U. Suthersanen, *Global Intellectual Property Law*, Cheltenham-Northampton: Edward Elgar, 2008, p. 349.

24 Andean Community Decision 486 of 14 September 2000, Art. 26 *i*. Online. Available: www.wipo.int/wipolex/en/details.jsp?id=9451 (accessed 5 December 2013). Decision 486 indicates a model-system to certify the licence or authorization to use TK.

25 Art. 71 ('Second Complementary Provision') of Law No. 27811, published in August 2002, introduces a 'Protection Regime for the Collective Knowledge of Indigenous Peoples derived from Biological Resources'. Online. Available: www.wipo.int/wipolex/en/details.jsp?id=3420 (accessed 5 December 2013). Peru Law No. 28216, 1 May 2004 established the Anti-Bio-Piracy Commission. Online. Available: www.wipo.int/wipolex/en/text.jsp?file_id=203365 (accessed 5 December 2013). See also the 2005 Indian Patent Amendment Act providing under Art. 25.4 the possibility of objection against registration for lack of novelty if knowledge 'oral or otherwise [is] available within any local or Indigenous community in India or elsewhere'. Online Available: www.wipo.int/wipolex/en/text.jsp?file_id=128116 (accessed 5 December 2013).

26 Regulation No. 511/2014(2014) OJ LA50/59ff.

provided the latter decides to make registration conditional upon the submission of the said permit. [27]

TK *versus* TRIPs

All the examined points are relevant in assessing the different approaches followed within the national legal orders that may lead to a conflict between TK-provider and TK-user countries and investors, the latter being interested in granting effectiveness to titles in keeping with the TRIPs rules, even though they might not fully conform with the rights of TK holders. However, it must be noted that the interests of GR-users and GR-providers do not necessarily conflict. TK-provider countries are also interested in avoiding isolation from the research and commercial centres of the more industrialized world as they would risk marginalization in terms of trade and investment.

Limits to the IPR concessions granted, or their invalidation in case of non-compliance with the rules on access to TK, can both be considered as inconsistent with TRIPs, implying an additional burden for IP protection. Up to now, no dispute has arisen before an international forum on this point although objections to the effectiveness of IPRs in respect of TK have been invoked before national courts.[28] The possibility that the problem may arise in due course cannot, however, be excluded.

One way of fostering the interplay between TK and IP is the adoption of a flexible approach in interpreting TRIPs provisions: Article 7 of the TRIPS Agreement lists among the objectives of the Agreement the promotion of technological innovation 'in a manner conducive to social and economic welfare', while Article 8.1 grants the right for Members to protect public health and nutrition, and to promote the public interest in sectors of vital importance. These provisions may give a GR-rich provider state arguments for the non-recognition of TK-related patents or trademarks when they contravene the principles which are designed to preserve the survival or identity of a given local community or its way of life. Exceptions in support of limits to patentability can be invoked under Article 27.2 of the TRIPs Agreement on grounds of public order or morality, 'including to protect human, animal or plant life or health or to avoid serious prejudice to the environment . . .', and may also find support in Article 27.3 of the TRIPS Agreement, which

27 In Switzerland, a Draft Federal Law submitted in 2012 to the CH Parliament for discussion provides for the duty to notify GRs use. Online. Available: www.env.go.jp/nature/biodic/abs/conf/conf01–03/ref03_1.pdf (accessed 26 May 2014). Other states (Japan, Norway, Denmark) are in the way of enacting measures in conformity with the Nagoya Protocol: no reference is made to sanctions for non-compliance.

28 For references to cases before the European Patent Office (EPO) see E. Bonadio, *Sistema brevettuale 'TRIPs' e risorse genetiche*, Napoli: Jovene, 2008, pp. 231 ff. On the applicability of the EPO rules against TK misappropriation see J. de Werra, 'Fighting against Biopiracy: Does the Obligation to Disclose in Patent Applications Truly Help?', *Vand. J. Transnat'l L.*, 42, 2009, 173.

states that 'Members may exclude from patentability . . . (*b*) plants and animals other than microorganisms, and essentially biological processes for the production of plants and animals other than non-biological and micro-biological processes', which is also relevant given the rural vocation of most Indigenous and local communities. Support for a flexible interpretation can be founded on the Doha Declaration of 14 November 2001 approved by the majority of the WTO Members, instructing the TRIPs Council to examine, among other issues, the relationship between the TRIPS Agreement and the CBD, the protection of TK and folklore. It was the stated intention of the WTO Members that proposed this measure that, in undertaking this task, 'the TRIPS Council shall be guided by the objectives and principles set out in Articles 7 and 8 of the TRIPS Agreement and shall take fully into account the development dimension'. [29]

However, the ambiguities of some provisions, such as Article 27.3 of the TRIPs Agreement, have been the subject of a heated debate within the TRIPs Council. Among the proposals for revision of that article, the African states suggested abolishing the distinction between non-biological and biological processes; other states recommended the introduction of a text expressly mentioning the need to protect TK in keeping with the CBD principles. Further proposals concerned adding a new Article 29*bis* to provide for the establishment of a duty on any applicant for a GRs-related patent 'to disclose the country and area of origin of any biological resources and TK used or involved in the invention, and to provide confirmation and compliance with all access regulations in the country of origin'.[30] The majority of industrialized countries have argued against such proposals, expressing their concern that disclosure could entail a burden, beyond the requirements of Article 29.1 of the TRIPs Agreement when applying for a patent.[31] In their opinion, this would constitute an element of legal uncertainty with a chilling effect on industrial innovation and research, thus also undermining the economic benefits for Indigenous and local communities. The lack of consensus is evident from the debates within WIPO where the same points have been considered. Industrialized states are only in favour of enhancing information exchanges and devising codes of conduct and databases to prevent the 'erroneous' granting of patents.[32] A less rigid, although essentially similar position, has been expressed by the EU, subject to the proviso that a disclosure

---

29   Doha Ministerial Declaration, 20 November 2001, para. 19, Doc. WT/MIN(01)/DEC/1, 20 November 2001.
30   Doc. WTO IP/C/W/404, 26 June 2003, III (*d*) and Doc. WTO/IP/C/W/474, 15 July 2006.
31   Norway is in favour of the faculty – not the duty to disclose (Doc. WT/IP/C/W/473, 14 June 2006, para. 10); less nuanced is the contrary position of the US (Doc. WTO/IP/C/W/449, 19 June 2005, para. 26 and, more recently, WIPO/GRTKF/IC/23/8 *Prov.*, 25 March 2013, para. 33) and Japan (WTO/IP/C/W/472, 13 June 2006, paras 42 ff.). For a more detailed analysis see A. Di Blase, 'I diritti di proprietà intellettuale applicabili alla cultura Indigena e tradizionale', *Comunicazioni e studi*, 23, 2007, 537 ff.
32   Doc. WIPO/IP/GR/05/INF/1, 28 February 2005.

regime would not give rise to substantial scrutiny during the patent exam-ination process.[33] Beyond that, the proposed amendments, aimed at reducing the impact of patents on GRs, may be insufficient to cope with the tendency towards privatization of immaterial resources.

National models for a TK title

It is evident from the debates at the World Trade Organization (WTO) that states representing the interests of biotechnology are not in favour of changes or amendments to the TRIPs Agreement nor are they interested in an overly flexible interpretation to meet the needs of TK-providing countries. Moreover, the proceedings within the World Intellectual Property Organization (WIPO), on-going for more than ten years, to discuss the proposals for a uniform international legal title as an instrument to safeguard TK,[34] show the lack of generalized support by the most industrialized members.[35] One has to remark that there are evident difficulties in constraining TK within the limits of a TRIPs-based IPR. TK has an overwhelmingly collective, rather than private, character and is sometimes shared by more than one single community, often located in different states. If we take patents as a model, there emerges the uncertainty over how to apply the standards of novelty, inventive steps and utility for claimed TK-associated inventions. The fixing of time-limits such as those provided for patents contradict the real purpose of TK, related as it is to tradition, maintenance and the protection of identity. From a technical point of view, a patent is only awarded when evidence of novelty is provided. This is obviously an obstacle when talking about practices and knowledge held over many generations. Profit sharing is not the main aim of TK-holders: they are more concerned with looking after the environment for future generations. Besides this, another practical problem is posed by the expense involved in the process of obtaining a patent and/or to oppose to the recognition of a patent applied for by a 'biotechnologist'. All things considered, TRIPs-based patents seem unfit for TK protection.[36] Similar arguments can be used for the TRIPs-based trade-mark model.

A general overview of the legislation of the majority of TK-provider countries (the so-called 'mega-diverse countries') which have introduced legislation to protect TK shows a very mixed bag that makes it difficult to

---

33 Doc. WIPO/GRTKF/IC/8/11, 17 May 2005.
34 See Doc. WIPO/GRTKF/IC/13/5(b) *Rev.*, 11 October 2008 ('The Protection of Traditional Knowledge: Draft Gap Analysis') and the *Draft Articles* in Doc. WIPO/GRTKF/IC/24/4, 10 January 2013, and WO/GA/43/14, 14 August 2013.
35 For an analysis of the different view expressed by the delegations see F. Lenzerini, 'Indigenous Peoples' Cultural Rights and the Controversy over Commercial Use of their Traditional Knowledge', *Cultural Human Rights*, op. cit., pp. 119 ff.
36 See H. Ullrich, 'Traditional Knowledge, Biodiversity, Benefit-Sharing and the Patent System: Romantics v. Economics?', in F. Francioni and T. Scovazzi (eds), *Biotechnology and International Law*, Oxford and Portland-Oregon: Hart, 2006, pp. 203 ff.

reach agreement on a coherent approach.[37] The only evident trend is the choice to provide for TK protection through ways and means that do not imply resorting to TRIPs-based titles, such as patents or trade-marks. This is particularly evident in the 1997 Philippines Indigenous Peoples' Rights Act, where reference is made to the CBD, the Universal Declaration of Indigenous Peoples' Rights, and the Universal Declaration of Human Rights.[38] In other countries, specific titles such as the collective right to confidentiality have been introduced. Once TK is coded in a public register, its infringement may give rise to an action for unfair competition, licence annulment and a ban on further commercialization of a product, or a monetary sanction.[39] A TK title may last for some time and be non-transmissible.[40] These titles, which sometimes involve Indigenous and local communities in the cumbersome duty of complying with the registration procedure in order to avoid TK entering the public domain, differ from TRIPs-based rights; such differences concern time-limits, the possibility of joint ownership and the duty to abstain from commercial use even in cases of wide-spread knowledge when duly documented (*i.e.* non-relevance of novelty), though some common features are present.[41] An even more serious problem is the prevalent locally-oriented approach, consisting in awarding protection uniquely to nationals of the country, unless an express reciprocity rule can be applied:[42] this represents an infringement of the core principle of national treatment under Article 3 of the TRIPs Agreement, which could be the object of complaints by non TK-provider states under the WTO Dispute Settlement Understanding.[43]

Worthy of note is the legislation enacted in some GR-provider countries when signing the International Convention for the Protection of New Varieties of Plants (UPOV Convention)[44] providing for the right of the title holder (the plant breeder) to exclude other subjects from trade and reproduction of plant

37 National laws and rules relating to TK and IP are in www.wipo.int/wipolex/en/. For a comparative overview see also doc. WIPO/GRTKF/IC/5/INF/4, 20 June 2003, *Annex*. The 2002 Bonn Guidelines. Online. Available: www.cbd.int/doc/publications/cbd-bonn-gdls-en.pdf (accessed 5 December 2013), should play a role as a tool – though not binding – to foster GR-provider states to implement the CBD principles.

38 1997 Philippines Indigenous Peoples' Rights Act. Online. Available: www.wipo.int/wipolex/en/details.jsp?id=5755 (accessed 5 December 2013).

39 Peruvian Law no. 27811, supra note 25.

40 See the 1999 *Thai Act on Protection and Promotion of Traditional Thai Medicinal Intelligence* provides for a special title for traditional medicine lasting all the lifelong + 50 years from death of the title-owner. Online. Available: www.wipo.int/wipolex/en/text.jsp?file_id=179713 (accessed 5 December 2013).

41 See Art. 39 of the TRIPs Agreement on the 'protection of undisclosed information'.

42 1999 *Thai Act on Thai Medicine*, Section 43. As regards Brazil, reference can be made to Art. 16 of the above-quoted 2001 Brazilian Provisional Measure, awarding private access to GRs only for nationals.

43 Understanding on Rules and Procedures Governing the Settlement of Disputes, Marrakesh Agreement Establishing the World Trade Organization, Annex 2, 33 ILM 1226 (1994).

44 International Union for the Protection of New Varieties of Plants, International Convention for the Protection of New Varieties of Plants (UPOV), adopted in Paris in 1961 and revised

varieties. This title, legitimized under Article 27.3(b) of the TRIPs Agreement, is not fit to protect the interests of the local and Indigenous communities and risks undermining traditional exchange practices and biodiversity: in fact the UPOV Convention limits farmers' freedom to save, exchange and sell seeds to neighbouring communities, to the detriment of farming practices and biodiversity.[45] This explains why the majority of GR-provider countries have introduced broad exceptions that allow the use of plant varieties for research and seeds' exchange,[46] thereby safeguarding the traditional right to share varieties for the conservation or development of local plants.[47] In this framework, the Peru Plant Variety Protection Act of 14 April 2011,[48] represents a step backwards as regards the protection of the traditional farmers (*campesinos*):[49] in fact, it conforms to the standards of the industrialized countries giving priority to the interests of the agro-industrial centres of the coast, more oriented towards transnational trade.[50]

TK-minus and TK-plus in bilateral agreements on trade and investments

Faced with legislation to protect TK against misappropriation in a GR-provider country, foreign investors might be tempted to obtain safeguards from the local state in order to reduce the risks of measures based on a flexible interpretation of TRIPs rules having the effect of limiting or removing the investors' IPRs. Note should be taken of the provisions of the bilateral agreements between the host and the investors' state and to the margins of flexibility left open with regard to the TRIPs-based titles. Sometimes, the parties seem to be committed to a rigorous implementation of the TRIPs

in 1972, 1978 and 1991. Online. Available: www.upov.int/upovlex/en/conventions/1961/content.html (accessed 5 December 2013).

45 In the UPOV Convention, as amended in 1991, the only admitted flexibility consists in the right for farmers to sow for their own harvest without the consent of the patent owner (the so-called 'farmers' privilege'). The unfavourable consequences of such restriction are evident from the recent decisions in the US, where farmers have been excluded from using patented seeds beyond the first crop. See the case *Bowman v. Monsanto*, US Supreme Court, 13 May 2013.

46 See the African model legislation. Online. Available: www.cbd.int/doc/measures/abs/msr-abs-oau-en.pdf (accessed 5 December 2013).

47 See the 2003 Philippines Administrative Rules, implementing the *Philippine Plant Variety Protection Act* of 2002. Online. Available: www.wipo.int/wipolex/en/text.jsp?file_id=225179 (accessed 5 December 2013), and the 1999 *Thailand Plant Varieties Protection Act*. Online. Available: www.wipo.int/wipolex/en/text.jsp?file_id=129781 and the 2001 *Indian Act on The Protection of Plant Varieties and Farmers' Rights*. Online. Available www.wipo.int/wipolex/en/text.jsp?file_id=128109) (accessed 5 December 2013).

48 *Peru Plant Variety Protection Act* of 14 April 2011. Online. Available: www.wipo.int/wipolex/en/text.jsp?file_id=244355 (accessed 5 December 2013).

49 The 2011 Act has been adopted to comply with to the commitment to accede to UPOV as provided in the 2006 Trade Promotion Agreement with the US: see infra, para. 4.

50 According to Art. 15, farmers have the right to sow for their own harvest the protected variety.

Agreement, in favour of the validity and effectiveness of the investor's IPRs, even though doubts might exist as to their compatibility with the CBD principles. For instance, under the bilateral US–Morocco Free Trade Agreement (FTA),[51] the parties have committed themselves to making 'patents available for plants and animals . . . for any new uses or methods . . ., including new uses of known product for the treatment of human and animals'.[52]

Some bilateral agreements give voice to the need to balance trade and investment against biodiversity protection. However, it is not always clear if this implies the recognition of limits to the investor's rights. For instance, although the US–Peru Trade Promotion Agreement[53] grants the faculty for the provider-country to use the flexibilities under Articles 27.2 and 27.3 of the TRIPS Agreement,[54] it sets down the commitment to make all reasonable efforts to extend patent protection. As regards other possible exceptions to a patent right, the TRIPs three-step formula is reproduced: this means that no special standard in favour of TK holders has been accepted by the Contracting Parties. The attached 'Understanding regarding biodiversity and traditional knowledge', whereby the contracting states explicitly recognize the basic principles concerning biodiversity and TK, does not seem to have a substantial impact on the patent regime:[55] the commitment of the parties to promote 'quality patent examination to ensure the conditions of patentability are satisfied' should be understood as merely consisting of granting information and giving access to publicly available databases. The Canada–Peru FTA[56] and the contemporary Agreement on Environmental Cooperation,[57] which are mutually supportive,[58] are also relevant, given the explicit reference in the latter agreement[59] to the commitments of the parties under the CBD Convention, even if it is still questionable whether this might substantially impact on

51   US–Morocco Free Trade Agreement, signed in 2004, in force since 2006. Online. Available: www.ustr.gov/trade-agreements/free-trade-agreements/morocco-fta (accessed 5 December 2013).

52   Art. 15.9 of the Morocco Free Trade Agreement seems to preclude a resort to the flexibilities under Art. 27.3 of the TRIPs Agreement, besides implying the risk of 'ever-greening', i.e. granting the right of 'stockpiling' patent protection by obtaining separate 20-year patents on multiple attributes of a single product.

53   US–Peru Trade Promotion Agreement, signed in April 2006, in force since 2009. Online. Available: www.ustr.gov/trade-agreements/free-trade-agreements/peru-tpa/final-text (accessed 5 December 2013).

54   US–Peru Trade Promotion Agreement, Art. 16.9 (2).

55   'Understanding regarding biodiversity and traditional knowledge'. Online. Available: www.ustr.gov/sites/default/files/uploads/agreements/fta/peru/asset_upload_file719_9535.pdf (accessed 5 December 2013).

56   Canada–Peru FTA, in force since 2009. Online. Available: www.international.gc.ca/trade-agreements-accords-commerciaux/agr-acc/peru-perou (accessed 5 December 2013).

57   Agreement on Environmental Cooperation. Online. Available: www.ec.gc.ca/caraib-carib/8F165B2F-6FE7–4C69-A160-E17CBA021540/2–3-b_Peru_Agreement_e.pdf (accessed 5 December 2013).

58   See Canada–Peru FTA, Art. 1703.1.

59   Agreement on Environmental Cooperation, Art. 5.6.

patenting in case of misappropriation. In the Economic Partnership Agreement of the EU with the Caribbean states,[60] the interplay between intellectual property and biodiversity is addressed in different sections of the same agreement,[61] although doubts remain as to the actual effect on patent registration.

A step forward is represented by the European Free Trade Association (EFTA)–Peru and EFTA–Colombia Free Trade Agreements (FTAs),[62] where the parties recognize the 'past, present and future contributions of Indigenous and local communities and their knowledge, innovations and practices to the conservation and sustainable use of biological and GRs and in general the contribution of the traditional knowledge of their Indigenous and local communities to the culture and economic and social development of nations'.[63] It has also been established that patent applications should contain a declaration of the GRs used by the inventor or patent applicant in accordance with the national law of the contracting states. That commitment is made more effective if the states concerned exercise their right to provide for administrative, civil or criminal sanctions against patent applicants wilfully making wrongful or misleading declarations. Reference is also made to the need to apply the national rules on prior informed consent and equitable sharing: this means that those principles have been indirectly accepted as standards of review to assess possible abuses by the investor and may be taken into account when evaluating the TK-provider state's behaviour in case of an investment dispute.

Conclusions

The emergence of a broad recognition of the need to provide for positive TK protection at international level is evident from the solemn declarations made at multilateral level, from the action of WIPO to build a universally-accepted TK title, and from the legislation of many GR-provider countries. An international uniform model would avoid the risk of competition between GR-rich countries and the pressure for commodification of products, which risks lowering the level of biodiversity. However, such an achievement still seems a long way off given the reluctance of the most industrialized states to accept more than merely formal amendments for fear it could cause flaws in the TRIPs system. On the other hand, a TRIPs-based title would not meet

60 Economic Partnership Agreement of the EU with the Caribbean states. Online. Available: http://eur-lex.europa.eu/LexUriServ/LexUriServ.do?uri=OJ:L:2008:289:0003:1955:EN:PDF (accessed 5 December 2013).
61 See Economic Partnership Agreement of the EU with the Caribbean States, Art. 150.
62 EFTA–Peru and EFTA–Colombia FTAs. Online. Available: www.efta.int/~/media/Documents/legal-texts/free-trade-relations/peru/EFTA-Peru%20Free%20Trade%20Agreement%20EN.pdf (accessed 5 December 2013). These Agreements entered in force on 1 July 2011 for Switzerland and Liechtenstein, on 1 October 2011 for Iceland, on 1 July 2012 for Norway.
63 Art. 6.5.

the demands of Indigenous/local communities, nor protect the general interests of mankind as they have been interpreted by the CBD and other multilateral conventions.

Nevertheless, the legislation adopted by some of the richest GR-provider countries, far from complying with the needs of homogeneity intrinsic to an internationally binding system, has a crucial role to play in the promotion and strengthening of a wide-spread awareness of the urgency with respect to the provision of TK protection. It shows their tendency to rely on a locally-oriented approach, befitting the different interests and characters of the local and Indigenous communities where TK is embedded, even if some provisions are definitely inconsistent with the TRIPs Agreement and the national treatment rule that is the core of the WTO/TRIPs uniform trade and profit-oriented approach. The national approach to TK suggests that a TK title should be built up outside the WTO/TRIPs system, on the basis of the principles applicable to intangible cultural heritage, and as such firmly linked to the protection of fundamental human rights. That could encourage the local and international courts to give more weight to the human-rights dimension when settling disputes where TK is involved.

The recent trend of reference to the CBD in some bilateral trade and investment agreements deserves special attention as here the principles relating to TK and TRIPs-based IPRs are indicated in a mutually supportive way. Such an attitude may contribute to reducing the pressure on less developed GR-provider countries to impose a profit-oriented pattern in transnational economic relations. The reference made to CBD in bilateral agreements means that those principles can be considered as standards of treatment, which may have a real impact in case of investor-state disputes. This can be regarded as a positive tendency, even if the outcome may be fragmentation and possible conflict between different regimes, depriving TRIPs of the character of a general and exclusive system for the protection of IP. It strengthens the awareness that essential interests which have a strong impact on the well-being of humankind cannot be confined within the strict borders of trade and commerce.

Bibliography

Bonadio E., *Sistema brevettuale 'TRIPs' e risorse genetiche*, Napoli: Jovene, 2008.

de Werra J., 'Fighting against Biopiracy: Does the Obligation to Disclose in Patent Applications Truly Help?', *Vand. J. Transnat'l L.*, 42, 2009, 143–179.

Di Blase A.,'I diritti di proprietà intellettuale applicabili alla cultura Indigena e tradizionale', *Comunicazioni e studi*, 23, 2007, 513–563.

Dutfield G., *Intellectual Property, Biogenetic Resources and Traditional Knowledge*, London: Sterling, 2004.

Dutfield G., Suthersanen U., *Global Intellectual Property Law*, Cheltenham-Northampton: Edward Elgar, 2008.

Francioni F., 'Cultural Heritage and Human Rights: An Introduction', in F. Francioni and M. Scheinin (eds), *Cultural Human Rights*, Leiden/Boston, MA: Martinus Nijhoff, 2008, pp. 1–15.

Lenzerini F., 'Indigenous Peoples' Cultural Rights and the Controversy over Commercial Use of their Traditional Knowledge', in *Cultural Human Rights*, Leiden/Boston, MA: Martinus Nijhoff, 2008, 119–149.

Macmillan F., 'The Protection of Cultural Heritage: Common Heritage of Humankind, National Cultural "Patrimony" or Private Property?', *Northern Ireland L.Q.*, (forthcoming 2013).

Taubman A., 'Saving the Village: Conserving Jurisprudential Diversity in the International Protection of Traditional Knowledge', in K.E. Maskus and J.H. Reichman (eds), *International Public Goods and Transfer of Technology under a Globalized Intellectual Property Regime*, Cambridge: Cambridge University Press, 2005, pp. 521–564.

Ullrich H., 'Traditional Knowledge, Biodiversity, Benefit-Sharing and the Patent System: Romantics v. Economics?', in F. Francioni and T. Scovazzi (eds), *Biotechnology and International Law*, Oxford and Portland-Oregon: Hart, 2006, pp. 201–229.

Vadi V., 'When Cultures Collide: Foreign Direct Investment, Natural Resources, and Indigenous Heritage in International Investment Law', *Columbia Human Rights L.R.*, 42, 2011, 797–889.

Vadi V., 'The Cultural Wealth of Nations in International Law', *Tulane J.I.L.* 21, 2012, 87–133.

10 Propertization, safeguarding and the cultural commons

The turf wars of intangible cultural heritage and traditional cultural expressions

Lucas Lixinski[1] *and Louise Buckingham*[2]

Introduction

This volume is premised on the idea of 'culture' being the subject of debate and law-making across different international and regional fora. Additionally, 'culture' means an array of different legal goods, one of which happens to be traditional culture, or cultural heritage. These two terms (traditional culture and cultural heritage), while practically synonymous in everyday usage, are employed divergently in the language of international law in this area. Indeed, the terms are often used in ways that are effectively diametrically opposed. To be sure, intangible cultural heritage (ICH) and traditional cultural expressions (TCEs) cover similar terrain in the sense that they are 'folkloric' manifestations in search of legal protection. Nevertheless, they each fall under the umbrellas of two very different organizations.

The United Nations Educational, Scientific and Cultural Organization (UNESCO) and the World Intellectual Property Organization (WIPO) are the governing institutions over these two synonymous yet different legal goods. ICH falls within UNESCO's remit, while TCEs are within that of WIPO. The two bodies have a history of working cooperatively towards the broader goals of safeguarding culture and heritage. Historically, they have cooperated on the issues at least since the 1970s.[3]

The work of WIPO in the field of folklore protection was, in the past, typically conducted jointly with UNESCO. In 1976, the two organizations jointly adopted the Tunis Model Law on the use of copyright for the protection

---

1 Senior Lecturer, Faculty of Law, UNSW Australia; PhD in Law, European University Institute (Florence, Italy).
2 BA (Hons)/LLB (Hons), LLM (Usyd); MSc (LSE); PhD Candidate, Faculty of Law, UNSW Australia.
3 For more on this relationship, see L. Lixinski, *Intangible Cultural Heritage in International Law*, Oxford: Oxford University Press 2013, pp. 56–58.

of folklore.[4] In 1982, the two organizations adopted Model Provisions for National Laws on the Protection of Expressions of Folklore against Illicit Exploitation and Other Prejudicial Action.[5] Then, in 1984, a Draft Treaty on the matter was elaborated. It was never approved, largely due to it being rejected by industrialized nations who objected to protecting community-based cultural expressions.[6]

During 1998 and 1999, WIPO appointed experts to conduct nine fact-finding missions to assess and identify the intellectual property (IP) needs of holders of folklore and Traditional Knowledge (TK). Following these missions it created an Intergovernmental Committee on Intellectual Property and Genetic Resources, Traditional Knowledge and Folklore in 2000 (the WIPO IGC).[7] The WIPO IGC is still engaged in text-based negotiations. At the time of writing, it is negotiating the Draft Provisions for the Protection of Traditional Cultural Expressions/Expressions of Folklore, which is one of the 'headings' given to the areas it deals with.[8]

As of the end of September 2013, and as a result of informal negotiations conducted during 2013 in particular, an intensive work plan for the WIPO intergovernmental committee was set out for the following two-year period.[9] Following the annual WIPO General Assemblies, the two-year mandate of the IGC will be renewed. In September 2014, the General Assembly marked a point of review to gauge the progress on the potential instruments. Commentators have also revealed that the three instruments may now become one.[10]

The draft agreement relating to these recent developments is instructive. In summary, after 'Bearing in mind the Development Agenda recommendations and acknowledging the progress made, the WIPO General Assembly

---

4 Tunis Model Law on Copyright for Developing Countries (UNESCO/WIPO, 1976). Article 6 refers to folklore.

5 Model Provisions for National Laws on the Protection of Expressions of Folklore Against Illicit Exploitation and Other Prejudicial Action (UNESCO/WIPO, 1982).

6 Draft Treaty for the Protection of Expressions of Folklore Against Illicit Exploitation and Other Prejudicial Action (UNESCO/WIPO, 1984).

7 J. Blake, *Commentary on the UNESCO 2003 Convention on the Safeguarding of the Intangible Cultural Heritage*, Geneva: Institute for Art and Law, 2006, at 3. Some of the Committee's latest work is the Draft Objectives and Principles. See WIPO Intergovernmental Committee on Intellectual Property, Genetic Resources, Traditional Knowledge and Folklore, *The Protection of Traditional Cultural Expressions/Expressions of Folklore: Draft Objectives and Principles*, WIPO/GRTKF/IC/10/4, of 2 October 2006.

8 The others being traditional knowledge (TK) and genetic resources (GR). Although, it should be emphasized that many participants in the forum believe the three categories – namely TCEs, TK and GR – are falsely separated and ought to be dealt with together. Further, as revealed in the commentary cited below, it appears that the IGC may ultimately recommend a treaty text that deals with TCEs, TK and GR in one single instrument.

9 See W. New, 'WIPO Members Reach Tentative Deal on TK Treaties; External Offices Mired', *Intellectual Property Watch*, 27 September 2013. Online. Available: www.ip-watch.org (accessed 4 October 2013).

10 Ibid.

agrees that the mandate of the WIPO Intergovernmental Committee . . . be renewed' . . . to:

- expedite its work 'with open and full engagement';
- follow 'a clearly defined work program, based on sound working methods';
- 'build on the existing work carried out by the Committee and use all WIPO working documents';
- 'submit to the 2014 General Assembly the text(s) of an international legal instrument(s) which will ensure the effective protection of GRs, TK and TCEs . . . the General Assembly in 2014 will take stock of and consider the text(s), progress made and decide on convening a Diplomatic Conference, and will consider the need for additional meetings'.[11]

In 2003, UNESCO adopted the Convention for the Safeguarding of the Intangible Cultural Heritage (the ICH Convention).[12] Consideration of the status of the WIPO IGC's debates, as outlined briefly above, and the *travaux préparatoires* of the ICH Convention, reveals many parallels. Many of the tensions and questions about the subject matter seem to have been replayed across fora. To put it simply, that both UNESCO and WIPO enact international instruments on the same matter would seem, on the face of it, to be repetitive and excessive.

However, close analysis of the most recent WIPO IGC draft articles concerning TCEs through the lens of safeguarding heritage suggests that the relationship between WIPO and UNESCO is not as synergistic or complementary as is often assumed. This analysis leads to questions about the nature of intellectual property and heritage regimes and the implications for the general regulation of culture internationally.

This chapter will explore this relationship between the two instruments (one already existing, the other in the making). We will not discuss the relationship between IP and traditional culture more broadly. This has been the object of much discussion elsewhere.[13] Instead, we will focus on the relationship between the two existing international regimes, and will argue

---

11 Ibid.
12 Convention for the Safeguarding of the Intangible Cultural Heritage (ICH Convention), opened for signature in Paris on 17 October 2003, in force 20 April 2006, 2368 UNTS 1.
13 See for instance J.E. Anderson, *Law, Knowledge, Culture: The Production of Indigenous Knowledge in Intellectual Property Law*, Cheltenham: Edward Elgar, 2009; Lixinski, op. cit., at 175–204; K. Bowrey, 'Indigenous Culture, Knowledge and Intellectual Property: The Need for a New Category of Rights?', in K. Bowrey, M. Handler, and D. Nicol (eds), *Emerging Challenges in Intellectual Property*, Oxford: Oxford University Press, 2011, 46–67; C.H. Farley, 'Protecting Folklore of Indigenous Peoples: Is Intellectual Property the Answer?', *Conn L Rev* 30, 1997, 1–57; D.J. Gervais, 'The Internationalization of Intellectual Property: New Challenges from the Very Old and the Very New', *Fordham Intellectual Property Media & Ent LJ* 12, 2002, 929–990; J. Gibson, *Community Resources: Intellectual Property, International Trade and Protection of Traditional Knowledge*, London: Ashgate, 2009; M. Halewood, 'Indigenous and Local Knowledge in International Law: A Preface to Sui Generis Intellectual Property Protection',

that ICH and TCEs are, in some very important respects, fundamentally at odds with each other, and that these incompatibilities go largely unnoticed, but can create serious problems for safeguarding this type of culture.

In order to substantiate this argument, we will first undertake an overview of the two systems, with a view to understanding what each defines as its object of protection, and how they envisage the relationship between the two systems. A close reading and limited comparative analysis of the recent treaty-text negotiations from WIPO, and the ICH Convention, will be conducted. We will then use this discussion to look more broadly at the promises and pitfalls of the propertization of culture.

UNESCO and WIPO in the safeguarding of intangible traditional culture

UNESCO and intangible cultural heritage

During the drafting of the 2003 UNESCO ICH Convention, the relationship between ICH and TCEs was still front and centre of debates. Francesco Francioni, Chair of the drafting meeting held in Turin (2001), presented a comprehensive report on issues that should be taken into account when drafting a definition of ICH. Among other things, the report outlined the possibility of legally protecting 'non-material' goods using the example of IP rights, but also drawing a line distinguishing between ICH and IP, in that IP focuses on the end product of the creative process, whereas ICH is the process itself.[14]

The 2003 UNESCO Convention thus defines intangible cultural heritage as follows:

> **Article 2 – Definitions.** For the purposes of this Convention, 1. The 'intangible cultural heritage' means the practices, representations,

McGill LJ 44, 1999, 953–996; H.C. Hanse, M. Blakeney, L.S. Lourie, P.E. Salmon, and C. Visser, 'Symposium: Global Intellectual Property Rights: Boundaries of Access and Enforcement: Panel II: The Law and Policy of Protecting Folklore, Traditional Knowledge, and Genetic Resources', *Fordham Intellectual Property Media & Ent LJ* 12, 2002, 753–803; P. Kuruk, 'Protecting Folklore under Modern Intellectual Property Regimes: A Reappraisal of the Tensions between Individual and Communal Rights in Africa and the United States', *Am U L Rev* 48, 1999, 769–849; S. von Lewinski, 'The Protection of Folklore', *Cardozo J Intl & Comp L* 11, 2003, 747–768; A. Lucas-Schloetter, 'Folklore', in Silke von Lewinski (ed.), *Indigenous Heritage and Intellectual Property*, The Hague: Kluwer Law International, 2003, 259–340; I.D. Obaldia, 'Western Intellectual Property and Indigenous Cultures: The Case of the Panamanian Indigenous Intellectual Property Law', *BU Intl LJ* 23, 2005, 337–394; H.-P. Sambuc, *La Protection Internationale des Savoirs Traditionnels: La Nouvelle Frontiére de la Proprieté Intellectuelle*, Paris: l'Harmattan, 2003[0], among others.

14 UNESCO, *International Round Table: 'Intangible Cultural Heritage – Working Definitions'*, meeting held in Turin Piedmont (Italy) on 14–17 March 2001. See also Lixinski, op. cit., at 7–10.

expressions, knowledge, skills – as well as the instruments, objects, artefacts and cultural spaces associated therewith – that communities, groups and, in some cases, individuals recognize as part of their cultural heritage. This intangible cultural heritage, transmitted from generation to generation, is constantly recreated by communities and groups in response to their environment, their interaction with nature and their history, and provides them with a sense of identity and continuity, thus promoting respect for cultural diversity and human creativity.

Intangible heritage, like Indigenous peoples' heritage, must be seen as holistic.[15] This holistic approach means, among other things, that the ICH Convention focuses on 'safeguarding', as opposed to 'protection' of intangible heritage. 'Safeguarding', in the context of the ICH Convention, means a shift away from strictly legal forms of protection and towards more holistic strategies to ensure the viability of heritage for present and future generations. In other words, the ICH Convention protects objects because they derive from a larger cultural practice, and not the other way around. The latter would be the traditional response of museums, for instance, in protecting the objects themselves and hoping, perhaps, to indirectly protect the culture behind them, or of IP.

Heritage here is seen as the cultural processes behind certain objects, and not the objects themselves (which are a commodified version of these processes). In this sense, any attempt to indirectly protect intangible heritage through protecting the end-results of these cultural and social processes must take into account that they are protecting the tangible manifestations of heritage, and not heritage itself, and necessarily fall short of fully protecting heritage.[16]

The safeguarding of intangible heritage at the international level happens primarily through intangible heritage lists. One such list is the 'Representative List of the Intangible Cultural Heritage of Humanity',[17] while the other is the 'List of Intangible Cultural Heritage in Need of Urgent Safeguarding'.[18] It is important to note that only the first list is called a 'representative' list, while the other includes, at least in theory, all forms of intangible heritage at grave risk of disappearing.

The listing mechanism was opposed by some member States during the negotiation of the Convention. Norway was one such notable example. It was of the opinion that a list-based mechanism would create a hierarchy of manifestations of heritage (the 'listed', which would somehow be 'better', and the 'unlisted'). Norway thought that a catalogue of best practices alone would

---

15   A. Kearney, 'Intangible Cultural Heritage: Global Awareness and Local Interest', in Laurajane Smith and Natsuko Akagawa (eds), *Intangible Heritage*, London: Routledge 2009, 209–226 at 217.

16   L. Smith, *The Uses of Heritage*, London: Routledge, 2006, at 54.

17   ICH Convention, Article 16.

18   ICH Convention, Article 17.

suffice to accomplish the objectives of the Convention. India, on the other hand, thought that the listing approach was an effective one, even though it should be approached carefully so as not to create any sort of hierarchy. This was generally the accepted argument, as the listing would help in the awareness-raising that was necessary for the achievement of the objectives of the Convention. Further, as highlighted by the Brazilian delegation, the listing mechanism at the international level mirrored the national obligation of inventorying, thus being also a desirable means to implement the Convention.[19]

There are several criteria imposed for a manifestation of heritage to be inscribed on the list of intangible heritage in need of urgent safeguarding and all of them must be met: (1) heritage must be intangible heritage in accordance with Article 2 of the Convention; (2) it must be in need of urgent safeguarding 'because its viability is at risk' or 'because it is facing grave threats as a result of which it cannot be expected to survive without immediate safeguarding'; (3) there must be a plan of safeguarding measures elaborated to enable the element to be practised and transmitted; (4) free, prior, and informed consent must be obtained from the concerned community, group, or individuals; (5) the element must be in the national inventory of intangible heritage of the concerned State Party; and (6) the State must give the authorization for such inscription.[20]

The criteria for inscription on the representative list are slightly different,[21] and in many ways impose a lesser burden on States seeking inscription. The criteria for inscription on the list of representative intangible heritage, which must be all met by States seeking inscription, are: (1) that the manifestation of heritage falls within the concept of Article 2 of the Convention; (2) that the inscription will contribute to the visibility and awareness of the significance of ICH and will encourage dialogue, thereby entangling cultural diversity and being a testimony to human creativity; (3) that safeguarding measures are elaborated to protect and promote the element; (4) free, prior, and informed consent of the affected communities, groups, and individuals; and (5) that the element is present in one of the inventories required from States Parties.[22] Also, communities must be involved in the preparation of the nominations for this list.[23]

Article 18 of the ICH Convention provides for programmes, projects, and other activities for the safeguarding of intangible heritage, and determines that

---

19 Blake, op. cit., at 79.
20 General Assembly, *Operational Directives*, Rule 1.
21 For a comparison, see Intergovernmental Committee for the Safeguarding of the Intangible Cultural Heritage, Second Extraordinary Session (Sofia, Bulgaria, 18–22 February 2008), *Decision 2.EXT.COM 17 (Report of the Intergovernmental Committee for the Safeguarding of the Intangible Cultural Heritage on its activities between the first and second sessions of the General Assembly of the States Parties to the Convention*, paras 11–19).
22 UNESCO General Assembly, *Operational Directives*, Rule 19.
23 UNESCO General Assembly, *Operational Directives*, Rule 21.

the Committee (upon approval by the Assembly) shall select those that best reflect the objectives of the Convention. In this way, an inventory of best practices, so important for the implementation of the Convention for the reasons listed above, can be created.[24] One of the issues raised regarding this repository of best practices was whether it should be a selective listing, or a more inclusive one.[25] It was decided early, in the first draft of this part of the Operational Directives, that the listing should be selective.[26]

The Operational Directives determine the criteria that must be met for the selection of a best practice: (1) the programme involves safeguarding, as defined in Article 2(3) of the Convention; (2) the programme coordinates efforts for safeguarding at the regional, subregional, and/or international levels; (3) the programme reflects the principles and objectives of the Convention; (4) it has demonstrated effectiveness in contributing to the viability of the ICH concerned; (5) it counts on the participation of the community, group, or individuals with free, prior, and informed consent; (6) it can serve as a subregional, regional, or international model for other safeguarding initiatives (that is, it can be 'transplanted' or emulated in other contexts); (7) the State(s), communities, groups, or individuals involved are willing to cooperate in the dissemination of best practices; (8) it is possible to assess the results of the programme, project, or activity; and (9) the programme 'is primarily applicable to the particular needs of developing countries'.[27] These criteria are further developed in a standardized form attached to the Operational Directives, accompanied by explanatory notes.[28] At the time of writing, there are ten programmes inscribed as best practices to promote the goals of the Convention.[29]

The ICH Convention's text is also very clear about the intention that the instrument is to be only one among many in the service of protecting ICH while respecting other important and existing rights. The idea behind Article 3 of the 2003 Convention enshrines this notion of complementarity. This provision determines that the ICH Convention is not to be interpreted in any way contrary to other international obligations, particularly those undertaken under the 1972 World Heritage Convention (Article 3.a) or other IP and environmental agreements (Article 3.b).[30]

24 Blake, op. cit., at 86–88.
25 See Intergovernmental Committee for the Safeguarding of the Intangible Cultural Heritage, First Extraordinary Session (Chengdu, China, 23–27 May 2007), *Discussion on the Implementation of Article 18 of the Convention for the Safeguarding of the Intangible Cultural Heritage,* Doc.ITH/07/1.EXT.COM/CONF.207/11, of 20 April 2007.
26 See Intergovernmental Committee for the Safeguarding of the Intangible Cultural Heritage, Second Session (Tokyo, Japan, 3–7 September 2007), *Preliminary Draft Directives for Implementing Article 18 of the Convention for the Safeguarding of the Intangible Cultural Heritage,* Doc.ITH/07/2.COM/CONF.208/12, of 30 July 2007.
27 General Assembly, *Operational Directives,* Rule 7.
28 See Form ICH-03 (2009) – Programmes, Projects and Activities.
29 See UNESCO, *The Intangible Heritage Lists.* Available: www.unesco.org/culture/ich/index. php?lg=en&pg=00559 (accessed 5 December 2013).
30 Blake, op. cit., at 42–43.

WIPO and traditional cultural expressions

At a recent meeting (in July 2013), the WIPO IGC redrafted a text, in its words, 'towards the development of an international legal instrument or instruments for the effective protection of traditional cultural expressions and traditional knowledge, and to address the intellectual property aspects of access to and benefit-sharing in genetic resources'.[31] In this chapter, the process of developing treaty texts about TCEs in particular will be referred to as 'TCE treaty-text negotiations'.[32]

The circumstances surrounding these negotiations differ markedly from the equivalent situation with respect to ICH. The ICH Convention was negotiated in the years up to 2003 and ratified predominantly by developing countries.

The outcomes that the TCE treaty-text negotiations and the ICH Convention envisage are fundamentally different in as far as the TCE treaty-text negotiations seem geared towards protection of the forms of expression that convey or enclose traditional or Indigenous identity, know-how, beliefs and heritage for the purpose of enabling their commercialisation (or 'propertization' via WIPO's IP paradigm). To use the examples provided on the WIPO website at the time of writing, these expressions may include music, dance, art, designs, names, signs, symbols, performances, ceremonies, architecture, handicrafts and narratives.

The draft work plan that came out of the recent WIPO General Assembly (GA) (and that is mentioned earlier in this chapter) concludes with the GA noting:

> the merits of studies and members of the IGC providing examples to inform the discussion of objectives and principles, and each proposed article, including examples of protectable subject matter and subject matter that is not intended to be protected, and examples of domestic legislation.[33]

The institutional imperative of achieving an outcome in this area is suggested by the sentence that follows: 'However, examples and studies are not to delay progress or establish any preconditions to the text based negotiations.'[34] While the tone of negotiations and States' positions can

---

31 WIPO TCE Portal. Online. Available: www.wipo.int/tk/en/folklore/ (accessed 5 December 2013).

32 The very recent developments in relation to the WIPO intergovernmental committee have led commentators to predict that what have, up until now, predominantly been discussed as potentially three treaty instruments – separating TCEs from traditional knowledge (TK) and genetic resources (GR) – may become one single instrument. Nevertheless, we shall discuss TCEs specifically here as it seems to us to be equally as likely that the WIPO intergovernmental committee will retain the tripartite separation it has worked with previously and TCEs represent the closest resemblance in terms of subject matter to ICH.

33 New, op. cit.

34 Ibid.

change according to governments in power and personnel deployed, it seems that currently wealthy developed countries are strongly backing the WIPO IGC initiatives concerning TCEs.

Comparison

The domains of ICH and TCEs have much in common. One of the main points of comparison is that both regimes arise out of gaps. The ICH regime emerges from a failure of the World Heritage Convention to address the concerns of 'non-Western' countries, including developing countries and Indigenous peoples, but also particularly Asian countries.[35] The proposed or likely regime for TCEs arises from the failure of copyright to satisfactorily protect traditional culture.

The subject matter is also very similar, at least on the surface. Both ICH and TCEs can be traced back to the now rejected idea of 'folklore'.[36] However, the definitions employed by both regimes also lead us in different directions as to the uses of these manifestations of culture: ICH focuses on social practices, whereas TCEs focus on the artefact. In this sense, ICH is the underlying culture, which comes to life through a song or a dance, for instance, whereas the TCE is the song or dance itself.

This difference in the definition significantly impacts the way the regimes around the two are constructed. Whereas the main objectives of the ICH regime are to 'safeguard', 'ensure respect', 'raise awareness', and 'provide for international cooperation',[37] the TCE (draft) regime aims at providing remedies for the misappropriation of traditional culture, and controlling the ways in which these expressions are used outside of traditional or customary contexts.[38]

This crucial distinction also affects the mechanisms of protection offered: while the ICH Convention looks at listing as its main mechanism for safeguarding and raising awareness, for the benefit of all of humankind, the TCEs draft focuses on the moral and economic rights of the holders of this culture.

Much of this divergence can be attributed to the different scopes of the two organizations within which each regime is housed. UNESCO focuses on culture as an element to contribute to world peace and security,[39] whereas the WIPO focuses on the promotion of IP protection.[40] Their different mandates inevitably affect the way they look at their subject matter, and the responses

---

35 Lixinski, op. cit., at 22–25.
36 The notion of folklore is largely rejected in academic and UNESCO circles because of its commodifying effects upon heritage. More specifically, 'folklore' is often read as 'tourism-oriented kitsch', and ICH and TCEs seek to distance themselves from that idea.
37 ICH Convention, Article 1.
38 WIPO, The Protection of Traditional Cultural Expressions: Draft Articles (Rev. 2, July 2013), Objectives.
39 UNESCO Constitution, Article 1(1).
40 WIPO Convention, Article 3.

they can devise. This is a phenomenon that happens across every organ, regional or international, that has attempted to protect this type of culture.[41]

In this way, the TCEs regime offers much 'harder', and more 'legal' mechanisms, which are appropriate in some instances. However, this approach may also stifle the circulation of ideas and cultural diversity. Because it effectively propertizes culture, the proposed regime may have the effect of preventing cultural borrowing and lending that has been so crucial for cultures across the world for so long. Some of these tensions are explored in the next section of this chapter.

Propertizing culture?

One of the consequences of an IP approach to traditional culture, it is often said, is the commodification of that culture, and its freezing at a certain point in time. The listing mechanisms of the ICH Convention, exemplifying a different approach, may also commodify and freeze culture, albeit to a smaller extent.

One of the concepts that can help explain this problem is that of the 'commons', or, in our case, the 'cultural commons'. The existence of a public domain is generally acknowledged in the field of culture (and particularly IP). There seems to be a tendency to think of the public domain as the end of the scope of application of the IP instrument. In other words, once the duration period associated with an IP right, such as copyright, has expired, material is then regarded as being in the public domain, to be freely exploited by anyone. As most IP instruments are concerned primarily with private rights, the public domain is usually not explored within them. One notable exception is the Universal Copyright Convention, which was an instrument adopted by UNESCO.[42] UNESCO's mandate as an organization for the protection and promotion of culture and cultural exchange led it to draft an instrument that, on top of conciliating different approaches to copyright protection, also had in mind the preservation of a robust public domain.[43]

The public domain is not necessarily the enemy of IP protection. Rather, the public domain is a natural part of the IP cycle, and something that must be carefully considered in the promotion of culture, which is after all one of the main reasons why IP protection exists in the first place.[44] If one looks at

---

41 Lixinski, op. cit., 233–234.
42 Universal Copyright Convention, opened for signature in Geneva on 6 September 1952, 216 UNTS 132.
43 R.L. Okediji, 'An Enduring Legacy For the Knowledge Economy: UNESCO and the International Copyright System', in A.A. Yusuf (ed.), *Standard-Setting in UNESCO Vol I: Normative Action in Education, Science and Culture*, The Hague: Martinus Nijhoff and UNESCO Publishing, 2007, 113–134, at 120.
44 See generally I. Alexander, *Copyright Law and the Public Interest in the Nineteenth Century*, Oxford: Hart, 2011.

intangible heritage as 'the common heritage of humankind',[45] the implication is that it is also a 'cultural common'.

When IP rights lapse over a certain work, this work passes into the public domain, and may be freely used by all of society. TCEs, under the prism of IP law, are usually considered to fall under the public domain, since they represent the manifestation of an often ancient (and by definition, traditional) practice. Such practices, when they can be traced back to a determined point in time, have usually exceeded the timeframe for protection under different categories of IP protection.[46]

A commitment to the concept of the public domain may shift the obligation for protection of manifestations of heritage from the creators to the State. The public domain can be divided in two: public domain, and *'domaine public payant'*. In both of these understandings, a national authority is designated for the defence of interests arising from the exploitation of intangible heritage by whoever intends to use it and does not belong to the custodial community. In the latter scenario, fees are paid over in order to be granted an authorization to use the work in question. These fees, once collected, usually go to a governmental fund oriented to cultural development, not reaching the custodial communities as copyrights or royalties. A country that exemplifies this system is Argentina.[47]

A regulated public domain can perform two functions: on the one hand, it can serve the desire to keep some level of protection for authors' moral rights (more specifically, the rights to attribution and integrity). On the other, it can be useful for the preservation of cultural heritage. While still predicated on the commodification of heritage, it is commodification that happens according to terms determined by the custodial communities. The *domaine public payant* is characterized by a stronger emphasis on the protection of cultural heritage, because it provides financial means for safeguarding intangible heritage (which revert to the custodial communities). The main drawback, however, is that there is little international recognition of public domain regulations. There is no international structure through which these mechanisms can be enforced, and, as the *domaine public payant* is more often than not aimed at preventing misuse by *foreign* third parties, it is of limited usefulness.[48]

---

45   On this concept, see generally K. Baslar, *The Concept of the Common Heritage of Mankind in International Law*, The Hague: Brill, 1998.

46   See D.E. Long, 'The Impact of Foreign Investment on Indigenous Culture: An Intellectual Property Perspective', *NCJ Intl L & Com Reg* 23, 1998, 229–243, at 269–270.

47   See for instance D. Lipszyc and C.A. Villalba, 'Preserving and Accessing our Cultural Heritage: Argentina's Experience through the *domaine public payant*', in E. Derclaye (ed.), *Copyright and Cultural Heritage: Preservation and Access to Works in a Digital World*, Cheltenham: Edward Elgar 2010, 179–192.

48   See C.A. Berryman, 'Toward More Universal Protection of Intangible Cultural Property', *J Intellectual Property L* 1 (1994), 293, reprinted in A. D'Amato and D.E. Long (eds), *International Intellectual Property Anthology*, Anderson, OH: Anderson Publishing Co., 1996, 76 at 77.

It is interesting to note that there has been a shift in attitudes about the general idea of the public domain in relation to exploitation of ICH, TCEs and TK. While traditional communities have often preferred the use of the public domain, some authors argue that the awareness of the economic potential of these resources seems to have created a shift: while corporations now try to make sure that these resources fall in the public domain (and can therefore be re-appropriated by corporate actors), traditional communities have largely abandoned the idea of a public domain to favour proprietary rights that can foster their development.[49] They use this argument not to discard the use of the public domain or the idea of commons, but simply to warn that these concepts should be considered carefully, rather than immediately jumped upon as the best solution.[50] In this sense, while the public domain allows for the 'regeneration and revitalization' of intangible heritage, it does not provide a strong economic incentive for creation and development.[51] It has been pointed out that economic exploitation of these resources is bound to happen asymmetrically, and that the potential for exploitation by a local community in comparison to that of a multinational corporate partner is unbalanced.[52]

The public domain has also been criticized as insufficient for the protection of ICH or TCEs on other grounds. First of all, the public domain fails to offer mechanisms to prevent the use of intangible heritage in certain circumstances. Such instances might include: falsely suggesting a connection to the custodial community; offensive, derogatory, or libelous uses; or attempts at using sacred or secret manifestations of intangible heritage. Also, other areas of legislation outside of IP law seem to be more effective than the total lack of regulation, and the conflicts with IP law are not so large that they exclude the application of IP law altogether.[53]

The public domain is in many ways different from the idea of commons; while the public domain is seen as 'free' and unregulated, the idea of commons rests on some form of control of distribution. While there are no financial benefits to be accrued from transactions involving the commons, there is still the need for a transaction, some form of authorization, before the commons can be used.[54] And this is very important for ICH or TCEs, since, as we have seen, communities are often less interested in financial benefits from the exploitation of their heritage by third parties than in actually controlling such use, to make sure it is not culturally offensive or harmful in any way.

---

49 A. Chander, and M. Sunder, 'The Romance of the Public Domain', *Calif L Rev* 92, 2004, 1331–1373, at 1335.
50 Ibid., at 1336.
51 See WIPO Intergovernmental Committee, *Consolidated Analysis*, para. 15.
52 See Chander and Sunder, op. cit., at 1351.
53 See WIPO Intergovernmental Committee, *Consolidated Analysis*, para. 23.
54 See J. Boyle, 'The Second Enclosure Movement and the Construction of the Public Domain', in James Boyle (ed.), *Collected Papers: Duke Conference on the Public Domain*, Chapel Hill, NC: Center for the Public Domain, 2003, 33–74, at 65–66.

The commons, however, requires some form of regulation.[55] A seemingly perennial problem with the commons is that any discussion of the concept seems to be overshadowed by the idea of 'the tragedy of the commons'.[56] This idea, articulated by Garrett Hardin originally, essentially dictates that (environmental) commons were bound to be subject to over-exploitation and therefore be destroyed.[57] This does not hold true when it comes to intellectual or cultural commons, however. The repeated use of informational or cultural commons does not lead to its depletion. On the contrary, such repetition can work to the advantage of certain groups who control these commons.[58] The central question is who should control these resources.

The plurality of social norms used to regulate the use of commons makes it very hard to design a model through which cultural commons should be governed. The sharing of benefits is an important element. There are other factors besides benefit-sharing that must be taken into account. For instance, there is the question of agency (that is, who gets to represent the ICH holders in the negotiation of these agreements). There are also pressing issues of free, prior and informed consent that must be taken into account.[59]

Concluding remarks

The two organizations at issue here, UNESCO and WIPO, certainly offer different responses to the protection of traditional culture. Generally, UNESCO has tended towards a more holistic, softer approach. WIPO, on the other hand, focuses more on the economics of culture, and adopts an overall approach that may be characterized as harder. Ultimately both organizations offer feasible alternatives, each promoting different perspectives on what culture is, and what role it should play in today's society. As long as they both coexist, there are options available for every State (and hopefully soon, every heritage holder) to manage their own culture. Ideally, any option adopted and promoted institutionally would manage the paradox of protecting the core or essential culture important to people in such a way as to avoid stifling, freezing or mummifying it. Further, fostering the free flow of ideas and genuine cultural exchange crucial for cultural diversity is clearly an important aspiration of both organizations. As WIPO makes yet another attempt to finalize

---

55 The regulation of the public domain fails to deal with the effects of colonialism, which is of course very relevant when it comes to use the public domain as an emancipatory tool for previously colonized custodial communities like Indigenous peoples. For this critique, see K. Bowrey and J. Anderson, 'The Politics of Global Information Sharing: Whose Cultural Agendas are Being Advanced?', *Social and Legal Studies* 18(4), 2009, 1–26.

56 See J. Boyle, 'Foreword: The Opposite of Property?', in J. Boyle (ed.), *Collected Papers: Duke Conference on the Public Domain*, Chapel Hill, NC: Center for the Public Domain, 2003), 1–32, at 7.

57 For a summary explanation of the idea, see Chander and Sunder, op. cit., at 1332.

58 Ibid., at 1337.

59 For a fuller analysis of these issues, see, among others, Lixinski, op. cit., at 197–232.

its work on these issues, we hope it takes fully into account the potentials and pitfalls of its regime, and engages in significant dialogue with other available solutions also.

Bibliography

Alexander, I., *Copyright Law and the Public Interest in the Nineteenth Century*, Oxford: Hart, 2011.

Anderson, J.E., *Law, Knowledge, Culture: The Production of Indigenous Knowledge in Intellectual Property Law*, Cheltenham: Edward Elgar, 2009.

Baslar, K., *The Concept of the Common Heritage of Mankind in International Law*, The Hague: Brill, 1998.

Berryman, C.A., 'Toward More Universal Protection of Intangible Cultural Property', *J Intellectual Property Law* 1 (1994), 293, reprinted in Anthony D'Amato and Doris Estelle Long (eds), *International Intellectual Property Anthology*, Anderson, OH: Anderson Publishing Co., 1996, 76.

Blake, J., *Commentary on the UNESCO 2003 Convention on the Safeguarding of the Intangible Cultural Heritage*, Geneva: Institute for Art and Law, 2006.

Bowrey, K., 'Indigenous Culture, Knowledge and Intellectual Property: The Need for a New Category of Rights?', in K. Bowrey, M. Handler, and D. Nicol (eds), *Emerging Challenges in Intellectual Property*, Oxford: Oxford University Press, 2011, 46–67.

Bowrey, K. and Anderson, J., 'The Politics of Global Information Sharing: Whose Cultural Agendas are Being Advanced?', *Social and Legal Studies* 18(4), 2009, 1–26.

Boyle, J., 'Foreword: The Opposite of Property?', in J. Boyle (ed.), *Collected Papers: Duke Conference on the Public Domain*, Chapel Hill, NC: Center for the Public Domain, 2003, 1–32.

Boyle, J., 'The Second Enclosure Movement and the Construction of the Public Domain', in J. Boyle (ed.), *Collected Papers: Duke Conference on the Public Domain*, Chapel Hill, NC: Center for the Public Domain, 2003, 33–74.

Chander, A. and Sunder, M., 'The Romance of the Public Domain', *California Law Review* 92, 2004, 1331–1373.

Farley, C.H., 'Protecting Folklore of Indigenous Peoples: Is Intellectual Property the Answer?', *Connecticut Law Review* 30, 1997, 1–57.

Gervais, D.J., 'The Internationalization of Intellectual Property: New Challenges from the Very Old and the Very New', *Fordham Intellectual Property Media & Ent LJ* 12, 2002, 929–990.

Gibson, J., *Community Resources: Intellectual Property, International Trade and Protection of Traditional Knowledge*, London: Ashgate, 2009.

Halewood, M., 'Indigenous and Local Knowledge in International Law: A Preface to Sui Generis Intellectual Property Protection', *McGill LJ* 44, 1999, 953–996.

Hanse, H.C., Blakeney, M., Lourie, L.S., Salmon, P.E. and Visser, C, 'Symposium: Global Intellectual Property Rights: Boundaries of Access and Enforcement: Panel II: The Law and Policy of Protecting Folklore, Traditional Knowledge, and Genetic Resources', *Fordham Intell Prop Media & Ent LJ* 12, 2002, 753–803.

Kearney, A., 'Intangible Cultural Heritage: Global Awareness and Local Interest', in L. Smith and N. Akagawa (eds), *Intangible Heritage*, London: Routledge 2009, 209–226.

Kuruk, P., 'Protecting Folklore under Modern Intellectual Property Regimes: A Reappraisal of the Tensions between Individual and Communal Rights in Africa and the United States', *Am U L Rev* 48, 1999, 769–849.

Lipszyc, D. and Villalba, C.A., 'Preserving and Accessing our Cultural Heritage: Argentina's Experience through the domaine public payant', in E. Derclaye (ed.), *Copyright and Cultural Heritage: Preservation and Access to Works in a Digital World*, Cheltenham: Edward Elgar 2010, 179–192.

Lixinski, L., *Intangible Cultural Heritage in International Law*, Oxford: Oxford University Press 2013.

Long, D.E., 'The Impact of Foreign Investment on Indigenous Culture: An Intellectual Property Perspective', *NCJ Intl L & Com Reg* 23, 1998, 229–243.

Lucas-Schloetter, A., 'Folklore', in S. von Lewinski (ed.), *Indigenous Heritage and Intellectual Property*, The Hague: Kluwer Law International, 2003, 259–340.

New, W., 'WIPO Members Reach Tentative Deal on TK Treaties; External Offices Mired', *Intellectual Property Watch*, 27 September 2013. Online. Available: www.ip-watch.org (accessed 4 October 2013).

Obaldia, I.D., 'Western Intellectual Property and Indigenous Cultures: The Case of the Panamanian Indigenous Intellectual Property Law', *BU Intl LJ* 23, 2005, 337–394.

Okediji, R.L., 'An Enduring Legacy For the Knowledge Economy: UNESCO and the International Copyright System', in A.A. Yusuf (ed.), *Standard-Setting in UNESCO Vol I: Normative Action in Education, Science and Culture*, The Hague: Martinus Nijhoff and UNESCO, 2007, 113–134.

Sambuc, H.-P., *La Protection Internationale des Savoirs Traditionnels: La Nouvelle Frontière de la Proprieté Intellectuelle*, Paris: l'Harmattan, 2003.

Smith, L., *The Uses of Heritage*, London: Routledge, 2006.

von Lewinski, S., 'The Protection of Folklore', *Cardozo J Intl & Comp L* 11, 2003, 747–768.

11 The digitization of public cultural heritage collections and copyright in public private partnership projects

Lucky Belder[1]

Introduction

Since the nineteenth century, the support of museums, libraries and archives is considered as a public task. This has resulted in the situation today in which cultural heritage institutions have become almost completely dependent on public policies (and public funding) related to cultural heritage protection. However, recent years have seen the winds of change. If we think of the 2005 UNESCO Convention on the Protection and Promotion of the Diversity of Cultural Expressions[2] proclaiming the principle that cultural expressions have both cultural and economic value,[3] it seems that this principle is becoming more valid every day. Cultural heritage institutions are increasingly expected to develop business models that are aimed to strengthen their financial position. This is also necessary because of the new developments in information and communication technology, and the high degree of importance the European Union (EU) has placed on the digitization of cultural heritage collections. To realize these costly projects, cultural heritage institutions are encouraged to participate in public private partnerships. The potential business models in these partnerships are based on the exploitation of the economic and cultural value of cultural information, mostly by the exploitation of copyrights.

This contribution focuses on some of the copyright issues of the digitization of cultural heritage collections in public private partnerships. A case study is provided by two agreements signed by Google in the course of 2010 with the Royal Library in The Hague and the British Library. After a short introduction on the EU's policy regarding the digitization of cultural heritage collections

---

1 Lucky Belder is Assistant Professor at Utrecht University, Molengraaff Institute for Private Law, the CIER (Center of Intellectual Property Law).
2 Convention on the Protection and Promotion of the Diversity of Cultural Expressions, 20 October 2005, in force 18 March 2007, in UNESCO, Records of the General Conference, 33rd session, Paris, 3–21 October 2005, (2 vols, 2005), vol. I, at 83.
3 Ibid., preamble.

and the role of public private partnerships between public cultural heritage institutions and private partners, the focus shifts to the position of the Google agreements with regard to recent developments in the EU regulatory framework on copyright law. One of the problems that needs to be solved is the practical issue of obtaining copyright over works of which the authors are unknown or cannot be traced. A more fundamental issue is the exploitation of copyrights in digital materials and the balance between protecting the public domain and open access to cultural heritage, on the one hand, and the protection of intellectual property rights by limiting access on the other. The recent 2012 Orphan Works Directive as well as the 2013 Revision of the Directive on the Re-use of Public Sector Information contain provisions that are relevant to the copyright provisions in Public Private Partnership contracts on the digitization of cultural heritage. The overall question is how these directives contribute to the digital access to public heritage collections.

Digitization and public private partnerships

The EU Digital Library

The digitization of European cultural heritage equates to the online representation of the European Union's diverse and multilingual cultural heritage and is aimed at supporting cultural heritage institutions in providing access to, preserving and researching cultural heritage.[4] The Digital Library initiative of 2005 aimed to provide access to the documentation of the first 30 million objects by 2015, and to arrive at the full disclosure of all public domain EU cultural heritage in public institutions by 2025.[5] The website Europeana.eu was launched in 2008,[6] and serves as the aggregation tool for providing access to digital heritage collections in the European Union today. Europeana does not have its own repository but offers links to digitized material hosted by cultural heritage institutions in the EU Member States.[7]

The digitization of their collections is designed to support cultural heritage institutions in their public service mission with regard to the preservation of

---

4   Commission Recommendation 2006/585/EC of 24 August 2006 on the digitization and online accessibility of cultural material and digital preservation. [OJ L 236, 31 August 2006]. See also 'i2010: Digital Libraries.' COM(2005) 465 final, p. 30, which refers to the provisions of the 2005 UNESCO Convention on Cultural Diversity, ratified in the EU in 2006, and the 2006 Commission Recommendation 'on the digitization and online accessibility of cultural material and digital preservation', C(2006) 3808 final, p. 5 (2006 Recommendation), in which it is underscored that providing access to cultural heritage online contributes to the EU Goals stated in the Lisbon Treaty concerning growth, employment and social cohesion.
5   European Commission, Communication to the European Parliament, the Council, i2010: Digital Libraries, COM(2005) 465 final.
6   Europeana, Online. Available: www.europeana.eu (accessed 1 June 2013).
7   See also N. Stroeker and R. Vogels, *Survey Report on Digitization in European Cultural Heritage Institutions 2012*, report by Panteia on behalf of the ENUMERATE Thematic Network, May 2012, p. 4.

the collection, the facilitation of research as well as providing access to the public. Yet, these are not the only objectives. The digitization of cultural heritage is also regarded as contributing to new initiatives, products and services related to education, research and tourism in the digital economy. The support given to creative industries is thereby part of the EU Digital Agenda and Europe 2020 with the overall aim 'to deliver sustainable economic and social benefits from a digital single market'.[8] This confirms a tendency to see the cultural heritage sector in its economic capacity and to consider services related to the Arts and Cultural Heritage as one of the creative industries.[9]

However, the digitization of cultural heritage collections is costly. In 2011, it was estimated that the cost for digitization (including rights clearance) would be more than €100 billion.[10] The recommendation therefore was that cultural heritage institutions should enter into Public Private Partnerships (PPPs). This recommendation is part of a process in the European Union policies to rely more on private initiatives in the realization of public policy objectives, which marks a fundamental shift away from the State as a direct operator to the State as organizer, regulator and controller.[11]

Yet, public private partnerships are as such undefined in law. There are some definitions in EU Reports related to cultural heritage institutions that cover a wide range of partnership contracts that may be considered as PPPs. The 2008 Report on the Digital Library referred to 'any partnership between a private-sector corporation and a public-sector body, through which the parties contribute different assets to a project and achieve complementary objectives'.[12] In 2011, the New Renaissance Report described PPPs as ranging 'from direct investment of funds in return for exclusive commercial exploitation of the digitised material to classical sponsorship schemes for advertising/marketing purposes'.[13]

---

8 European Commission, Communication to the European Parliament, the Council, A Single Market for Intellectual Property Rights. Boosting Creativity and Innovation to Provide Economic Growth, High Quality Jobs and First Class Products and Services in Europe, COM(2010) 245 final, Introduction.

9 UNESCO Convention on the Protection and Promotion of the Diversity of Cultural Expressions, 2005; UNCTAD Creative Economy Report 2008: The Challenge of Assessing the Creative Economy towards Informed Policy-making, pp. 11–13. Online., Available: http://unctad.org/en/docs/ditc20082cer_en.pdf. (accessed 1 June 2013) and UNCTAD Creative Economy Report 2011: A Feasible Development Option, p. 7. Online. Available: http://unctad.org/en/Docs/ditctab20103_en.pdf (accessed 1 June 2013).

10 See generally N. Poole, UK Report of the Study into the Cost of Digitisation by the UK Collections Trust, Annex 5 to Comité des Sages, The New Renaissance 2011.

11 Green paper on Public-Private Partnerships and Community Law on Contracts and Concessions, COM(2004) 327 final.

12 *Final Report on Public Private Partnerships for the Digitization and Online Accessibility of Europe's Cultural Heritage*, High Level Expert Group on Digital Libraries, Sub-group on Public Private Partnerships, i2010 European Digital Libraries Initiative 2008, para. 2.

13 Comité des Sages, *The New Renaissance, Report of the Reflection Group on Bringing Europe's Cultural Heritage Online*, Brussels, 10 January 2011, para. 9.1.1.

The EU 2004 Green Paper presented an inventory of the beneficial aspects of PPPs, with particular emphasis on financial aspects, stating that by sharing investments, public expenses may be limited. However, other aspects like the sharing of technology and know-how between the public and private partners were also considered relevant. Moreover, the sharing of past experiences is considered to lead to the development of best practices, which generate an optimum contribution to creativity and innovation. Finally, the willingness of a private partner to invest, participate and share the risk is considered as contributing to political legitimation. This aspect works two ways: not only will it make the public partner even more aware of its social responsibility to establish working relations with private partners, but also the private partner will be interested in linking its business with a public partner, especially a strong brand like a national museum or library. Public private partnership may also be seen as a form of corporate social responsibility. Increasingly, private corporations consider it part of their brand identity to engage in projects with public interest aspects.[14]

Issues in public private partnerships

If PPPs are not defined in law as such, they can be considered as collaborative projects by undertakings that make use of both public and private resources. In EU competition law PPPs are therefore seen as projects by undertakings that share public and private resources, making the general rules of EU competition law, namely articles 101–105 TFEU/ 107–109 TFEU, relevant.[15] This means that, first and foremost, the public institutions that are engaged in these partnerships are subject to the general principles of equal treatment, objectivity, as well as proportionality and transparency.

The general rule is that, when a public institution enters into a public contract regarding works or services which are relevant to the internal market, the EU legal framework on public procurement is relevant. Equally important is that economic activities of the state or through state resources are not to interfere with competition in the internal market. The rules on state aid provide the legal framework in which these partnerships are to operate. [16]

Digitization contracts

In a first inventory of existing PPPs on the digitization of cultural heritage collections in 2011, it became clear that a few major players such as Google

---

14 Green paper on Public-Private Partnerships and Community Law on Contracts and Concessions, COM(2004) 327 final, para. 15.
15 Treaty on the Functioning of the European Union, Consolidated version, 53 OJEU 30 March 2010, 2010 C83/01.
16 See also, L. Belder (ed.) *Cultivate! Cultural Heritage Institutions, Copyright and Cultural Diversity in the European Union and Indonesia*, CIER Report, Utrecht: Utrecht University November 2013. Delex Amsterdam 2014.

are actively engaged in contracting with museums and libraries.[17] This section will discuss the content of the Cooperative Agreement between Google Ireland Inc. and two libraries – the Dutch Royal Library and the British Library – as case studies.

The contracts between Google Ireland Inc. and the two libraries are almost but not completely similar.[18] Both contracts are based on a standard contract predisposed by the company, with changes made after negotiating with the individual Library. It is of note that both contracts contain the provision that the parties are independent contractors, and that this agreement does not create an agency, partnership or joint venture (General Provisions, sub g).

The 'Cooperative Agreement' is a framework contract with a focus on public domain materials, although it does not specify the exact materials that are to be digitized. The parties agree to identify 'in good faith' the content to be digitized, provided that the Library commits to making at least a significant number of titles available for digitization. The Dutch Royal Library agreed to the digitization of 160,000 items while the British Library committed to 250,000 items. The company is to digitize the content, make one digital copy available to the Library, and if public domain material is made part of Google Books Services, Google is to provide a service at no cost to end-users for access to the display of the full text of the Digital Copy of that public domain work. The Agreement with the Royal Library stipulates the non-exclusive character of the Agreement in paragraph 2.1. The British Library has no such clause.

The most important part of a PPP agreement is the arrangement on the investments to be made by the respective parties. As both Libraries are public sector institutions, their investments are to be considered as a state resource. Not only does the making available of the collection represent a value, but the organization and collection of the titles in metadata may also have a value as a database. Yet, this value as such is not calculated. The contract only calculates the value of the physical books, as the company can decide whether or not to remove the books from the Libraries' premises in order to digitize them. This provision seems guided by motives related to the insurance of the value of physical books during their transportation and custody. There is also an agreement on the general costs for the Library. As stipulated in paragraph

17 Constructed by two Ivy League Stanford students in 1996, the search engine aims to 'organize the world's information and make it universally accessible and useful'. Google, *Google's mission is to organize the world's information and make it universally accessible and useful*. Online. Available: www.google.com/intl/en/about/company/ (accessed 1 June 2013).

18 The British Library contract was published after a procedure under the Freedom of Information Act by the Open Rights Group. See G. Ruiz, *Access to the Agreement between Google Books and the British Library*. Online. Available www.openrightsgroup.org/blog/2011/access-to-the-agreement-between-google-books-and-the-british-library (accessed 1 June 2013). Similarly, the Royal Library published the Google contract after an official procedure based on the Act on the access to public information. See Royal Library, *Contract signed, after a 'WOB' procedure*, 12 September 2011. Online. Available: www.kb.nl/nieuws/2011/contract-google-kb.html (accessed 1 June 2013).

3.1 of the respective contracts, these costs include those related to the locating, pulling and moving the materials to and from the designated location on the Library premises as well as re-shelving; the work done by Library employees and their agents; the network bandwidth and data storage required by the Library to receive the digital copy; if works are digitized on the Library premises, the necessary bandwidth as well as the physical space; and the conservation efforts on the books if so wished for by the library.

On the side of the company, the investment made is in the form of the work of its employees on the digitization and the making available of the digital copy; the hardware and software required to digitize the content; the space required to digitize content outside of the library; the transportation of the selected content; and the insurance against the risk of loss, damage or destruction of materials during transport and custody.

Do such arrangements comply with the general standards in EU Competition law? There may be issues of transparency and exclusivity with regard to the exploitation of the digitized materials which may add up to more than 15 years. Another issue is that the terms of these contracts are drafted by the company. For instance, the Dutch Agreement is to be covered by California law and the jurisdiction is set in the Courts of Santa Clara County, California USA. A similar provision in the contract with the British Library sets the choice of law on English law and the jurisdiction in English courts.[19]

Copyright aspects

The digitization of cultural heritage objects affects the copyright over the originals and the exploitation of the digitized materials. Copyright grants rights to the authors of original literary, scientific or artistic works, including books, letters, magazines, newspapers, photographs, paintings, sculptures, drawings, films, and music. Neighbouring rights are vested in performances, fixations thereof in sound or film, and in broadcasts. Structured collections of (meta)-data are protected by database rights, as long as there has been a substantial investment in the obtaining, verification or presentation of these data. During the protection period, the right-holder has the exclusive rights to forbid or allow others to copy the protected content, or to make this content accessible for others.

In the process of digitization, a digital copy is the reproduction of copyright and neighbouring rights protected content. Providing public access to content protected by copyright or neighbouring rights can either be done through 'communication to the public' or by 'making available to the public' in such a way that members of the public may access the content in a place and at a

19 British Library Contract, para. 12.11.

time individually chosen by them ('pull-' communication, or making available 'on demand'). Digitization of content qualifies as 'reproduction', or 'extraction', and placing content on a public website, for instance, constitutes 'making available to the public', or as 're-utilization'. In the terminology of databases rights, the reproduction of a digital copy is referred to as an 'extraction'. Making a database accessible for others involves the 're-utilization' thereof.

In the European Union, intellectual property (IP) rights are understood to provide an incentive for investments in innovation and creativity, and therefore contribute to economic growth.[20] Furthermore, IP protection is expected to contribute to 'European cultural creativity',[21] and to cultural diversity. The EU copyright policy is to seek a balance between a high level of intellectual property protection,[22] and measures to promote learning and culture,[23] including the preservation and dissemination of Europe's cultural heritage.[24]

Copyright is to ensure the protection of the creators of this content and also the related creative industries. Of equal interest to the flourishing of the digital single market is the access to content. On the other hand, cultural heritage institutions are key actors in the digital access to cultural heritage. As such cultural heritage institutions are to come to terms with the obstacles and challenges provided by the current regime of copyright law, and the economics of access to public information.

In principle, the right-holder has the exclusive right to the digitization and online dissemination of protected content. Directive 2001/29/EC provides for optional limitations to exclusive rights based on considerations related to the protection of freedom of speech, cultural diversity, privacy, the support of democracy and the correction of market failures. This allows for certain conditions under which content protected by copyright and neighbouring rights may be partially reproduced and communicated or made available to the public in quotations, or as an illustration to non-commercial teaching without the consent of the right-holder. Furthermore, it may be permissible to make a 'private copy' for non-commercial, private purposes.[25]

The 2001 Directive provides for two optional exceptions with regard to the creation, preservation and the disclosure of cultural content by cultural heritage institutions. There is a notable exception to the reproduction right

---

20 European Commission, Communication to the European Parliament, the Council, A Single Market for Intellectual Property Rights. Boosting Creativity and Innovation to Provide Economic Growth, High Quality Jobs and First Class Products and Services in Europe, COM(2010) 245 final, pp. 3–4.

21 Directive 2001/29/EC of the European Parliament and of the Council of 22 May 2001 on the harmonisation of certain aspects of copyright and related rights in the information society, cons. 11, 12 and 14.

22 Directive 2001/29/EC, cons. 4, 9. See also the EC Green Paper Copyright in the Knowledge Economy, COM(2008) 466/3, p. 4.

23 Directive 2001/29/EC, cons. 14.

24 COM(2010)245 final, p. 13.

25 Directive 2001/29/EC, Art. 5.

for specific acts of reproduction.[26] Another provision provides for an exception to both the reproduction right and the right of communication/making available to the public for purposes of research or private study through dedicated in-house (computer) terminals.[27] These two optional exceptions address public and non-commercial cultural heritage institutions, which are defined as 'publicly accessible, non-profit making libraries, museums, educational establishments or archives'.[28] The non-profit nature of cultural heritage institutions, along with the fact that they remain publicly accessible, is crucial to the availability of these exceptions. This means that, for instance, libraries housed in or used by companies that operate for direct or indirect economic or commercial advantage may not, in principle, rely on these exceptions to digitize a work for preservation purposes.[29]

The first exception allows for the digital reproduction of (analogue) individual collection items in need of restoration or for other preservation purposes. This exception may not be taken to provide for a blanket mass-digitization licence.[30] No remuneration is required for the reproductions made under this exception. It is notable that the optional nature of the two exceptions drafted for cultural heritage institutions, has led to implementation in (only) 18 of the EU's 28 Member States, who moreover have implemented these provisions differently.[31]

Copyright in the digitization contracts

A standard provision in the PPP digitization contracts is that both parties intend to perform the Agreement in compliance with national copyright law.

---

26   See Directive 2001/29/EC, Art. 5(2)(c) (stating that 'Member States may provide for exceptions to the reproduction right [. . .] in the following cases: [. . .] (c) In respect of specific acts of reproduction made by publicly accessible libraries, educational establishments or museums, or by archives, which are not for direct or indirect economic or commercial advantage.').

27   See Directive 2001/29/EC, Art. 5(3) (stating that 'Member States may provide for exceptions and limitations to the rights provided for in Articles 2 and 3 [*reproduction right* and *right of communication to the public of works and right of making available to the public of other subject matter*] in the following cases: [. . .] (n) use by communication or making available, for the purpose of research or private study, to individual members of the public by dedicated terminals on the premises of establishments referred to in para. 2(c) of works and other subject matter not subject to purchase and licensing terms which are contained in their collections [. . .]').

28   See also Directive 2001/29/EC, cons. 40.

29   See also S. von Lewinski and M.M. Walter, 'Information Society Directive', in M.M. Walter and S. von Lewinski (eds), *European Copyright Law. A Commentary*, Oxford: Oxford University Press 2010, pp. 1036–1037.

30   See Directive 2001/29/EC, preamble (4).

31   See L. Guibault, G. Westkamp, T. Riber-Mohn, P.B. Hugenholtz, *Study on the Implementation and Effect in Member States' Laws of Directive 2001/29/EC on the Harmonisation of Certain Aspects of Copyright and Related Rights in the Information Society*, Amsterdam: IvIR February 2007 (Guibault *et al.* 2007), pp. 46–47; G. Westkamp, *Part II: Country Reports on the Implementation of Directive 2001/29/EC in the Member States*, London: Queen Mary Intellectual Property Research Institute 2007, pp. 22–27.

Each party remains responsible for determining how to protect intellectual property rights in the relevant jurisdiction. If either party determines that a work should be treated as an in-copyright work in a jurisdiction, after notifying the other party, this work is to be treated as an in-copyright work by both partners. This is also relevant in view of the rights clearance of orphan works, the diligent search requirements, and the licence agreement with the national rights organizations. As for the protection of right-holders, the company is to implement software that accommodates any person who calls for a cessation in the making available of the digital materials, as long as the company determines that the copyright holder or his representative is responsible.

Copyright issues 1: rights clearance of works in view of large-scale digitization projects

To comply with national copyright law, it is necessary to operate a system of rights clearance, especially in view of the significant share of out-of-commerce works and orphan works in European cultural heritage collections. This resulted in the draft of the voluntary Memorandum of Understanding [. . .] Out of Commerce Works, and the recently adopted Orphan Works Directive.

The Brussels Memorandum of Understanding

The Brussels Memorandum of Understanding containing Key Principles on the Digitization and Making Available of Out-of-Commerce Works 2011 (Brussels Memorandum) is aimed to counter the problem of high transaction costs involved in the process of digitizing and making available of the category of copyright works that are 'out-of-commerce' by providing an 'extended collective licence'. The main objective of the Brussels Memorandum is to create a platform for clearing all necessary rights in certain types of copyrighted works that are no longer in commercial circulation. It was signed by six European and international collective management organizations (CMOs) and publishers' organizations representing right-holders to books and journals,[32] and three associations representing libraries in Europe.[33] Although the European Commission endorses the initiative, the Brussels Memorandum is to date not legally binding.

32 These are the European Federation of Journalists (EFJ), the European Publishers Council (EPC), the European Writers' Council (EWC), European Visual Artists (EVA), the Federation of European Publishers (FEP), the International Association of Scientific, Technical & Medical Publishers (STM) and the International Federation of Reprographic Rights Organisations (IFRRO).

33 These are the Association of European Research Libraries (LIBER), the Conference of European National Librarians (CENL) and the European Bureau of Library, Information and Documentation Associations (EBLIDA).

184   *Lucky Belder*

According to the Memorandum, publicly accessible, non-commercial cultural institutions[34] may obtain a single licence for the mass-digitization and online disclosure of out-of-commerce books and journals, including embedded images.[35] Out-of-commerce works are those which 'in all [. . .] versions and manifestations [. . .] no longer commercially available in customary channels of commerce', including the orphan works of which the authors are unknown or cannot be traced. Copies of works held by individuals, stored in libraries or on sale in second hand shops do not count as 'commercially available'. How to determine the commercial availability should be determined in the country in which the book or journal was first published, and depends on the specific availability of bibliographic data infrastructure. Publicly accessible cultural institutions may, on a voluntary basis, negotiate agreements for digitizing and making available out-of-commerce works in their collections with 'all relevant parties', which should in any case include collective management organizations representing authors and publishers.[36]

Orphan Works Directive

Although the Memorandum may be considered as an important step towards solving the problems related to the digitization of out of commerce works in cultural heritage institutions, the problem that more than 13 per cent of the works in cultural heritage collections are so called 'orphan works' made it necessary to develop an EU wide legislative tool.

The recent Orphan Works Directive (OWD) on certain permitted uses of orphan works regulates that all EU Member States are to provide for a limitation or exception regarding orphan works in favour of cultural heritage institutions.[37] This would seem to be a licence for the digitization and making available online of orphan works.[38] A work is regarded as an 'orphan work' if 'none of the right holders in that work or phonogram is identified or [. . .] none is located despite a diligent search'[39]. The 'diligent search' should be carried out in good faith, 'in respect of each work or other protected subject-matter, by consulting the appropriate sources for the category of works and other protected subject matter' in the Member State of first publication or broadcast.[40] Member States should develop lists of sources to be consulted in

34 The first preamble to the MoU refers to the definition of cultural institutions given in ISD, Art. 5(2)(c).
35 J. Axhamn, L. Guibault, *Cross-border Extended Collective Licensing: A Solution to Online Dissemination of Europe's Cultural Heritage?*, IViR Report for Europeana Connect, August 2011. Online. Available: http://bit.ly/oDLCAd (accessed 1 June 2013).
36 Principle 1(1) Brussels Memorandum.
37 Directive 2012/28/EU (Orphan Works Directive or OWD), OJ C 376, 22 December 2011, p. 66.
38 The scope of the limitation or exception is limited to published books, journals, newspapers, magazines or other writings (OWD, Art. 1(2)(a)); cinematographic or audiovisual works and phonograms (OWD, Art. 1(2)(b) & (c)) in the collections of cultural heritage institutions.
39 OWD, Art. 2.1.
40 OWD, Art. 3.1; 3.2.

this respect, and in any case the sources listed in the Annex to the Orphan Works Directive must be searched.[41]

The provisions of the Orphan Works Directive, however, do not provide a solution to the practical hurdle of the transaction costs that are involved in the 'diligent' search operations for right-holders. Cultural heritage institutions are still expected to invest time and effort into trying to identify and locate right-holders of all the individual works contained in heritage collections. In combination with the measures in the Brussels Memorandum of Understanding that provide for the introduction of a one-stop-shop for collective rights clearance on the basis of an Extended Collective Licensing model, these challenges may be effectively addressed. The Orphan Works Directive is to be considered as 'without prejudice to that Memorandum of Understanding',[42] and 'without prejudice to the arrangements in the Member States concerning the management of rights such as extended collective licenses, legal presumptions of representation and transfer, collective management or similar arrangements or a combination of them, including for mass digitization'.[43]

This means that, although the Brussels Memorandum and the Orphan Works Directive are intended to solve some of the problems regarding copyright in the digitization of cultural heritage collections, the costs of rights clearances and diligent searches, as well as the remuneration costs for right-holders are still a major issue in new digitization projects.[44]

The Orphan Works Directive is designed to support the work of cultural heritage institutions, defined in Art. 1.1 as 'publicly accessible libraries, educational establishments and museums, archives, film or audio heritage institutions and public service broadcasting stations, established in the Member States, in order to achieve aims related to their public-interest missions'. It is, however, considered that the major digitization projects may not be realized without collaborative projects with private partners. The Directive therefore allows these non-profit institutions to generate revenues for the exclusive purposes of covering their costs of digitizing and making available to the public, based on the digital copies of the orphan works.[45]

Furthermore, the exception for orphan works is to be regarded as being 'without prejudice to the freedom of contract' of cultural heritage institutions that are in the pursuit of their public interest missions, particularly in respect of public-private partnership agreements'.[46] This means that the commercial activities of the private partners are not to stand in the way of the exception for orphan works.

---

41 OWD, Art. 3.2.
42 OWD, cons. 4.
43 OWD, cons. 24.
44 M. Favale, *et al.*, 'Copyright, and the Regulation of Orphan Works: A Comparative Review of Seven Jurisdictions and a Rights Clearance Simulation', Report Commissioned by the Intellectual Property Office, 2013, p. 24.
45 OWD, Art. 6.2.
46 OWD, Art. 6.4.

Directive 2013/37/EU on the Re-use of Public Sector Information

The new Directive 2013/37/ EU amending Directive 2003/98/EC on the Re-use of Public Sector Information (RPSID) marks a new step in access to public domain information. The Directive makes it mandatory to regulate the re-use of public sector information. From now on, European national governments will be required to provide access to all public sector information data – from digital maps to population data to traffic statistics – at only marginal cost.[47]

While the 2003 Directive exempted cultural heritage institutions, the new Directive takes into account that libraries, museums and archives hold a significant amount of valuable public sector information resources, in particular since digitization projects have multiplied the amount of digital public domain material.[48] These cultural heritage collections and related metadata are seen as a potential base for digital content products and services that, by innovative re-use, can contribute to sectors such as learning and tourism.[49] The revised Directive, therefore, specifically includes the information contained in or created by libraries, museums and archives. The data generated in the digitization projects are to be made available in machine-readable and open formats. An exception is made for documents on which third parties hold intellectual property rights.[50]

The new RPSI Directive explicitly refers to the new business models that are being developed by cultural heritage institutions in public private partnerships. The Directive states that 'practice has shown that such public private partnerships can facilitate worthwhile use of cultural collections and at the same time accelerate access to the cultural heritage for members of the public'.[51] However, the Directive takes into account that these public private partnerships may require specific arrangements with regard to a period of exclusivity for the re-use of the digital copy as well as an arrangement regarding the revenues related to the making available of the digital copy. It is, therefore, set out that a certain period of exclusivity is to be allowed, but that these exclusive arrangements shall be transparent and made public.[52] The Directive stipulates that in case an agreed exclusive right relates to the preferential commercial exploitation necessary to digitize cultural resources, the period of such preferential exploitation shall not exceed in principal in general ten years. When that period exceeds ten years, its duration shall be subject to review during the eleventh year, and if applicable, every seven years thereafter.[53]

---

47   RPSID, Art. 3.1.
48   RPSID, Art. 3.2.
49   RPSID, cons. 15.
50   RPSID, cons. 9.
51   RPSID, cons. 30.
52   RPSID, Art. 10 (b).
53   RPSID, Art. 10 (b).

The basic rule in the Directive on what may be taken into account in view of the recovery of costs for the making available of public sector information is that public sector bodies can charge, at maximum, the marginal cost for reproduction, provision and dissemination of the information.[54] However, in view of the position of cultural heritage institutions, it is permissible for cultural heritage institutions to aim for full cost recovery plus a reasonable return on investment.[55] It is unclear, however, what this means. First problem is that the investment share of the libraries and the investment share by the private partner can be calculated in more than one way. How does one calculate the making available of a unique cultural heritage collection for digitization? Which costs should one include? Moreover, the reasonable return on investment seems to relate to the new business models that may be developed by the libraries *based* on the digital copies, in partnership with relevant corporate partners, and not *to the making available of the heritage collections* by public heritage institutions to such partners in the first place.

Looking at the provisions on the transparency regarding the digitization contracts, it is to be remembered that the Agreements scrutinized above as case studies have only been made public by the relevant Libraries after a court order, and they have some confidentiality clauses. Another aspect is the exclusive arrangements in terms of preferential commercial exploitation, because they are all based on the automatic extension of a first period of six years of preferential exploitation.

Other issues

Another problem with partnership agreements is related to the sustainability of the technology involved. A digital copy that is made in the year 2013 will need to be updated and adapted several times to new formats in order to be compatible with hardware and software in the year 2023. The partnership agreements that were examined as case studies however only refer to a Library copy, which will become the property of the Library. Although the RPSID encourages open data and formats, there is no provision in the RPSID that supports the public institutions in demanding access to the content on the level of the original digital copy during the whole of the contract period.

A second issue is that of 'social sustainability', related to the protection of fundamental rights, such as the right to privacy or cultural rights. Digitization agreements should include safeguards in this regard. Digitization projects may cover information and/or personal data that need to be handled with care and consideration. If anything, there should be an opt-out regime for parties who can demonstrate a personal interest in stopping the publication of certain information.

54 RPSID, Art. 6.2.
55 RPSID, Art. 6.4.

A third aspect is the economic sustainability of public private partnership contracts. An end clause should address the state of affairs after the partnership has ended, including the division of assets, claims and rights. Also, some regulation is required to govern how problems arising during the project term will be solved in a manner that is satisfactory to both parties.

In economic terms, PPPs are based on commercial contracts between two undertakings, with the added characteristic that public cultural heritage institutions are to be considered as public bodies, and under a specific regime of public procurement and state aid. These public bodies are, however, still in the early stages of exploring the potential of PPPs. Major problems are to be found not only in the differences in cultures and practices between the public and private sector, but also relating to the uncertainty as to the legal and normative framework in which these business models operate.

Conclusions

The Orphan Works Directive and the Re-use of Public Sector Information Directive represent the first steps. It cannot be said that the OWD makes life easier for cultural heritage institutions. Some libraries have already made it clear that it is difficult to comply with the rules on digital search.[56] One positive element is the emphasis in the RPSID on transparency in the contracts. However, this is not new, but merely confirms standard rules. Any confidentiality clause is in breach of those rules. However, it would seem that the RPSID does not provide sufficient rules on the conditions upon which public institutions can enter into partnerships with commercial partners in the first place. The focus is on the re-use of the digital copy that is the result of such a partnership and not on the creation of the digital copy.

More fundamentally both Directives consider that museums, libraries and archives are to be allowed to develop business models expecting a reasonable return on investment based on the digital copies regarding public domain cultural heritage collections. This marks a shift in thinking on the position of cultural heritage institutions in society, and the right of access to cultural heritage that they are expected to provide. If first their ambition was to focus on the protection of cultural objects, the focus has since turned towards the social function of cultural heritage and we see a trend towards an increased emphasis on the economic relevance of cultural heritage. This access may be guaranteed for a public far larger than could ever have been reached without digital technology; it is however reserved for those that can afford it. More guidance is needed at the European level in order to safeguard a minimum standard of free access to cultural heritage.

---

56 See e.g. Royal Library, *KB stelt publiek belang boven privaat auteursrecht.Tijdschriften tot 1940 online via opt out.* 22 October 2012. Online. Available: www.kb.nl/sites/default/files/docs/over wegingen_kb_optoutaanpak.pdf (accessed 1 June 2013).

Bibliography

Axhamn, J., and Guibault, L., *Cross-Border Extended Collective Licensing: A Solution to Online Dissemination of Europe's Cultural Heritage?*, IViR-Report for Europeana Connect, August 2011.

Belder, L., De Cock Buning, M., and de Bruin, R., Cultivate! *Cultural Heritage Institutions, Copyright and Cultural Diversity in the European Union and Indonesia*, CIER Report. Online. Available: www.cier.nl (accessed 1 June 2013).

Comité des Sages, *The New Renaissance. Report of the Reflection Group on Bringing Europe's Cultural Heritage Online*, Brussels 10 January 2011. Online. Available: http://ec.europa.eu/information_society/activities/digital_libraries/doc/refgroup/final_report_cds.pdf (accessed 1 June 2013).

European Commission, Green paper on Public-Private Partnerships and Community Law on Contracts and Concessions, COM(2004) 327 final.

European Commission, Communication to the European Parliament, the Council, i2010: Digital Libraries, COM(2005) 465 final.

European Commission Recommendation 2006/585/EC of 24 August 2006 on the Digitization and Online Accessibility of Cultural Material and Digital Preservation. COM(2006) 3808 final.

European Commission, EC Green Paper Copyright in the Knowledge Economy, COM(2008) 466/3.

European Commission, Communication to the European Parliament, the Council, A Single Market for Intellectual Property Rights. Boosting Creativity and Innovation to Provide Economic Growth, High Quality Jobs and First Class Products and Services in Europe, COM(2010) 245 final.

Europeana. Online. Available: www.europeana.eu (accessed 1 June 2013).

Favale, M., Homberg, F., Kretschmer, M., Mendis D., and Secchi, D., 'Copyright, and the Regulation of Orphan Works: A Comparative Review of Seven Jurisdictions and a Rights Clearance Simulation', Report Commissioned by the Intellectual Property Office, 2013.

Google, *Google's mission is to organize the world's information and make it universally accessible and useful*. Online. Available: www.google.com/intl/en/about/company/ (accessed 1 June 2013).

Guibault L., Westkamp, G., Riber-Mohn, T., Hugenholtz, P.B., *Study on the Implementation and Effect in Member States' Laws of Directive 2001/29/EC on the Harmonisation of Certain Aspects of Copyright and Related Rights in the Information Society*, Amsterdam: IvIR February 2007.

High Level Expert Group on Digital Libraries, Sub-group on Public Private Partnerships, *Final Report on Public Private Partnerships for the Digitization and Online Accessibility of Europe's Cultural Heritage*, i2010 European Digital Libraries Initiative, Brussels, 2008.

Poole, N., *The Cost of Digitising Europe's Cultural Heritage, A Report for the Comite des Sages of the European Commission*, the Collections Trust, Annex 5 to the Comité des Sages, The New Renaissance. Report of the Reflection Group on bringing Europe's Cultural Heritage Online, Brussels 10 January 2011.

Royal Library, *Contract signed, after a 'WOB' procedure*, 12 September 2011. Online. Available: www.kb.nl/nieuws/2011/contract-google-kb.html (accessed 1 June 2013).

Royal Library, *KB stelt publiek belang boven privaat auteursrecht.Tijdschriften tot 1940online via opt out*. 22 October 2012. Online. Available: www.kb.nl/sites/default/files/docs/overwegingen_kb_optoutaanpak.pdf (accessed 1 June 2013).

Ruiz, G., *Access to the Agreement between Google Books and the British Library*. Online. Available: www.openrightsgroup.org/blog/2011/access-to-the-agreement-between-google-books-and-the-british-library (accessed 1 June 2013).

Stroeker, N., Vogels, R., *Survey Report on Digitization in European Cultural Heritage Institutions 2012*, EUMERATE Thematic Network, May 2012.

UNCTAD, *Creative Economy Report 2008: The Challenge of Assessing the Creative Economy towards Informed Policy-making*. Online. Available: http://unctad.org/en/docs/ditc2008 2cer_en.pdf. (accessed 1 June 2013).

UNCTAD, *Creative Economy Report 2011: A Feasible Development Option*. Online. Available: http://unctad.org/en/Docs/ditctab20103_en.pdf (accessed 1 June 2013).

Von Lewinski, S., Walter, M.M., 'Information Society Directive', in M.M. Walter and S. von Lewinski (eds), *European Copyright Law. A Commentary*, Oxford: Oxford University Press 2010, pp. 1036–1037.

Westkamp, G., *Part II: Country Reports on the Implementation of Directive 2001/29/EC in the Member States*, London: Queen Mary Intellectual Property Research Institute 2007, pp. 22–27.

Part IV

Culture and economic interests in European law

12 Market integration and cultural diversity in EU law

Bruno De Witte

Introduction

The European Union has recently become more actively engaged, on the international scene, in cultural cooperation with third countries. In doing so, it has remained very cautious in proposing policy initiatives that could impact negatively on cultural diversity, or in accepting obligations that would constrain its own cultural policies or those of its Member States.[1] In particular, the European Union has consistently sought to exclude cultural goods and services from trade liberalization in the context of the WTO. This position was recently confirmed when the European Commission's mandate for the negotiation of a Transatlantic Trade and Investment Partnership (TTIP) was defined, and on this occasion the French minister of Culture Aurélie Filippetti repeated the traditional mantra: '*la culture n'est pas une marchandise comme les autres*'.[2] That same policy logic explains why the European Union was an enthusiastic participant in the negotiation of the UNESCO Convention on the Diversity of Cultural Expressions,[3] whose text insists on the right of states to define their cultural policies according to their own policy preferences. The Convention envisages the protection of cultural diversity essentially as the protection of each country's autonomy in deciding its own policy priorities in the cultural domain.

One may wonder, however, whether the European Union's *internal* legal regime corresponds to its external positions. Does it also accept internally that the EU Member States define their cultural policies in the way they wish?

---

1 On the practice of the European Union in the external domain, see the chapter in this volume by Evangelia Psychogiopoulou.

2 A. Filippetti, 'La France, fer de lance de l'exception culturelle face au marché libre', *Le Monde* 14 June 2013, p. 17. The EU's position in the trade-and-culture debate is examined in Mira Burri's contribution to this volume.

3 See E. Psychogiopoulou, 'The Convention on the Diversity of Cultural Expressions and the European Union – The Quest for Competence and Implementation', in T. Kono and S. Van Uytsel (eds), *The Unesco Convention on the Diversity of Cultural Expressions – A Tale of Fragmentation in International Law*, Antwerp: Intersentia, 2012, pp. 365–394.

Does it consider that cultural goods or services should not be subject to the logic of the internal market, or at least not in the same way as other goods and services? These are the questions that this chapter will deal with.

Cultural diversity in the system of European Union competences

The powers of the European Union in the field of culture are defined, by the European Treaties,[4] in a way that places heavy emphasis on their subsidiary nature. According to Article 167 TFEU, action by the Union in relation to culture shall (only) be for 'supporting and supplementing' the action of the Member States. Moreover, the Union is not allowed to enact 'any harmonisation of the laws and regulations of the member states' in this field. In the three-level system of EU competences which was codified by the Lisbon Treaty, culture is ranked in the lowliest category, namely the 'competence to carry out supporting, coordinating or complementary action' (Article 6 TFEU); in those areas, the main responsibility to define and implement policies remains with the Member States.[5]

Within this rather restrictive constitutional framework, the role of the European Union is limited to taking so-called 'incentive measures' in order to achieve the cultural policy aims set out in Article 167. Whereas incentive measures may not amount to harmonization, it is not clearly spelled out, in a positive way, what they are. In practice, they have taken the form essentially of multi-annual funding programmes through which the European Union supports projects proposed either by the Member State authorities or by private actors and organizations within the framework of policy objectives set at the European level. Under this funding mechanism, a number of trans-national cooperation projects, set up between cultural operators established in different European countries, benefit from additional EU funding. The EU funding mainly relates to performing arts and cultural heritage projects, but also supports projects in the visual arts, books and translations. Its aim is to promote the creation of cross-national cultural networks and thereby to promote cultural interaction across intra-EU borders. The name of the cultural policy programme of the EU changed over time for no obvious other reason than to denote some idea of policy dynamism: it was called *Culture 2000* in the period between 2000 and the end of 2006,[6] then simply the *Culture Programme (2007–2013)* in the following seven-year period,[7] and since 1 January 2014

---

4 With the plural term 'European Treaties', I refer to the Treaty on European Union (TEU) and the Treaty on the Functioning of the European Union (TFEU).

5 On this category of EU competences, see R. Schütze, 'Co-operative Federalism Constitution-alised: The Emergence of Complementary Competences in the EC Legal Order', *European Law Review* 31 (2006), 167–184.

6 The programme was established by Decision 508/2000 of 14 February 2000 (OJ 2000, L 63/1) and ran until the end of 2006.

7 Decision 1903/2006 of 12 December 2006 (OJ 2006, L 378/22).

a new seven-year programme called *Creative Europe* is in operation and incorporates the previously separate *Media* programme (which funds the production and Europe-wide distribution of audiovisual material).[8] Despite the gradual increase of the sums allocated to those programmes, they continue to form a tiny part of the overall EU budget.[9] Therefore, although the cultural programmes may make an important difference for the participants in the individual projects funded by it, their overall contribution to cultural diversity in Europe is rather limited.

The funding programmes are, however, only one part of the Union's policy impact on cultural diversity. Paragraph 4 of Article 167 TFEU hints, in fact, at the existence of a broader range of indirect cultural policies, in providing that '[T]he Union shall take cultural aspects into account in its action under other provisions of the Treaties, in particular in order to respect and to promote the diversity of its cultures.' This seemingly anodyne phrase points to an important phenomenon, namely the fact that cultural policy objectives may be achieved, and policy effects may be caused, under other headings than under the heading of cultural policy *per se*. This indirect approach faces an inherent limitation, though. In the system of EU competences as it was patiently constructed by the ECJ through its many 'legal basis' cases, the main content of EU legislation should always correspond to the specific aims or object mentioned in the Treaty article that serves as its legal base.[10] Therefore, in contrast with incentive measures based on Article 167 TFEU, all other European cultural policy measures may not be enacted *primarily* for the sake of promoting cultural diversity, but only as an integral part of laws and policies whose central aim is defined otherwise.

When pursuing these policies with an ancillary cultural dimension, the EU institutions should 'take into account' (in the terms of Article 167) the need to respect cultural diversity. This requirement stems not only from the language of Article 167(4), quoted above, but it is also a result of the wording of Article 3 TEU, and of Article 22 of the Charter of Fundamental Rights which makes respect of cultural diversity a duty for the EU institutions in *all* their actions (and also, incidentally, for the Member States when they implement EU policies).[11]

---

8 Regulation 1295/2013 of 11 December 2013 establishing the Creative Europe Programme (2014 to 2020) (OJ 2013, L 347/221).

9 The *Creative Europe* programme has a budget of €1.46 billion for its entire seven-year period of existence, which corresponds to an increase of 9 per cent compared to the funding of its two predecessor programmes, *Culture* and *Media*, but still amounts to no more than 0.15 per cent of the total EU budget.

10 K. St. C. Bradley, 'Powers and Procedures in the EU Constitution: Legal Bases and the Court', in P. Craig and G. de Búrca (eds), *The Evolution of EU Law* (2nd ed.), Oxford: Oxford University Press, 2011, pp. 85–109.

11 See the commentary of this Charter article by R. Craufurd Smith, 'Article 22', in S. Peers, T. Hervey, J. Kenner and A. Ward (eds), *The EU Charter of Fundamental Rights – A Commentary*, Oxford: Hart, 2014, pp. 605–631.

The protection of cultural diversity is thus 'mainstreamed' in all the policies of the EU, in theory at least. But there is little evidence of such mainstreaming in most EU policy domains, partly because this particular mainstreaming obligation is one of many that are imposed by the European Treaties, and partly because the cultural one is formulated less forcefully than those relating to environmental protection, gender equality or social protection; therefore, its neglect in day-to-day European policy making goes unnoticed and unsanctioned.[12] A recent example of the alleged neglect of cultural diversity mainstreaming is the EU's Roma Integration Framework,[13] which focuses on economic integration as a means for the social inclusion of the Roma minority, whereas the question of cultural diversity is not expressly considered in the Commission's document.[14]

In the remainder, I will focus on the impact on cultural diversity of one EU policy domain, albeit a very central one: the domain of the internal market. In assessing the impact of market integration, I will follow the traditional distinction, in EU law, between *negative integration* and *positive integration*, which will be looked at in the two following sections. By negative integration, I mean the role of the free movement of goods, services and persons, and of competition law, in *removing* obstacles caused by national rules and practices to the functioning of the internal market; by positive integration, I refer to the activity of the EU legislator to *harmonize* national regulations, by means of common European Union norms, in order to allow for the smooth functioning of the internal market. Thus, the effects of negative and positive integration are similar in requiring national policies that obstruct the functioning of the internal market to be modified; but the means through which this happens are different: negative integration consists in the abolition (or at least the non-application) of national laws, whereas positive integration consists in their (partial) replacement by new European norms. In both cases, questions arise as to how cultural diversity concerns are accommodated.

The internal market and cultural diversity: negative integration

Although the original text of the Treaty establishing the European Economic Community (Treaty of Rome, 1957) did not mention the word culture, it soon

---

12 For an overall analysis of the cultural mainstreaming requirement and its translation into practice, see E. Psychogiopoulou, *The Integration of Cultural Considerations in EU Law and Policies*, Leiden: Martinus Nijhoff, 2008.

13 European Commission Communication, *An EU Framework for National Roma Integration Strategies up to 2020*, COM(2011) 173 of 5 April 2011.

14 This absence of consideration of cultural diversity 'strongly suggests that the Framework's authors view any barriers that cultural practices may pose to economic integration as unacceptable and therefore to be overcome by thinking differently'. (M. Goodwin and R. Buijs, 'Making Good European Citizens of the Roma: A Closer Look at the EU Framework for National Roma Integration Strategies', *German Law Journal* 14 (2013), 2041–2056, at 2046).

became clear that the economic law concepts and principles contained in that treaty could affect cultural products and activities to the extent that these had an economic dimension. The EEC Treaty could, in fact, be said to have had an implicit 'cultural programme' from the very beginning, namely the elimination of national obstacles to the *free flow of cultural goods and activities* within the common European market. Only one little phrase of the original text of the EEC Treaty revealed this, and only in an indirect way: Article 36 (now Article 36 TFEU) allows the Member States to retain barriers to the free movement of goods for reasons of 'protection of national treasures possessing artistic, historic or archaeological value'. There would have been no need for that derogation in favour of a limited category of cultural goods if the basic principle of free movement did not apply to all cultural goods in the first place. Indeed, the European Court of Justice confirmed at an early stage of the life of the European Community that all products forming the object of a commercial transaction (including works of art, music recordings, newspapers and books) come under the Treaty rules on *free movement of goods*. Cultural activities are similarly subsumed within broader economic concepts as regards the *freedom to provide services*, which includes, for example, the cross-border distribution of television programmes. Similarly, the *free movement of persons* grants a right to mobility and non-discrimination to economic operators (whether employed or self-employed) in the cultural sector. Finally, the rules on *state aid and competition law* apply to undertakings in the cultural sector as in any other economic sector.

Free movement of goods, persons and services

Over the years, the issue of the relevance to be given to cultural diversity in the context of market integration became controversial as a subset of a broader question – whether, and to what extent, non-economic values can be accepted as a ground for preserving regulatory diversity among the Member States of the European Union, even when this diversity creates market barriers. Cultural diversity came to be seen as a value threatened by the impact of market integration, rather than as a value that underlies the free movement rights and is boosted by their effective application. [15]

In a long string of cases, the Court of Justice has accepted cultural policy justifications for restrictions of economic trade and personal mobility on condition that those restrictions are not discriminatory and not disproportional. It also held that the specific circumstances that may justify recourse to a restriction may vary from one country to another and from one era to another, [16]

---

15 Indeed, the way in which cultural diversity is usually problematized in this area of EU law does not mean that market integration and cultural diversity are necessarily antithetic values. To a large extent, it can be argued that market integration promotes the circulation of cultural products and activities and thus increases cultural diversity within each country of Europe.

16 ECJ, Case C-38/02, *Omega v. Bonn*, judgment of 14 October 2004, para. 31.

which means, in fact, recognizing the diversity of national value systems. Still, the European Court's record on issues of cultural diversity is patchy and unpredictable[17], and there is some diffidence among national courts as to whether the European Court will strike the right balance if asked to do so.

An example of this diffidence is the *Fun Radio* case, decided by the French *Conseil d'Etat* on 8 April 1998. It concerned the compatibility with European Union law of the French radio quotas regulation, according to which at least 40 per cent of songs broadcast on French radio stations must be *chansons d'expression française*. Similar types of linguistic requirements can, in fact, be found in many European countries. The supreme administrative court acknowledged that this constituted a restriction of intra-European trade, both of the free movement of goods (namely, of music recordings) and of the free movement of services (namely, of pre-packaged music programmes). It held, however, that these restrictions were justified for reasons of national cultural policy, and that the 40 per cent requirement was not disproportional. In doing so, the *Conseil d'Etat* formally applied the test formulated by the European Court of Justice for such situations, but it omitted to refer a preliminary question to the ECJ, for fear probably that the ECJ would reach a different conclusion as to the necessity of the restriction.[18]

The uncertainty involved, and the lack of predictability of the European Court's rulings, can be illustrated by comparing the reasoning and outcomes of the *UTECA* and *Las* judgments of the ECJ, which both involved linguistic requirements impeding free trade and free movement in the internal market.

The *UTECA* case concerned a Spanish law compelling all Spanish TV stations to spend 3 per cent of their revenue on the acquisition of films originally produced in one of the languages of Spain. This was challenged by an association of private broadcasters who argued that this reduced their business freedom by directing them towards the acquisition of films produced in Spain rather than films produced in other European countries, thereby also causing an unjustified restriction of the freedom to provide services. The case was referred by the Spanish administrative court to the ECJ. The European Court readily agreed that the Spanish law constituted a restriction of the freedom to provide services, but held that it was justified by the legitimate aim of defending and promoting the national languages of the country.[19] According to the Court, the fact that the language criterion operates, in

---

17 For an overall description of the Court's case-law in this field see R. Craufurd Smith, 'Community Intervention in the Cultural Field: Continuity or Change?', in R. Craufurd Smith (ed.), *Culture and European Union Law*, Oxford: Oxford University Press, 2004, pp. 19–80, at pp. 28–40; and S. de Vries, *Tensions within the Internal Market: The Functioning of the Internal Market and the Development of Horizontal and Flanking Policies*, Groningen: Europa Law Publishing, 2006, at pp. 85–96.

18 Conseil d'Etat, 8 April 1998, *Sté SERC Fun Radio*, (1999) *Revue française de droit administratif* 209 (and the conclusions of the *commissaire* Sylvie Hubac, *id.*, 194).

19 ECJ, Case C-222/07, *Unión de televisiones comerciales asociadas (UTECA)*, judgment of 5 March 2009; among the commentaries to this judgment, see I. Urrutia, 'Approach of the European

practice, to the advantage of Spanish film producers, 'cannot, of itself, constitute proof of the disproportionate nature of the measure (. . .) without rendering nugatory the recognition, as an overriding reason in the public interest, of the objective (. . .) of defending and promoting one or several of its official languages'.[20] This comes close to accepting that the EU's commitment to the protection of cultural and linguistic diversity may go as far as justifying the discriminatory treatment of goods, services or persons from other EU countries.

The *Anton Las* judgment of 2013 struck a rather different note. The case concerned employment legislation in the Flemish Community of Belgium, which requires the exclusive use of the Dutch language (the official language of the region) for the conclusion of employment contracts. This piece of legislation, dating from the early 1970s, was originally meant to protect employees against the practice of some employers imposing French as the language of communication within the firm. That original concern is no longer pressing, and the requirement now acts, arguably, as a deterrent to cross-border mobility of persons: non-Dutch speaking EU citizens might be reluctant to conclude an employment contract whose terms they do not understand. Upon a preliminary reference by a Belgian labour court, the ECJ ruled that this legislative requirement was indeed 'liable to have a dissuasive effect on non-Dutch-speaking employees and employers from other Member States and therefore constitutes a restriction on the freedom of movement of workers'.[21] When comparing with the facts of *UTECA*, this restriction of cross-border economic activity seems rather mild (would anyone really refrain from taking up a job in Flanders because they would not be able to understand the official version of the labour contract?), and not as severe as the restriction caused by the Spanish legislation on acquisition of films. And yet, although the Court of Justice explicitly referred to the recognition of cultural and linguistic diversity in Article 3(3) TEU and Article 22 of the Charter of Rights, and confirmed that Member States (or autonomous regions within them) may protect and promote their official languages,[22] it eventually struck down the Flemish law for imposing a disproportionately harsh restriction of free movement. The proportionality reasoning of this judgment was rightly criticized as open-ended and ad-hoc, giving little guidance for further cases involving conflicts between market integration and cultural diversity.[23]

Court of Justice on Accommodation of the European Language Diversity in the Internal Market: Overcoming Language Barriers or Fostering Linguistic Diversity?', *Columbia Journal of European Law* 18 (2012), 243–276, at 265 ff.; D. Ferri, 'Il principio di protezione e promozione della diversità culturale quale parametro di legittimità delle misure a tutela delle lingue nazionali nel settore audiovisivo', *Diritto pubblico comparato e europeo* (2009), 1381–1388.
20 *UTECA* judgment, para. 36.
21 ECJ, Case C-202/11, *Anton Las v PSA Antwerp NV*, judgment of 16 April 2013, para. 22.
22 *Las* judgment, paras 26 and 27.
23 E. Cloots, 'Respecting Linguistic Identity within the EU's Internal Market: *Las*', *Common Market Law Review* 51 (2014), 623–646.

From a comparative examination of the *UTECA* and *Las* cases, it appears that the Court of Justice does recognize, in principle, the importance of the value of cultural diversity in the post-Lisbon EU, but that, when balancing that value against the conflicting requirements of free movement rights law under its proportionality review, the outcome varies and is quite unpredictable.

State aid and tax benefits

From the point of view of EU law, public financial support to specific categories of firms may constitute *state aid*, and may be prohibited by the Commission if it is held to have a detrimental effect on the conditions of competition in the internal market. Small amounts of funding are automatically considered not to have such a detrimental effect, so that the European scrutiny of state subsidies is limited to large sums paid to individual firms, and to subsidy schemes with a large number of small beneficiaries.

State subsidies to the cultural sector, or with a cultural aim such as the strengthening of the national or regional language, are not excluded from the scope of the state aid regime, but the Maastricht Treaty introduced a new clause in the relevant Treaty article (this is now Article 107 para. 3(d) TFEU) according to which financial aid to promote culture and heritage conservation will be held compatible with EU law 'where such aid does not affect trading conditions and competition in the Union to an extent that is contrary to the common interest'. This 'culture clause' would appear to cover the many cultural subsidy schemes existing in all European countries, but it does not solve all the problems, since the sentence just quoted still leaves a very wide margin of discretion for the Commission to decide which schemes are compatible with, or contrary to, the 'common interest'. However, it is undeniable that the Member State governments, when inserting this clause in the EC Treaty back in 1992, wanted to convey a signal to the European Commission that it should tread carefully when examining state subsidies in the cultural domain, and it seems that the Commission is indeed acting cautiously and that cultural subsidy regimes in the Member States are not in danger of being challenged by the Commission.[24] It has been argued that the European Commission for a long time showed insufficient sensitivity to cultural diversity concerns in its state aid policy in connection with the funding of cinema production and distribution.[25] The Commission did, however, gradually adopt a more lenient approach, and its

---

24 See, for example, Commission Decision 1999/133/EC of 10 June 1998 concerning state aid in favour of the *Coopérative d'exportation du livre français*, OJ 1999, L 44/37: the Commission did not object to a French financial support mechanism that facilitated the acquisition of French language books by customers living abroad. It accepted that the objective of this aid scheme was 'to promote culture' in the sense of (then) Article 87(3)(d) EC Treaty and that it did not unduly affect competition in the common market. For similar reasoning, see the Commission decision on various schemes for the promotion of the Basque language, *State Aid N 161/2008 – Spain*, 16 July 2008.

25 See discussion of this point in A. Herold, 'Between Art and Commerce: Constitutional Contradictions within the Framework of the EU Film Policy', in F. Palermo and G.N.

current policy framework leaves considerable freedom to Member States to organize their film support schemes in the way they like, including in the definition of cultural criteria for funding. They are even allowed to impose so-called 'territorial spending obligations' which would seem – at first blush – to be antithetical to the idea of an internal market.[26]

The case of *tax exemptions* is more complicated than that of direct subsidies, as is illustrated by a judgment of the EFTA Court of 2002 in the *Einarsson v. Iceland* case in 2002.[27] Since, in that case, the EFTA Court applied rules of EU law, its judgment is also relevant for similar situations that would occur within an EU Member State rather than in the EFTA state Iceland. In Iceland, the sale of books in the Icelandic language (both original publications and translations from foreign languages) was subject to a VAT rate of 14 per cent, whereas the sale of foreign language books was subject to the normal VAT rate of 24.5 per cent. Einarsson, a private person who bought foreign language books, and was charged the higher VAT rate, complained that this constituted a breach of Article 14 of the EEA Agreement which provides that EFTA states shall not impose higher tax rates, directly or indirectly, on imported products compared to domestic products. The EFTA Court found that the language criterion created an indirect discrimination against imported books (since almost all books published in Icelandic were produced inside the country) and declared the differential rates to be contrary to the EEA Agreement. Since Article 14 of the EEA Agreement is an exact copy of (what is now) Article 110 TFEU, one could think that the legal position under EU law would be the same as outlined in the *Einarsson* judgment. This outcome may seem logical, in the light of the applicable legal rules, but it does not seem fair that European law should impede a country from taking measures to support the use of a small European language, and to protect the country's cultural distinctiveness. So, here is a specific point on which internal market law, as currently interpreted, does not leave enough room for cultural distinctiveness and linguistic diversity.

The internal market and cultural diversity: positive integration

Turning now from negative integration to positive integration, the task of combining the value of cultural diversity with that of market integration rests

Toggenburg (eds), *European Constitutional Values and Cultural Diversity*, Bozen/Bolzano: European Academy, 2003, 71–85, and in E. Psychogiopoulou, 'EC State Aid Control and Cultural Justifications', *Legal Issues of Economic Integration* 33 (2006), 3–28.

26 European Commission, *Communication on State aid for films and other audiovisual works*, OJ 2013, C 332/1. See in particular section 4(3) of the Communication, which deals with territorial spending obligations. Those are requirements for the beneficiaries of public funding to spend a given percentage of the production budget within the territory of the granting country.

27 EFTA Court, Case E-1/01, *Hördur Einarsson v The Icelandic State*, judgment of 22 February 2002. See the case note by G. Toggenburg, 'Sprache versus Markt: is die EFTA vielfalts- oder einfallslos?', *European Law Reporter* 6 (2002), 217–223.

on the shoulders of the EU legislative branch rather than the Court, or the Commission in its competition-monitoring role. The starting point of the analysis, as I have argued elsewhere, is the existence of a competence for the European Union to pursue an unspecified number of non-market aims by means of internal market legislation.[28] Seen in the context of the overall constitutional framework of the European Union as revised by the Lisbon Treaty, there is no reason why single pieces of internal market legislation should prioritize market-making rather than market-correction, or should privilege producer interests over broader societal interests. Deciding the appropriate mix of both ingredients is a matter for the internal market legislator – that is, for the political institutions participating in the law-making process.

The legal ground for this broad competence to regulate the internal market is the existence (discussed in the previous section) of mandatory requirements that may justify restrictions to free movement. If the Member States are allowed to maintain restrictions to the free movement of goods, persons or services when justified for the protection of language policy, media pluralism or the national artistic heritage (to name but a few of the interests recognized by the Treaty text or by the ECJ), then the European Union may, and must, address those same concerns when adopting harmonization measures designed to eliminate the restrictions. To illustrate this reasoning, consider the following example.

As part of its internal market programme, the European Community adopted, in the early 1990s, a Directive on the return of illegally exported cultural objects to their country of origin.[29] The legal basis of the Directive was Article 95 EC (the predecessor of the current Article 114 TFEU), as it pursued the aim to remove the impediment to market integration caused by the divergent, but mostly legitimate, national rules restricting the export of works of art.[30] The Directive provides for a mechanism for the physical return of cultural goods removed from the territory of a Member State in contravention of its cultural heritage laws. Before 1993, many states sought to enforce these laws by means of border controls on exported goods. In view of the aim to remove all border controls on goods by 1 January 1993, the Directive was enacted as a 'compensatory measure' offering an alternative means of enforcing national heritage laws in a border-free Europe. So, in this instance, the protection of the cultural heritage acted, first, as a legitimate national interest

---

28   B. De Witte, 'A Competence to Protect: The Pursuit of Non-Market Aims through Internal Market Legislation', in P. Syrpis (ed.), *The Judiciary, the Legislator and the Internal Market*, Cambridge: Cambridge University Press, 2012, pp. 25–46.

29   Directive 93/7 on the return of cultural objects unlawfully removed from the territory of a Member State (OJ 1993, L 74/74). The Directive was recently amended and strengthened, and published in a recast version: Directive 2014/60 of 15 May 2014 (OJ 2014, L 159/1).

30   For further elaboration of this example, see A. Biondi, 'The Merchant, the Thief and the Citizens: the Circulation of Works of Art within the European Union', *Common Market Law Review* 34, (1997), 1173–1195.

limiting the operation of the internal market recognized under Article 36 TFEU, and, second and later, as an objective pursued by the internal market legislator when adopting a harmonization measure designed to remove that barrier.

This example of Directive 93/7 reveals another, and rather surprising, facet of the constitutional framework of internal market legislation, namely the fact that non-market policy concerns can be pursued through internal market legislation even when those concerns cannot directly be addressed *as such* by the European legislator. As the introduction of this chapter recalled, cultural policy is an area in which the Union is barred by Article 167(5) TFEU from adopting legislation that harmonizes national laws and regulations. However, that prohibition does not prevent the harmonization of national laws that regulate cultural activities, when such harmonization appears necessary for the smooth functioning of the internal market. In such a case, the harmonization measure does not *directly or principally* pursue the cultural policy aims of Article 167, but rather aims at improving the functioning of the internal market *while taking into account* cultural policy considerations, as is indeed allowed by the mainstreaming clause of Article 167(4).

A further, and classic, example of this reasoning is provided by the Directive on Television without Frontiers, which was first adopted in 1989, revised in 1997 and again revised in 2007, and is now entitled the Directive on Audiovisual Media Services.[31] It is legally based on the internal market objective of facilitating the provision of media services from one European country to the others, but it is also, at the same time (and among other things), a cultural policy instrument, as is most clearly apparent from its Article 16, which seeks to promote the diffusion of television programmes of European origin.[32] Similarly, the Directive of 2001 harmonizing the national rules concerning the resale rights of artists (that is, their right to obtain a percentage of the proceeds of any later sales of their work)[33] was based on Article 95 EC and justified as a measure that would create a level playing-field for the trade in works of art. By extending the resale right to all EU countries, including for example the United Kingdom where it did not exist before, this Directive aimed at reducing the phenomenon of 'auction shopping', whereby the sale of works of art is displaced to countries that do not provide for a *droit de suite* of artists. Obviously, a level playing field could also have been achieved in the

---

31 A codified version of this Directive, incorporating the various amendments, was adopted as Directive 2010/13 of 10 March 2010 (OJ 2010, L 95/1).

32 For further discussion of the cultural policy dimension of this Directive, and of EU media law in general, see Rachael Craufurd Smith's chapter in this volume.

33 Directive 2001/84 of 27 September 2001 on the resale right for the benefit of the author of an original work of art (OJ 2001, L 272/32). See K. Lubina and H. Schneider, 'The Implementation of Droit de Suite – An Inventory and Reflection in the Light of the Community's Cultural Competence', in H. Schneider and P. Van den Bossche (eds), *Protection of Cultural Diversity from a European and International Perspective*, Antwerp: Intersentia, 2008, pp. 317–354.

opposite way, by abolishing the resale right in the countries where it existed. So, the choice made by the authors of the Directive reflects a cultural policy concern to strengthen the legal position of artists as against that of the art trade sector.

The constitutional *limit* that the Union legislator must observe in such cases is that the non-market objective or effect of the measure may never be the only and exclusive one. There is always a *threshold* requirement that the measure must *also* adequately contribute to improve the conditions for the establishment and functioning of the internal market. Internal market legislation, to be constitutionally valid, must satisfy a specific internal market test, in the sense that the authors of the act must make a plausible case that the act either helps removing disparities between national provisions that hinder the free movement of goods, services or persons, or helps removing disparities that cause distorted conditions of competition. However, as argued before, these need not be, and cannot logically be, the only purposes of internal market legislation. Such legislation also invariably and legitimately pursues other public policy objectives. Internal market legislation is always also 'about something else', and that something else may in fact be the main reason why the internal market measure was adopted.

This legal framework does not guarantee, obviously, that cultural policy concerns will be adequately, or sufficiently, taken on board in specific pieces of European legislation. The EU institutions will face the same choices as in other areas of internal market legislation as regards the appropriate mix of deregulation of national regimes and re-regulation by means of Europe-wide rules. That choice may be contested, but the Court of Justice is not likely to call into question the balance struck by the legislator.

Consider, in this regard, the recent seals products dispute. On 16 September 2009, the EU adopted a regulation on trade in seal products,[34] whose legal basis was Article 95 EC Treaty (since then renumbered as Article 114 TFEU). This is, therefore, a piece of internal market legislation whose *object* is defined as 'harmonising the rules across the Community as regards commercial activities concerning seal products, and thereby prevent the disturbance of the internal market in the products concerned'.[35] The main *objective* or aim of this measure, though, is the protection of the welfare of animals in conjunction with the protection of cultural diversity; the regulation introduces a general ban on the marketing of all products made from seals because of the conditions, considered to be unacceptable, under which those animals are hunted and killed (animal welfare concern), but this is accompanied by a conditional derogation for products resulting from hunts traditionally conducted by Inuit and other Indigenous communities. The latter may be termed a cultural diversity concern, as the preamble of the Regulation states that 'the hunt is an integral part of the culture and identity of the members of the Inuit society, and as

34   Regulation 1007/2009 of 16 September 2009 on trade in seal products (OJ 2009, L 286/36).
35   Preamble of the Regulation, recital 8.

such is recognised by the United Nations Declaration on the Rights of Indigenous Peoples'.[36] However, the Inuit organizations, seals traders, and Canada and Norway challenged the EU regime for striking the wrong balance by imposing an excessive restraint on the traditional activity of the Inuit (and the somewhat less traditional activity of the fur traders), but both the EU's General Court and the WTO's Appellate Body essentially upheld the validity of the EU's regime, and the issue of cultural diversity barely surfaced in those rulings.[37]

Once EU legislation is in place, then the possibility for States to argue for derogations inspired by cultural diversity concerns is constrained by the text of that legislation. A good illustration of that mechanism is provided by an ECJ judgment regarding linguistic requirements for lawyers in Luxembourg. The European Commission had brought before the ECJ an infringement action against Luxembourg in relation to the application, in that country, of Directive 98/5 on the professional establishment of lawyers in Member States other than the one in which they obtained their qualifying professional degree.[38] This Directive is one of the many legislative measures designed to facilitate the free movement of persons within the EU, in this case by requiring all Member States to recognize the professional qualifications of lawyers from other EU countries. The Commission argued that Luxembourg had created a number of undue obstacles to the correct application of the Directive by imposing additional barriers not expressly allowed by it. One such barrier was a language requirement. Foreign lawyers could only be registered at the Luxembourg bar if they could show their proficiency in the three national languages, French, German and Luxembourgish. It is clear that this condition, especially that of knowing Luxembourgish, acts as an effective barrier against the establishment of most if not all foreign lawyers. In its Grand Chamber judgment of 19 September 2006, the Court of Justice held that the Directive 98/5 listed all the requirements that foreign-trained lawyers had to meet in order to be allowed to practise their profession under their home title, and that the Member States could not add any other conditions such as a language knowledge requirement. That requirement was therefore held to be in breach of EU law.[39]

---

36 Preamble of the Regulation, recital 14.
37 General Court of the EU, Case T-526/10, *Inuit Tapiriit Kanatami and others v. European Commission*, judgment of 25 April 2013; WTO Appellate Body Report, European Communities – Measures Prohibiting the Importation and Marketing of Seal Products, WT/DS400/AB/R and WT/DS401/AB/R, 22 May 2014. For a discussion of the legal and policy issues involved in those disputes, see T. Perišin, 'Is the EU Seals Products Regulation a Sealed Deal? EU and WTO Challenges', *International and Comparative Law Quarterly* 62 (2013), 373–405; see also Valentina Vadi's chapter in this volume.
38 Directive 98/5 of 16 February 1998 (OJ 1998, L 77/36).
39 ECJ, Case C-193/05, *Commission v Luxembourg*, judgment of 19 September 2006. The same issue was raised in a preliminary reference which originated in legal action taken by a British lawyer against the Luxembourg bar; that case was decided on the same day and the Court's

Conclusion: how much cultural diversity in the European Union's internal market?

Defining the rightful place of the value of cultural diversity in the context of the EU's market integration regime remains a controversial question. Recent Treaty reforms, in particular the Lisbon Treaty, have given more salience to cultural diversity, by inscribing it among the main objectives of the European Union, in Article 3 TEU, and by including respect for cultural diversity in the (now binding) text of the EU's Charter of Fundamental Rights. This growing salience is reflected in the *external* domain by the European Union's conclusion and ratification of the Unesco Convention on Cultural Diversity and by the increased attention to cultural cooperation clauses in the EU's external agreements. *Inside* the EU, though, cultural diversity plays a more ambiguous role. On the one hand, it is treated with due respect in Court judgments and policy documents of the EU institutions, and the Union's budget supports projects that favour the mutual exchange of cultural creations between the Member States. On the other hand, though, the pursuit by the Member States of their cultural or linguistic policies occasionally clashes with the principles of market integration, thus requiring the intervention by the Court of Justice or the Commission, in the context of negative integration, and regulatory choices by the European legislator, in the context of positive integration. When confronted with the Union's 'core idea' of market integration, the lofty statements about the protection of cultural diversity often – but not always – take second place.

Bibliography

Biondi, A., 'The Merchant, the Thief and the Citizens: the Circulation of Works of Art within the European Union', *Common Market Law Review* 34 (1997), 1173–1195.

Bradley, K. St. C., 'Powers and Procedures in the EU Constitution: Legal Bases and the Court', in P. Craig and G. de Búrca (eds), *The Evolution of EU Law* (2nd ed.), Oxford: Oxford University Press, 2011, pp. 85–109.

Cloots, E., 'Respecting Linguistic Identity Within the EU's Internal Market: Las', *Common Market Law Review* 51 (2014), 623–646.

Craufurd Smith, R., 'Community Intervention in the Cultural Field: Continuity or Change?', in R. Craufurd Smith (ed.), *Culture and European Union Law*, Oxford: Oxford University Press, 2004, pp. 19–80.

Craufurd Smith, R., 'Article 22', in S. Peers, T. Hervey, J. Kenner and A. Ward (eds),*The EU Charter of Fundamental Rights – A Commentary*, Oxford: Hart, 2014, pp. 605–631.

de Vries, S., *Tensions Within the Internal Market: The Functioning of the Internal Market and the Development of Horizontal and Flanking Policies*, Groningen: Europa Law, 2006.

ruling on the language issue was identical: Case C-506/04, *Graham J. Wilson v Ordre des avocats du barreau de Luxembourg*. On both these judgments, see the comments by J. Vanhamme, 'L'équivalence des langues dans le marché intérieur; l'apport de la Cour de Justice', *Cahiers de droit européen* 2007, 359–380, at 373–378.

De Witte, B., 'A Competence to Protect: The Pursuit of Non-Market Aims through Internal Market Legislation', in P. Syrpis (ed.), *The Judiciary, the Legislator and the Internal Market*, Cambridge: Cambridge University Press, 2012, pp. 25–46.

Ferri, D., 'Il principio di protezione e promozione della diversità culturale quale parametro di legittimità delle misure a tutela delle lingue nazionali nel settore audiovisivo', *Diritto pubblico comparato e europeo* (2009), 1381–1388.

Filippetti, A., 'La France, fer de lance de l'exception culturelle face au marché libre', *Le Monde* 14 June 2013, p. 17.

Goodwin, M. and Buijs R., 'Making Good European Citizens of the Roma: A Closer Look at the EU Framework for National Roma Integration Strategies', *German Law Journal* 14 (2013), 2041–2056.

Herold, A., 'Between Art and Commerce: Constitutional Contradictions within the Framework of the EU Film Policy', in F. Palermo and G.N. Toggenburg (eds), *European Constitutional Values and Cultural Diversity*, Bozen/Bolzano: European Academy, 2003, 71–85.

Lubina, K. and Schneider, H., 'The Implementation of Droit de Suite – An Inventory and Reflection in the Light of the Community's Cultural Competence', in H. Schneider and P. Van den Bossche (eds), *Protection of Cultural Diversity from a European and International Perspective*, Antwerp: Intersentia, 2008, pp. 317–354.

Perišin, T., 'Is the EU Seals Products Regulation a Sealed Deal? EU and WTO Challenges', *International and Comparative Law Quarterly* 62 (2013), 373–405.

Psychogiopoulou, E., 'EC State Aid Control and Cultural Justifications', *Legal Issues of Economic Integration* 33 (2006), 3–28.

Psychogiopoulou, E., *The Integration of Cultural Considerations in EU Law and Policies*, Leiden: Martinus Nijhoff, 2008.

Psychogiopoulou, E., 'The Convention on the Diversity of Cultural Expressions and the European Union – The Quest for Competence and Implementation', in T. Kono and S. Van Uytsel (eds), *The Unesco Convention on the Diversity of Cultural Expressions – A Tale of Fragmentation in International Law*, Antwerp: Intersentia, 2012, pp. 365–394.

Schütze, R., 'Co-operative Federalism Constitutionalised: The Emergence of Complementary Competences in the EC Legal Order', *European Law Review* 31 (2006), 167–184.

Toggenburg, G., 'Sprache versus Markt: ist die EFTA vielfalts- oder einfallslos?', *European Law Reporter* 6 (2002), 217–223.

Urrutia, I., 'Approach of the European Court of Justice on Accommodation of the European Language Diversity in the Internal Market: Overcoming Language Barriers or Fostering Linguistic Diversity?', *Columbia Journal of European Law* 18 (2012), 243–276.

Vanhamme, J., 'L'équivalence des langues dans le marché intérieur; l'apport de la Cour de Justice', *Cahiers de droit européen* (2007), 359–380.

13 EU media law

Cultural policy or business as usual?

Rachael Craufurd Smith

Introduction

This chapter considers how the European Union (EU) has accommodated cultural concerns in its regulation of the audiovisual sector. It argues that the EU pursued cultural objectives from the very start of its engagement with the mass media but that these objectives were ones that fitted neatly with, and indeed were used to support, its primary economic goals. Domestic cultural policies were largely inward-looking and created barriers to the establishment of an integrated European audiovisual market. In seeking to open up domestic markets to foreign audiovisual goods and services, the EU thus promoted cultural diversity and exchange, but also potentially undermined Member State capabilities in the cultural field. The EU has sometimes been depicted as unable to push through positive measures in support of cultural objectives but to a significant extent negative integration was seen as adequately responding to its specific economic and cultural concerns.

The EU has generally presented its European cultural objectives as complementing those at domestic level and in the following sections I consider to what extent this has indeed been the case. The first two sections focus on EU attempts to stimulate the development of European television services and an integrated television market, while the remaining sections briefly discuss EU intervention in the fields of industrial policy and competition law. Throughout this chapter I consider how the EU's evolving competence in the field, coupled with technological changes, have affected the rationales for, and way in which, the EU engages with the mass media.

EU media policy and the European polity

Given the economic focus of the 1957 EEC Treaty it may seem surprising that the Community's initial engagement with the media sector had such a pronounced political and cultural focus. The European Parliament ('EP'), directly elected from 1979 and acutely aware of the democratic dimension to European politics, set the initial frame of reference in a number of influential advisory papers.[1] The 1982 Hahn Report observed that for 'European unification' to be successful Europeans needed access to reliable information: '[a] European identity will only develop if Europeans are adequately informed. At present information via the mass media is controlled at national level.'[2] The Report thus called for the development of a European television company or European television channel that would sit alongside domestic stations and take advantage of the possibilities of satellite broadcasting.[3] It also called on the Commission to advise as to the legal basis for Community action in the media field; the need for such action; and the practicalities of creating a European television channel.

The Commission responded in 1983 with its interim report 'Realities and Tendencies in European Television: Perspectives and Options'.[4] This concluded that Community engagement with the audiovisual sector was required on industrial, political and cultural grounds. Industrially, the Community could facilitate the creation of a European broadcasting market through adopting technical standards, removing domestic barriers to trade and stimulating the production of television programmes to fill the new cross-border channels. Politically, the creation of a common television service was required as 'a first step towards a more European perception of the prospects and problems of tomorrow', a perception that would not be fully reflected in domestic services. '[L]ast but not least', action was needed 'to maintain the pluralism of national identities that go to make up the cultural unity of Europe.'[5]

Because the creation of an independent European broadcasting organisation was considered neither financially nor politically feasible, the Commission proposed that the Community should support the development of satellite services by the European Broadcasting Union ('EBU'), a consortium of Europe's public service broadcasters. The EBU had already carried out a short trial of a collaborative satellite television service, 'EURIKON', in 1982, very much in line with the Commission's objectives.[6] The preference for a public service initiative reflected a degree of scepticism as to the ability of private commercial broadcasters to then provide the 'balanced and all round European programme of news, politics, education, culture, entertainment and sport' that both the

---

1 Discussed in R. Collins, *Broadcasting and Audiovisual Policy in the European Single Market*, London: John Libbey, 1994, ch. 2. On the influence of the EP in the media field see K. Sarikakis, 'Defending Communicative Spaces: The Remits and Limits of the European Parliament', in J. Harrison and B. Wessels (eds), *Mediating Europe: New Media, Mass Communications and the European Public Sphere*, Oxford: Berghahn Books, 2009, pp. 239–261.
2 EP Committee on Youth, Culture, Education, Information and Sport, Report on Radio and Television Broadcasting in the EC, February 1982, Doc. 1–1013/81, Explanatory Statement at p. 8.
3 Ibid. at p. 10, though the EP was itself divided over EEC competence in the media field, see Collins, op. cit., p. 39, n. 1.
4 Commission, Realities and Tendencies in European Television: Perspectives and Options, COM(83) 229 final.
5 Commission, Realities and Tendencies, op. cit., p. 5.
6 Commission, Realities and Tendencies, op. cit., p. 18.

Commission and EP considered to be required.[7] Despite Community support, the EBU's follow-on satellite service, Europa, was not successful, with audiences displaying little appetite for culturally unfamiliar foreign content.[8] David Ward has noted that financial and administrative difficulties also dogged the EBU's early satellite venture so that its demise cannot be entirely attributed to the 'cultural discount'.[9]

Despite the Community's initial failure to realise a 'European' television channel and ongoing doubts as to whether a genuine European public sphere can be created given Europe's cultural and linguistic diversity, the EU institutions have not yet given up on the task.[10] The EP in its September 2010 Resolution on Journalism and New Media identified a key goal of the EU institutions 'to create together a European public sphere'.[11] The internet undoubtedly offers citizens enhanced opportunities to access foreign media services produced with a non-national frame of reference and to engage in dialogue with citizens from other countries. News websites, such as the *European Daily*,[12] now offer informed, dedicated coverage of European affairs and national media increasingly report on a range of European matters, though often from a 'foreign affairs' perspective.[13] Access to reliable sources of information is particularly important in countries such as Britain where sections of the media have adopted an increasingly 'nationalist and . . . xenophobic approach to the coverage of European affairs'.[14] The Commission has consequently continued to support collaborative European media initiatives, notably the multi-lingual Euronews service, which seeks to be both impartial and to avoid distinctively national perspectives.[15] Yet, EU support for independent media of this type is politically risky, always open to characterisation by a hostile press as an attempt to 'rig' the news agenda and create positive publicity for its policies.

7   Commission, Realities and Tendencies, op. cit., p. 23. The EU's approach to public service broadcasting has varied over time and with the DG concerned, see section 5.
8   Collins, op. cit., p. 48.
9   D. Ward, *The European Union Democratic Deficit and the Public Sphere: An Evaluation of EU Media Policy*, Amsterdam: IOS Press, 2002, p. 51.
10 Collins, op. cit. ch. 3; Ward, op. cit., ch. 1; R. Koopmans and J. Erbe 'Towards a European Public Sphere?', *Innovation*, 2004, vol. 17, 97–118.
11 European Parliament, Resolution on Journalism and New Media – Creating a Public Sphere in Europe, 7 September 2010, P7_TA(2010) 0307, para. 1.
12 European Daily. Online. Available: http://europeandaily.com/ (accessed 25 November 2013).
13 L.B. Adam, 'The Significance of EU Topics in National Media. Has There Been an Europeanization of Reporting in the National Media?', *Bruges Political Research Papers*, No. 27, November 2012.
14 O. Daddow, 'The UK Media and 'Europe': From Permissive Consensus to Destructive Dissent', *International Affairs* 2012, vol. 88, 1219–1236 at 1219.
15 EurActiv, 'Commission wants to Boost Euronews TV Channel', 28 October 2010. Online. Available: www.euractiv.com/future-eu/commission-wants-boost-euronews-news-499198 and see Euronews website. Online. Available: www.euronews.com/media/download/mediapack/media-kit-201307-English.pdf (both accessed 25 November 2013).

When the EEC began to lay the foundations of its audiovisual policy in the early eighties, the Treaty basis for socio-political initiatives of this type was far from clear. The legal position of the EU is now more robust, with potential bases for action, alongside the established economic rationales, in the fields of citizenship, the protection of democratic principles, and human rights. The status of European citizen, formally recognised in the 1992 Maastricht Treaty, affords the right to stand and vote not only in European elections but also in municipal elections when resident in other EU countries.[16] The Court of Justice has developed this status further, holding in its *Ruiz Zambrano* ruling that Article 20 TFEU precludes 'national measures that have the effect of depriving citizens of the Union of the genuine enjoyment of the substance of the rights conferred by virtue of their status as citizens of the Union'.[17] *Ruiz Zambrano* indicated that European citizenship might afford protection even in a purely internal situation and was relied on by the High Level Group ('HLG'), set up by the Commission in 2011 to examine the scope for EU action to protect media freedom and pluralism. The HLG concluded that '[t]he EU should be considered competent to act to protect media freedom and pluralism at State level in order to guarantee the substance of the rights granted by the Treaties to EU citizens, in particular the rights of free movement and to representative democracy. The link between media freedom and pluralism and EU democracy, in particular, justifies a more extensive competence of the EU with respect to these fundamental rights than to others enshrined in the Charter of Fundamental Rights.'[18] Von Bogdandy *et al.* also suggest that where a Member State systematically violates human rights, citizens may rely on Article 20 TFEU to seek direct redress in national courts and at EU level.[19]

In relation to democratic principles, the TEU calls on Member States to respect 'liberty, democracy, respect for human rights and fundamental freedoms, and the rule of law', and establishes a procedure for review and ultimate political sanction where there is a risk of serious breach by a Member State of these principles.[20] There is no indication that these powers apply solely in the context of the application of EU law. In addition, the Lisbon Treaty added a new Title II to the TEU on Democratic Principles, which affirms the right of every citizen 'to participate in the democratic life of the Union'.[21] It also established the citizens' initiative, whereby one million citizens, with sufficient cross-country support, can call on the institutions to take forward

---

16 See now Art. 20 TFEU.
17 Case C-34/09, *Ruiz Zambrano* (2011) ECR I-1177, para. 42. See also A. Von Bogdandy, M. Kottmann, C. Antpöhler, J. Dickschen, S. Hentrei and M.Smrkolj, 'Reverse Solange – Protecting the Essence of Fundamental Rights Against EU Member States', *Common Market Law Review*, 2012, vol. 49, 489–520.
18 High Level Group on Media Freedom and Pluralism, Report: A Free and Pluralistic Media to Sustain European Democracy, January 2013, at p. 21.
19 Bogdandy *et al.*, op. cit.
20 Now Arts 2 and 7 TEU.
21 Art. 10.3 TEU.

legislation in specific fields, and enhanced the role of national parliaments in overseeing Union action and ensuring respect for the principle of subsidiarity. Without access to accurate information, particularly from the media, such rights become largely meaningless.

Human rights, incorporated into the Community system by early judgments of the European Court of Justice,[22] were given additional political protection through Articles 2 and 7 TEU discussed above. More recently, the Lisbon Treaty has afforded Treaty status to the rights contained in the Charter of Fundamental Rights of the EU (the 'Charter').[23] The Charter explicitly calls for respect for '[t]he freedom and pluralism of the media' and for 'cultural, religious and linguistic diversity'.[24] Article 51 of the Charter importantly limits its application to the EU institutions and agencies and to Member States when 'implementing Union law'.

The gradual strengthening of the provisions relating to citizenship, democracy and human rights in the EU treaties has had a palpable effect on how specific media issues are now being characterised and addressed at the EU level. Nowhere is this more apparent than in the field of media ownership. During the course of the eighties, political and civil society organisations in a number of EU countries became increasingly alarmed at the high levels of media consolidation in their countries and the close links between powerful media groups and political factions. Unable to obtain a solution domestically, they looked to Europe for redress and found a willing champion in the EP, which repeatedly called on the Community to address media ownership concentration.[25] This in turn led to the publication by the Commission in 1992 of a Green Paper on media pluralism.[26] The Commission concluded that media pluralism was primarily a matter for the Member States but that minimum controls on media ownership could be established on the basis of the Treaty Internal Market rules: different domestic limits on media holdings could distort competition and impede freedom of establishment and the provision of services.[27] Agreeing common standards was complicated, however, by the diversity of approaches to regulating media ownership in the Member States and very different market contexts. Faced with intense lobbying from private broadcasters and divergent positions among the Commission Directorates General and Member States, the Commission dropped the project prior to submitting a formal legislative draft.[28]

22   Case 11/1970, *Internationale Handelsgesellschaft* [1970] ECR 1125.
23   Art. 6.1 TEU.
24   Arts 11 and 22 of the Charter.
25   A. Harcourt, 'EU Media Ownership Regulation: Conflict Over the Definition of Alternatives', *Journal of Common Market Studies*, 1998, vol. 36, 369–389.
26   European Commission, Pluralism and Media Concentration in the Internal Market, An Assessment of the Need for Community Action, COM(92) 480 final.
27   Ibid. at 59. See also Commission, Follow-up to the Consultation Process Relating to the Green Paper on 'Pluralism and Media Concentration in the Internal Market – An Assessment of the Need for Community Action', COM(94) 353 final.
28   For detailed coverage see Harcourt (1998), op. cit.

The EP was not, however, prepared to leave the issue and began to focus instead on those TEU provisions (notably Articles 2 and 7 TEU), which call on Member States to respect democratic principles and fundamental rights. EU intervention on this basis appeared increasingly compelling given that the 1993 Copenhagen criteria for Community membership required candidate countries to have in place adequate guarantees of democracy, the rule of law and human rights.[29] Double standards would have been apparent if candidate countries were required to protect freedom of speech and information within their domestic orders while existing members were not. In its 2004 *Resolution on the Risks of Violations, in the EU and especially in Italy, of Freedom of Expression and Information*, the EP therefore asserted that 'any legal or administrative measures instituted by a Member State and affecting the pluralism of the media or the freedom of expression and information, as well as the absence of action by a Member State to protect these fundamental rights could fall within the scope of Article 7(1) or Article 7(2) of the Treaty on European Union'.[30]

The result has been the gradual development of a human rights dimension to EU media law and policy, on which the monitoring of, and intervention in, individual state practice can be built.[31] Rather than engage in difficult negotiations with 28 Member States with a view to agreeing common legislative standards, the EU can take targeted action, responding to the distinctive political, cultural and economic features of the state in question. Given the potentially negative political ramifications of intervention, both for the state concerned and also the EU, targeted action is likely to take place only where there are serious and well substantiated concerns. In 2011, for example, the Commission put pressure on the Hungarian government to amend some of the more troubling aspects of the 2010 Hungarian Media Law, which had raised concerns among Council of Europe and EU experts, journalists and civil society groups both within and outside Hungary.[32] Commissioner Kroes justified such action not only on the basis of ensuring compliance with EU free movement principles but also from the broader perspective of freedom of expression.[33]

Nevertheless, the Commission adopted a more conservative view of its competence than some authors and the HLG on media pluralism have

29 See A. Harcourt, 'The Regulation of Media Markets in Selected EU Accession States in Central and Eastern Europe', *European Law Journal*, 2003, vol. 9, 316–340, at 323.

30 European Parliament, Resolution on the Risks of Violation, in the EU and especially in Italy, of Freedom of Expression and Information (Article 11(2) of the Charter of Fundamental Rights), P5_TA-PROV(2004) 0373, para. 83.

31 P. Iosifidis, *Global Media and Communication Policy*, Basingstoke: Palgrave/Macmillan, 2011, ch. 7.

32 See CoE Parliamentary Assembly, Committee on Culture, Science, Education and Media (Rapporteur Mats Johansson), 'The State of Media Freedom in Europe', June 2012, paras 72–76; Center for Media and Communication Studies, 'Hungarian Media Laws in Europe. An Assessment of the Consistency of Hungary's Media Laws with European Practices and Norms', 2012 Central European University, Budapest.

33 N. Kroes, 'Hungary's New Media Law', Speech/11/6 at the EP, Brussels, 11 January 2011.

suggested.[34] Rather than focus on Articles 2 and 7 TFEU, the Commission appears to have relied on the EU Charter of Fundamental Rights, as incorporated by Article 6 TEU, and thus imported the limitation in Article 51 that Charter rights apply to the Member States only when 'implementing EU law'. Commissioner Kroes considered that the EU could only act to enforce fundamental rights in areas covered by EU law, for instance when covered by the Audiovisual Media Services Directive.[35] Issues arising outside this field were thus left to be determined at the national level and were ultimately addressed by the Hungarian Constitutional Court, with ongoing engagement also by the Council of Europe.

But intervention, even on a case-by-case basis, requires reference to agreed criteria and a central question moving forward is whether the EU will develop its own benchmarks or collaborate with other international organisations, such as the Council of Europe, in their development.[36] In the pluralism field the Commission has supported the development of indicators that can be used to assess the potential risks to media pluralism in the Member States.[37] The resultant multi-faceted monitoring tool, comprising economic, socio-demographic and legal indicators, is currently being trialled by the Centre for Media Pluralism and Media Freedom (based at the European University Institute) in relation to specific states. How the 'media pluralism monitor' will then be employed, if at all, has yet to be determined, particularly since states such as the Netherlands and the UK are developing alternative systems of review and may well resist oversight on subsidiarity grounds. Member States could be required, for example, to apply the monitor themselves or the Fundamental Rights Agency or an independent research centre, such as the EUI Centre for Media Pluralism could be engaged to carry out regular reports, with identified deficiencies addressed by the Commission in discussion with the state concerned. The EP Civil Liberties Committee (Rapporteur Renate Weber) in a recent Motion for an EP Resolution on the EU Charter, underlined the importance of annual monitoring and the compilation of reports regarding media pluralism in all Member States.[38]

These new approaches may supplement as opposed to supplant potential legislative initiatives, creating a more diverse EU 'regulatory toolbox'. Thus

---

34 See text accompanying nn. 18–19 above.
35 N. Kroes, 'Defending Media Pluralism in Hungary', 5 January 2012. Online. Available: http://ec.europa.eu/commission_2010–2014/kroes/en/blog/media-pluralism-hungary (accessed 25 November 2013).
36 See J-C. Juncker, 'Council of Europe-European Union: A Sole Ambition for the European Continent', 11 April 2006. Online. Available: www.coe.int/t/der/docs/RapJuncker_E.pdf (accessed 25 November 2013) and CoE Committee of Ministers, 123rd Session, Co-operation with the European Union – Summary Report, 22 April 2013, CM(2013) 43.
37 K.U. Leuven, Jönköping International Business School, Central European University, Ernst & Young, Independent Study on Indicators for Media Pluralism in the Member States. Towards a Risk-Based Approach, Leuven, July 2009. Online. Available: https://ec.europa.eu/digital-agenda/sites/digital-agenda/files/final_report_09.pdf (accessed 25 November 2013).
38 EP Civil Liberties Committee, Motion for an EP Resolution on the EU Charter: Standard Settings for Media Freedom across the EU, 23 March 2013, P7_TA(2013) 0203, para. 32.

the EP Civil Liberties Committee in their Motion on the EU Charter also call for 'a legislative framework for media ownership rules introducing minimum standards for the Member States'.[39] Similarly, the re-launched Citizens' European Initiative for Media Pluralism calls for a directive to address concentration of media ownership; the independence of media regulators; rules on conflicts of interest; and media ownership transparency and the Commission has already initiated a consultation on the independence of media regulators with a view to possible legislative action.[40]

The internal market – in pursuit of cultural objectives?

Despite the marked socio-political dimension to the Community's early engagement with the media sector, the Community began to exert real influence in the field only through the application of the Treaty free movement provisions. Such initiatives were also informed by distinctly European cultural objectives. The basis for Community intervention was established by the ECJ in the early seventies in the *Sacchi* case, which confirmed that the provision of media goods and services could fall within the scope of the Treaty provided the necessary commercial and cross border elements were present.[41] This encouraged commercial operators to challenge domestic media regulations in domestic courts, relying on the directly effective free movement Treaty rules.[42]

These actions were facilitated by the line of ECJ rulings, dating back to *Dassonville*, which extended the scope of the free movement principles beyond directly discriminatory measures to cover rules that apply regardless of origin, such as advertising limits and programme content requirements, yet which make it more difficult for broadcasters to target multiple markets.[43] Although the Court accepted that indistinctly applicable measures of this type could be justified by genuine general interest goals, such as media pluralism or consumer protection, such measures had to be shown to be necessary and proportionate.[44] Countries such as the Netherlands, which sought to prevent their segmented and plural domestic broadcasting system from being undercut by commercial satellite broadcasters based in neighbouring Luxembourg, found it difficult to convince the Court that their rules were other than protectionist.[45] Only in the *TV10* case did the Court rather belatedly accept that the Netherlands

---

39 Ibid., para. 19.
40 See European Initiative website. Online. Available: www.mediainitiative.eu/about/ and Commission, Public Consultation on the Independence of Audiovisual Regulatory Bodies, March 2013. Online. Available: https://ec.europa.eu/digital-agenda/en/public-consultation-independence-audiovisual-regulatory-bodies (both accessed 25 November 2013).
41 Case 155/73, *Italy v. Sacchi* [1974] ECR 409, para. 427.
42 For example, case C-288/89, *Stichting Collectieve Antennevoorziening Gouda and others v. Commissariaat voor de Media* [1991] ECR I-4007.
43 Case 8/74, *Procureur du Roi v. Dassonville* [1974] ECR 837.
44 As in case C-288/89, op. cit.
45 Ibid.

could take action against foreign satellite services that had deliberately located abroad in order to escape the more exacting Dutch advertising restrictions.[46]

The questions that these cases raised as to the viability of domestic broadcasting systems made the Member States more willing to work towards a legislative solution where they could regain an element of control over developments: although the Commission had sole power to propose legislation, it was the Member States that, at this point, held the ultimate power of adoption. Legislation in the form of the 'Television Without Frontiers' Directive ('TWFD'), based on the service provisions in the EEC Treaty, was finally agreed in 1989.[47] The Directive reflected the Community's 'new approach' to regulation: rather than attempt to establish a comprehensive set of common standards, the Directive focussed only on those domestic measures most restrictive of trade and established minimum standards with which all traders had to comply. Member States were, however, allowed to impose more exacting requirements in these areas but only on their own domestic producers. Broadcasters that complied with the rules in their 'home state' were guaranteed access to all other states, even those that had chosen to impose more exacting rules internally, resulting in television services subject to different regulatory systems competing in the same market.

The basis for the Directive was undoubtedly economic: a single television market was seen as enabling broadcasters to reap economies of scale; create firms large enough to compete with powerful foreign competitors; and enhance consumer choice.[48] But in establishing minimum rules to facilitate trade, the Commission could not ignore the broader framework of cultural and political concerns that influenced domestic broadcasting regulation.[49] In the 1984 Television Without Frontiers Green Paper, which set out the Commission's initial thinking on a legislative measure, the Commission noted that '[t]he citizens of the Community will welcome the extension of the potential coverage and content of television all the more if the Community is in a position to view the opportunities offered by these new broadcasting techniques as a cultural challenge and to place them within the context of a broad plan for the future of Europe not based on economic precepts alone'.[50]

Yet, if we consider the terms of the 1989 Directive as ultimately adopted there is very little reflection of these cultural considerations in the operative

---

46   Case C-23/93, *TV10 v. Commissariaat Voor de Media* [1994] ECR I-4795.

47   Council Directive 89/552/EEC on the coordination of certain provisions laid down by law, regulation or administrative action in Member States concerning the pursuit of television broadcasting activities (1989) OJ L298/15.

48   Commission, Green Paper on the Establishment of the Common Market for Broadcasting, Especially by Satellite and Cable, COM(84) 300 final.

49   For discussion of the incorporation of non-market objectives into Internal Market legislation see B. De Witte, 'A Competence to Protect. The Pursuit of Non-market Aims Through Internal Market Legislation', in P. Syrpis (ed.), *The Judiciary, The Legislator and the EU Internal Market*, Cambridge/New York: Cambridge University Press, 2012, pp. 25–46.

50   Commission, 1984 Green Paper, op. cit., p. 23.

part of the text. Cultural concerns are most apparent in the European content quota, designed to contain the penetration of US content and maintain demand for domestic content. The quota was, however, heavily qualified and widely regarded as a merely political rather than legal requirement.[51] Programmes capable of inclusion in the quota did not need to meet any specific content requirements, though certain genres such as news and sport were excluded. Perhaps most strikingly, there was no requirement to include content from other Member States, thereby enhancing greater understanding by the public of their European partners. Two other provisions were designed to protect the cinema industry, through a requirement that there should be a two-year period after initial theatrical release before a film could be broadcast on television, and the maintenance of domestic linguistic policies, through an acknowledgement that states could continue to impose language requirements on television broadcasters under their jurisdiction.

Why were there so few overtly cultural provisions in the Directive? Political and procedural reasons played an important part but it is also arguable that the Directive was seen, at least by certain actors within the EU institutions, as pursuing an implicit cultural agenda – though not one that the Member States would necessarily have recognised. From a political and procedural perspective, Littoz-Monnet has cogently explained how the position of individual Member States in influencing the final regulatory package was weakened by the ability to pass a Directive with a qualified majority in the Council.[52] Given that the interests of the Member States varied widely depending on domestic politics and the nature of their respective media markets, it was difficult for countries such as France, which favoured a more exacting set of European benchmarks in support of culture, to build sufficient consensus for its position. Intervention of this type was opposed by countries such as the United Kingdom, with a more liberal agenda and desire to keep open trade with the United States, and Denmark, which rejected EU competence in the cultural field. Once regulation moved from the domestic to the European level, therefore, France was unable to gain sufficient support for binding quotas, though it did manage to push through the provisions on language policy and film releases, as well as obtain a number of 'side payments' in the form of European aid for the film industry, discussed further below.

From a cultural perspective, the Commission adopted a distinctly 'European' approach to broadcasting's cultural potential. On this view, market liberalisation was seen as giving Europeans access to a richer, more culturally diverse, range of programmes. This would support further European integration,

51 J. Harrison and L. Woods, *European Broadcasting Law and Policy*, Cambridge: Cambridge University Press, 2007, ch. 11.
52 A. Littoz-Monnet, *The European Union and Culture. Between Economic Regulation and European Cultural Policy*, Manchester: Manchester University Press, 2007, ch. 4; see also T. Gibbons and P. Humphreys, *Audiovisual Regulation Under Pressure. Comparative Cases from North America and Europe*, Abingdon: Routledge, 2012, ch. 7.

strengthen 'mutual understanding, trust and rapprochement' among the peoples of Europe and enable them to 'make a more objective assessment of the situation in the Member States and hence in the Community'.[53] In addition, the free flow of information across borders as mandated by Article 10 of the European Convention on Human Rights was seen as necessitating the opening-up of 'the Member States' self-contained broadcasting systems' so that each could complement and influence the other.[54] The Commission concluded that, with very few exceptions, it was simply illegitimate both from the perspective of Community and human rights law for Member States to impose domestic programme standards on foreign television services. Examples of the sort of illegitimate requirements it had in mind were:

> those relating to the nature and quality of programmes (e.g. information, entertainment, education; high quality entertainment), to the orientation of programmes (e.g. impartiality, representation of a particular tendency in society), to the reliability of information (e.g. prior examination of source, content or accuracy), to the programmes available generally from a broadcasting organization (e.g. minimum requirements as regards the expression of different opinions or the balance of programmes).[55]

The Commission's 'European take' on cultural and free speech objectives thus dovetailed conveniently with the Directive's central market-building rationale. Cultural exchange across borders was to be facilitated by removing from Member States such capacity as they had to regulate foreign broadcasts on content grounds, while states would remain competent to regulate domestic broadcasters according to their own political and cultural objectives. From the European perspective, the 'independence of cultural developments in the Member States and the preservation of cultural diversity in the Community therefore remained unaffected'.[56] From the perspective of states such as the Netherlands, it was less apparent that foreign broadcasts were simply complementing, as opposed to undermining, the established broadcasting order.

The TWFD was adopted prior to the introduction of the culture article in the EC Treaty in 1992.[57] To what extent has this article, which calls on the Union to take culture into account in its actions under other Treaty provisions (para. 4), influenced the subsequent scope and nature of EU intervention in the media field? Subsequent Internal Market initiatives, notably the Electronic-Commerce Directive and revisions to the TWF Directive in the form of the

53 Commission, 1984 Green Paper, op. cit., p. 29.
54 Commission, 1984 Green Paper, op. cit., p. 171.
55 Commission, 1984 Green Paper, op. cit., p. 174.
56 Council Directive 89/552/EEC, op. cit., recital 13.
57 Art. 128 EC, now 167 TFEU.

Audiovisual Media Services Directive ('AVMSD'),[58] continued to push a market-building agenda with its latent integrationist goals and included very few explicitly cultural provisions.[59] It is, however, possible to detect in these measures rather more acknowledgement of the concerns of certain Member States that EU initiatives could in fact be undermining, rather than simply complementing, domestic cultural policies.

The Electronic Commerce (E-Commerce) Directive of June 2000 does not apply to broadcast services covered by the TWFD but covers a range of on-demand electronic communication services, such as on-demand radio, books, and newspapers. The Directive originally applied to on-demand television services but these are now covered by the AVMSD, discussed further below. The E-Commerce Directive also adopts a home-state-control, minimum harmonisation, approach but its broad scope and focus on online contracting and the protection of intermediaries meant that it did not attempt to establish specific programme content requirements. The Directive therefore allows Member States to maintain restrictions on *foreign* services on a range of specified general interest grounds, including public policy, defined to include the protection of minors and human dignity; public health; public security; and the protection of consumers. These domestic measures are subject to a process of prior notification, both to the state where the provider is established and the Commission, which decides on the legality of the measure under EU law, without prejudice to possible judicial review. The E-Commerce Directive thus incorporates a different approach to market-building based on an 'authorisation' procedure. Though administratively demanding, it obviates the need to obtain consensus on common standards, is flexible and also reduces the risk that states will be faced with unexpected legal challenges to domestic measures. In deterring states from introducing covert protectionist rules, it also encourages wider trust in the overall regulatory package.

Alongside this system of authorised derogations, the E-Commerce Directive also contains a specific provision relating to culture, Article 1.6. This provides that the Directive 'does not affect measures taken at Community or national level, in the respect of Community law, in order to promote cultural and linguistic diversity and to ensure the defence of pluralism'. The adoption of a separate provision on culture in the operative part of the Directive suggests that Member States remain free to apply cultural measures to foreign information society services without the need to submit these for prior authorisation. Such measures would, however, still be subject to potential

---

58   Directive 2000/13/EC, On Certain Legal Aspects of Information Society Services, in particular Electronic Commerce in the Internal Market (2000) OJ L178/1 and Directive 2010/13/EU (consolidated version), On the Coordination of Certain provisions Laid Down by Law, Regulation of Administrative Action in Member States Concerning the Provision of Audiovisual Media Services (2010) OJ L95/1.

59   M. Burri-Nenova, 'The New Audiovisual Media Services Directive: Television Without Frontiers, Television Without Cultural Diversity', *Common Market Law Review*, 2007, vol. 44, 1689–1725.

challenge for infringement of EU law by the Commission or by commercial operators in domestic courts relying on their directly effective free movement rights. Alternatively 'national level' could be interpreted restrictively to exclude measures that affect foreign providers.

The use of an authorisation procedure had in fact been employed in the initial revision to the TWFD in 1997.[60] The 1997 revision process underlined the continuing difficulty of agreeing cultural measures at European level, even with the new cultural title in the EC Treaty and enhanced legislative powers of the EP under co-decision. Thus France, backed by the EP, was unable to strengthen the existing European quotas. The revisions did, however, authorise Member States to designate certain sporting or other events as being of major social importance with a view to ensuring their coverage on free-to-air television.[61] The provision is interesting in subjecting such measures to a system of Community review and registration, and for its recognition that the action of broadcasters in other Member States can undermine the operation of such domestic regimes, necessitating controls by the country of establishment. The Community thus regularizes but importantly also offers protection to domestic cultural measures, potentially undermined by the operation of foreign broadcasters. Given the cultural aspect of the provision the Commission's role is limited to checking for 'manifest errors'.[62]

The TWFD was revised again in 2007 to cover on-demand audiovisual media services (previously within the scope of the E-Commerce Directive).[63] The preamble to the AVMSD emphasises the relevance of Article 167(4) TFEU and that audiovisual media services are 'as much cultural services as they are economic'.[64] In relation to on-demand services, the Directive combined the two approaches to content regulation that had characterised the TWF and E-Commerce Directives. First, such services were subjected to a number of minimum content standards relating to child protection, human dignity, European content and advertising in line with, though not as exacting as, those for broadcast services. Second, Member States remained free to regulate *foreign* on-demand providers on the general interest grounds identified in the E-Commerce Directive, subject to Commission review.[65] The AVMSD did not, however, carry over the culture clause in Article 1.6 of the E-Commerce Directive, leaving it therefore unclear whether Member States remain free to regulate foreign on-demand services specifically on cultural grounds – something the Commission appears to have intended to exclude in the original TWFD but to have accepted in the context of the E-Commerce Directive.[66]

---

60 Discussed in Littoz-Monnet, op. cit., 90–96.
61 See now Art. 14 AVMSD.
62 Case C-205/11 P, *FIFA v. Commission*, judgment 18 July 2013, nyr, paras 15, 20–21.
63 Directive 2007/65/EC, consolidated in Directive 2010/13/EU, op. cit.
64 Recitals 5 and 6 of the preamble.
65 Art. 3.4.
66 Recital 19 AVMSD, which affirms that the 'independence of cultural developments in the Member States . . . remain unaffected' was present in the TWFD. For further discussion see

Growing dissatisfaction on the part of certain (mainly small) states with the operation of the country of origin principle can also be detected in the addition of Article 4(2)-(5) to the AVMSD.[67] This authorises states, subject once again to Commission review, to take action against broadcasters that have located abroad 'in order to circumvent' stricter domestic rules. Although the TWFD had affirmed the continuing independence of Member States in the cultural field, forum shopping by broadcasters unleashed a process of deregulatory competition. Countries such as Luxembourg and the UK with relatively light regulatory regimes had considerable success in encouraging firms to relocate to their jurisdictions.[68] Gibbons and Humphreys doubt whether the evasion principles in the AVMSD will adequately address state concerns but as more broadcast services move online and on-demand the relevance of these provisions will diminish, just as the relevance of the authorisation procedures in Article 2.4 will grow.[69] Indeed, as the EU moves to address ongoing technological and market developments in the communications sector, greater emphasis is likely to be placed on EU accreditation procedures and informal standard setting in relation to both state and, increasingly, private regulatory regimes.

Taking culture into account in EU industrial policy

Alongside its policy of market opening the EU has pursued a policy of market strengthening, also with a pronounced cultural dimension. The Internal Market initiatives discussed above were designed to break down the barriers to audiovisual trade but the Commission was aware that Europe's production industries were highly fragmented along national lines and resistant to change. It therefore sought to stimulate a secondary market, built around cooperation among firms from different Member States. Not only did this offer the prospect of the development of players of European, if not international, stature, it would also create competition for the established public service broadcasters, which had traditionally produced in-house: a policy already pursued through the independent production quotas in Article 5 TWFD (now Article 17 AVMSD). Trial projects commenced in the late eighties, with the first formal programme, MEDIA 1991–1995, based on the general 'catch-all provision', Article 235 EEC (now Article 352 TFEU).[70]

R. Craufurd Smith, 'Determining Regulatory Competence for Audiovisual Media Services in the EU', *The Journal of Media Law*, 2011, vol. 3, 263–285.
67 Gibbons and Humphreys, op. cit., p. 148.
68 A. Harcourt, 'Institution-driven Competition: the Regulation of Cross-border Broadcasting in the EU', *Journal of Public Policy*, 2007, vol. 27, 293–317.
69 Gibbons and Humphreys, op. cit., p. 148.
70 Decision No. 90/685/EEC, Concerning the Implementation of an Action Programme to Promote the Development of the European Audiovisual Industry (Media 1991–1995), (1990) OJ L380/37.

Although the audiovisual sector was seen as 'a strategic sector for the services industry' in the Community, its cultural dimension was also acknowledged.[71] By 'guaranteeing solidarity between countries and markets of different sizes', the programme would carry out 'balancing operations' in favour of the less widespread cultures and languages in Europe. Producers in less developed countries would benefit from collaborating with established partners in the major producing countries, while specific support was provided for dubbing and subtitling, thereby stimulating the circulation of culturally distinct films and programmes.[72] The MEDIA Programme was again designed to complement Member State cultural policies, which focused on production aid, by assisting firms at the pre and post-production stages.

This combination of industrial and cultural objectives has been a constant feature of the subsequent MEDIA programmes, with MEDIA 2007 aiming to enhance 'European cultural and linguistic diversity', 'intercultural dialogue' and support for 'countries or regions with low audiovisual production capacity and/or a restricted geographic and linguistic area'.[73] Cultural solidarity is, however, less explicit in the media stream of the new Creative Europe Programme, based on the culture, industry and training provisions in the TFEU, replacing the existing Culture and MEDIA programmes in 2014.[74] The Commission continues to see the cultural and linguistic fragmentation of Europe as a major stumbling block to the development of internationally successful European audiovisual industries.[75] Though a key object of the programme is to safeguard European cultural and linguistic diversity, the new programme focuses on 'structuring actions with maximum systemic impact' and support for projects with 'high commercial and circulation potential'.[76] The programme does, however, bring together for the first time under one framework the EU's cultural and media-related support measures, recognising the links between these two initiatives that, for largely historical reasons, have developed in isolation.

In relation to international trade, the EU's approach has been heavily influenced by the strength of US content in domestic film and television markets and has refused to make market-opening commitments under the General Agreement on Trade in Services (GATS).[77] Concern by countries such

71 Commission, Communication Relating to an Action Programme to Promote the Development of the European Audiovisual Industry 'MEDIA' 1991–1995, COM(90) 132 at 1.
72 Ibid. at 7, 11 and 18.
73 Decision No. 1718/2006/EC, MEDIA (2007), (2006) OJ L 327/12, Arts 1.2 (a)-(b) and 1.4(c). For assessment of the actual economic and cultural impact of early European support measures see V. Henning and A. Alpar, 'Public Aid Mechanisms in Feature Film Production: The EU Media Plus Programme', *Media, Culture and Society* 2005, vol. 27, 229–250.
74 Regulation No 1295/2013 establishing the Creative Europe Programme (2014 to 2020), (2013) OJ L 347/221.
75 Commission Staff Working Paper, Impact Assessment, SEC(2011) 1399 final, pp. 67–69.
76 Ibid. at 81–82.
77 C. Pauwels and J. Loisen, 'The WTO and the Audiovisual Sector: Economic Free Trade vs Cultural Horse Trading?', *European Journal of Communication*, 2003, 291–312 and on the US

as France that the EU might waver in this regard led to the introduction of Article 207 TFEU, which requires Council unanimity to authorise the negotiation and conclusion of agreements relating to culture and audiovisual services. The EU's desire to maintain its ability to protect domestic audiovisual markets from external competition also led it to be a key participant in the drafting and adoption of the 2005 UNESCO Convention on the Protection and Promotion of the Diversity of Cultural Expressions.[78] The Convention's emphasis on equitable exchange of cultural goods and services and cultural diversity found reflection in the Commission's subsequent 2007 communication 'A European Agenda for Culture in a Globalizing World' and the MEDIA Mundus programme, designed to reinforce cooperation between EU and third country professionals.[79] At the international, as opposed to Member State, level, therefore, the EU has been markedly less willing to see exposure to external trade as inevitably diversity enhancing and has here worked with a range of third sector organisations and lobby groups to achieve its ends.[80]

EU Competition law and culture

Competition law focuses on protecting the interests of consumers through maintaining open and contestable markets and there is limited scope (and to date limited willingness) to take into account cultural concerns in the context of Articles 101 and 102 TFEU as drafted.[81] The HLG on Media Freedom and Pluralism has, however, called for 'the European competition authorities to take into account the specific value of media pluralism in the enforcement of competition rules'.[82]

In relation to state aid law the position is very different, given the scale of financial assistance that states specifically allocate to cultural activities. Even

audiovisual industry more generally: P.S. Grant and C. Wood, *Blockbusters and Trade Wars*, Vancouver/Toronto: Douglas and McIntyre, 2004.

78 Convention on the Protection and Promotion of the Diversity of Cultural Expressions, 20 October 2005, in force 18 March 2007, in UNESCO, Records of the General Conference, 33rd session, Paris, 3–21 October 2005, (2 vols, 2005), vol. I, at 83. For commentary, see R. Craufurd Smith, 'The UNESCO Convention on the Protection and Promotion of the Diversity of Cultural Expressions: Building a New World Information and Communication Order?', *International Journal of Communication*, 2007, 24–55.

79 Commission, Communication on a European Agenda for Culture in a Globalizing World, COM(2007) 242 final and Decision No 1041/2009/EC, MEDIA Mundus (2011–2013), (2009) OJ L288/10.

80 A. Harcourt, '"Cultural Coalitions" and International Regulatory Co-operation', *Journal of Common Market Studies*, 2012, vol. 50, 709–725.

81 Though note the General Court's review of the Commission's 'CISAC' decision on the basis of article 167(4)TFEU in case T-451/08, *Stim v Commission*, nyr. For discussion of 'cultural mainstreaming' in the competition field see E. Psychogiopoulou, *The Integration of Cultural Considerations in EU Law and Policies*, Leiden/Boston, MA: Martinus Nijhoff, 2008, 245–331 and M. Wheeler, 'Supranational Regulation: The EU Competition Directorate and the European Audio-visual Marketplace', in Harrison and Wessels (eds), op. cit., 262–285.

82 High Level Group, op. cit., Recommendation 8.

before the introduction in 1992 of a specific derogation to the state aid provisions for aid for 'culture and heritage conservation',[83] the Commission had indicated that, for cultural and economic reasons, it intended to take 'a positive attitude' to state aid for the audiovisual sector.[84] Indeed, the EU MEDIA programmes were, as discussed above, explicitly designed to complement domestic aid for the film sector. In practice, however, although the Commission affords Member States considerable freedom to grant aid in line with domestic cultural policies, it has imposed a number of important procedural constraints designed to ensure that such aid is proportionate and predictable for private competitors.[85] Particularly in the context of public service broadcasting, Commission oversight was seen as so potentially threatening that the Member States felt it necessary to adopt the Amsterdam Protocol, which affirms the legitimacy of funding for public service broadcasting 'as conferred, defined and organised by each Member State', albeit this must not be contrary to the common interest (now protocol 29 to the TFEU).[86] EU state aid rules have undoubtedly put public service broadcasters on the defensive, with the market seen as the norm and services of general economic interest requiring specific justification.[87] Even where aid has been accepted the Commission has looked closely at the ultimate basis for financial support, most recently, for example, questioning the French tax on providers of electronic communications services, intended to produce funds for public broadcasting.[88]

Conclusions

EU engagement with the media sector has throughout pursued political and cultural, as well as economic, goals. It has never been simply 'business as usual'. In particular, attempts to open up domestic markets on Internal Market grounds have been seen as promoting cultural diversity and cultural exchange, complementing cultural policy at the domestic level. Though EU law has indeed often complemented domestic measures, most notably through the MEDIA programmes, there have also been tensions, notably in the field of state aid and as a result of forum shopping in the context of the TWFD/ AVMSD. Although the EU has tended to recognise the threat of cultural imperialism 'only when it is imposed by external actors',[89] its defence of

83 Now Art. 107.3(d) TFEU.
84 Commission, Communication on Audiovisual Policy (1990), op. cit., at p. 20.
85 Commission, Communication on the Application of the State Aid Rules to Public Service Broadcasting (2009), (2009) OJ C257/1; K. Donders, *Public Service Media and Policy in Europe*, Basingstoke/New York: Palgrave/Macmillan, 2012; Wheeler, op. cit.
86 (2010) OJ C83/312.
87 Wheeler, op. cit., at p. 276.
88 This technical challenge based on Directive 2002/20/EC was overturned by the Court of Justice in case C-485/11, *Commission v. France*, 27 June 2013, nyr. The aid itself was approved in Commission Decision C27/09, (2011) OJ L59/44.
89 Sarikakis, op. cit., p. 253.

cultural measures in the context of international trade underlines the potential legitimacy of such measures also at the domestic level. And, as the listed event provisions in the AVMSD indicate, EU law may even be desirable to support such initiatives.

The context and framework for EU intervention has evolved significantly from the eighties. Reaching agreement on minimum standards among 28 Member States will be extremely difficult, particularly given the enhanced emphasis on subsidiarity in the TEU. Yet, without structured EU intervention media service providers will find Europe an increasingly unattractive forum for their operations and Member States will once again face the uncertainty of domestic rules being subjected to European challenge. With a gradual shift to on-demand delivery of audiovisual services it is possible to anticipate increasing reliance on EU accreditation of state and even private rules, backed by a system of EU guidance and soft law standard-setting, to address these issues.

The EU is also beginning to deploy more targeted tools based directly on the democratic and human rights principles in the Treaty. Fields previously addressed from an Internal Market perspective, such as media ownership, are now being considered with a view to introducing monitoring procedures. As the EU moves into areas occupied by established international players, such as the Council of Europe, the importance of collaboration to prevent undue duplication of effort and to maintain consistency in the standards employed becomes increasingly important. Citizens and 'cultural coalitions' are also beginning to exert a palpable influence on EU policy and practice. It is too early to tell whether this new environment will prove less threatening to states such as France that seek to maintain significant support for their audiovisual sector on cultural grounds. To prevent such conflict, the EU will need to keep in mind not only how its cultural objectives can strengthen Europe's audiovisual industries and support European integration but also cut across, and even undermine, cultural initiatives at the domestic level.

Bibliography

Adam, L.B., 'The Significance of EU Topics in National Media. Has There Been an Europeanization of Reporting in the National Media?' *Bruges Political Research Papers*, No. 27, November 2012.

Burri-Nenova, M., 'The New Audiovisual Media Services Directive: Television Without Frontiers, Television Without Cultural Diversity', *Common Market Law Review*, 2007, vol. 44, 1689–1725.

Center for Media and Communication Studies, 'Hungarian Media Laws in Europe. An Assessment of the Consistency of Hungary's Media Laws with European Practices and Norms', 2012, Central European University, Budapest.

Collins, R., *Broadcasting and Audiovisual Policy in the European Single Market*, London: John Libbey, 1994.

Council of Europe, Parliamentary Assembly, Committee on Culture, Science, Education and Media (Rapporteur Mats Johansson), 'The State of Media Freedom in Europe', June 2012.

Council of Europe Committee of Ministers, 123rd Session, Co-operation with the European Union – Summary Report, 22 April 2013, CM(2013)43.

Craufurd Smith, R., 'The UNESCO Convention on the Protection and Promotion of the Diversity of Cultural Expressions: Building a New World Information and Communication Order?', *International Journal of Communication*, 2007, 24–55.

Craufurd Smith, R., 'Determining Regulatory Competence for Audiovisual Media Services in the EU', *The Journal of Media Law*, 2011, vol. 3, 263–285.

Daddow, O., 'The UK Media and 'Europe': From Permissive Consensus to Destructive Dissent', *International Affairs* 2012, vol. 88, 1219–1236.

De Witte, B., 'A Competence to Protect. The Pursuit of Non-market Aims Through Internal Market Legislation', in P. Syrpis (ed.), *The Judiciary, The Legislator and the EU Internal Market*, Cambridge/New York: Cambridge University Press, 2012, pp. 25–46.

Donders, K., *Public Service Media and Policy in Europe*, Basingstoke/New York: Palgrave/Macmillan, 2012.

EurActiv, 'Commission wants to Boost Euronews TV Channel', 28 October 2010. Online. Available: www.euractiv.com/future-eu/commission-wants-boost-euronews-news-499198 (accessed 25 November 2013).

European Commission, Realities and Tendencies in European Television: Perspectives and Options, COM(1983) 229 final.

European Commission, Green Paper on the Establishment of the Common Market for Broadcasting, Especially by Satellite and Cable, COM(1984)300 final.

European Commission, Communication relating to an Action Programme to Promote the Development of the European Audiovisual Industry 'MEDIA' 1991–1995, COM (1990)132.

European Commission, Pluralism and Media Concentration in the Internal Market, An Assessment of the Need for Community Action, COM(1992) 480 final.

European Commission, Follow-up to the Consultation Process Relating to the Green Paper on 'Pluralism and Media Concentration in the Internal Market – An Assessment of the Need for Community Action.', COM(1994) 353 final.

European Commission, Communication on a European Agenda for Culture in a Globalizing World, COM(2007) 242 final.

European Commission, Communication on the Application of the State Aid Rules to Public Service Broadcasting (2009), (2009) OJ C257/1.

European Commission, Proposal for a Regulation Establishing the Creative Europe Programme, COM(2011) 785/2.

European Commission, Public Consultation on the Independence of Audiovisual Regulatory Bodies, March 2013. Online. Available: https://ec.europa.eu/digital-agenda/en/public-consultation-independence-audiovisual-regulatory-bodies (accessed 25 November 2013).

European Commission Staff Working Paper, Impact Assessment concerning the Creative Europe Programme, SEC(2011) 1399 final.

European Parliament, Committee on Youth, Culture, Education, Information and Sport, Report on Radio and Television Broadcasting in the EC, February 1982, Doc. 1–1013/81.

European Parliament, Resolution on the Risks of Violation, in the EU and especially in Italy, of Freedom of Expression and Information (Article 11(2) of the Charter of Fundamental Rights), 22 April 2004, P5_TA-PROV(2004) 0373.

European Parliament, Resolution on Journalism and New Media – Creating a Public Sphere in Europe, 7 September 2010, P7_TA(2010) 0307.

European Parliament Civil Liberties Committee, Motion for an EP Resolution on the EU Charter: Standard Settings for Media Freedom across the EU, 23 March 2013, P7_TA(2013) 0203.

Gibbons, T. and Humphreys, P., *Audiovisual Regulation Under Pressure. Comparative Cases from North America and Europe*, Abingdon: Routledge, 2012.

Grant, P.S. and Wood, C., *Blockbusters and Trade Wars*, Vancouver/Toronto: Douglas and McIntyre, 2004.

Harcourt, A., 'EU Media Ownership Regulation: Conflict Over the Definition of Alternatives', *Journal of Common Market Studies*, 1998, vol. 36, 369–389.

Harcourt, A., 'The Regulation of Media Markets in Selected EU Accession States in Central and Eastern Europe', *European Law Journal*, 2003, vol. 9, 316–340.

Harcourt, A., 'Institution-driven Competition: the Regulation of Cross-border Broadcasting in the EU', *Journal of Public Policy*, 2007, vol. 27, 293–317.

Harcourt, A., '"Cultural Coalitions" and International Regulatory Co-operation', *Journal of Common Market Studies*, 2012, vol. 50, 709–725.

Harrison, J., and Woods, L., *European Broadcasting Law and Policy*, Cambridge: Cambridge University Press, 2007.

Harrison, J. and Wessels, B., (eds), *Mediating Europe: New Media, Mass Communications and the European Public Sphere*, Oxford: Berghahn Books, 2009.

Henning, V., and Alpar, A., 'Public Aid Mechanisms in Feature Film Production:The EU Media Plus Programme', *Media, Culture and Society*, 2005, vol. 27, 229–250.

High Level Group on Media Freedom and Pluralism, Report: A Free and Pluralistic Media to Sustain European Democracy, January 2013.

Iosifidis, P., *Global Media and Communication Policy*, Basingstoke: Palgrave/Macmillan, 2011.

Juncker, J-C., 'Council of Europe-European Union: A Sole Ambition for the European Continent', 11 April 2006. Online. Available: www.coe.int/t/der/docs/RapJuncker_E. pdf (accessed 25 November 2013).

Koopmans, R. and Erbe, J., 'Towards a European Public Sphere?', *Innovation*, 2004, vol. 17, 97–118.

Kroes, N., 'Hungary's New Media Law', Speech/11/6 at the EP, Brussels, 11 January 2011.

Kroes, N., 'Defending Media Pluralism in Hungary', 5 January 2012. Online. Available: http://ec.europa.eu/commission_2010–2014/kroes/en/blog/media-pluralism-hungary (accessed 25 November 2013).

K.U. Leuven, Jönköping International Business School, Central European University, Ernst & Young, Independent Study on Indicators for Media Pluralism in the Member States. Towards a Risk-Based Approach, Leuven, July 2009. Online. Available: https://ec. europa.eu/digital-agenda/sites/digital-agenda/files/final_report_09.pdf (accessed 25 November 2013).

Littoz-Monnet, A., *The European Union and Culture. Between Economic Regulation and European Cultural Policy*, Manchester: Manchester University Press, 2007.

Pauwels, C., and Loisen, J., 'The WTO and the Audiovisual Sector: Economic FreeTrade vs Cultural Horse Trading?', *European Journal of Communication*, 2003, 291–312.

Psychogiopoulou, E., *The Integration of Cultural Considerations in EU Law and Policies*, Leiden/Boston, MA: Martinus Nijhoff, 2008, 245–331.

Sarikakis, K., 'Defending Communicative Spaces: The Remits and Limits of the European Parliament', in J. Harrison and B. Wessels (eds), *Mediating Europe: New Media, Mass Communications and the European Public Sphere*, Oxford: Berghahn Books, 2009, pp. 239–261.

Von Bogdandy, A., Kottmann, M., Antpöhler, C., Dickschen, J., Hentrei, S., and Smrkolj, M., 'Reverse Solange – Protecting the Essence of Fundamental Rights Against EU Member States', *Common Market Law Review*, 2012, vol. 49, 489–520.

Ward, D., *The European Union Democratic Deficit and the Public Sphere: An Evaluation of EU Media Policy*, Amsterdam: IOS Press, 2002.

Wheeler, M., 'Supranational Regulation: The EU Competition Directorate and the European Audio-visual Marketplace', in J. Harrison and B. Wessels (eds), *Mediating Europe: New Media, Mass Communications and the European Public Sphere*, Oxford: Berghahn Books, 2009, pp. 262–285.

14 Culture in the EU external economic relations

Evangelia Psychogiopoulou[1]

Introduction

Culture has formed part of the EU competences since 1993, when the Treaty establishing the European Community (TEC) entered into force.[2] Article 3(1)(q) TEC required the European Community (EC) to contribute to 'the flowering of the cultures of the Member states', and Article 128 TEC assigned to the EC an express but *complementary* competence in the cultural field. Currently, according to the Treaty on the Functioning of the European Union (TFEU),[3] culture belongs to the policy areas in which 'the Union shall have competence to carry out actions to support, coordinate or supplement the actions of the Member States'.[4] Pursuant to Article 167(1) TFEU, the EU is to 'contribute to the flowering of the cultures of the Member States, while respecting their national and regional diversity and at the same time bringing the common cultural heritage to the fore'. EU action, 'aimed at encouraging cooperation between the Member States and, if necessary, supporting and supplementing their activity',[5] may take the form of incentive measures and recommendations, and any harmonisation of the laws and regulations of the Member States is excluded.[6]

The external dimension of EU cultural powers emanates from Article 167(3) TFEU, which mandates the EU and its Member States to 'foster cooperation with third countries and the competent international organisations in the field of culture'. Beyond this, in exercising its external powers in general, the EU must heed the repercussions of its activities on cultural diversity.

1 Marie Curie Post-doctoral Research Fellow, Maastricht Centre for European Law, Department of International and European Law, Faculty of Law, Maastricht University, Maastricht, the Netherlands.
2 Consolidated version of the Treaty Establishing the European Community, OJ C 325, 24/12/2002, p. 33.
3 Consolidated version of the Treaty on the Functioning of the European Union, OJ C 115, 9/5/2008, p. 47.
4 See Art. 6 TFEU.
5 See Art. 167(2) TFEU.
6 See Art. 167(5) TFEU.

This derives from Article 167(4) TFEU, which requires the EU to take cultural aspects into account under the various internal and external policy areas within its purview 'in order to respect and to promote the diversity of its cultures'.[7] Importantly, besides this broad 'cultural mainstreaming' mission, an express recognition of the duty of the European institutions to afford consideration to the cultural implications of their external action can be found in the TFEU provisions on common commercial policy, where the EU enjoys an exclusive competence.[8] In relation to the negotiation and conclusion of EU agreements with third countries and international organisations in the field of trade in cultural and audiovisual services, and reflecting Member States' sensitivity on the issue, Article 207(4) TFEU states that the Council shall act by unanimity 'where these agreements risk prejudicing the Union's cultural and linguistic diversity'.

For the most part, the treatment of cultural and audiovisual services in the EU's trade agreements has so far been cautious. The World Trade Organization (WTO)'s General Agreement on Trade in Services (GATS)[9] is worthwhile mentioning in this regard because audiovisual and cultural services fall under the scope of its rules. What merits attention, in particular, is the way in which the EU has been confronted with the most favoured nation (MFN) principle of the GATS, and the scheduling of market access and national treatment commitments for foreign services and service suppliers, in the progressive pursuit of a higher level of trade liberalisation.[10] Whereas during the Uruguay round negotiations, the EC and the Member States scheduled some commitments in the field of cultural services (mostly incorporated under the so-called *entertainment services* of the WTO's services classification list), in the area of audiovisual services, they abstained from making any market access and national treatment commitments. In addition, in line with Article II(2) of the GATS, they listed exemptions from the application of the MFN principle[11] –

7   On this see generally E. Psychogiopoulou, *The Integration of Cultural Considerations in EU Law and Policies*, Leiden/Boston, MA: Martinus Nijhoff, Brill, 2008.
8   See Art. 3 TFEU.
9   Agreement establishing the World Trade Organization, Annex 1B, General Agreement on Trade in Services and Annexes, 15 April 1994. Online. Available: www.wto.org/english/docs_e/legal_e/26-gats.pdf (accessed 23 September 2013).
10 See Arts II, XIX and XX of the GATS.
11 The EC's MFN exemptions concern: a) measures that define works of European origin in such a way as to extend national treatment regarding access to broadcasting or similar forms of transmission to audiovisual works originating in states that are parties to the *European Convention on Transfrontier Television*; b) measures based on bilateral and plurilateral agreements between the Member States and third countries that confer national treatment to co-productions coming within the scope of these agreements, in particular in relation to distribution and access to funding; and c) measures granting access to support programmes to audiovisual works, and suppliers of such works, meeting certain European origin criteria. See European Communities and their Member States, Final list of Article II (MFN) Exemptions, GATS/EL/31, 15 April 1994.

a means to preserve, among others, avenues for preferential audiovisual cooperation with third countries.[12]

Besides its WTO-related action, during the past few years, the EU has strengthened the support offered to the cultural activities of the United Nations Educational, Scientific and Cultural Organization (UNESCO). It has played, for instance, a key role in the negotiations of the UNESCO Convention on the Protection and Promotion of the Diversity of Cultural Expressions (the UNESCO Convention or the Convention),[13] and it has also become a party to it.[14] According to the Convention, parties, and thus also the EU, shall endeavour to reinforce international cooperation for the promotion of cultural diversity, integrate culture in their development policies, cooperate with developing countries, and encourage collaborative partnerships.[15] Developed countries are specifically required to facilitate cultural exchanges with developing countries by providing preferential treatment to their artists and other cultural professionals and practitioners, and to their cultural goods and services.[16] Parties also undertake to foster mutual supportiveness between the Convention and the other treaties they have adhered to, and to pay consideration to the provisions of the Convention when applying and interpreting their existing international obligations or when entering into new ones.[17]

In light of the Convention's entry into force on 18 March 2007, the European Commission (Commission)'s *Communication on a European Agenda for Culture in a Globalizing World* (the Cultural Agenda)[18] identified the *promotion of culture as a vital element in the EU's international relations* as a key objective that should henceforth determine EU cultural activity. The Council endorsed the Cultural Agenda[19] and, in its 2008 *Conclusions on the promotion of cultural diversity and intercultural dialogue in the external relations of the Union and its Member States*,[20] it called on the Member States and the Commission to

12 European Commission, Staff working document on the external dimension of audiovisual policy, SEC(2009) 1033, 14 July 2009, p. 8.

13 UNESCO Convention on the Protection and Promotion of the Diversity of Cultural Expressions, 20 October 2005, in force 18 March 2007, in UNESCO, Records of the General Conference, 33rd session, Paris, 3–21 October 2005 (2 vols., 2005), vol. I, at 83.

14 Council Decision of 18 May 2006 on the conclusion of the Convention on the Protection and Promotion of the Diversity of Cultural Expressions, OJ L 201, 25/7/2006, p. 15.

15 See Arts 12, 13, 14 and 15 of the Convention.

16 Ibid., Art. 16.

17 Ibid., Art. 20.

18 Communication from the Commission on a European agenda for culture in a globalizing world, COM(2007) 242, 10 May 2007.

19 Council resolution of 16 November 2007 on a European agenda for culture, OJ C 287, 29/11/2007, p. 1.

20 Council conclusions on the promotion of cultural diversity and intercultural dialogue in the external relations of the Union and its Member States, 20 November 2008. Online. Available: www.consilium.europa.eu/ueDocs/cms_Data/docs/pressData/en/educ/104189.pdf (accessed 23 September 2013).

encourage the ratification and implementation of the Convention; pursue political dialogue with third countries, especially on legislative and regulatory aspects; foster balanced exchanges of cultural goods and services, especially with emerging economies; and strengthen the contribution of culture to sustainable development and the capacity of developing countries to protect and promote cultural diversity. Moreover, the Member States and the Commission were invited to draw up a European strategy for systematically incorporating culture in the external relations of the EU, and to establish specific strategies for the EU's external cultural relations, tailored to the characteristics of the cultural industries of the third countries concerned, their socio-economic features, sustainable development and the state of their cultural exchanges with the EU.

The aim of this chapter is to work towards a better understanding of the ways in which the EU addresses culture and cultural diversity in its external relations, particularly its external *economic* relations. What is the place occupied by culture in the EU's trade or trade-related agreements, and has the UNESCO Convention exercised any influence in this respect? The next sections discuss, in particular, recent EU efforts to protect and promote cultural diversity through the negotiation of *protocols on cultural cooperation* that accompany EU bilateral and regional trade and economic agreements. The analysis explores the main features and characteristics of these protocols; investigates the means and tools through which they seek to advance cultural cooperation; and places them within the broader *trade versus culture* debate that has marked their elaboration.

The protocols on cultural cooperation

Against the background of the UNESCO Convention, the Commission's Cultural Agenda and the 2008 Council conclusions, a new cultural cooperation instrument was developed in the form of a *protocol on cultural cooperation*, to be appended in the EU's trade and economic agreements concluded with third countries and regions. Shortly after the entry into force of the UNESCO Convention, the Commission announced the elaboration of a draft model text for a specific *title on cultural cooperation*,[21] which should serve as a basis for future and ongoing bilateral and regional trade negotiations. According to the Commission, the model text, which could be adjusted in order to take into account the nature and the level of cultural exchanges between the EU and the third countries concerned, would guarantee the prompt implementation of the UNESCO Convention and would promote its ratification by the EU's negotiating partners. Also, it would recognise the importance of the cultural industries and the multifaceted nature of cultural goods and services as

---

21 See European Commission, 'Argumentaire on the Title on Cultural Cooperation in future EU trade agreements', 11 May 2007. Online. Available: http://trade.ec.europa.eu/doclib/docs/2007/may/tradoc_134655.pdf (accessed 23 September 2013).

activities of cultural, economic and social value; facilitate cultural exchanges; ensure the treatment of the audiovisual sector under a 'cooperation' perspective; and safeguard the parties' capacity to elaborate and develop their cultural policies.

So far, cultural cooperation protocols have been integrated in three trade and trade-related agreements entered into by the EU: the Economic Partnership Agreement signed with the Cariforum group of countries[22] on 15 October 2008,[23] the Free Trade Agreement (FTA) signed with Korea on 6 October 2010,[24] and the Association Agreement signed with the Central America (CA) group of countries[25] on 29 June 2012.[26] All three protocols follow the same structure: they consist of a preamble, horizontal provisions addressing cultural cooperation in general and sectoral provisions concerning cooperation in specific cultural sectors. They are discussed in detail below.

General framework and institutional structures

The preamble of all three protocols indicates the parties' intention to effectively implement the UNESCO Convention and to cooperate on the basis of its principles and provisions. Whereas the EU-Cariforum and EU-CA protocols expressly refer to Articles 14, 15 and 16 of the Convention on 'cooperation for development', 'collaborative arrangements' and 'preferential treatment for developing countries', the EU-Korea protocol builds on Article 12 of the Convention on the 'promotion of international cooperation'.[27] For the purposes of cultural cooperation, the protocols stress the need to take into account the degree of development of the parties' cultural industries, the level and structural imbalances of their cultural exchanges, and the existence (or not) of preferential schemes for the promotion of local/regional cultural content.

22 Comprising Antigua and Barbuda, the Commonwealth of the Bahamas, Barbados, Belize, the Commonwealth of Dominica, the Dominican Republic, Grenada, the Republic of Guyana, the Republic of Haiti, Jamaica, Saint Christopher and Nevis, Saint Lucia, Saint Vincent and the Grenadines, the Republic of Suriname and the Republic of Trinidad and Tobago.
23 Economic Partnership Agreement between the Cariforum States, of the one part, and the European Community and its Member States, of the other part, OJ L 289/I, 30/10/2008, p. 3.
24 Free Trade Agreement between the European Union and its Member States, of the one part, and the Republic of Korea, of the other part, OJ L 127, 14/5/2011, p. 6.
25 The countries concerned are Panama, Guatemala, Costa Rica, El Salvador, Honduras and Nicaragua.
26 Agreement establishing an association between Central America, on the one hand, and the European Union and its Member States, on the other: Online. Available: http://trade.ec. europa.eu/doclib/press/index.cfm?id=689 (accessed 23 September 2013).
27 See European Commission, 'Concept paper: Cultural cooperation protocol with Korea', 18 February 2009. Online. Available: http://trade.ec.europa.eu/doclib/docs/2009/march/tradoc_142542.pdf (accessed 23 September 2013). The concept paper also refers to Article 20 of the Convention ('relationship to other treaties: mutual supportiveness, complementarity and non-subordination').

They also stipulate that the objectives they pursue are complemented and supported by additional (existing or future) policy instruments, aimed at reinforcing the parties' cultural industries; promoting local/regional cultural content; protecting and promoting cultural diversity and cultural heritage; and in the case of the EU-Cariforum protocol, integrating cultural considerations in development cooperation, particularly in the field of education. Korea's ratification of the UNESCO Convention is a prerequisite for the entry into force of the EU-Korea protocol.[28] The provisions of the EU-CA protocol, in turn, are to be progressively applied between the EU and each signatory CA country that ratifies the Convention, unless all signatory CA countries ratify the Convention prior to the completion of their internal legal procedures for the approval of the EU-CA Association Agreement, in which case the protocol shall apply from the date of entry into force of the agreement.[29] The Convention is also recognised as the reference point for all definitions and concepts used in the protocols.

According to Article 1 of the protocols, the main objectives of the cultural cooperation frameworks so established are to facilitate cultural exchanges, including in the audiovisual sector, to improve the conditions governing the parties' cultural exchanges, to address and redress any imbalances and asymmetrical patterns that may exist in cultural exchanges, and to preserve and further develop the parties' capacity to elaborate and implement cultural policies in support of cultural diversity. Evidently, the protocols share the same objectives.

However, the institutional arrangements made to facilitate the attaining of these objectives differ considerably. According to Article 203 of the EU-Cariforum EPA, Part III of the EPA on 'dispute avoidance and settlement' applies to any dispute concerning the interpretation and application of the EPA and thus also to disputes concerning the interpretation and implementation of the protocol. Key tasks in this respect are assigned to the Trade and Development Committee, established by Article 230 of the EPA with a view to supervising the implementation of the agreement and evaluating its application.

Contrasting the EU-Cariforum protocol, the EU-Korea protocol separates cultural and trade disputes, precludes cross-retaliation with the FTA,[30] and creates, by means of Article 3, a Committee on Cultural Cooperation (CCC) to oversee its implementation. The CCC, which is to meet at least once a year, shall comprise senior officials from the administration of each party with expertise and experience in cultural matters and practices and shall exercise all functions of the Trade Committee, established to ensure the smooth

---

28   See Art. 15.10(3) of the EU-Korea FTA.
29   See Art. 9 of the EU-CA protocol.
30   The suspension of the obligations emanating from the provisions of the protocol is permitted only in relation to disputes that arise on their basis. See Art. 3bis(d) and (e) of the EU-Korea protocol.

operation of the FTA,[31] where such functions are relevant for the purposes of implementing the protocol. In particular, the parties may request consultations in the CCC regarding any matter of mutual interest arising under the protocol. The CCC must make every attempt to arrive at a satisfactory solution, and may also seek the advice of the parties' Domestic Advisory Groups (DAGs) on cultural cooperation.[32] Should the matter not be resolved, a request for the establishment of an arbitration panel can be made to the party complained against and the CCC,[33] which is responsible for establishing and maintaining a list of arbitrators with knowledge and experience on the subject matter of the protocol.[34] In the event of parties' disagreement on the composition of the arbitration panel, the selection of arbitrators shall take place by lot on the basis of the CCC's list.[35]

The EU-CA protocol similarly distinguishes between cultural and trade disputes but provides fewer details on the issue. First, it stipulates that its provisions do not fall under the scope of Title X on 'dispute settlement' of Part IV of the Association Agreement focusing on trade.[36] Second, it states that the Co-operation Sub-Committee, set up to monitor, among other things, the implementation of Part III of the Association Agreement on 'cooperation',[37] shall consist of officials with 'competence in cultural matters and practices' when dealing with the implementation of the protocol.[38]

Horizontal strands for cultural cooperation

All three protocols include horizontal provisions on 'cultural exchanges and dialogue' and 'artists and other cultural professionals and practitioners'.[39] With respect to cultural exchanges, the parties shall aim to strengthen their capacity to determine and implement cultural policies, develop their cultural industries and enhance exchange opportunities for their cultural goods and services.[40] Whereas the EU-Cariforum and EU-CA protocols emphasise preferential treatment in this respect,[41] the EU-Korea protocol refers to the parties' respective 'entitlement to benefit from schemes for the promotion of local/ regional cultural content' operated by the other party.[42] The parties further

31 See Art. 15.1 of the EU-Korea FTA.
32 See Art. 3(5) of the EU-Korea protocol. The DAGs shall consist of representatives of cultural and audiovisual stakeholders.
33 See Art. 14.4 of the EU-Korea FTA in conjunction with Art. 3bis of the EU-Korea protocol.
34 See Art. 3bis(c) of the EU-Korea protocol.
35 Ibid., Art. 3bis(b).
36 See note no. 1 of the EU-CA protocol.
37 See Art. 8(7) of the EU-CA Association Agreement.
38 See preamble to the EU-CA protocol.
39 See Arts 2 and 3 of the EU-Cariforum protocol, Arts 2 and 4 of the EU-Korea protocol, and Arts 2 and 3 of the EU-CA protocol.
40 See Art. 2 of the EU-Cariforum, EU-Korea and EU-CA protocols.
41 See Art. 2(1) of the EU-Cariforum and EU-CA protocols.
42 See Art. 2(1) of the EU-Korea protocol.

commit to cooperate, through dialogue, in order to foster a common understanding and the exchange of information on cultural and audiovisual matters and on good practices in the field of intellectual property protection.[43]

The provisions pertaining to artists and other cultural professionals and practitioners[44] affirm the parties' endeavour to facilitate, in conformity with their domestic regulations, the entry into and temporary stay in their territories of their partners' artists and other cultural professionals and practitioners.[45] According to the EU-Cariforum and EU-Korea protocols, a temporary stay amounts to a maximum of 90 days over a 12-month period.[46] Relevant provisions target artists, actors, technicians and other cultural personnel engaged in the shooting of cinematographic films and television works, visual, plastic and performing artists and instructors, composers, authors, providers of entertainment services and other similar professionals involved, for example, in the recording of music or cultural events such as literary fairs, festivals and so on.[47] To benefit from the provisions of the protocols, relevant artists and cultural professionals/practitioners must not be engaged in selling or supplying their services, they must not receive any remuneration from a source located in the host country and they must not be engaged in the supply of a service in the framework of a contract concluded between a legal person without commercial presence in the host country and a consumer therein.[48] In all three protocols, the parties further endeavour to facilitate training and increased contacts between their artists and cultural professionals/practitioners.[49]

Crucially, in the case of the EU-Cariforum EPA, the provisions of the protocol concerning artists and other cultural professionals and practitioners must be read in conjunction with Article 83 and Annex IV of the EPA, which grant binding EU market access[50] for the supply of entertainment services (other than audiovisual services) by Cariforum *contractual services suppliers* (CSS),[51] through the presence of natural persons. The EPA provides quota-

---

43 See Art. 2(2) of the EU-Cariforum, EU-Korea and EU-CA protocols.
44 These are defined in Article 1 of the protocols as the 'natural persons that perform cultural activities, produce cultural goods or participate in the direct supply of cultural services'.
45 See Art. 3(1) of the EU-Cariforum protocol, Art. 4(1) of the EU-Korea protocol and Art. 3(1) of the EU-CA protocol.
46 See Art. 3(2) of the EU-Cariforum protocol and Art. 4(2) of the EU-Korea protocol.
47 See Art. 3(1) of the EU-Cariforum protocol, Art. 4(1) of the EU-Korea protocol and Art. 3(1) of the EU-CA protocol.
48 Ibid.
49 See Art. 3(3) of the EU-Cariforum procotol, Art. 4(3) of the EU-Korea protocol and Art. 3(2) of the EU-CA protocol.
50 With the exception of Belgium.
51 'Contractual services suppliers' are defined as the natural persons employed by a juridical person who has no commercial presence in the territory of the other party and who has concluded a bona fide contract (other than through an agency) to supply services to a final consumer in the latter party, requiring the presence on a temporary basis of its employees in that party in order to fulfil the contract.

free market access,[52] subject to some qualification requirements and the conducting of an economic needs test,[53] on the basis of the following conditions: a) the natural persons concerned must be engaged in the supply of a service on a temporary basis as employees of a juridical person, who has obtained a service contract for a period not exceeding 12 months; b) they must be offering entertainment services as an employee of the juridical person for at least the year preceding the date of submission of an application for entry into the EU and possess at the date of the submission of the application a minimum of three years of professional experience in the sector of the activity that is the subject of the contract; c) they must not receive remuneration for the provision of services other than that paid by the CSS during their temporary stay; and d) their number must not be larger than necessary to fulfil the contract. Subject to specific provisos, temporary entry and stay may cumulatively amount to six months in any 12-month period.[54] The unparalleled market access commitments made, unprecedented in previous EU trade agreements, seek to facilitate the circulation of Cariforum artists and cultural professionals/practitioners in the EU, which might generate important capacity building effects.

The EU-Cariforum and EU-CA protocols also lay down provisions for technical assistance, so as to assist the developing countries concerned in the development of their cultural industries, the formulation and implementation of cultural policies and the production and exchange of cultural goods and services.[55] The measures in question are many and varied, ranging from training and the exchange of information and expertise to counselling on the elaboration of policies and legislation, and on the usage and transfer of technologies and know-how. Technical assistance may also facilitate cooperation between private companies, non-governmental organisations and public-private partnerships.

Sectoral strands for cultural cooperation

Under their sectoral facet, all three protocols include provisions on audiovisual cooperation, performing arts, publications and the protection of heritage sites

52 Note that the market commitments made do not confer an entitlement to exercise the professional title of the party where the service is provided. In addition, they do not apply to measures affecting natural persons seeking access to employment in the EU, nor do they prevent the EU Member States from applying measures to regulate the entry and temporary stay of natural persons in their territory, provided that such measures are not applied in a manner that nullifies or impairs the benefits accruing to the Cariforum countries under the commitments made. See Arts 60(5) and 83(2)(f) of the EU-Cariforum EPA.

53 With the exception of Greece and Slovenia. For the conduct of an economic needs test, the main criterion is the assessment of the relevant market situation in the EU Member State concerned or the region where the service is to be provided (also with respect to the number of, and the impact on, existing services suppliers).

54 See Art. 83(2)(e) of the EU-Cariforum EPA. In the case of Luxembourg, it may amount to 25 weeks.

55 See Art. 4 of the EU-Cariforum and EU-CA protocols.

and historic monuments. The provisions are more or less standardised with the exception of those concerning cooperation in the audiovisual sector.

More specifically, all three protocols state that the parties shall encourage the implementation of the existing, as well as the negotiation of new, co-production agreements between one or several EU Member States and one or several of the signatory Cariforum and CA countries, as well as Korea.[56] Also, they affirm the parties' commitment to facilitate the access of co-produced works to their respective markets. While the EU-Cariforum and EU-CA protocols refer to the organisation of festivals, seminars and other similar initiatives as one of the means to be used for that purpose,[57] the EU-Korea protocol provides that the EU Member States and Korea may grant financial benefits to co-produced works as defined in relevant existing or future bilateral co-production agreements to which one or several EU Member States and Korea are party.[58] More importantly, both the EU-Cariforum and EU-Korea protocols grant EU-Cariforum and EU-Korea co-productions preferential access to the EU market, albeit under different conditions.[59]

The EU-Cariforum protocol states that EU-Cariforum co-productions qualify as 'European works' within the meaning of the EU Audiovisual Media Services (AVMS) Directive.[60] EU-Cariforum co-productions accordingly fall under the scope of the provisions of the directive mandating the EU Member States to ensure, where practicable and by appropriate means, that broadcasters reserve the majority proportion of their transmission time for European works and that on-demand audiovisual media services also promote the production of and access to European works.[61] To benefit from the EU preferences, EU-Cariforum co-productions need to comply with three cumulative conditions.[62] First, they must be realised by undertakings which are owned directly or by majority participation by an EU Member State or a signatory Cariforum state and/or by nationals of an EU Member State or a signatory Cariforum state. Second, the director(s) or manager(s) of the co-producing undertakings must have the nationality of an EU Member State and/or of a signatory Cariforum state. Third, the total financial contribution of the producer(s) of the EU party

56   See Art. 5(1) of the EU-Cariforum protocol, Art. 5(2) of the EU-Korea protocol and Art. 5(1) of the EU-CA protocol.
57   See Art. 5(2) of the EU-Cariforum and EU-CA protocols.
58   See Art. 5(2) of the EU-Korea protocol.
59   See Art. 5(2)(a) of the EU-Cariforum protocol and Art. 5(4) of the EU-Korea protocol.
60   See Art. 1(1)(n) of Directive 2010/13/EU of the European Parliament and of the Council of 10 March 2010 on the coordination of certain provisions laid down by law, regulation or administrative action in Member States concerning the provision of audiovisual media services, OJ L 95, 15/4/2010, p. 1. According to the directive, 'European works' encompass works co-produced within the framework of agreements related to the audiovisual sector concluded between the EU and third countries, provided that these fulfil the conditions defined therein.
61   Ibid., Arts 13 and 16.
62   See Art. 5(2)(a) of the EU-Cariforum protocol.

on the one hand and of the signatory Cariforum states on the other must range between 20 per cent and 80 per cent of the total production costs.

The EU-Korea protocol is underpinned by reciprocity. In accordance with Article 5 of the EU-Korea protocol, EU-Korean co-productions enjoy reciprocal access to the parties' support schemes by qualifying both as 'European works' within the meaning of the AVMS Directive and as 'Korean works' within the meaning of existing audiovisual support instruments in Korea. To fall under the scope of the EU and Korean preferences, the protocol lays down more exacting conditions when compared with those of the EU-Cariforum protocol.[63] In addition to safeguards intended to obstruct the circumvention of the system by third parties (i.e. provisions concerning the ownership of the co-producing undertakings, the nationality of producers/managers,[64] etc.), the EU-Korea protocol requires the participation of producers from two EU Member States in the co-produced works, with a minimum financial contribution for each Member State set at 10 per cent of the total production costs.[65] Moreover, the overall financial contribution of the EU and Korean parties must respectively amount to at least 30 per cent of the total production costs,[66] and the technical and artistic participation of each party must be balanced: it must not vary by more than 20 per cent compared with the parties' respective financial contribution and in any case, it cannot exceed 70 per cent of the overall artistic and technical features of the project. Interestingly, third party participation is allowed on condition that the third countries concerned have ratified the UNESCO Convention and that their participation does not exceed 20 per cent of the total production costs and/or of the entire technical and artistic contribution to the project.[67] In the field of animation where Korea has assumed an important position in the world market, more stringent conditions are laid down. The participation of producers from three EU Member States is required and the minimum financial contribution of the EU and Korean producers must respectively be at a minimum of 35 per cent of the total production costs.[68] Also, the technical and artistic contribution of the producer(s) of each party must not vary by more than 10 per cent compared with the parties' financial contribution and must not exceed more than 65 per cent of the overall technical and artistic contribution to the co-produced work.[69]

63 See Art. 5(6) of the EU-Korea protocol.
64 Note that in the case of the EU-Korea protocol, in addition to having the nationality of an EU Member State and Korea, the respective director(s) or manager(s) of the co-producing undertakings must also be able to demonstrate their domicile therein (see Art. 5(6)(b) of the EU-Korea protocol).
65 See Art. 5(6)(c) of the EU-Korea protocol.
66 Ibid., Art. 5(6)(d).
67 Ibid., Art. 5(6)(e).
68 Ibid., Art. 5(6)(c)–(d).
69 Ibid., Art. 5(6)(e).

240   *Evangelia Psychogiopoulou*

In order to ensure that the system works properly and that mutual benefits accrue for both parties, the protocol limits the duration of the preferential system established to a provisional period of three years.[70] This can be renewed, following a review by the CCC of its effects on cultural diversity and the promotion of mutually beneficial cooperation between the parties, upon advice by the DAGs.[71] Each party enjoys the right to end the preferential market access granted before the expiry of the initial or any subsequent period, as well as the right to request the CCC to evaluate the scheme and to suspend preferences when changes to the preferences operated by the other party undermine reciprocal benefits.[72] The parties are also required to monitor the implementation of reciprocal preferences, with the involvement of civil society through the DAGs, and raise any issues that may arise with the CCC.[73]

Further, the EU-Korea protocol provides that each party shall promote the audiovisual works of its partner through the organisation of festivals, seminars, etc.,[74] and lays down provisions for cooperation specifically in the field of broadcasting.[75] Collaborative measures include the exchange of views and information on broadcasting policy and regulation between competent authorities, broadcasters' cooperation, the exchange of audiovisual works and participation in international broadcasting events held by the other party. All three protocols additionally stipulate that the parties shall encourage the promotion of their respective territories as a location for the shooting of audiovisual works[76] and that they will examine, in conformity with their domestic legislation, and allow the temporary importation of the technical material and equipment necessary for that purpose.[77] With the exception of the EU-CA protocol, the EU-Cariforum and EU-Korea protocols also indicate that the parties shall cooperate in order to facilitate the rental and leasing of such material and equipment, enhance the use of international and regional audiovisual standards and encourage the digitalisation of audiovisual archives.[78]

The sectoral provisions targeting other cultural sectors are much less detailed. In the field of performing arts, the parties agree to cooperate in order to increase contacts and professional exchanges, promote training, encourage joint productions and foster the development of international theatre technology standards and the use of stage signs.[79] Cooperation in the field of

70   Ibid., Art. 5(8)(a).
71   Ibid., Art. 5(8)(b), in conjunction with Art. 5(8)(a).
72   Ibid., Art. 5(8)(b), (9) and (10).
73   Ibid., Art. 5(9).
74   Ibid., Art. 6(1).
75   Ibid., Art. 6(2).
76   See Art. 6(1) of the EU-Cariforum procotol, Art. 7(1) of the EU-Korea protocol and Art. 5(3) of the EU-CA protocol.
77   See Art. 6(2) of the EU-Cariforum protocol, Art. 7(2) of the EU-Korea protocol and Art. 5(4) of the EU-CA protocol.
78   See Art. 5(3)–(5) of the EU-Cariforum protocol and Art. 6(3)–(5) of the EU-Korea protocol.
79   See Art. 7 of the EU-Cariforum protocol, Art. 8 of the EU-Korea protocol and Art. 6 of the EU-CA protocol.

publications focuses on facilitating the exchange and dissemination of partner countries' publications, particularly through the organisation of fairs, seminars and other literary events, co-publications, translations, and increased contacts and training for librarians, writers, translators, booksellers and publishers.[80] Finally, the parties shall cooperate in order to share expertise and best practices for the protection of heritage sites and historic monuments, for instance through increased contacts between experts, collaboration on professional training and for raising the awareness of local populations, and counselling on heritage protection and heritage legislation, covering implementation aspects among other issues.[81]

Culture and trade: a difficult symbiosis?

The elaboration of cultural cooperation protocols and their incorporation in the EU's trade and economic agreements have been followed closely by national cultural policy-makers and other cultural stakeholders, generating a heated debate about the place culture should or should not occupy in trade negotiations. Criticism emerged when the Commission appeared to be systematically including cultural cooperation protocols in the EU's trade agreements with the EU-Korea FTA. The EU-Korea protocol was harshly criticised for circumventing the well-established EU position of not making any trade commitments in the field of audiovisual services.[82] In any case, cultural cooperation protocols, it was argued, should only be proposed to countries that are party to the UNESCO Convention, and different protocol formats should be devised, in partnership with the Member States and civil society, to account for the different categories of EU partner countries.[83] Unsurprisingly, France intervened in the debate and advocated the development of a broad, comprehensive negotiating strategy on EU cultural cooperation with third countries on the basis of protocols to be appended to the EU's economic and trade agreements *and* separate EU cultural cooperation agreements.[84]

---

80 See Art. 8 of the EU-Cariforum protocol, Art. 9 of the EU-Korea protocol and Art. 7 of the EU-CA protocol.

81 See Art. 9 of the EU-Cariforum protocol, Art. 10 of the EU-Korea protocol and Art. 8 of the EU-CA protocol.

82 European Coalitions for Cultural Diversity, 'Comments on the Concept Paper on the Draft Cultural Cooperation Protocol with Korea', 18 March 2009. Online. Available: www.coalition francaise.org/wp-content/uploads/2009/11/Barroso-Coree-18–03–09.pdf (accessed 23 September 2013).

83 Ibid.

84 Communication by France, 'For a New European Union External Cultural Strategy'. Online. Available: www.diplomatie.gouv.fr/fr/IMG/pdf/2009–12–21_Communication_France_ Strategie_culturelle_exterieure_ENG.pdf (accessed 23 September 2013). On this see also L.R. Hanania, 'Cultural Diversity and Regional Trade Agreements – the European Union Experience with Cultural Cooperation Frameworks', 28 September 2012. Online. Available: http://papers.ssrn.com/sol3/papers.cfm?abstract_id=2087639 (accessed 23 September 2013).

Some of the above mentioned concerns and proposals appear to have influenced the drafting of the EU-Korea and EU-CA protocols.[85] The final text of the EU-Korea protocol reveals that in establishing a framework for EU cultural cooperation with Korea, attention was given to both the degree of development of the Korean cultural industries and the existence of preferential schemes in Korea for the promotion of cultural content in the audiovisual field. In addition, cultural and trade disputes were separated, a solution that was followed by the EU-CA protocol as well. Significantly, the latter protocol was not appended to the trade provisions of the EU-CA Association Agreement but was linked to Title VIII on 'Culture and Audiovisual Cooperation' under part III of the EU-CA agreement on 'cooperation'.[86] Also, an attempt to assuage concern, in a 'statement' accompanying the signature, on behalf of the EU, of the EU-Korea FTA,[87] the Commission expressly noted that the EU-Korea protocol, drawn up and negotiated with reference to Korea's cultural policy, in particular its support for the audiovisual sector, should not be taken as a precedent in future trade negotiations.

Despite these 'assurances', the *trade vs culture* dilemma that has characterised the negotiation of the protocols seems to have played a key role for the negotiation of a stand-alone cultural cooperation agreement (CCA) with two Andean countries, Colombia and Peru,[88] separate from the trade agreement agreed with the same countries.[89] Although this might be considered a welcome move by cultural diversity advocates, the EU-Colombia Peru CCA contains, for the most part, identical provisions to those of the three protocols,[90] which indicates that there was no thorough assessment of the potential for

---

85 On this see also J. Loisen and D. De Ville, 'The EU-Korea Protocol on Cultural Cooperation: Toward Cultural Diversity or Cultural Deficit?', *International Journal of Communications*, 2011, vol. 5, 254, at 264; European Coalitions for Cultural Diversity, 'Contribution to the Public Consultation on a Future Trade Policy', 28 July 2010. Online. Available: www.coalition francaise.org/wp-content/uploads/2010/09/CEDC-Contribution-future-trade-policy-28.7.2010-final3.pdf (accessed 23 September 2013), p. 2.

86 See Art. 74(7) of the EU-CA Association Agreement and the preamble to the EU-CA protocol.

87 See Council Decision of 16 September 2010 on the signing, on behalf of the European Union, and provisional application of the Free Trade Agreement between the European Union and its Member States, of the one part, and the Republic of Korea, of the other part, OJ L 127, 14/5/2011, p. 1, at p. 4.

88 See Agreement on Cultural Cooperation between the European Union and its Member States, of the one part, and Colombia and Peru, of the other part. Online. Available: http://ec.europa. eu/culture/policy/strategic-framework/documents/agreement-cultural-colombia-peru_en.pdf (accessed 23 September 2013).

89 See Council Decision of 31 May 2012 on the signing, on behalf of the Union, and provisional application of the Trade Agreement between the European Union and its Member States, of the one part, and Colombia and Peru, of the other part, OJ L 354, 21/12/2012, p. 1.

90 With limited exceptions. Note, for instance, the provisions of the EU-Colombia Peru CCA aimed at preventing and mitigating illegal trade in cultural heritage goods and the more extensive list on the types of artists and other cultural professionals and practitioners that may benefit from collaborative training measures (Arts 5(4) and 10(3) of the EU-Colombia

EU-Colombia Peru cultural cooperation prior to its drafting. The CCA, however, does downplay the emphasis on audiovisual cooperation – evident at least in the EU-Cariforum and EU-Korea protocols, and contains more detailed provisions on the tasks of the Cultural Cooperation Committee established to monitor its implementation.[91] Similar to the protocols, nonetheless, it is drafted in a weakly binding language (e.g. parties shall 'aim to', 'encourage', 'facilitate', 'endeavour to', etc.).

Conclusions

The provisions of the UNESCO Convention encouraging increased international cooperation in the field of culture have induced the EU to develop novel approaches concerning the place and treatment of culture in its external economic relations. The integration of cultural cooperation protocols in the EU-Cariforum EPA, the EU-Korea FTA and the EU-CA Association Agreement marks a qualitative shift in the interaction of trade and economic objectives with cultural diversity concerns. The three agreements have proven sufficiently flexible to accommodate, through the protocols, provisions that safeguard the ability of the EU and its Member States to adopt and maintain measures that promote cultural interaction and exchange. The EU-Cariforum EPA, underpinned by a genuine development perspective, has gone a step further, providing Cariforum contractual suppliers of cultural services other than audiovisual services binding market access in the EU subject to conditions. From this perspective, the three agreements develop new methods and means for the EU to address the trade/culture quandary, in conformity with the UNESCO Convention and its WTO obligations.

This has not happened without objection, and the concerns voiced seem to have influenced the policy choices made. It is significant, for instance, that the EU-CA protocol has been linked to the 'cooperation' chapter of the EU-CA Association Agreement and not to its trade provisions. It is also significant that, in the case of Colombia and Peru, a separate cultural cooperation agreement was agreed with no link whatsoever to the trade agreement entered into by the parties. The ongoing trade negotiations with other third countries, such as India, the ASEAN countries[92] and Canada, will in all likelihood further qualify the EU's position on the interface of culture with trade. What is important to stress here, by way of conclusion, is that the UNESCO Convention itself requires mutual supportiveness and complementarity between its provisions and the international obligations of the countries party

---

Peru CCA). In endeavouring to exchange best practices for the preservation and digitalisation of audiovisual archives, the EU-Colombia Peru CCA also states that the parties shall encourage cooperation between their cinematheques (Art. 7(5) of the EU-Colombia Peru CCA).

91   See Arts 4 and 7 of the EU-Colombia Peru Cultural Cooperation Agreement.
92   These are Burma-Myanmar, Brunei, Cambodia, Indonesia, Laos, Malaysia, Philippines, Singapore, Thailand and Vietnam.

to it.[93] In order to achieve such mutual supportiveness and complementarity, there is a need for changes to, and a rethinking of, the agreements the EU opts to negotiate – including those of a trade and economic nature.

Bibliography

Agreement establishing an association between Central America, on the one hand,and the European Union and its Member States, on the other. Online. Available: http://trade.ec.europa.eu/doclib/press/index.cfm?id=689 (accessed 23 September 2013).

Agreement establishing the World Trade Organization, Annex 1B, General Agreement on Trade in Services and Annexes, 15 April 1994. Online. Available: www.wto.org/english/docs_e/legal_e/26-gats.pdf (accessed 23 September 2013).

Agreement on cultural cooperation between the European Union and its Member States, of the one part, and Colombia and Peru, of the other part. Online. Available: http://ec.europa.eu/culture/policy/strategic-framework/documents/agreement-cultural-colombia-peru_en.pdf (accessed 23 September 2013).

Communication from the Commission on a European Agenda for Culture in a Globalizing World, COM(2007) 242, 10 May 2007.

Communication by France, 'For a new European Union External Cultural Strategy'. Online. Available: www.diplomatie.gouv.fr/fr/IMG/pdf/2009–12–21_Communication_France_Strategie_culturelle_exterieure_ENG.pdf (accessed 23 September 2013).

Consolidated version of the Treaty Establishing the European Community, OJ C 325, 24/12/2002, p. 33.

Consolidated version of the Treaty on the Functioning of the European Union, OJ C 115, 9/5/2008, p. 47.

Council Conclusions on the Promotion of Cultural Diversity and Intercultural Dialogue in the External Relations of the Union and its Member States, 20 November 2008. Online. Available: www.consilium.europa.eu/ueDocs/cms_Data/docs/pressData/en/educ/104189.pdf (accessed 23 September 2013).

Council Decision of 18 May 2006 on the conclusion of the Convention on the Protection and Promotion of the Diversity of Cultural Expressions, OJ L 201, 25/7/2006, p. 15.

Council Decision of 16 September 2010 on the signing, on behalf of the European Union, and provisional application of the Free Trade Agreement between the European Union and its Member States, of the one part, and the Republic of Korea, of the other part, OJ L 127, 14/5/2011, p. 1.

Council Decision of 31 May 2012 on the signing, on behalf of the Union, and provisional application of the Trade Agreement between the European Union and its Member States, of the one part, and Colombia and Peru, of the other part, OJ L 354, 21/12/2012, p. 1.

Council resolution of 16 November 2007 on a European agenda for culture, OJ C 287, 29/11/2007, p. 1.

Directive 2010/13/EU of the European Parliament and of the Council of 10 March 2010 on the coordination of certain provisions laid down by law, regulation or administrative action in Member States concerning the provision of audiovisual media services, OJ L 95, 15/4/2010, p. 1.

---

93 See Art. 20 of the UNESCO Convention.

Economic Partnership Agreement between the Cariforum States, of the one part, and the European Community and its Member States, of the other part, OJ L 289/I, 30/10/2008, p. 3.

European Coalitions for Cultural Diversity, 'Comments on the Concept Paper on the Draft Cultural Cooperation Protocol with Korea', 18 March 2009. Online. Available: www.coalitionfrancaise.org/wp-content/uploads/2009/11/Barroso-Coree-18–03–09.pdf (accessed 23 September 2013).

European Coalitions for Cultural Diversity, 'Contribution to the Public Consultation on a Future Trade Policy', 28 July 2010. Online. Available: www.coalitionfrancaise.org/wp-content/uploads/2010/09/CEDC-Contribution-future-trade-policy-28.7.2010-final3.pdf (accessed 23 September 2013).

European Commission, 'Argumentaire on the Title on Cultural Cooperation in Future EU Trade Agreements', 11 May 2007. Online. Available: http://trade.ec.europa.eu/doclib/docs/2007/may/tradoc_134655.pdf (accessed 23 September 2013).

European Commission, 'Concept Paper: Cultural Cooperation Protocol with Korea', 18 February 2009. Online. Available: http://trade.ec.europa.eu/doclib/docs/2009/march/tradoc_142542.pdf (accessed 23 September 2013).

European Commission, Staff working document on the external dimension of audiovisual policy, SEC(2009) 1033, 14 July 2009.

European Communities and their Member States, Final list of Article II (MFN) Exemptions, GATS/EL/31, 15 April 1994.

Free Trade Agreement between the European Union and its Member States, of the one part, and the Republic of Korea, of the other part, OJ L 127, 14/5/2011, p. 6.

Hanania, L.R., 'Cultural Diversity and Regional Trade Agreements – the European Union Experience with Cultural Cooperation Frameworks', 28 September 2012. Online. Available: http://papers.ssrn.com/sol3/papers.cfm?abstract_id=2087639 (accessed 23 September 2013).

Loisen, J., and De Ville, D., 'The EU-Korea Protocol on Cultural Cooperation: Toward Cultural Diversity or Cultural Deficit?', *International Journal of Communications*, 2011, vol. 5, 254.

Psychogiopoulou, E., *The Integration of Cultural Considerations in EU Law and Policies*, Leiden; Boston, MA: Martinus Nijhoff, Brill, 2008.

UNESCO Convention on the Protection and Promotion of the Diversity of Cultural Expressions, 20 October 2005, in force 18 March 2007, in UNESCO, Records of the General Conference, 33rd session, Paris, 3–21 October 2005 (2 vols., 2005), vol. I.

Index

The letter 'n' refers to a footnote.